© 2001 Sarah Spain Mosier

About the Author

JOHN MOSIER is full professor of English at Loyola University in New Orleans, where, as chair of the English department and associate dean of the College of Arts and Sciences, he taught primarily European literature and film. His background as a military historian dates from his role in developing an interdisciplinary curriculum for the study of the two world wars, a program funded by the National Endowment for the Humanities. From 1989 to 1992, he edited the *New Orleans Review*.

THE MYTH
OF THE
GREAT WAR

THE MYTH OF THE GREAT WAR

A NEW MILITARY HISTORY OF WORLD WAR I

John Mosier

Perennial

An Imprint of HarperCollins*Publishers*

First Perennial edition published 2002.

Designed by The Book Design Group

Maps by Robert Laurent

The Library of Congress has catalogued the hardcover edition as follows:

Mosier, John.
    The myth of the Great War: a new military history of World War I / John Mosier—1st ed.
         p.   c m.
    Includes bibliographical references and index.
    ISBN 0-06-019676-9
    1. World War, 1914–1918—Campaigns. I. Title.
D521.M86   2001
940.4'1—dc21   00-046103

ISBN 0-06-008433-2 (pbk.)

02 03 04 05 06 ❖/RRD 10 9 8 7 6 5 4 3 2

The general had so wished to do this, and was so sorry he had not managed to do it that it seemed to him as if it had really happened. Perhaps it might have been so? Could one possibly make out amid all this confusion what did or did not happen?

—Tolstoy, War and Peace, Book 2, Chapter 16

CONTENTS

ILLUSTRATIONS

Maps

Photographs   Pages 39, 40, 42, 43, 46, 47, and 340

PREFACE

For American readers the First World War is a distant and faded memory. Given the number of histories dealing with the war that have appeared in Great Britain in recent years, this is clearly not the case for the English reader, who as a result perhaps has certain expectations about what such a history should cover. On picking this volume up, and seeing it has little to say about the Eastern Front, and nothing at all to say about the fighting in Africa or Asia Minor, or the war at the sea, the reader may conclude that it is hardly fair to call this a story of the Great War.

In truth, however, every history of this war excludes a great deal. No British or American account deals adequately with the war between France and Germany on the Western Front. So to the reader who feels the book is incomplete because it omits an account of, say, Gallipoli, I would reply that this tragic adventure had much less of an impact on the course of the war than did the Battle of Woëvre Plain in the spring of 1915. I also think that reader who reflects on that part of this book that does deal with military operations in the East will realize that Allied hopes that such operations would bring about a decisive end to the war were entirely delusionary.

No history of the war is complete; mine at least has the merit of relating a part of it which is mostly new. If would be foolishly pretentious of me or of any historian to lay claim to some profoundly original or novel insight into the war. What I do claim is this. This history reveals to the interested reader a great deal that has been ignored or supressed by other historians, and it demonstrates connections that have either been ignored or denied. Moreover, while much of it may be well known to a handful of specialists, their insights have not filtered down either to the general reader or even to the standard accounts.

Claims about the German and French casualties sustained during the Battle of Verdun, for example, continue to be wildly misreported, even in the works of specialists, although extremely accurate estimates have been available since immediately after the war. Accordingly there is much here that the thoughtful reader will find surprising.

It may fairly be said that this narrative is more concerned with the events of the first half of the war than the second. There is a reason. The patterns of combat were established early on, and they remained surprisingly constant throughout the war. The Allied tendency to attack the strongest parts of the German line in almost suicidal fashion began in 1914 and was still a feature of late 1917. So too with the surprise—and surprisingly successful—German offensives, the last of which was in the summer of 1918.

This is not to suggest that there was no change, no improvement, no tactical development. The Allied armies of 1918 were far better than the armies of 1914. Unfortunately the Germans, who had begun the war with better equipment and better tactics, improved as well.

Readers will discover as they near the end of the book that the intervention of the United States in the war looms large. This is not American chauvinism, because, as I say in the introductory chapter, I had always assumed that the contribution of the United States to winning the war was more on the order of Canada's, and I was quite astonished by what my research uncovered. My aim in writing this book was to introduce the reader to a largely unknown side of the war, to explain how it was that the Germans were almost invariably victorious on the battlefield, and to show how the Allies consistently misrepresented what was happening.

However, as I worked, I found that part of the misrepresentation involved grossly underestimating the impact that the United States had on the war. For American historians, the neutrality of the United States until it was reluctantly forced into the war is virtually a holy writ. Consequently there has been a certain coyness about the extent to which American finance and American industry supported the Allies long before the formal declaration of war.

On the other side of the Atlantic, there has been an equal reluctance to admit the extent to which American intervention in 1918 was decisive. For many analysts, the idea that the BEF broke the back of the German Army in summer and fall of 1918 is the only illusion about the war left to them, and I suspect it is one that will be clung to fiercely. In fact the AEF was much more successful than is commonly allowed, even, or particularly, by American historians. The concluding chapters of the book address those achievements. The great war monuments of the British Empire and of France are ossuaries and memorials to the dead. The great American monuments in France are victory columns.

History is not amenable to controlled testing. Consequently we have no way of knowing if the United States actually won the war for the Allies. My own contention is more modest: without those millions of pounds sterling, those millions of tons of high explosives, and those two million American soldiers, the Allies would have lost the war. But such arguments trouble me because they obscure a more fundamental issue. In this war there were no real victors. If the United States intended to impose a new world order on Europe, it failed abysmally. If France and Great Britain intended to create a new balance of power, they failed as well. That they certainly failed to destroy Germany as a great power is a fact so painfully obvious it hardly bears mention.

The narrator of Ford Madox Ford's brilliant novel *The Good Soldier* (first published in 1915) begins his narrative by opining that the story he is about to tell is the saddest he has ever heard. He was wrong. The story of the Great War is the saddest story ever heard. He who tells it differently does no service to the memory of the millions of soldiers whose remains lie in France and Belgium. As a young French soldier wrote in April of 1915:

> Whosoever curses not war shall be cursed! Amen. By the blood and by the
> bruise; by the cries of terror and agony with which the darkness shivers; by
> the freezing wind of the shell which makes the hairs stand up and the hor-
> rible flame which scorches them; but the hairs which dry on the face of
> the dead shall be cursed.

In a book that was eleven years in the writing, and even more years in the thinking, the number of people whose contributions should be acknowledged becomes so great it is impossible to list them all.

I owe a profound intellectual debt to three people in particular, the spiritual godparents of this book. I learned about diplomatic affairs of the times from David Amacker (formerly a lieutenant in the U.S. Army), one of President Wilson's interpreters at Versailles. Frank Byerley, Jr. (formerly a captain in the U.S. Army), a pioneer aviator, was one of the country's first autogyro pilots, and probably the only aviator ever to be grounded by the president of the United States. It is to him that I owe my knowledge of all things mechanical. I was introduced to France by Vera Volmane, who was at the time president of the French Film and Television Critics Association. Getting to know Vera, a formidable film critic and an outspoken journalist, was getting to know France, with all its strengths and weaknesses.

Any teacher owes a great deal to his colleagues, and I was fortunate to work with two men, both fine scholars, who encouraged me to teach and write about military affairs; C. Joseph Pusateri, a talented historian, and Richard Frank, a brilliant young teacher of German.

I regret that Frank, David, Vera, Joe, and Richard did not live to see the publication of this book.

I pass from the dead to the living. Over the years I have been greatly assisted by countless archivists and librarians, from the War College at Carlisle Barracks to the Austrian Army Museum in Vienna, and by scores of caretakers and groundsmen throughout France. But one person in particular has assisted me over the last twenty odd years (surely a record of some sort) and deserves special mention: Patricia Doran of the J. Edgar and Louise S. Monroe Library of Loyola University in New Orleans.

Bernard A. Cook, Loyola's Professor of Modern European History, was kind enough to take the time to read a very early version of this manuscript. Mary McCay, who succeeded me as chair of the Department of English at Loyola, was particularly supportive during the many years I was at work on this project. In Washington, D.C., Albert and Annick Casciero were kind enough to put me up—and to put up with me over the course of many visits to the National Archives.

It is a common courtesy for an author to acknowledge the work of his agent and his editor. In my case it is a pleasure to do so. Without the tireless energy and enthusiasm of James D. Hornfischer, this book would have never happened. And I'm grateful for the early support of Paul McCarthy and in having Cass Canfield, Jr., as my editor. His work greatly improved the manuscript.

Last, I want to acknowledge the contributions of my wife. Sarah Spain Mosier, an accomplished editor in her own right, read and corrected the many versions of this manuscript; she also happens to be the great love of my life.

INTRODUCTION

The War on the Western Front

The reports passed on to the ministers were, as we all realized much later, grossly misleading. Victories were much overstated. Virtual defeats were represented as victories, however limited their scope. Our casualties were understated. Enemy losses became pyramidal. That was the way the military authorities presented the situation to Ministers—that was their active propaganda in the Press. All disconcerting and discouraging facts were suppressed in the reports received from the front by the War Cabinet—every bright feather of success was waved and flourished in our faces.

—*Lloyd George* [1]

The First World War is one of the most written about subjects in modern history, and probably in military history. The West's most distinguished historians have written accounts of the war, some of them, like Winston Churchill, historical figures of great importance. That anyone might have anything new to say on the subject seems on the face of it most unlikely, all the more so since the century came to an end with the publication of massive works by two British writers, the distinguished military historian John Keegan and the younger but equally talented economic historian Niall Ferguson.

My own aim, when I began work a decade ago, was consequently quite modest. As a literary-historian-turned-film-critic who had a good deal of familiarity with France, I thought I might introduce the interested reader to a few hitherto unremarked aspects of the Great War—unremarked only insofar as the English language reader went, I hasten to add, since little of note about this war had failed to escape the hundreds of French military historians, army experts, and participants.

It certainly never occurred to me to doubt the main outlines of what everyone agreed was a bloody and inconclusive struggle in which the Germans and the Allies fought for fifty-two months, with neither side having much of an advantage. I heartily agreed with A.J.P. Taylor that if Napoleon had returned at the start of 1917, he would "have found nothing which surprised him or which, at any rate, he could not understand: much the same European powers as in his day fighting much the same war on a rather larger scale."[2]

Ten years on, however, I am forced to conclude it was in most respects a war that Napoleon, or anyway Professor Taylor, would have found full of surprises: it differed dramatically from all previous wars, for example, in being the first war in which the medical services of the combatants recorded that the overwhelming majority of casualties were caused by artillery projectiles rather than by bullets. As late as 1870, for example, nine out of every ten soldiers killed in action died as a result of bullets fired by other soldiers (rifles, muskets, and pistols), and nine out of ten wounded soldiers were injured the same way: wars were settled by rounds of musketry. The only thing that had changed was the increase in the killing power of the infantry's main weapon, as breech-loading rifles replaced muzzle-loaded smoothbores, and were in turn replaced by bolt-action magazine weapons.[3]

But in the Great War, about two out of every three German fatalities were caused by artillery fire, and only a little over half the live wounded were caused by rifle and machine gun bullets. The figures for the Allies revealed a similar trend, although there the imbalance was more striking: Seven out of every ten British casualties and three out of every four French were caused by artillery. For the soldiers of the American Expeditionary Force, the figures were equally skewed. As the authors of the American Army's medical report put it, "It is clearly apparent that the gunshot missiles of the greatest military importance during the World War were those of the artillery, and that during the Civil War, of small arms."[4]

Since this was a war in which, for the first time in the history of warfare, most casualties were caused by artillery, my conclusion was that something had changed dramatically on the battlefield. I was equally surprised to learn that the change was entirely to the advantage of Germany.

Over the course of the war on the Western Front the German Army suffered many fewer casualties than their adversaries. There is hardly a time period or a battle in which the losses came anywhere near equality; generally they were in the ratio of two or three to one. The French combat veteran and legislator André Maginot observed while the war was still going on that "the losses of the enemy on all fronts put together is not noticeably greater than our losses alone on one front."[5]

A war in which the cause of fatalities changes so dramatically, and in which one side is enormously more successful at killing than the other, is clearly a war in which something strikingly new took place, and it was disturbing to find only one English account—that of Winston Churchill—that attempted to answer the most pressing question arising from this data: why were the Germans so much more successful than the Allies at killing soldiers with artillery?

Churchill had noticed the casualty imbalance in the 1920s, and had explained it by arguing that the Germans did better because they almost always remained on the defensive while the Allies were almost always attacking.[6] When the Germans attacked, he opined, they got slaughtered just as the Allies did. Not so. Whenever the German Army gathered its resources and attempted an offensive, it was—by the standards of the Allies—extremely successful.

Given that there were always many more Allied troops in France than there were German troops, the record was remarkable. In 1917, the BEF spent four horrific months trying to break out of the Ypres salient (Third Ypres, or Passchendaele), had four hundred thousand men killed, wounded, or missing, and gained hardly any ground, none of it of much value. In late September 1914, well after the end of the Battle of the Marne, a German offensive took more territory in one week than the Allies managed in the succeeding four years of fighting.

It was by no means a unique event. On the Western Front, with three exceptions during 1917, the Allies spent almost four years exactly to the day engaging in offensives that were futile and costly. Time and again, a desperate Allied attack would seize a few kilometers of the first-line German positions, and a victory would be declared—as at Cambrai in 1917, when the church bells in England were rung to celebrate the great triumph. Within a few days, the defenders had mounted a counterattack that not only erased the gains but drove the attacking infantry out of half of its own forward positions.

Cambrai was supposed to be a victory, or at least a bloody stalemate, but on close examination most Allied triumphs turned out to be falsely contrived, and Lloyd George's litany of how the news was manipulated by Great Britain's Imperial General Staff is quite exact. But even in the privileged position of prime minister he was unaware of the extent to which the really unwelcome news, like the massive British casualties caused in July 1917 by the new German dichloroethylsulfide gas, was suppressed completely. Like most of us, he supposed that the French had reclaimed the ground lost at Verdun during 1916 by a brilliant offensive conducted at the end of the year. I had never read anything to contradict that, and when I first saw a list of the twenty-one French military cemeteries at Verdun, I supposed that, like the great cemetery before the ossuary of Douaumont, they contained the remains of men killed in that horrific ten-month battle in 1916.[7] I was dumbfounded to see, in the other twenty cemeteries, graves from all four years of the war, and whole cemeteries where the majority of the marked graves were from August 1917 and September 1918.

The collapse at Saint-Mihiel in September 1914; the loss of the Channel ports, of Antwerp, and of Lille, all in October of that year; the fiasco of the Battle of the Woëvre in April 1915, the loss of the Argonne in July; the massacres of France's elite troops in the Vosges are a sad litany of slaughter, not counting what Lloyd George called the virtual defeats dressed out as victories. That list included the First Battle of the Marne, First and Second Champagne, the Somme, all three of the Ypres battles—in fact, if one used what seems to be the unexceptionable criteria for military success of winning both strategic ground and the casualty exchange, it emerges that in the first four years of the war, there were possibly five Allied offensives that might fairly be called victories, and probably only three.

Perhaps more surprising, however, is how often the German Army conducted offensive operations. Sometimes, as at Cambrai, these took the form of vigorous countering attacks that ejected the exhausted British (or French) soldiers from the positions they had won at such great cost, and, in the case of Cambrai, half of their jumping-off line as well. But there were other operations that were clearly offensives, and using the same criteria of casualty exchange and territory gained, these were invariably successful. Compared to the Allied "victories" the German ones were real. With each year of the war, the Central Powers eliminated a major adversary, destroying its army completely and occupying enormous amounts of its territory: Belgium in 1914, Serbia in 1915, Rumania in 1916, Italy in 1917, and at the end of 1917, Russia as well. Whenever the Germans could throw the resources together to mount a major offensive operation in the West, it was successful. In July 1916, for example, at the end of their Verdun offensive, the German Army was master of the battlefield: The last major fort on the right bank, Souville, was a heap of rubble held by a few desperate infantry units.

The data led me to try to answer two questions that logically followed: Why was the German Army so successful, and why did Germany ultimately lose the war? In terms of technology, it soon became apparent that the German Army entered the war using weapons that the British and the French simply didn't possess (hand grenades, mortars, motorized super-heavy artillery), and had both a qualitative and quantitative superiority in key weapons both sides did possess (like the German 210 millimeter howitzer), and rapidly brought even more new and untested weapons into play (flamethrowers and gas shells in the first quarter of 1915).

But the use of new weapons in combat does not automatically confer an advantage. The French deployed hundreds of tanks in their April 1917 offensive, and the British deployed even more at Cambrai in November. Moreover, although the Allies were late in producing weapons like mortars—and probably never had as many deployed as the Germans did—the technological edge in weaponry for Germany was probably at its peak in the early spring of 1915. But Allied failures and German successes continued more or less unchecked for three years after that, which suggests that the basis of the German advantage was as much tactical as technical. Four years of success on such a large scale is clearly the result of leadership and training, not the brilliance of one or two leaders, a few lucky accidents, or the use of some secret weapon.

The evidence that those tactics did in fact exist was noticed soon enough, by ordinary captains and gunnery sergeants serving in the French Army right up to its generals: "Thanks to the new German system of making their attacks," Joffre recounts that Pétain wrote him on 7 May 1916, "we were slowly but surely being used up, and he advanced the theory that if the Allies did not soon intervene we would finish by being beaten."[8]

Put that way, it seems clear enough, and there is no shortage of firsthand testimony from eyewitnesses that the basis for the success of the

German Army was not purely technological, but reflected superior offensive and defensive tactics that in turn rested on a superior system of training and leadership. But to Joffre, Pétain's insight was simply another sign of his defeatism and pessimism.

What was wanted on the Allied side was dash and discipline, not a cold assessment of the alternatives. Here was how the Allied leadership thought the war should be fought:

> They advanced in line after line, dressed as if on parade, and not a man shirked going through the extremely heavy barrage, or facing the machine-gun and rifle fire.... I have never seen, I would never have imagined, such a magnificent display of gallantry, discipline, and determination. The reports I have had from the very few survivors of this marvelous advance bear out what I saw with my own eyes, viz., that hardly a man of ours got to the German front line.[9]

Such passages are often used to evoke the horrors of this war, and the folly of the senior commanders, in this case British. True enough, and no one can read a passage like this without feeling a shock of utter disbelief as well as pure horror.

But close investigation reveals a more profoundly disturbing reality: this sort of slaughter of the infantry is almost exclusively a British achievement. After the summer of 1916, instances of French soldiers attacking like this decrease markedly. French soldiers at the Chemin des Dames in April 1917 were massacred not because they marched across the terrain as though on parade, but because they were given an impossible objective, their artillery was impotent, and the tanks on which they had placed such reliance were quickly destroyed.

Outside of the fantasies of Allied propagandists, instances of the Germans attacking like this at any point during the war—including August 1914—are few and far between. As one French historian puts it, with a certain bitter irony: "cases where the masses of *Feldgrau* advanced shoulder to shoulder, to the beat of drums and fifes, are a great deal rarer than legend would have it.[10] So German success on the battlefield was not simply a function of tactics and technology, it was also the product of military competence. An officer who loses all of his men may possess many wonderful qualities, but military competence is not one of them. The system that leaves him there has lost sight of what the Soviet general

Volkogonov called "the fundamental principle of the military art, namely, that the objective should be gained at minimal cost in human life."[11]

That standard seems an eminently reasonable one. Wellington remarked after Waterloo that he was disappointed to find Napoleon little more than a butcher. Agincourt and New Orleans were great victories precisely because the objective was gained at a minimal cost. There were certainly engagements where the Germans were massacred—as one would expect in a war involving millions of men that went on for over four years. But the general trend was constant, and always in Germany's favor. Why then did they lose the war?

As an American, I was surprised to find that Germany lost the war because by October 1918 there were two million American soldiers in France. Without ever considering the fact, I had always assumed that our participation in the war was roughly equivalent to Canada's, which is to say, honorable and significant, but not determining. Over the four years of the war, 624,964 Canadians enlisted, 422,405 were in the field, and there were 56,625 war dead—this last close to the battlefield deaths suffered by the AEF.[12] Canada's record in the Great War was one of distinction, but, given the fact that Great Britain alone put nearly five and a half million men into the field, it could hardly be said that Canada's role was decisive.

But America's role in the war was absolutely decisive. The string of German battlefield successes stopped abruptly on the entry into the line of the newly formed American divisions, the course of the war changed drastically, and members of the *Oberste Heeresleitung*, the General Staff of the German Army (the OHL), recommended that Germany seek terms. When Wilson hinted to the Allies that he would seek his own peace unless his famous Fourteen Points were adopted, they caved in.[13] The Great War was won on the ground by American soldiers deployed as an American force, and operating largely against the wishes and suggestions of the senior French and British commanders, who thought American troops should be distributed into Allied units as replacements for Allied losses to minimize their importance.

Why the Allies were so inept on the battlefield, and how they managed to fool the world, and, much of the time, their own governments as well, is a fascinating topic worthy of study on its own. But the story of how the war unfolded is complex enough, and I have confined myself to that, with the aim of making clear what actually happened there, and how the fighting in the East and West were related. The Western Front was the center of decision for the war; events in Italy, the Balkans, and Russia are discussed only when they impacted on the West—which they did much more often and to much greater effect than is generally supposed.

This argument suggests that the basis for the success of German arms on the battlefield in the second World War was systematically developed by the officers and men of Wilhelmine Germany in the first, and the tactics employed, far from being radically new innovations, were simply direct extensions of what had been done earlier. The striking successes in the early years of World War II should be credited to the achievements of the German Army of 1914 and, to an equal extent, the foolishness of Germany's adversaries. Not only had they failed to prepare, they had hardly bothered to absorb any of the lessons of the previous war, the Soviet Union under Stalin no less than France or Great Britain. Nikita Khrushchev, who presumably knew, observes that the U.S.S.R. was "unprepared in an elementary respect. . . . The Tsar . . . in 1914 had a larger supply of rifles than we did the day after Hitler invaded. And our economic potential was incomparably higher . . . we had no excuse."[14]

So this book concludes that Hitler's initial military successes were largely a function of the systematic innovations of his commanders in an earlier war, and hardly the result of his genius; I would add to that an observation that lies far outside the subject of this book, but one that flows from it quite logically, to the effect that Germany in November 1918 was hardly a beaten country; to twist one of Mark Twain's aphorisms around, the rumors of its death were greatly exaggerated.

Germany won the military struggle against its adversaries because Germany used its resources more intelligently. Aside from the superiority that one would naturally anticipate in a wealthy country with a high level of scientific achievement and an educated citizenry, the German Army was more competent than its opponents because its training was better, its officers were better, and the men who directed its endeavors were more familiar with the basics of the military art.

How the contrary view of the war became holy writ among historians is a fascinating and complex subject deserving a separate study. The military commands of Great Britain and France had complete control over the news that came out of the war, particularly on the Western Front. In public, they recounted the war as they wished. The first histories of the war, published while it was still going on, were written by Allied propagandists who went to great lengths to represent their works as objective histories.[15] Their works were all the more convincing because they rested on what appeared to be a solid factual base—facts supplied by the staffs of the French and British armies, and endorsed by their commanders.

In private, the Allied staffs fed their governments only such information as supported their views on what was happening. To a great extent, they believed their own misinformation. As this account makes clear, the information was wrong, and to a great extent it backfired. In France, the nature of this, although not all of the particulars, was gradually brought out during the war. In the United Kingdom, it remained obscured in such controversy as to color all subsequent accounts.[16] So much so that even today most English and Americans assume that the argument is a purely subjective one of how the data is interpreted.

Casualty data are complex, but basic comparisons can be made. Immediately after the war, an official government publication compiled by the researchers and statisticians of the United Kingdom's War Office made the comparison between British and German losses. In 1915, the British War Office calculated that 42,940 British soldiers were killed in combat against the Germans, who for their part had 20,652 killed in combat against the British.[17] In 1916, the year of the Somme, the same figures were 109,399 British to 49,450 Germans. In 1917, the year of Arras, Passchendaele, and Cambrai, the figures were 136,141 British to 72,668 Germans. Only in the last year of the war, 1918, did the figures approach equality: 108,539 British to 108,508 Germans.

Although no French agency did comparable calculations for relative French and German losses on a year-by-year basis, the same pattern of relative loss prevails throughout the first forty-eight months of the war. The great myth of the war, then, is that Great Britain and France won it. As we shall see, it is not the only one.

NOTES

1. David Lloyd George, *War Memoirs* (London: Odhams, 1938), 2:1313.

2. A.J.P. Taylor, *Illustrated History of the First World War* (New York: G.P. Putnam's Sons, 1964), 125.

3. The German medical services analyzed the data from previous wars whenever possible; see

Tables 64 and 65 in Heeressanitätsinspektion des Reichsministeriums, *Sanitätsbericht über das deutsche Heer im Weltkrieg 1914/18,* 3 vols. (Berlin: Reichsministerium, 1935), vol. 3. Both the Canadian and Australian medical historians found the data supplied by the various combatants to be congruent in almost every respect. See Andrew Macphail, *Official History of the Canadian Forces in the Great War: The Medical Services* (Ottawa: Acland, 1925), 253–54; Arthur Grahame Butler et al., *The Australian Medical Services in the War of 1914–18* (Melbourne: Australian War Memorial, 1930–43), 2:878.

4. *Surgeon General's Report of 1920:* W1.1/20:1:495.

5. See the text of Maginot's speech to a secret session of the Chamber, as reprinted in Paul Allard, *Les Dessous de la guerre révélés par les comités secrets* (Paris: Éditions de France, 1932), 15. (Unless otherwise specifically noted, all translations from French to English are my own.) Postwar, British War Office statisticians computed that on the Western Front, omitting 1914 and the end of the war, about two British soldiers fell for every German (see the discussions in note 16 and 17). The table compiled in the official Australian Medical History shows the ratio to be much worse than this (Butler, 3:873). The confusion arises when German losses from other fronts are factored in: fighting in France, Italy, Russia, Serbia, Rumania, and Russia over the course of the war, the German Army lost about the same number of men the Allies did on the Western Front alone.

6. "Though the Germans invaded, it was more often the French who attacked," is his memorable phrase: Winston Churchill, *The World Crisis, 1916–1918* (New York: Charles Scribner's Sons, 1927), 1:8–9.

7. The graves in the cemeteries of Fromeréville, Arrancy, and Monthairons were all reinterred at other, larger cemeteries, so today there are only eighteen, officially containing 56,105 remains. In addition to the largest, Douaumont (14,856 graves), the others are Avocourt, Belleray, Bras sur Meuse, Brocourt en Argonne, Chattancourt, Dombasle en Argonne, Dugny-sur-Meuse, Esnes en Argonne Haudainville, Landrecourt, Senoncourt les Majouy, Les Souhesmes-Rampont, Vadelaincourt, Verdun Bevaux, Verdun Faubourg Pavé, Verdun Glorieux, and Ville sur Cousances.

8. Joffre, *The Personal Memoirs of Joffre, Field Marshal of the French Army,* trans. T. Bentley Mott (New York: Harper, 1932), 2:451.

9. Brigadier General Rees, describing the action of his 94th Infantry Brigade on 1 July 1916, on the Somme, as quoted by John Laffin, *British Butchers and Bunglers of World War One* (Gloucestershire, England: Sutton, 1988), 9. This passage has been widely quoted by historians of the war.

10. The quote is from Henry Contamine, *La Revanche, 1871–1914* (Paris: Berger-Levrault, 1957), 277. Pierre Joseph Camena Almeida can list only twelve cases in the German Army where "heavy" casualties had been incurred by the end of the Marne in *L'Armée allemande avant et pendant la guerre de 1914–18* (Paris: Berger-Levrault, 1919), 160, 171–73. Joseph Bedier finds only one instance of the Germans advancing in this fashion (the 21st Bavarians at La Marfée on 27 August 1914) in *L'Effort française* (Paris: Renaissance du Livre, 1919), 16. Numerous claims were, of course, made (and will be discussed below), but none of them seem to have much evidentiary value.

11. Dmitrii Antonovich Volkogonov, *Stalin: Triumph and Tragedy,* trans. and ed. Harold Shukman (New York: Grove Weidenfeld, 1988), 475. Patton and Montgomery, two highly

regarded Allied generals of World War II, felt the same way. See the summary of Patton on this in John Nelson Rickard, *Patton at Bay: The Lorraine Campaign* (Westport, Conn.: Praeger, 1999), 6.

12. Figures taken from Charles Edwin Woodrow Bean, *Anzac to Amiens, A Shorter History of the Australian Fighting Services in the First World War.* 5th ed. (Canberra: Australian War Memorial, 1968), 532.

13. Robert H. Ferrell, *Woodrow Wilson and World War One* (New York: Harper and Row, 1985), 131–33.

14. Strobe Talbott, trans., *Khrushchev Remembers* (Boston: Little, Brown, 1970), 159. The problem with the Russians in 1914 wasn't that they were unprepared, but that they, like everyone else, were woefully unprepared for the war that followed. By prevailing standards, they were prepared. See the analysis in Norman Stone, *The Eastern Front 1914–1917* (New York: Charles Scribner's sons, 1975), esp. 49.

15. On the Allied censorship of, and control over news emanating from, the front, see Jean Galtier-Boissière, *Histoire de la grande guerre* (Paris, Crapouillot, 1932, 295–304, and the firsthand account of the censorship in action by Jean de Pierrefeu, *G.Q.G. Secteur 1.* 1st ed. (Paris: Les Éditions G. Crés et cie., 1922). For accounts of how the Allies manipulated the news, see Stewart Halsey Ross, *Propaganda for War: How the United States Was Conditioned to Fight the Great War of 1914–1918* (Jefferson, N.C.: McFarland, 1996); M.L. Sanders and Philip M. Taylor, *British Propaganda During the First World War, 1914–18* (London: Macmillan, 1982). The first histories of the war were written by men either known to be uncritical Allied supporters. (Frank Simonds, whose history appeared while the war was still going on) or propagandists (John Buchan, the second head of the U.K. propaganda operation).

16. When Churchill tried to base an argument on these figures, he was pilloried, most notably by the eminent medieval historian Sir Charles Oman. See the discussion by Robin Prior in *Churchill's World Crisis as History* (London: Croom Helm, 1983), 212–26. See also the article by Williams, "Treatment of the German Losses on the Somme in the *Official History: Military Operations France and Belgium, 1916, Volume Two*," *RUSI Journal*, 5:111 (February 1966), 70ff. Prior makes several minor errors in his text but his discussion makes the point clear enough. The discussion in Churchill is in *The World Crisis, 1916–1918*, 1:23–32. The attack by Oman is in Lord Sydenham of Combe et al., *The World Crisis by Winston Churchill, A Criticism* (London: Kennikat, 1970 [1928]).

17. These figures are to be found in War Office [United Kingdom], *Statistics of the Military Effort of the British Empire During the Great War, 1914–1920* (London: His Majesty's Stationery Office, 1922), 359–62. Curiously, although most British analysts derive their basic data from this text, they ignore this portion of it. As noted in the text, the French did not try to compute relative losses in this manner; total losses for all the combatants are given in the epilogue (see the discussion in notes 4 and 5). Here–and elsewhere in this text–I have used the numbers for those killed in action only, and excluded the wounded and the missing. The figures for the wounded are ambiguous. Sometimes the figure refers to the number of cases, and sometimes the number of individuals. As the American data make clear, soldiers were wounded more than once; additionally, some soldiers were wounded and then later were killed or were missing. Moreover, we have much good evidence suggesting that the German wounded, as a group, had a higher rate of recovery than the French and British wounded.

The number of missing is likewise ambiguous: although some soldiers are blown to pieces or buried, and never found, many of those listed as missing were actually taken prisoner (or deserted). At the end of the war, the Allies were able to calculate a figure for the category "missing in action, presumed dead," but the German records had been lost. Although a book could be written on the subject, the point here is simple: the categories of wounded and miss-ing vary as a function of the type of report as well as national record keeping. Consequently, I have used the figures for soldiers killed whenever possible; however, British records for 1914 are a shambles (which is why the comparison omitted 1914), and French records for the first year or so of the war are little better. Such cases, where the broader fig-ures are the only ones available, are noted.

Casualty Tables

1. Casualties by Nation, Western Front

Country	Deaths	Missing	Totals	Wounded
Belgium	35,000	63,000	98,000	n.a.
France	1,070,000	314,000	1,384,000	3,481,000
Great Britain	564,715	319,824	884,539	1,837,613
United States	116,950	4,452	121,402	239,787
Total	1,786,665	701,276	2,487,941	5,558,400
Germany	669,263	623,260	1,292,523	1,214,327

2. Deaths by Year and Nation, Western Front

Country	1914	1915	1916	1917	1918	Totals
Belgium	8,199	2,996	2,072	2,414	9,048	24,729
France	304,124	210,879	295,368	169,430	210,162	1,189,963
Great Britain	17,174	66,415	150,131	226,450	162,613	622,783
United States	0	0	0	0	85,252	85,252
Total	329,497	280,290	447,571	398,294	467,075	1,922,727
Germany	85,021	113,438	142,823	121,622	206,359	669,263

Sources: See notes 4, 5, and 6 in the Epilogue.

Notes: (1) The figures for the Missing in Table 1 include live prisoners of war later repa-triated. (2) The figure for the wounded is for cases, not individuals (soldiers who were wounded more than once, or were wounded and then died or went missing would be included in these totals. (3) French data in Table 2 adjusted to factor out the missing and prisoners. (4) German data for 1918 include Churchill's adjustment for incomplete report-ing by the German Medical Services after July 1918. (5) Not listed are the approximately 16,000 Italian, Portuguese, Russian, Czech, and Polish deaths on the Western Front, as well as the roughly 600 Austro-Hungarian soldiers killed in action there.

1

France and the Failures of National Defense, 1870–1914

An examination of the army before 1914 reveals that it was ruled more by confusion than by logic, afflicted by institutional malfunctioning rather than from the neat application of a coherent but wrongheaded system of thought inspired by professional principles and right-wing sentiments.... In the final analysis, the radical Republic got the army it deserved....

—*Douglas Porch*[1]

The issues that determined how the Great War would be fought stemmed from the French war with Germany in 1870, the postwar responses to the defeat by the new French government, and the responses of the German Army to meet France's constantly shifting war plans. France's confused and volatile national defense policies forced the German military to adopt a set of weapons, a military doctrine, and a plan of action that determined how it would fight a future war.

On 19 July 1870, France declared war on Prussia, which immediately caused the German states allied with Prussia to declare war on France. Although France had forced the war on Prussia (something Bismarck had skillfully encouraged), and was thus the aggressor, the country had no coherent plan of action. Engels, writing in a London newspaper, pointed out that it hardly made any sense to declare war without then launching an invasion, but this is exactly what had happened.[2]

Three weeks after the French declaration of war, the French were still organizing at their frontier. The initial battles of early August were all fought right on the border, and mostly inside France: Wissembourg (the fourth), Wörth (the sixth), and Spicheren (the sixth). The French Army of the Northeast, defeated in all three engagements, retired in the direction of Châlons, a city located on the Marne River to the southeast of Reims. On the fifteenth, the French Army of the Center, based around Metz, was defeated at Vionville, and then, on the eighteenth, at Gravelotte, both small towns to the west of Metz.

The surviving French regrouped in Metz, waiting to be relieved. When the Germans defeated the relief forces on the thirtieth (at Beaumont), MacMahon left Bazaine to hold out in Metz, and withdrew to Sedan. There, in September 1870, he was wounded at the start of what both sides hoped would be the decisive battle of the war. Unlike Metz, Sedan is a city located in a bowl. Troops penned up there were helpless. The next day the emperor, Napoleon III, was forced to surrender, along with most of what was left of France's army.

Broadly put, after 1870, France had three aims: to develop the capability to mount an effective defense of the frontier, to strengthen France militarily through alliances, and to develop a loyal and effective military. The initial effort was impressive. The first military planners of the Third Republic, of whom the military engineer Raymond-Adolphe Séré de Rivières was the most important, sought to build a coherent policy of national defense for the new post-1870 frontier. Séré de Rivières, who from 1872 to 1880 was France's minister of war, laid down the basic plans that would determine France's defense policy: a belt of fortifications that would protect the country from an invasion and allow France time to bring its armies onto the field. Over the next thirty years, starting with an appropriation of the then staggering sum of eighty-eight million francs in 1874, France poured an unprecedented amount of its resources into this project.[3] By 1914 there were over one hundred independent forts on the northeastern frontier alone, and the Belgians, under the direction of another brilliant engineering officer, Brialmont, had mounted a parallel effort that they felt would ensure their neutrality in the event of a future conflict: the three most strategically important Belgian cities (Namur, Liège, and Antwerp) were encircled by no less than forty forts.

The main forts were supplemented by dozens of small reinforced structures, called *fortins* or *ouvrages*, and carefully sited so as to dominate the terrain. The French encircled key cities that lay at critical transportation junctures with fortifications. From north to southeast, the cities of Lille, Maubeuge, Reims, Verdun, Toul, Épinal, and Belfort were, like the three Belgian cities, turned into what the French termed *places forti-fiées,* or fortified positions. A town like Verdun was the unfortified administrative center of a two-hundred-square-kilometer area protected by some twenty major forts and about twice that many smaller *ouvrages.*[4]

The most important path into France lay along the Meuse River, which began in the Vosges Mountains down by Switzerland and ran up through France and Belgium into Holland. Major rail and road links ran alongside, and the river itself, with its connecting canals, was an important transportation artery. In Belgium, the fortified areas surrounding Liège and Namur sat astride the Meuse, as did Verdun. But from Verdun on down the river there were no fewer than twelve isolated forts on the heights of the Meuse, guarding the major crossings.

In addition, there were fortified towns and single forts stretching along the Belgian frontier from Lille to the new German frontier, and along that frontier down to Switzerland. The scheme of fortifications gave the Germans difficult choices. From the easternmost fort of Reims (Pompelle) to the westernmost fort of Verdun (Bois Bourrus) was only about forty kilometers, most of which was taken up by the Argonne Forest, a rough and dense tract of the sort European armies had traditionally avoided.

Below Verdun, there was another stretch between the river forts along the Meuse and the Moselle. But the French considered this area, the plain of the Woëvre, a swamp as unsuitable for maneuver as the Argonne. And from Épinal on down to Belfort, the forts formed a dense barrier. An invader (which could only be Germany) would either have to develop out of heavily forested areas (the Ardennes and the Argonne), try to move through the passes of the Vosges Mountains, blunder through major urban areas (such as Nancy), or mount a direct attack on one of the fortified areas.

All of the options would force an attacker to move slowly. The American Civil War had made it fairly clear that assaults against fortified positions, even when they were fortified only at the rudimentary level of, say, Vicksburg, were difficult propositions, and, as the decades wore on, the experiences in the Boer War and the Russo-Japanese War reinforced this lesson.

Although there were successful sieges made, none of them were accomplished very quickly, and all of the developments in firepower after 1870 seemed to convey an advantage to the defender, who increasingly had the capability to stand back at long range and destroy the invader, first with artillery and then with infantry fire, since the rifles coming into widespread use were all accurate out to distances of four and five hundred meters (with much greater killing ranges).

This greater range (the killing range of the muskets of the turn of the century had been about fifty meters) forced gunners to stand back, while advances in explosives and metallurgy made for considerably more potent weapons. During the 1870s and 1880s most of the developments that made the breech-loading rifle a feasible mass weapon were applied to artillery pieces. Napoleon had been a gunner, and the French were anxious to assert their historic supremacy in the field. The military engineers DeBange and Baquet both perfected breech-locking mechanisms, which enabled the gun barrel to withstand very high stresses, and DeBange's 120 millimeter gun of 1878, which fired an eighteen-kilogram shell containing over four kilograms of high explosive out to distances of slightly over eight thousand meters, was a remarkable weapon.

Such guns were powerful. But they were also extremely heavy, with a massive swollen casting at the rear of the gun, which was necessary for the mounts, since this was the place where all the rearward force generated by the firing of the gun was transmitted to the gun carriage. So DeBange's gun, which weighed over eight thousand kilograms, couldn't be pulled into action by the usual team of six horses. For the defenders, this was fine: the guns could be shipped in by rail, unloaded, mounted almost permanently, and then sighted in on possible targets.

But for an attacking army, simply moving such weapons onto the battlefield would take a great deal of time, and would involve the construction of roads and railroad spurs, as well as the strengthening of bridges—and obviously, very careful positioning. Even without the defenders taking any action, it might take ten days or more simply to transport the gun and get it into position. And the really heavy weapons, such as DeBange's 270 millimeter siege mortar of 1878, weighed nearly twenty metric tons and had to be shipped to the site in pieces and then assembled, a procedure that took days.

Even when the barrel was of modest bulk, the process of assembly was cumbrous. After the site was prepared, the barrel, which weighed several tons on its own, had to be unloaded from its traveling mount and then mated with the mount, a process which one contemporary military journal called slow and laborious at best. At every level, technology favored the defense. Even though advances in explosives had made the original masonry forts of the 1870s seriously vulnerable to shellfire, a systematic program of reinforcement and modernization kept the key forts largely invulnerable to artillery fire.

By the turn of the century, France had one of the largest artillery parks in Europe. Screened by the forts, French gunners would simply destroy the enemy's siege artillery before he was able to bring it onto the field, and infantry operating in the intervals between the forts would ensure the impossibility of infiltration. While the enemy laboriously moved up his own siege artillery—a process that in itself might take weeks—an army in the field would be mobilized and brought into play. But the army itself was subsidiary to the garrisons and the guns.

Napoleon III's talented wife had desperately tried to enlist the support of foreign powers during the 1870 war. None of Bismarck's neighbors were particularly keen on seeing Prussia beat France, but after Prussia's triumphs over Denmark and Austria, neither were they keen to enter the field. After 1870, it was clear that no European power, on its own, could match Germany.

Bismarck had made Russo-German alliance the cornerstone of his foreign policy, and when he was dismissed in 1890 by the young emperor Wilhelm II, the coalition headed by his new chancellor, Caprivi, was either incapable or unwilling to preserve this alliance. Wilhelm II, for all his mental instability, understood clearly enough the catastrophic effect of this shift on Germany's national security. When Nicholas II assumed the Russian throne in 1894, Wilhelm intervened personally in an attempt to forestall the new alliance, but to no avail. By 1894, the French had slipped deftly into the middle, and signed a treaty with Russia.

Overnight the new treaty changed France's defense policy. If Germany attacked, Russia would come to France's aid. France and Russia together were considerably more powerful militarily than Germany. It did not take a major strategist to see that while the Germans tried to batter their way through France's fortifications, Russian field armies would be invading East Prussia.

There was another side to this equation, of course. If Germany attacked Russia, France was bound to come to her aid. That meant standing on the offensive. And that in turn meant the development of an army that was able to mobilize promptly and take to the field. Consequently, the next logical priority was the development of the army.

But the triumphs of French foreign policy were far from over. In 1902, France concluded a secret agreement with Italy that effectively ruled out any Italian military action against France (or vice versa). As Germany had invested a good deal of effort in developing an alliance with Italy and Austria-Hungary, this was another significant setback for the Germans. The Italian arrangement was so secret that the central staff of the French Army, the *Grand Quartier Général* (GQG), didn't find out about it until 1909, seven years after the Foreign Ministry had concluded the bargain.[5]

As secret arrangements went, the best was yet to come. In January 1906, a series of talks began between representatives of the French and British high commands regarding the landing of a British force in France or possibly Belgium. Although these talks were supposedly secret, unofficial, and nonbinding, by June 1906, the Committee of Imperial Defence had decided that, in the event of a war breaking out,

> Any military cooperation on the part of the British Army, if under-
> taken at the outset of the war, must take on the form of an expedition
> to Belgium or in direct participation of the defense of the French fron-
> tier. A German violation of Belgian territory would apparently neces-
> sitate the first course. The possibility of such violation taking place
> with the consent of the Belgian government must not be overlooked.
> In any case, the views of the French would have to be considered, as it
> is essential that any measure of co-operation on our part should har-
> monize with their strategic plan. Whichever course was adopted, a
> preliminary landing on the French northwestern coast would be
> advantageous.[6]

Thus, while officially denying it, Great Britain had tied its entry into a Continental war to whatever the French policy of the moment was, and committed itself to land an expeditionary force in support. As most of the people present at the meeting were aware—some of them more gloomily than others—this was a commitment to a Continental war, particularly since the document quoted begins by ruling out any immediate naval action.

The only country that might conceivably go to war with France and be in a position to invade French soil was Germany. So now France had a formal alliance with Russia, a secret agreement of neutrality with Italy, and an even more secret understanding with Great Britain that committed

Great Britain to fight Germany on the Continent. France's advantage in this was quite clear: Germany could hardly expect to emerge victorious in a war against all three of the other major powers. It would face a war on two fronts with no real allies to speak of. How any advantage accrued to Great Britain is difficult to explain.

Henry Wilson, Director of Military Operations and the *eminence grise* behind these talks, of course felt he was right to involve his country in a Continental war. He envisioned a great Continental war in which the sides would be so evenly matched that six divisions of the BEF would provide the margin of difference. His arithmetic was faulty on three or four different levels, but no one felt able to challenge him, so his theory prevailed. Both the idea and the way it was pushed would prove symptomatic of a military mindset in the British General Staff which elevated numbers (usually the wrong ones) over all else.

But Great Britain's and Germany's loss was France's gain. The country had a formidable defensive network of fortifications, which was now matched by a formidable network of alliances. What it needed was an army capable of enforcing its will on the battlefield.

THE ARMY

While the engineers had fortified and the government ministers had negotiated, the French Army had devolved. In reality, there were two armies, or maybe half a dozen. When military experts spoke of the French Army, they meant the 172 infantry regiments of the regular army in metropolitan France, together with its attached regiments of cavalry and artillery. But after 1870, there was another army as well. By 1910, France had one of the largest colonial empires in the world. However, the Colonial Army was not, as might be supposed, composed of native troops. Instead, it encompassed a bewildering array of exotically named units: omitting the nineteen battalions of native troops, there were twelve regiments of colonial infantry, two of the Legion, four of *zouaves,* nine of *tirailleurs,* six mixed *zouaves* and *tirailleurs,* and five *bataillons légères d'Afrique.*

The term *regiment* or *battalion* should be taken loosely. A regiment generally consisted of three battalions, and at its full mobilized strength it came to roughly twenty-five hundred men. But the two regiments of the

Legion had seventeen thousand men between them, and the colonial units had a much higher peacetime strength than their regular army counterparts. This was also true of the other enclave within the regular army, the *chasseurs*. Like many elite units of this period, they were organized by battalions as well, but the battalions were overstrength. So although France technically only had 172 infantry regiments, in reality the number was much higher: each of the twelve alpine battalions, the *chasseurs alpins* (BCA), for example, had the same firepower as an infantry regiment.

Given the mountainous nature of much of the French frontier, the need for alpine troops was clear, but it is also clear that France had way too many "elite" units of one sort or another. Too many specialist troops and not enough commanders. In fact, there was no real overall commander. Instead, there was a committee, the CSG (*Conseil Supérieure de la Guerre*), composed of those generals who would be the army commanders in the event of a war. The chairman of the committee was the minister of war, and the vice chair was the man who in wartime would be the commander in chief. The vice chair had his own job: in 1910, General Michel was the head of the commission in charge of the fortifications. One searches in vain for the word "staff" in these lists of titles. The arrangement was deliberate: if one man controlled the military in peacetime, he might be tempted to use it.

By 1910, it had become obvious that this was not a good arrangement, and when Messimy became minister of war in 1911, he aimed at a reform in which the future commander in chief would also be chief of staff, and thus have real power. But only in theory, as the government was still leery of letting a senior army officer actually have control over matters military. But Messimy's reform was a major step in putting someone in control of the army. The question was who.

In 1910, Gallieni, who had been in charge of the Madagascar expedition, was the most well known of the senior officers. The second most obvious candidate, General Michel having been summarily retired, was General Pau. But the only candidate Gallieni would support who was also acceptable to the government—and who would take the job with all its strings—was Joffre, whose new title would be Chief of the General Staff.

The General Staff already had a head, General Dubail, who would continue, but with even fewer rights than before, since in the event of a war, the *chef d'état-major général* (Joffre) would assume command of the armies in the field, taking with him as *major-général* (chief of his staff) the *premier sous-chef d'état-major*. So Dubail, as *chef d'état-major de l'armée*, had no authority at all. Not that Joffre himself had all that much. The technical bureaus that controlled the development of weapons all reported to the minister of war, who also had final say on the budget. Thus the end result of the disgrace at Sedan and Metz, the Boulanger coup, and the squalor of the Dreyfus affair all came home to roost. The government had every piece of the national defense puzzle in place except one: an army.

When Joffre assumed command, such as it was, in July 1911, he was faced with separate but interrelated problems: the condition of the army, the deficiencies of its equipment, and the need for a new strategic plan. After 1870, France's plan had been primarily defensive, and its emphasis had been to ensure a rapid mobilization, which would match the troops with their units at the right time and in the right place. Given the size of the country, and the length of the border, it was important to know where exactly the Germans would attack.

Over the course of the decades, the French had settled on the hypothesis that the main German attack would develop from around Metz, trying to break into the French lines in the area from Verdun to Toul. As a result, the fortifications there were the most modern, and the French plan of mobilization, Plan 16, had the greater part of the army mobilized with an eye to operating there.

Joffre's predecessor, General Michel, had become increasingly concerned about an attack from a different quarter, and had wanted to reorganize defense plans to deal with the possibility of an attack through Belgium. The Belgian fortifications at Namur and Liège, although blocking efforts to move eastward, would be unable to prevent a southwesterly slide of German armies that would enable a massive attack across the French frontier west of Verdun.

Joffre and his staff realized that the best way to block a German invasion was to move aggressively into Belgium. Accordingly, one of his first proposals to the government was to mobilize French forces so they could move directly across the frontier. Like General Michel, Joffre assumed Belgium would be invaded in the event of a war; the question was simply who would get there first.

Joffre's ideas were quite sound, but the government dithered.

Poincaré, then in one of his many premierships (he didn't become president until 1913) was unwilling to risk a violation of Belgian neutrality,
since the Belgians were extremely sensitive about alliances and entanglements. His fear was that if the Germans got wind of any French plans to
move into Belgium, they would use this to drive a wedge between
England and France.

An expeditionary force of six divisions would constitute the greater
part of the British Army's available troops in the United Kingdom. Once
in France, the United Kingdom would be committed to a French war, and
Poincaré wasn't willing to give the Germans any opening at all.[7] And
Belgium was irrevocably opposed to any entanglements with France or
the United Kingdom—to a level that in retrospect seems foolish. Certainly
the Belgian minister of war in September 1914 was not anxious to remind
anyone that in 1912 he had made it clear to the British naval attaché that
"in his opinion the dangers of a breach of Belgian neutrality lay more
from England than anywhere else."[8] But he said it, and his government
felt it. There were attempts to deneutralize Belgium and turn it into a convenient staging area for French armies. But they were never well executed,
they failed entirely, and the French, on their own, were not prepared to
violate Belgian neutrality.

So Poincaré passed on Joffre's option, and the staff moved on to the
next one, which became Plan 17. Like its predecessor, this was not a plan
of attack, but a scheme of mobilization, although obviously the areas the
army assembled would dictate future theaters of operations. The frontier
was big, and the Germans had several options. They could, for example,
simply stand on the defensive in the West and conduct offensive operations in the East, where they had an ally, Austria-Hungary. Or they could
do it the other way around. And if they attacked in the West, they had
three main possibilities: an advance through Belgium, an attack developing out of the Metz bridgehead (as Plan 16 had been disposed against), or
an attack out of southern Alsace.

Put that way, the French choices became much simpler. The Germans
had built forts as well, and their fortifications around Metz and to the
west of Strasbourg made any offensive action there impossible. Nothing
could be done to give an impression of impinging on Belgian neutrality.
So defensively, the best plan was to cluster forces so they would be in a
position to strike back against a German invasion out of Metz or
Belgium. And here an accident of geography favored the French: troops

located in front of the Verdun forts could move to block either offensive, since the Germans would be hung up on the Meuse forts in Belgium or have to cross over the river below Namur. In any of the possible scenarios, the French would have less distance to travel than their adversaries. They could either be there first or strike directly into the side of an advancing force that was shifting to the West.

If armies were mobilized from Belfort up along the Vosges, they could either block a German advance or mount their own offensive operations. Increasingly, the French favored this last. The reasons were sensible enough. The Alsatians were culturally, linguistically, and socially a Germanic people. This hardly meant they were enthusiastic recruits to the *Kaiserreich*, any more than the Sudeteners of Bohemia wanted to become Bavarians, but Wilhelmine Germany after 1870 had pumped an enormous amount of money into both Alsace and Lorraine in an attempt to integrate it into the Reich. When, in 1918, French soldiers advanced into the region, they were amazed at how developed it was compared to France, and even today, the dividing line of 1870 can be divined almost by sight, simply by an inspection of the infrastructure of the towns and villages.[9]

In a word, Alsace was as German as Pomerania: the Germans were going to have to defend Obernai and Munster just as vigorously as Posen. Militarily, the Alsatian plain was promising. Once an army got into it from the south, it could rapidly surge up along the Rhine and make its way into Germany itself. Strasbourg was a fortified city, like Verdun (or Belfort). But the bulk of the fortifications faced west, as that was where the main threat lay. There was no particular reason why a French army couldn't fight its way north at greater speed than a German army could fight its way south through Belgium and Champagne-Ardennes.

The French General Staff could afford to be grandiose in its planning because France would be able to field an enormous army. In the event of a general mobilization, its peacetime army of some 884,000 men would expand to a field army of 1,689,000, with another 1,092,00 men in the pipeline in the interior and the colonies.[10] If the Germans attacked through Belgium, they would face a force of over a quarter of a million Belgian soldiers as well.[11] There was no way Germany could put that many troops into the Western Front.

Unfortunately, during its decades of garrison and fortification duty, the army had totally lost touch with the basics. When Joffre viewed the maneuvers of 1911, here is what he saw:

> The infantry, hardly maneuvering, demonstrated the gaps in their instruction, the fronts of attack were disproportionate to the means at hand, the ground badly used. The artillery and the infantry did not look for a way to coordinate their efforts.... In sum, the mass of the army, for a long time maintained in the defensive mold, had neither doctrine nor instruction.[12]

General Percin, Inspector General of French Artillery, was hardly surprised. After the 1910 maneuvers he had written a detailed complaint about the deficiencies. The infantry might practice, but the gunners had other ideas: "I never saw an army corps with more than eighteen batteries of four pieces," Percin wrote. "In the maneuvers I directed last September, of the Thirteenth Corps, I had twenty-three batteries, each with one gun."[13] In fact, so few guns were involved in most exercises that Percin recorded that senior artillery officers were employed as umpires because there was really nothing for them to do. And the few gunners who were around (who had very little ammunition) were determined to deploy their weapons at ranges Percin judged suicidal, given an adversary armed with bolt-action rifles. But when he protested, a member of the Superior War Council overruled him.

Joffre did his best to equip the army with weapons, plans, and doctrines. But weapons development was in the hands of a bureau that reported to the War Ministry, not the army. The experts there, who had allies among the gunners, refused to develop the guns Joffre felt the army needed, principally a 105 millimeter howitzer to complement the 75 millimeter gun. The Balkan wars had made it clear that shells would be fired at a rate far beyond what had been previously calculated. Joffre tried to get the shell supply increased. But the budget was controlled by the War Ministry, which was in turn subject to the Chamber of Deputies.

Unfortunately, the Chamber was simply unwilling to spend any more money than they had already spent. Although France's treaty with Russia had dramatically changed the equation of national defense, the government had no intention of allocating the money to support the new defense policy. Joffre was turned down on basically every major request he made, from mobile kitchens to new uniforms. In 1914, French soldiers went to war wearing red pants because the Chamber had refused to spend the money for less visible uniforms, and they went to war hungry because the French Army had no way to supply its soldiers with cooked meals.

Over plans and doctrines, however, Joffre had some say. The new plan of mobilization and deployment, Plan 17, was approved by the General Staff and put into effect in April 1913, less than fifteen months before the start of hostilities.[14] New infantry regulations designed to remedy the problems Joffre had observed during maneuvers took longer to develop. In fact, they were not introduced until 20 April 1914, with an all too obvious result, as Joffre himself observed.

> Unfortunately, these regulations were still in study within the army when the war broke out. It takes a long time for a doctrine to penetrate into the last echelons, above all after a period of moral anarchy.... From the point of view of tactics, the cadres still did not grasp offensive necessities....They had, in particular, a general tendency not to take into account sufficiently the conditions of modern war, which does not permit many attacks like those made in the time of the muzzle loading musket and cannon.[15]

Unfortunately, "moral anarchy" was an excellent term to describe the French Army.

The new regulations hardly helped solve the problem. In the army before mobilization, each regiment operated at half strength. Mobilization meant that each combat unit in the regular army doubled in size, the new arrivals being men who had completed their military service in years past. This was true of everyone else's army as well. Omitting from consideration the reserve and third-line units, about half of all the soldiers in all the regular armies of August 1914 were civilians who had just put on their uniforms.

Along with the uniforms, they had to learn a new doctrine expressly designed to counteract the bad habits they had learned earlier—assuming anyone remembered and there wasn't anyone to teach them. Part of the moral anarchy was that the army was desperately short of officers. General Weygand estimated the army was short eight hundred lieutenants, but extant documents suggest this figure is far too low. The fifth infantry division had only sixteen of the sixty lieutenants it was supposed to have, and about half of its sub and reserve lieutenants, for a shortage of junior officers.[16]

All the evidence suggests this situation was typical. Admissions to military school were down, the pay of officers was miserable, and promotions were held up indefinitely or blocked owing to politics. Emil Driant, who would be the first senior officer to fall at Verdun in 1916, had graduated fifth in his class at Saint-Cyr in 1875, served in three Tunisian campaigns, and ended up commanding the elite first battalion of *chasseurs à pied* in 1899—and was then summarily retired, as he had the misfortune of having married General Boulanger's daughter.[17]

The government persecuted Roman Catholics in the officer class with the same fanaticism that members of that class had persecuted Dreyfus. Senior officers were instructed to report those officers serving under them who went to Mass. The then-Colonel Pétain's alleged response to such an instruction, to the effect that as he sat in the front row he had no idea who was behind him, was thus calculated to infuriate both left and right alike (Pétain was hardly an exemplary Roman Catholic).

As anarchy had descended on the army—whatever its cause—its professional officers had fragmented into small groups—to the extent that they even had a name for them, *chapelles*. On 22 January 1919, General Fayolle had dinner with Colonel Rimailho and General Saint-Clair-Deville. Rimailho was a gunnery expert responsible for the development of some of France's best weapons, and he and Saint-Clair-Deville showed Fayolle pictures of some of their innovations. "Why weren't those adopted during the war?" asked one of France's few successful generals. "Rivalries among the *chapelles*," they replied.[18]

Thus each *chapelle*, each clique, had its own ideas, carefully nurtured and protected from outside influences. One clique—which subsequently became the most famous—favored the cult of the offense; another, the power of field artillery. Would the war be long or short, decided by cavalry or the bayonet, by magazine rifles or shrapnel? And who was most qualified to lead? For each viewpoint, a clique, each one almost hermetically sealed.

Joffre, to give him credit, was trying to impose order. The new regulations, like Plan 17, were the sign of that. But when the soldiers finally began to absorb the new doctrines, what would they learn?

> The attack implies, on the part of all combatants, the will to come to grips with the enemy and remove him from combat with the bayonet....When one considers all the dispositions made, and the effectiveness of other arms, the success of the attack always depends, in the final analysis, on the bravery, the energy, and the obstinacy of the infantry."[19]

Clearly, this was a doctrine that, if applied, would eliminate moral anarchy. Unfortunately, it would do so by the process of eliminating most of the combatants, who would be blown apart or shot to pieces before they ever even saw their adversary. During the Great War, casualties caused by edged weapons came to roughly one quarter of one percent for each of the combatants.[20]

NOTES

1. The conclusion to Douglas Porch, *The March to the Marne: The French Army 1871–1914* (Cambridge: Cambridge University Press, 1981), 249–54.

2. As reported by Michael Howard, whose *The Franco-Prussian War* (New York: Collier, 1961) is the standard account—and the best. For Engels, see 76; unfortunately, Howard's sensible remark on 57 that "by a tragic combination of ill luck, stupidity, and ignorance France blundered into war . . . in a bad cause . . . It was not due simply to the machinations of Bismarck that France had to go, alone and unpopular, to meet her fate," seems to have been routinely ignored by historians of the 1914–18 conflict.

3. The most comprehensive discussions of these fortifications are those of Guy Le Hallé, *Verdun, les forts de la victoire* (Paris: CITÉDIS, 1998); Colonel Robert Normand, *Défense de Liège, Namur, Anvers en 1914* (Paris: L. Fournier, 1923). See also Étienne Anthérieu, *Grandeur et sacrifice de la ligne Maginot* (Paris: G. Durassié, 1962); Louis Claudel, *La Ligne Maginot: Conception—Réalisation* (Saint-Maurice: Association Saint-Maurice: 1974); Jean-Yves Mary, *La Ligne Maginot: Ce qu'elle était, ce qu'il en reste* (Paris: SERCAP, 1980).

4. See the extensive discussion in Stéphane Gaber, *La Lorraine fortifiée* (Metz: Éditions Serpenoise, 1997), esp. 150.

5. See Maréchal Joffre, *Mémoires du maréchal Joffre* (Paris: Plon, 1932). There are enormous differences between Joffre's French original and the standard two-volume translation, *The Personal Memoirs of Marshal Joffre,* trans. T. Bentley Mott (New York: Harper, 1932), and where possible, I have translated the passage from the French edition, particularly for those passages left out of the English. Curiously, the two-volume French edition is so rare as to be almost unavailable, so I have used Mott's translation for those passages. To simplify, the French version will be referred to as *Mémoires* and the English version by the translator's name, Mott. For the Italian reference, see Mott 1: 37.

6. As quoted by Niall Ferguson, *The Pity of War* (New York: Basic Books, 1999), 64. After the fact, British apologists would hide behind a technicality, claiming that the CID decision was not binding on the government, and Maurice Hankey would claim that no decision had actually been reached. Not so. As Viscount Esher, a member of the CID, observed: "The mere fact of the War Office plan having been worked out in detail with the French General Staff has certainly committed us to fight" (as quoted by Ferguson, 66). For the Belgian appreciation, see Roger Keyes, *Outrageous Fortune, The Tragedy of Leopold III of the Belgians* (London: Secker and Warburg, 1984), 5–7.

7. S.R. Williamson, in "Joffre Reshapes French Strategy, 1911–1913," sees this as a more focused discussion than I do. See his essay in Paul M. Kennedy, ed., *The War Plans of the Great Powers 1880–1914* (Boston: Allen and Unwin, 1985), esp. 138. My reading of the passage (109–126) is that Joffre is deliberately vague about whether France would only respond, or whether it would actually initiate on its own.

8. As quoted by Williamson in ibid., 132.

9. See Alain Peyrefitte, *The Trouble with France* (Le Mal Français), trans. William R. Byron (New York: New York University Press, 1986), 27. The use of such details to differentiate sections of France is from Xavier de Planhol, *An Historical Geography of France* (Géographie Historique de la France), trans. Janet Lloyd (Cambridge, England: Cambridge University Press, 1994).

10. Mobilization figures taken from Service Historiques des Armeés, *Inventaire sommaire des archives de la guerre* N 24 (Troyes: La Renaissance, 1967), 1: 206. Estimates of the total size of the army generally fail to include the colonial army; with the European troops of that force added, France's peacetime army was actually larger than Germany's.

11. In August 1914, Belgium mobilized an army of 234,000 men, of whom 117,000 composed a field army of six infantry divisions and one cavalry division, the remainder being the troops who manned the forts. See Major Tasnier and Major R. van Overstraeten, *L'Armée belge dans la guerre mondiale* (Brussels: Henri Bertelles, 1923), 316, and Henri Bernard, *L'An 14 et la campagne des illusions* (Brussels: La Renaissance du Livre, 1983), 59. The Belgian Army was a force considerably larger than the BEF's 90,000-odd men. Published sources in France estimated this would have been the case as early as 1900. See the discussion in [Sidney Rau], *L'État militaire des principales puissances étrangères en 1900* (Nancy: Berger-Levrault, 1900), 279. In 1912 Joffre was counting on a Belgian field army of six divisions and a BEF of seven divisions (*Mémoires*, 118).

12. *Mémoires*, 33. This passage is missing from the English translation.

13. Général Percin, *L'Artillerie aux manouevres de Picardie en 1910* (Paris: Berger-Levrault, 1911), v.

14. So anyone who was behind the informational curve and thought Plan 16 was still in effect would assume the French were blind to an attack through Belgium, which explains why so many early writers did just that.

15. *Mémoires*, 40. Unfortunately, the Mott translation of this passage is somewhat misleading, since Mott uses the term "moral inertia" instead of Joffre's "moral anarchy" (1.34–35). Here as elsewhere it can be argued that the tendency of English analysts to depend on translations has either led them astray or confirmed their prejudices. Anarchy is hardly the same thing as inertia.

16. Leonard V. Smith, *Between Mutiny and Obedience: The Case of the French Fifth Infantry Division During World War I* (Princeton, N.J.: Princeton University Press, 1994), 37–38. The basic shortages of officers had already been discussed both in Général Weygand, *Histoire de l'armée française* (Paris: Flammarion, 1961), 310–14, and in Jean Feller, *Le Dossier de l'armée française: La Guerre de cinquante ans, 1914–1962* (Paris: Perrin, 1966), 35.

17. See the summary in Gaston Jolivet, *Le Colonel Driant* (Paris: Delagrave, 1919).

18. Fayolle, *Carnets secrets de la grande guerre*, ed. Henry Contamine (Paris: Plon, 1964), 323.

19. Quote from *Inventaire sommaire des archives de la guerre N 24*, 1.60. British regulations said the same thing: "It is the spirit of the bayonet that captures the position . . . the rifle and the bayonet is [sic] the main infantry weapon." As quoted by Martin Samuels, *Doctrine and Dogma: German and British Infantry Tactics in the First World War* (New York: Greenwood, 1992), 49.

20. See the analysis of French medical data by Michel Huber, *La Population de la France pendant la guerre* (New Haven, Yale University Press, 1931), 430–31. Although little noted, the figure is routinely accepted by military historians as being true for all combatants during the war, whose frequency was so low that the Germans didn't even bother to keep data on this type of casualty.

2

Germany and the Development of Combined Arms Tactics

The theory of strategy scarcely goes beyond the first principles of common sense.

—*Moltke the Elder*[1]

Helmuth Karl Bernhard, Graf von Moltke, chief of the Prussian General Staff from 1857 to 1871, and then chief of the Great General Staff, the *Oberste Heeresleitung* (OHL) from 1871 to 1888, was of the opinion that in the event of a two-front war, Germany should strike East, and stay on the defensive in the West. Nor had he been enamored of the acquisition of Metz and the Alsace. But during most of his tenure as chief, Russia was, nominally at least, Germany's ally, and France's military power—and its aggressive tendencies, such as they were—projected into Africa and Asia.

Von Moltke the Elder retired at the age of eighty-eight and died three years later, before the first of France's secret pacts had even come into being. His successor, Alfred, Graf von Schlieffen, soon had to face the results of the first of Germany's foreign policy disasters: after 1894, in the event of a war with either France or Russia, Germany would have to face them both, and thus fight a war on two fronts. Militarily, this would be a catastrophe. Germany's only reliable ally, Austria-Hungary, spent hardly any money on its military at all. Nor was there any hard evidence that the Austrians would actually fight.

So Germany faced the prospect of a two-front war in which its army would be vastly outnumbered. In 1900 there were nearly two million

Frenchmen and Russians in uniform, and a little over half a million Germans. Over the next twelve years the German numbers crept slowly upward, but so did the numbers for France and Russia. In the event of a war, Germany would have to fall back on the tactics of Frederick the Great: destroy one enemy before it was itself destroyed by the other one. Defeat the enemy in detail before he can combine against you, as Napoleon would say. Put this way, the only sensible plan was to attack France first, get an overwhelming force into France as quickly as possible, driving on toward Paris, and knocking France out of the war in a great battle of annihilation.

The fastest way into France was by way of Belgium and Holland. Von Schlieffen hoped that Germany would be able to secure a passage through Belgium, or that it would simply capitulate—and as the discussions in London make clear, the British and French were curious themselves. But everyone knew the only practicable route into northern France for a large army was through Belgium. Like the French and British General Staffs, the German General Staff assumed that Belgium would have to fight on one side or the other, and planned accordingly.

THE VON SCHLIEFFEN PLAN

Unlike his French counterparts, von Schlieffen was not bound to present his plans to the government for approval. And wisely so, because as he himself soon concluded, his plan was unfeasible. Although militarily sound, Germany lacked the manpower to make it work. Over the years, he kept on tinkering with the basic idea, and his troop dispositions give a good idea of his desperation. He was planing on defending the two-hundred-odd-kilometer frontier in Alsace with six battalions of *Jäger*, an infantry division of the reserves, supported by a division of *Landwehr*, the German designation for units that would consist of men too old (or untrained) even to be added to the reserves. The German defenses in the East would basically be left to the *Landwehr* as well. The entire right bank of the Moselle would be defended by four divisions, two of them reserves.

There would be no troops at all in reserve. Von Schlieffen didn't have enough men to sweep through Belgium, outflank Paris, defeat the French

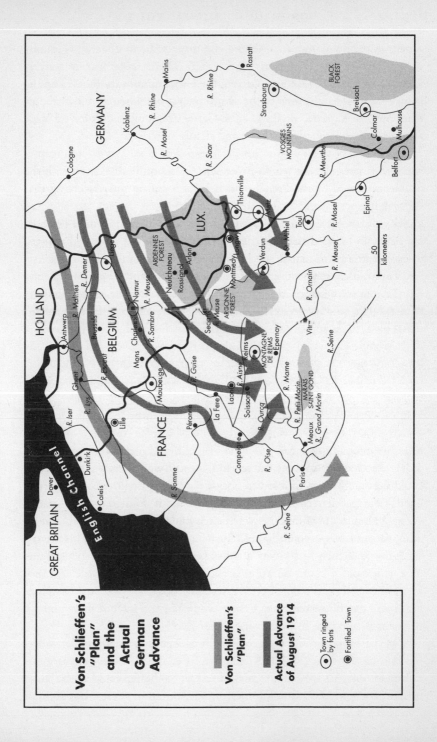

Von Schlieffen's "Plan" and the Actual German Advance

Von Schlieffen's "Plan"

Actual Advance of August 1914

⊙ Town ringed by forts
◉ Fortified Town

50 kilometers

GREAT BRITAIN

English Channel

HOLLAND

GERMANY

BELGIUM

FRANCE

LUX.

BLACK FOREST

VOSGES MOUNTAINS

ARDENNES FOREST

ARGONNE FOREST

MARAIS SAINT GOND

MONTAGNE DE REIMS

Dover
Calais
Dunkirk
Ghent
Antwerp
Malines
Brussels
Liege
Namur
Mons
Charleroi
Maubeuge
Lille
Péronne
La Fère
Laon
Soissons
Compiègne
Paris
Meaux
Reims
Epernay
Vitry
Soissons
Arlon
Rossignol
Neufchateau
Longwy
Montmedy
Verdun
St. Mihiel
Toul
Thionville
Epinal
Belfort
Mulhouse
Colmar
Breisach
Strasbourg
Rastatt
Mains
Koblenz
Cologne

R. Rhine
R. Mosel
R. Saar
R. Meurthe
R. Mosel
R. Meuse
R. Ornain
R. Seine
R. Marne
R. Petit Morin
R. Grand Morin
R. Ourcq
R. Oise
R. Somme
R. Aisne
R. Guise
R. Sambre
R. Meuse
R. Escaut
R. Lys
R. Iser
R. Demer
R. Meuse
R. Seine
R. Aisne
R. Meuse
Second

armies in the field, and do anything else. In fact, he discovered Germany didn't have the troops even to do that. There were just too many Frenchmen. Over in London, Wilson, the only top military thinker on the British General Staff, came to the same conclusion: when all the available manpower was totaled on both sides, Germany simply didn't have a large enough army for the plan to have any chance of success.

So von Schlieffen kept adjusting the assumptions, trying to create a scenario where his plan would make sense. He simply dispensed with the problems caused by the French and Belgian fortifications, assuming that German troops would march around them. If the French actually did attack, say, in Alsace, he also assumed that the Germans would be moving so much faster than their enemies that they would fight and win the decisive battle before the French could get into Germany proper.

The political implications of writing off Alsace, northern Lorraine, and East Prussia were staggering, but even then von Schlieffen found he didn't have enough infantry to execute his plan. If one assumes that an operational plan, to be approved and made the basis for operations, has to offer at least some chances of success, Germany did not have a plan at all. At least Yamamoto could say that if the American aircraft carriers were in port on 7 December 1941, a successful air attack would leave the United States without any naval capabilities in the Pacific to speak of. Moreover, in the vastness of the Pacific, it was possible to mount a surprise attack. Once the Japanese fleet left home waters, they could be headed anywhere. It would be rather difficult to conceal a million men in the Rhineland.

Once German soldiers started moving through Belgium, the French could reasonably be supposed to notice them, and deploy troops accordingly.[2] Von Schlieffen could claim that German soldiers would simply sweep all before them, but this was clearly clutching at straws. The shakiest of these straws—which actually formed the first sentence of his memorandum—was this: "In a war against Germany, France, particularly as long as it cannot count on an effective support of Russia, will probably first limit itself to the defensive."[3] Actually, this was two large ifs combined into one blithe sentence: France would stay on the defensive and the Russians would take forever to mobilize.

As Austrian and German military intelligence were gloomily aware, this was hardly the case. The Russians were in the midst of an enormous railroad boom. In 1893, two years after von Schlieffen had become chief of staff, Russia had 31,200 kilometers of track, an increase from 1883 of about a third; but by 1903, the track had increased to 58,400 kilometers, and anyone who cared to could see that the increases were going to continue. By 1913, Russia had nearly 71,000 kilometers of track in service. By every other measure, the Russian Army would be able to mobilize and transport its troops into action within a matter of two or three weeks, not the six to eight weeks that von Schlieffen's plan demanded.[4]

As the complications mounted, von Schlieffen took refuge in still more military fantasies. If Great Britain intervened, its expeditionary force would land in Antwerp, where a few German units could keep it penned up until the war was over, and if it broke out, the army would simply have to defeat it. New units would have to be raised. If the Belgians refused to grant the German Army passage through their country, they should threaten the country at large, terrify it into submission.

Traditionally, the senior generals of the German emperors, both Hohenzollern and Habsburg, had soldiered on until they were too feeble to mount a horse: Radetzky and Prince Eugene in Austria, Blücher and Steinmetz in Prussia. Von Moltke the Elder had continued to run the German General Staff (and the army) until well into his eighties and hadn't retired until he was eighty-eight. But in 1906 von Schlieffen, although he was only seventy-three, was replaced. So was his plan.

His successor, Johannes Ludwig, Graf von Moltke, was, at fifty-eight, a much younger man. He and the chief of Section Two (responsible for mobilization), an obscure major named Ludendorff, set about trying to devise an actual plan of operations for the German Army in the event of a war, one that would reflect military realities.

By 1906, twelve years into the Franco-Russian Alliance, it was pretty clear that a war with France would be a war on two fronts. Von Moltke, however, was gloomily aware that the actual situation might be much worse than even that rather disastrous scenario suggested. In the margin beside his predecessor's blithe assumption about France's intentions, von Moltke wrote, sensibly enough, that what France did would depend on the causes of the war. In his own opening sentence, he opined that there was only one thing that would be certain in the event of such a war: Germany would have to fight on three fronts.[5] The basic equations had all been changed: more fronts, a more rapid Russian mobilization, the ambiguity about France's intentions. And then there were all of von Schlieffen's desperate gambles.

Von Moltke and Ludendorff saw that Alsace could hardly be abandoned. A French attack there could do untold mischief, roll up the plain of Alsace and spill over into Germany, while remaining far south of Strasbourg's protective belt of forts. From the peaks of the upper Vosges, an observer could look across the Rhine into Germany. In that sense Bismarck had been prescient (although probably for the wrong reasons): the best place to defend southwestern Germany was in the Vosges Mountains, which separated France from German-occupied Alsace.

Nor could they write off East Prussia to the Russians. Ludendorff, born in Posen, could hardly have been enthusiastic about that possibility, but it was politically impossible to abandon the East to an invading Russian army. The German Army was a popular and respected institution: the country counted on the army to defend it against an invasion, not abandon it and go into France. Any plan had to leave sufficient forces in the East to hold off the Russians.

Then there was the matter of logistics. Modern armies demanded enormous amounts of supplies: whole trains were needed simply to keep the horses fed. Moreover, the evidence of the Balkan wars made clear that any modern war would involve a heavy expenditure of shells, and in the German Army soldiers expected, not unreasonably, to be fed and clothed, their wounded cared for and sent quickly back home for medical care. By 1910, all of those things depended on railroads. German soldiers might very well march around the Belgian fortifications (or the French ones), but without the ammunition and supplies they needed, they would quickly become nothing more than a mob in uniform.

So von Moltke began with a set of constraints, and those constraints suggested that it was imperative to neutralize the Belgian fortifications astride the Meuse at Liège and Namur. And quickly. There wasn't time for a protracted siege, another Port Arthur. If the army's advance was blocked there, it would be funneled down the eastern part of Belgium, where it would cross the frontier and run smack into the great fortifications at Verdun, collectively the largest—and most modern—of all the fortified areas. For the offensive to be able to develop into France, the Germans had to be able to slide down the Meuse and shift westward, relying on the highly developed Belgian transportation system for support. That of course suggested another need for speed: the whole Meuse corridor was a mass of bridges and tunnels. At some point an alert defender would begin destroying them. They had to be seized intact.

So far so good, but the troubling fact remained that the Germans would still be grossly outnumbered. Von Schlieffen's tinkering with the assumptions, and his highly questionable decisions, had all been predicated on the conventional wisdom of the time about the need for a superiority in numbers. It was the same logic that had led General Wilson to the idea that the intervention of the BEF would prove decisive. Both he and von Schlieffen had agreed that there was no way to get around the basic problem: Germany's numbers were too small.

Not of course because Germany was smaller than France. In the long haul, if the war continued for more than a few months, Germany's larger population would give it a decisive advantage. In order to keep a large peacetime army, France's system of universal military service had encompassed 85 percent of the eligible males. Essentially, by 1910 or so, every male over twenty-one had completed a service obligation. This enabled France to keep a large peacetime army and to double and then triple it at mobilization.

But the governments of Germany and Austria-Hungary had never appropriated enough money for their armies to do the same. Although in theory every male was eligible for military service like his French counterpart, there was only enough money available to train a percentage of the men eligible. The rest formed what was called the *Ersatz-reserv*. As the best estimate was that less than half of the eligibles had military training (and perhaps only a third in the Habsburg lands), there was an enormous manpower pool that the armies had not yet tapped: in August 1914, Germany had nearly four million men who were capable of being mobilized, but had never been trained, and the annual *Ersatz-reserv* for 1914 alone was nearly a quarter of a million men.[6]

In this sense, time was on Germany's side. The two German empires had an enormous manpower pool on which to draw if the war went on, and France did not. Moreover, if the Germans could carry the war into France, and occupy Belgium, they would cripple France's industrial capacity. Great Britain might mount a blockade, but the British and the French were heavily dependent on German raw materials for their military. The explosives in French shells were made with chemicals that came from Germany. Even if Germany couldn't win the war outright in two months, its advantages would soon come into play—and if German troops were on enemy soil, all the better. It was the same calculation that had led the French and the *stavka* (the czarist General Staff) to make plans to get into Germany as soon as possible.

The Germans had reason to believe, however, that they possessed a great equalizer that would enable them simultaneously to smash through the fortifications and invade France, defeat the Russians in the East, and the French in Alsace. Not through superior numbers, but through superior firepower. Because in the decade after 1900, the German Army had developed an entirely new family of weapons and the tactics to use them. In combination, the two gave their soldiers a firepower unprecedented and completely unrecognized.

The difference was striking. As we noted in the last chapter, both the French and the British believed the key element on the battlefield was the rifle with a bayonet attached to it, wielded by a determined soldier. The comparable German doctrine introduced a new concept: firepower. The infantry was supreme on the battlefield, but the German regulations brought in a new wrinkle: "In combination with the artillery, it [the infantry] defeats the opponent....The attack consists of the carrying forward of fire against the enemy, if necessary up to the closest range."[7] So the German Army saw an attack not as the assault of the infantry with their bayonets, but as the advance of fire, and fire coming from both artillery and riflemen.

There is a large gap between theory and practice, and soldiers in the field do not necessarily read textbooks or attend lectures. But, uniquely among the major powers, the German and Austrian armies had developed the weapons to make such tactics possible. Additionally, the German Army already had the specialized troops in place to deploy its new weapons. And no wonder: when the German General Staff looked to the West, the first thing they saw was a thicket of concrete, masonry and earthenwork fortifications, too numerous to march around, and specifically designed to be proof against the older tactics of siege and storm. So there was a reason von Moltke could choose to begin the war in the West by a *coup de main* against the Liège forts. He and Ludendorff knew they had the weapons and the tactics to break through the fortifications. It was these weapons and tactics that gave the new German planners the confidence that von Schlieffen had lacked.

The nature of war had changed. It was no longer the numbers of riflemen that counted, it was the guns. The German Army wasn't any larger than the French Army. But in firepower it had an advantage of somewhere between four to one to twelve to one. When the war began, the Germans deployed weapons the Allies did not possess, weapons they had refused to build, and weapons they believed could not be built.

THE FIREPOWER REVOLUTION

In 1898 there was a revolution in gun design equivalent to the shift from propeller planes to jet aircraft. Before the introduction of the French seventy-five millimeter field gun in 1898, the backward force generated by the rapidly expanding gases in the gun barrel had to be absorbed mechanically, and the engineers of the 1870s used a combination of mass, emplacement, and mechanical brakes in generally vain attempts to keep the gun from moving backward each time it was fired.[8]

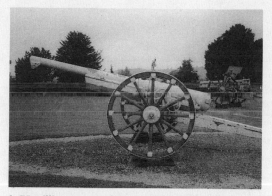

The famous **French 75 millimeter gun**, developed in 1897, had the first long hydraulic recoil mechanism. An excellent design, it was the wrong gun for this war, because its maximum angle of fire was only sixteen degrees. The gun shown is from 1917. American troops were largely equipped with the French 75.

French 155 millimeter short-barreled gun, developed in 1877. In modern terms this gun would be called a howitzer, owing its short barrel and high angle of fire. The short barrel meant a short range. Notice the bulk, the high profile, and the lack of a recoil mechanism.

French 155 millimeter Long, model 1877. In the model shown the barrel was cast in 1878, and the mount fabricated in 1917. The lack of a recoil mechanism on these weapons made accurate indirect fire an impossibility. Like its cousin, the 120 millimeter Long, the 155 Long was too heavy and had too short a range.

In all guns made before 1898, the gun barrel was mounted directly to the gun carriage, and the mounting—as well as the breech end of the barrel—was heavily reinforced, since this was the point that had to absorb the most force from the blast. The resulting weapons could fire powerful shells out to long ranges, but the weapons were incredibly heavy: sheer mass was needed to take the stress and dampen the movement of the weapon. The movement of the gun itself when fired meant that the guns were inherently inaccurate: at six thousand meters, a deviation of even one degree in repositioning would mean that the second shell would land nearly two hundred meters from the first. Even at half that range the deviation would be a hundred meters. And at closer distances, the gunners would be picked off by the opposing infantry.

All of this—once the improvements in shell construction and explosives of the 1880s had taken place—was a function of the recoil problem. In 1897 French engineers used hydraulics to solve it. The gun barrel slid along a trough, and as the barrel moved backwards, it compressed a cylinder filled with air and oil, which absorbed the force generated by the expanding gases in the barrel. In 1898 the first of these new weapons, the famous French 75, went into production.

Since the hydraulic cylinder absorbed the force of the blast, the gun barrel and the carriage could be much lighter. Consequently the gun could be set up quickly and fired rapidly. When fired, it remained in exactly the same position: "On this carriage the gun recoils without objectionable derangement of its laying [sic], returning after firing to a position so near its former one that it may be layed accurately without loss of time," was how the *United States Army Manual* put it.[9]

The change was dramatic. The 75 could fire up to twenty rounds in a minute (fifteen to sixteen being more usual). The gun it replaced could fire only three. So one of the new guns could lay down as much high explosive or shrapnel in a minute as an entire battery of six of the older weapons. The improvement was even more dramatic than that, however. The magazine rifle and the machine gun vastly increased the depth of the killing field. The old smoothbore musket had a lethal range of about fifty meters and its operator was lucky to get off one round a minute in actual combat. Consequently, gunners could stand off at two or three hundred meters and fire their guns directly at their targets. At those distances, shifts in the angle of the gun had a negligible effect on its accuracy.

At such close ranges, charges by infantry with bayonets, or by horsemen, were practicable: a horse could cover fifty meters in less time than it took the rifleman to reload, and a determined charge on foot could rapidly close the gap, at fifty meters, and possibly even at a hundred. But the new bolt-action magazine rifles enabled the infantryman to fire four or five rounds at a range of four hundred meters: a charge across open ground would be suicide.

Gunners were affected as well. They had to move their guns well back, since the killing range of these new rifles was in theory the limit of human eyesight: if the rifleman could see a target, he could hit it and kill it. But when they moved their guns back out of range of the infantry, they could no longer fire directly at their opponents—something would always be in the way. Thus indirect fire became the norm, replacing the older concept of direct fire in which gunners sighted their weapons just like the infantry.

So now the standard method of fire was to fire on coordinates relayed to the gunners by an observer. Precision of aim became all important. With the new long-recoil gun, a battery could be aligned precisely on a target—and stay aligned on it. Once the range was taken for the target, a battery could dump over a hundred rounds on the target in a minute. This left the defenders no time to seek cover, and very little warning before a strike. In one minute a battery of 75s could saturate a one-hundred-meter-target square, with virtually every shell landing within the grid.

The situation was thus roughly analogous to the shift from musket to rifle. As early as 1842, it had been found that at longer distances (of say four hundred meters), the rifle was over twelve times as likely to hit the target as the musket. A soldier firing a bolt-action rifle with five rounds in it could thus lay down five times as much fire as the man with a musket, and each round would have twelve times the probability of hitting the target.[10] At four hundred meters, one rifleman had the killing power of sixty musketeers. At three thousand meters, a battery of four 75s had the killing power of about seventy of the older field guns, and at longer distances the ratio went up even further. Not surprisingly, by 1910, the armies of all the major powers had discarded their mechanical-recoil field guns and pressed new long-recoil weapons into service.

But the German Army went on to the next level in firepower. Guns larger than 75 to 105 millimeters were traditionally thought of as siege artillery. The standard British howitzer was so heavy that "the breechloading six inch thirty cwt equipment had to be unshipped from its main traveling carriage and mounted on a ground platform for firing, a slow and laborious process at best," as a Canadian manual put it.[11] Given that the barrel assembly weighed three metric tons, the fact that it was moved in sections and set up on site is hardly surprising.

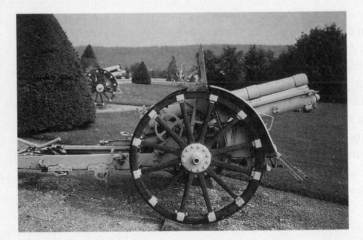

German 105 millimeter howitzer, 1913. The hydraulic mechanism is clearly visible beneath the barrel. A light and portable weapon that weighed the same as the standard field gun, it was issued to infantry divisions even before the war began. The angle of fire for this gun was approximately 45 degrees, making it far more versatile than the French 75. The Allies had nothing comparable.

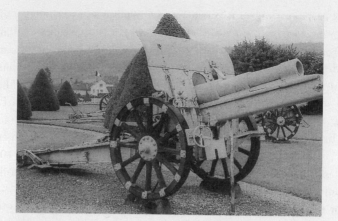

German 150 millimeter howitzer, 1913. Hardly larger than the 105 millimeter howitzer, this hydraulic recoil weapon was initially assigned to each army corps: Together with its larger relative the 210 millimeter howitzer, it allowed the Germans to dominate the battlefields of the war. The gun shown was made in 1914.

By contrast the total weight of the new long-recoil German 150 millimeter howitzer was about twenty-six hundred kilograms, and the gun was almost indistinguishable from the 105 millimeter weapon, which in turn was almost the same size as the standard 77 millimeter field gun: when both weapons were parked side by side, only an expert could tell them apart. All three could be pulled by a team of six, set up and fired immediately.[12]

A howitzer—a weapon that fires a shell at a steeper angle over a shorter range than a gun does—was the ideal weapon for besieging a fort, a fact that had been known for centuries. But with mechanical recoil, the downward force of the explosion meant the weapon required a sizable platform. Howitzers were weapons that, like the British example above, took time and effort to emplace. That was one reason the French and the Belgians had put so much faith in their fortifications. But if a 150 millimeter howitzer was as mobile as an ordinary field gun, this clearly changed the equation considerably.

There was another reason why howitzers were extremely potent weapons. When the French had developed the 75, they had kept the same limited elevation capability (sixteen degrees) as in their older weapons, and everyone else had done the same. So a field gun fired a shell on what was very close to a flat trajectory. Since the artillery doctrines of the day

were all based on field guns firing shrapnel shells against infantry and cavalry maneuvering in the field, this was hardly a problem. But Joffre had
already noticed that northeastern France, and particularly the heights
along the Meuse River valley, was not the sort of terrain where that was
likely to happen. A much more likely scenario was troops deployed
behind the ridges or small hills that were a distinctive feature of the
ground.

A battery of 75s could fire hundreds of rounds at a battery of 105s
emplaced in the dead space behind a two-hundred-meter hillock, and
never land a hit. Conversely, howitzers could toss shells right over the
obstacle and hit infantry sheltering on the other side—or the enemy
artillery themselves. Plunging fire (as this sort of shell tossing at high
angles was called) could reach behind ridges, forests, and buildings, and
drop shells directly into trenches and onto the turrets of forts. Instead of
shooting at the earthen and concrete walls of the fort, the gunners could
land shells directly on top of the gun turrets and observation cupolas.

Since the howitzer shell was subject to less stress (as its range was
less), it had a greater explosive payload. At ranges of two to three thousand meters, a battery of four 105s could do as much damage as ten 75s.[13]
And the figures went up once again for the 150 millimeter weapon.
Comparing the older mechanical recoil weapons to the 75 was comparing
a musket to a rifle; comparing them to the new hydraulic-recoil howitzer
was comparing a musket to a machine gun.

The high angle of fire had another advantage in siege work. The weak
spot in any fort of the era was the steel gun emplacement, whether it was a
turret or an embrasure, and the same held true for the armored observation cupola. Since the forts were basically dug into the ground, the
observers needed those turrets to see. The Belgians, in constructing their
turrets, had built them to withstand the 210 millimeter shells of the 1880s.

But a 210-howitzer shell would have four times the explosive payload of the older weapon. A direct hit on a turret would be devastating:
even if it didn't destroy the turret, it would damage the gun barrel. French
engineers had been worrying about this weak spot, and in 1888 Major
Bussière created a turret that could be retracted into the concrete shell of
the fort. His turret housed two 155 millimeter guns. It was installed in an
annex at Fort Souville (Verdun), and is still there today, practically the
only part of the fort that is identifiable.

Only one was made, because in 1890 Major Galopin developed a much more modern disappearing turret which was so well designed that it was used in postwar fortifications as well. Initially, Galopin's retractable turrets housed only 57 millimeter guns, but by 1905, the engineers had managed to fit the famous 75 into the retractable turret, producing a formidable weapon. Fourteen turrets were installed at Verdun, five at Toul, and four at Épinal. By 1912, the engineers had managed to fit two different models of 155 millimeter gun into disappearing turrets, and five were installed at Verdun, with a handful more installed at the forts along the Meuse below Saint-Mihiel.

The disappearing turret was clearly the best solution. Once retracted, the turret was basically invulnerable even to direct hits from the heaviest weapons, as Verdun's retractable turrets bear witness. But it was an expensive solution, and funds were lacking. By 1914, the French had installed less than three dozen for their whole frontier and the Belgians hadn't installed any at all.

This was a fatal error, because the recoil principle could be applied to very large guns as well as smaller ones. In the years before the war the Germans had developed an incredible new weapon, a 210 millimeter howitzer, which was moved in one piece and could be deployed like its smaller siblings. It took more horses to pull, but the Germans, like the French, had already started using four-wheel drive tractors whenever possible to pull such weapons. They also had developed larger horses. The 210 would be deployed in the field just like the 105 and the 150 millimeter weapons.[14]

In 1912, a 210 millimeter howitzer (or a 150 millimeter gun) was the upper limit of firepower that could be moved by road and deployed immediately into action. Above that even in the German Army the weapon had to be broken down into separate components and assembled on site. But there was an obvious exception. The 210, with a range of 9,500 meters, was a formidable weapon. But if one was willing to trade off range, the size of the weapon went down dramatically. A smaller weapon could be moved in much closer. If it had a high angle of fire, the gunners could position it in a safe place and toss large packages of high explosive onto the fort.

The resulting weapon, which the Germans called a *Minenwerfer*, or mine thrower, was not, properly speaking, an artillery piece at all. It had a very short range—nine hundred meters or less. So it was deployed not by gunners, but by a peculiarly German branch of the army, the *Pioniere*. These were combat engineers. They would be the main siege troops, since

German 170 millimeter *Minenwerfer,* or medium mortar. Each shell the 1913 model fired contained as much high explosive as eighteen French 75 millimeter shells. Notice the protrusion for the wheels. The weapon could be pulled by two horses or handled by twenty men.

as engineers they had the picks and ladders, and the explosive charges, needed to storm a fort. But they would also deploy the *Minenwerfer.* Originally, the *Pioniere* had been assigned to siege trains, but by 1914 they had been broken up into battalions, and parceled out among the infantry divisions, each regular division getting at least one company. This was not a trivial force. Once the war began, the thirty-five peacetime battalions, which had a strength of some twenty-one thousand men, quadrupled to eighty thousand men in seventy battalions.[15] But practically speaking, the *Pioniere* were spread out in 379 companies, providing the support for the infantry.

Mortars had been around a long time. But these new weapons used the recoil system as well. They were light enough to be pulled by two horses, or handled by the men of the *Pioniere.* The explosive charge was incredible. The French 75 fired an explosive shell with a payload of .688 kilograms of high explosive. The German 105 millimeter howitzer fired shells with only slightly more high explosive—just above 1 kilogram. But from there the explosive payload increased enormously. The German 150 millimeter howitzer delivered a 6 kilogram payload, while the 210 delivered 18 kilograms.[16] But the 170 millimeter *Minenwerfer* fired a shell with an explosive payload of 37 kilograms. In the words of one observer, it was like having a satchel of dynamite thrown at you. No gun turret in existence would withstand a direct hit.

By September of 1915 the French were deploying this **58 millimeter mortar.** Notice the absence of any recoil mechanism, in contrast to the German *Minenwerfer* shown.

German 210 millimeter howitzer. Although substantially larger than the German 150 millimeter howitzer, this surprisingly portable weapon could be towed on existing roads like its smaller cousins. From August 1914 on it was the backbone of German heavy artillery: Roughly one-fourth of all German heavy weapons were variants of the 210 millimeter howitzer. Although little known, it may fairly be called the best heavy weapon of the war. *(National Archives)*

The Austrians had taken a different approach. Why not build a very large gun and design it so that it could be quickly assembled? At the Daimler factory in Wiener Neustadt, a young engineer named Ferdinand Porsche had developed a twenty-metric-ton 305 millimeter howitzer, which was transported by three heavy trucks. The trucks could transport the gun at a steady ten kilometers an hour. Once the site was reached, the weapon was so designed that in four hours it would be throwing thirty-seven kilograms of high explosive out to distances of twelve thousand meters.[17]

Larger weapons of 420 millimeters were feasible, and were being built, but they had to be moved on site and assembled, and this took time. To speed up the process, the Germans had developed a new quick-drying concrete, so that the gun would have a stable base within forty-eight hours. None of these larger 420 millimeter weapons were actually in service when the war began, but the Austrian weapons had been in service from 1909 on, so the OHL planned on borrowing the Austrian weapons and their crews, and deploying them against the fortifications in the West.

THE UNITY OF THEORY AND PRACTICE

The possession of a few new and untried weapons is one thing; deploying them in combat is something entirely different. The German General Staff had made these guns organic to their administrative structure, and in that they differed radically from the Allied idea about heavy weapons. A French Army corps commander had only one kind of weapon: one hundred twenty 75 millimeter field guns. A German divisional commander deployed fifty-four 77 millimeter field guns, but he also had eighteen 105 millimeter howitzers, and the corps commander had an additional sixteen 150 millimeter howitzers.

Given the higher explosive payload and inherent accuracy of the howitzer on the likely battlefield, for all practical purposes, a German division had as much killing power in its eighteen howitzers as its French counterpart did in its 75s. At the corps level, the Germans deployed vastly more firepower. Not only did the corps have a complement of 150 millimeter howitzers that the French lacked, but its divisions had units of *Pioniere* assigned to them with their own special weapons.

France's six army groups deployed three hundred heavy weapons, almost all of them mechanical-recoil guns dating from around 1878, and all were controlled at the army group level. Not counting the Austrian 305 millimeter howitzers, the experimental 420 millimeter mortars, and the weapons of the combat engineers, the German Army deployed 848 heavy weapons, a quarter of them the 210 millimeter howitzer, and all of them modern long-recoil weapons. These weapons, rather than being held in reserve, were assigned down to the corps (and sometimes the division) level.

The decentralization of command was probably more important than the qualitative and quantitative superiority. At the army corps level, the 150 millimeter howitzers were assigned to whichever division needed them, and the even heavier guns were controlled at the corps level. Relatively low-level German commanders thus had direct control over extremely heavy artillery, just as each division had its own complement of *Pioniere*. On the battlefield, the German Army gave operational control over its heavy weapons to whatever group needed them, generally, the division.[18] By contrast, the only way a local French commander could get heavy weapons support was by going up two levels to the army group staff.

The ultimate proof of a working doctrine is not its existence in writing, but the extent to which it can be used in the field. That the German Army had worked all these things out in some detail comes from an analysis of what happened on the battlefield. When the Germans began to plan for a war in the West, they had a certain confidence in the instrument that would execute the plan. To smash through the forts, the Germans would deploy an integrated array of weapons, all of them specifically designed to be used against fortifications. Since the Allies didn't have any of these guns themselves, the Germans would have the advantage of surprise as well as of firepower, and in von Moltke's plan, this would translate into a quick success.

So von Moltke and Ludendorff now had a plan that allowed them to do the three tasks that von Schlieffen had been trying to accomplish. Counting men with rifles, they were still woefully short. But they had their opponents seriously outgunned. They had the firepower to handle Alsace and the East, and still mount a major offensive thrust right through the Belgian forts and into France. What then?

Von Schlieffen, following the plan of 1870, had his heart set on Paris.

He wanted a repeat of 1870, only in quick time. Von Moltke and the General Staff had a clever idea, which was also a more basic one. Germany would be horribly outnumbered. The ideal strategy was to defeat each enemy in detail before they could close in. In the classical military conception of things, this meant fighting two enormous battles of annihilation, cutting off the invading Russian armies and destroying them as they drove into East Prussia, and at the same time destroying the French armies in the field. Both involved strategies of encirclement.[19]

But what if that failed? Armies of millions of men are not so easily surrounded, nor are they easily defeated. But France and the United Kingdom and Russia had two basic problems. The first was that France and the United Kingdom were heavily dependent on German imports. Prewar, it had never occurred to Allied military planners that—for example—France got most of the raw materials for its ammunition from Germany.[20] Although the Admiralty had always planned to mount some sort of blockade if there was a war, the British General Staff had never seriously looked into the extent to which the British were dependent on Germany. They might have an inexhaustible reservoir of manpower, but for those men to be an effective army, they needed German chemicals.

Second, most of France's industrial capacity was along its northeastern frontier. Amputate that—and Belgium, France's main trading partner—and the French would have a major problem catching up. A sobering loss might change public opinion. In a long war, the advantage would go to the side that was sitting on the other side's assets, and if the Germans could survive the first months of the war without a major defeat, the pendulum would swing in their direction almost automatically.

A calculus of desperation. But Germany had no choice. As early as 1910, von Moltke had described the war which he assumed Germany would have to fight as "a lengthy campaign with numerous hard, lengthy battles until we force down one of our enemies; the strain and consumption of resources will increase as we have to win in several theaters in the West and East one after another."[21] As in France, the military didn't determine foreign policy, it simply tried to win whatever war the government had forced it to fight. In this, both General Staffs were alike. The French, sensibly enough, preferred to fight in Belgium. The Germans, with equal sense, would have preferred a war on one front. Neither group got its wish. Joffre would have to fight in France, and von Moltke would have to fight a war on three fronts. Only in the United Kingdom had the military trumped the government, forcing it to become involved in a Continental war that no British politician in his right mind could have been enthusiastic about fighting—regardless of the provocation.

NOTES

1. As quoted by Gerhard Ritter in his edition of von Schlieffen's writings, *Der Schlieffenplan: Kritik eines Mythos* (Munich: Oldenbourg, 1956), 54. Unless specifically noted, all translations from the German are my own.

2. The fact that in August 1914 the French command failed to prod its armies into moving rapidly enough in no way vitiates this point, which is frequently misunderstood: the problem wasn't that there weren't any (or enough) French troops who could easily have been moved deep into Belgium, the problem was that they failed to move there.

3. In my translation this passage, found in Ritter (145), is not quite so dogmatic as in the usual English translation: "In a war against Germany, France will probably at first restrict herself to defense, particularly as long as she cannot count on effective Russian support." See Gerhard Ritter, *The Schlieffen Plan: Critique of a Myth,* trans. Andrew and Eva Wilson (New York: Praeger, 1958), 134–35.

4. In *A History of Russian Railways* (London: Allen and Unwin, 1964), J.N. Westwood summarizes the relevant figures (taken from Russian sources) in appendix 4 (track), 5 (tonnage of freight), and 6 (passengers transported). As Westwood points out, most Russian railway construction had a military objective, and the Russians steadily doubled their track and lengthened their sidings so as to speed up mobilization (170–73).

5. The Wilsons mistranslated this key passage: "three" became "two." See Ritter (179) for the original.

6. See the extensive discussion in Eugene Carrias, *L'Armée allemande: Son histoire, son organisation, sa tactique* (Paris: Berger-Levrault, 1938), 83–96.

7. As quoted by Martin Samuels, *Doctrine and Dogma: German and British Infantry Tactics in the First World War* (New York: Greenwood, 1992), 33–34. The regulations speak of the attack as being "sealed" by the bayonet, not accomplished by it. The infantry regulations of 1906 also specified procedures for attacks against fortifications, which made the German Army unique. See the excellent discussion in Bruce I. Gudmundsson, *Stormtroop Tactics: Innovation in the German Army, 1914–1918* (New York: Praeger, 1989), 27–29.

8. For detailed drawings and discussions of the recoil principles, including the wheel braking system, see Lieutenant-Colonel Jules Paloque, *Artillerie de campagne* (Paris: O. Doin et Fils, 1909), 147–48. The ramp system was still in use in the French Army in 1915. See the picture of the 120-millimeter gun in Yves Buffetaut, *La Bataille de Verdun, de l'Argonne à la Woëvre*

(Tours: Éditions Heimdale, 1990), 44. There is an excellent discussion of the development of French guns after 1870 in Lieutenant-Colonel Émile Rimailho, *Artillerie de campagne* (Paris: Gauthier-Villars, 1924), 5–106. This discussion is of particular interest since Rimailho developed the only modern heavy gun the French Army had in quantity in August 1914.

9. Field Artillery Board, U.S. Army, *Gunnery and Explosives for Field Artillery Officers* (Washington, D.C.: U.S. Government Printing Office, 1911), 9. See the diagram and explanation in Paloque, 150; rates of fire are discussed on 146–54.

10. William Wellington Greener, *The Gun and Its Development,* 9th ed. (London: Cassell and Company, 1910), 633.

11. Leslie W.C.S. Barnes, *Canada's Guns* (Ottawa: Canadian War Museum, 1979), 79. The excessive weight of British field guns had been observed by Paloque as well (410): by his reckoning, the standard British field gun weighed in at only a few hundred kilograms less than the 150 millimeter German howitzer.

12. In this book, in an effort to simplify matters for the reader, the following conventions are used with regard to artillery: (1) German weapons are identified as 77, 105, 150, and 210 millimeter weapons, rather than by their German designations of 7.7, 10.5, 15, and 21 centimeter guns (I am aware that the German weapons were not precisely those dimensions); (2) the term "mortar" is restricted to man-portable weapons (German *Minenwerfer,* French *artillerie de tranche,* or *crapouillots*), even though both the Germans and the French used the word to describe extremely heavy guns with barrels were less than ten times the diameter of the weapon (the gunnery definition of caliber is the length of the barrel divided by its diameter—the bigger this number, the greater the range of the weapon). So, for example, the gun referred to in the text as the German 210 millimeter howitzer was known officially in the German Army as a 21 centimeter *Mörser.*

13. Figures based on tests conducted by the U.S. Army, as discussed in Bruce I. Gudmundsson, *On Artillery* (New York: Praeger, 1993), 30.

14. The larger horses for German heavy weapons were noticed as early as 1900 by [Sidney Rau] *L'État militaire des principales puissances étrangères en 1900* (Nancy: Berger-Levrault, 1900), 97.

15. Numbers taken from Paul Heinrici, *Das Ehrenbuch der Deutschen Pioniere* (Berlin: Wilhelm Rolf, 1931), 47.

16. Data on the explosive payload of shells taken from État-Major, 2eme Bureau et Artillerie, Grand Quartier Général des Armées du Nord et du Nord-Est, *Artillerie Allemande: Les Projectiles* (Paris: Imprimerie National, 1917), which lists all shells by size and date of manufacture. See also the discussion in Général [Firmin Émile] Gascouin, *L'Évolution de l'artillerie pendant la guerre* (Paris: Flammarion, 1920), which is probably the definitive accounting for French artillery.

17. Ludwig Jedlicka, *Unser Heer: 300 Jahre österreichisch Soldatentum im Krieg und Frieden* (Vienna: Fürlinger, 1963), 288 (and photograph). There are excellent photographs of this weapon in Joseph Jobé, ed., *Guns, An Illustrated History of Artillery* (New York: Crescent, 1971), 35, 174.

18. Rau had noticed this tendency as well—at the turn of the century (114). Thus German practice made hash of the Allied idea that reserve divisions would be grossly underequipped with artillery.

19. The best discussion of this is in Jehuda L. Wallach, *The Dogma of the Battle of Annihilation* (Westport, Conn.: Greenwood, 1986), who explains why the traditional charge that von Moltke fatally weakened the German right wing is incorrect (54, 92–93). Not coincidentally, Wallach is one of the few serving officers (in the Israeli Defense Forces) to write about the war.

20. See the discussions in Arthur Conte, *Joffre* (Paris: Oliver Orban, 1991), 261; Fernand Gambiez and Martin Suire, *Histoire de la première guerre mondiale* (Paris: Fayard, 1968), 257.

21. As quoted by Niall Ferguson, *The Pity of War* (New York: Basic Books, 1999), 97. Although von Moltke was lobbying for ammunition supplies, the comment hardly supports the notion that the OHL aimed to win the war in the West in six weeks.

3

1914: The Fall of the Forts

The metronomes at headquarters were always set at too slow a speed.
—Marc Bloch[1]

Serbia was the first of the combatants to declare a general mobilization, on 25 July 1914. Later the same day, Austria-Hungary responded with a partial mobilization along the frontier with Serbia, to be followed by the Russians in two rather confusing steps. The Russians had declared a preparatory or intermediate step toward complete mobilization on the twenty-sixth, followed by an order for a general mobilization on the twenty-ninth, which was canceled and then approved on the thirtieth. Russia and France, by previous agreement, were to coordinate their declarations, so France gave its own intermediate step toward complete mobilization the same day that Russia ordered its general mobilization.

The problem with these mobilizations was that once one went to the last stage–which could happen quickly—the country had no easy way to disengage. Not only were millions of men dislocated from their jobs, but the railroad system was completely taken over so the armies could be assembled. A great many of the trucks, buses, and automobiles were commandeered, along with a sizable proportion of the nation's horses. It would take twenty-four thousand horses simply to pull France's four thousand 75 millimeter guns, and most of them would be borrowed from private owners.

So mobilization was an incredibly disruptive event. How could one begin it and then stand down without becoming vulnerable to attack? So the act of mobilization meant the country intended to go to the next step, and fight. If France and Russia both mobilized, they could have only one common enemy, Germany. The same logic held true for Great Britain. Once the Expeditionary Force landed in France and began to operate, the country was at war—although clearly the British had more options along the way than did the Continental powers. But mobilization clearly and unambiguously meant war.[2] Once it became obvious that their enemies had actually begun mobilization, Germany and Austria-Hungary mobilized as well, and by 1 August 1914, all the major powers were on the move.

Curiously, the order to mobilize didn't mean the start of a shooting war. Since every unit in every army was operating at only half to two-thirds strength, no unit could go into action until it had received its complement of reservists, and the actual process was even more complex than this suggests: during mobilization, both the French and the Germans spun off reserve units, whose cadres came from the existing units of the peacetime army. Moreover, the basic peacetime unit in the Continental armies, which was also the recruiting unit, was the regiment. So as each regiment was filled out (or created) it had to be matched up with its twin to form a brigade, and that brigade had to be matched up with its corresponding division, and that division had to be mated with its army corps. It was a complex process, and no one had ever done it before. For obvious reasons, it was impossible to have an actual rehearsal.

Belgium was squarely in the center of the target. The Belgians already knew that in the event of a conflict, if they let the Germans pass through their country, it would promptly be appropriated in one way or another by France (or by Great Britain). Conversely, if they refused, they would have to face Germany. Two bad choices. There was a third choice, militarily speaking. The country could have built up its defenses to the extent that no great power would be willing to fight it. This had been Brialmont's aim in building the forts.

But once the forts had been built, not much was done in the way of national defense. Belgium was a fair-sized country, and a wealthy one. Through conscription, it could easily have had an army of well over half a million men, equipped with the best of weapons, since it had a thriving armaments industry. Instead, by scraping the barrel, the country had enough manpower for an army of under a quarter of a million, with a field army of about 115,000.[3] So the third option had been ruled out long before the war started. There was a fourth option as well, one that worried the Allies considerably—and accounted for much of their propagandizing about the Rape of Belgium. The Belgians could offer token resistance and let the Germans simply overrun the country so there wouldn't be any serious fighting. Whether this was possible or not is a moot point, as was joining France in an alliance and working out joint plans for the defense of the country.

In a word, the Belgians couldn't make up their mind, and now that the war had begun, their only real option was to fight. The country's leaders counted heads and decided to go with the probable winner: in a contest pitting Germany against France, Russia, and Great Britain, Germany seemed likely to lose. Moreover, Belgium was a small country. If the British landed an expeditionary force in France on the twenty-first, they could be in Belgium in a few days, and France's Plan 17 mobilized a powerful army, the Fifth, right below the frontier. Commanded by France's most experienced general, Lanrezac, it had half of all French cavalry, and some of the country's best troops. In a week or less, those troops could be in Belgium holding the line of the Meuse, since a German offensive that ran down the right bank of the river into France would run into both the extensive Verdun positions and the Fourth Army, which had formed up below Verdun.

THE FALL OF LIÈGE

Belgium's defensive system was hardly negligible. The Liège defenses comprised twelve forts of varying sizes, finished in 1891, forming a fifty-two-kilometer perimeter around the city, which, as von Moltke had noticed earlier, was the major road, rail, and water transport junction in the region. Unlike the original fortifications of the late 1870s, which were masonry, the forts were reinforced concrete, but built to a specification capable of withstanding only 210 millimeter shells.

But they were respectable fortifications, and heavily armed. The six large forts had either eight or nine turrets: one turret with two 150 millimeter guns, two each with two 120 millimeter guns, two each with one 210 millimeter howitzer, three or four with new 57 millimeter guns for defense, and other 57s located in embrasures to protect the forts from assault. The six smaller forts were equally equipped, but had only half the heavy weapons turrets.[4] The *place* (a French word used to denote the sum of the fortifications) was supported by a heavily reinforced division, the third, which had about

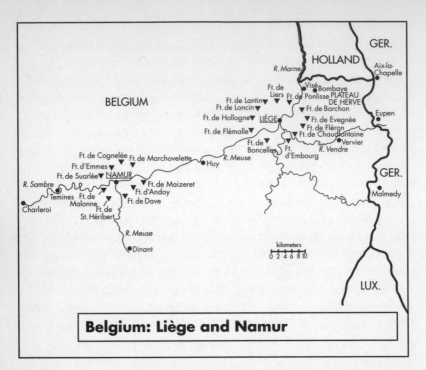

Belgium: Liège and Namur

twenty-four thousand infantry, five hundred cavalry, seventy-two field guns, and thirty machine guns.[5] With the fortress troops added in, Leman, the commander, had nearly thirty-two thousand men and two hundred and fifty guns. By the standards of 1914, this was a formidable force, as well equipped as anything the British or French would bring into battle.

Behind the Meuse fortifications, there was little to stop an invader, but Lemann only needed to hold out for a couple of weeks and the position could be heavily reinforced, which was why von Moltke had written of a need for a *coup de main*. The Germans needed to get through the positions before the Allies could bring up reinforcements to block them.

Initially, the Germans were actually outnumbered. Von Emmich, the German officer charged with the operation, had only been given six mixed brigades, the composition of which reveals exactly what the tactics would be. He had five *Jäger* battalions (almost a third of the active units available), six companies of *Pioniere,* and seven artillery units. Four of these were armed with 105 millimeter howitzers, two with the bigger 210 millimeter howitzers, and one unit with the standard field guns. Coming up behind was a company of *Pioniere* equipped with the 250 millimeter mortars, and a hastily thrown together outfit transporting the still experimental 420 millimeter guns. Unlike the other weapons, these could be moved in only by rail, and required time to set up and bring into action. The Austrian guns, which could be moved by road, were moving south and west, along with the tractor-drawn 210 millimeter howitzers and the regular heavy weapons.

The Germans, of course, had never actually done any of this before, and they made mistakes. Troops got lost, infantry assaults went astray, and a number of senior officers managed to get themselves killed. On 6 August the batteries at Evegnée and Fléron killed the general of the Fourteenth Brigade, von Wussow, and his chief of staff (at which point Ludendorff took command). But after sorting through all the fog and confusion, the progression was simple enough. The Belgian forts, like the French ones, had been designed as part of an integrated defense system, so Lemann's twenty-four thousand infantry, with their field guns, were a key component of the defense. The forts themselves had no infantry. All they could do was fire their guns to interdict the German advance.

Fighting began in earnest on the sixth, and by the seventh, Lemann, unwilling to lose his infantry, retreated. Liège itself fell into German hands. Allegedly this last was due to the prompt action of Ludendorff, who took command after the deaths of the senior commanding officers. This illustrates an important point about the way the German Army operated: Ludendorff, as von Moltke's planning chief, had helped plan the operation; now he was on hand to see that it actually happened—and presumably to authorize changes dictated by the situation on the battlefield. It was this unity of theory and practice, with staff officers out in the field, that would give the Germans one of their major advantages: a relatively quick two-way flow between the battlefield and the German General Staff. Here, right at the beginning of the war, was the classic instance, with the man who planned the operation intervening to make sure it was carried out.

The hasty departure of the infantry freed the gunners to go into operation. On the eighth, the German howitzers opened up on Fort Barchon, and at 1600 hours French time (or 1700 hours German) the fort surrendered. Barchon was one of the five large triangular shaped forts of the *place*, and these forts were the only ones that were truly armored, so its abrupt fall was disquieting, and doubly so since the fort was still capable of resistance. German gunners had blown off one of the 57-millimeter turrets, but the fort was pretty much intact.

Moreover, Barchon, on the south side of the Meuse, was the key to the whole position. Once it was gone, the forts on either side were deprived of covering fire, and the Germans simply peeled the forts back from both sides. On the ninth, the howitzers opened fire on Evegnée, on Fléron, and then on Pontisse. By the eleventh, Barchon's neighbor, Fort de Evegnée, about two kilometers to the south, had surrendered as well: Direct hits from the 210s had popped rivets loose in the turrets, killing gunners, wrecking the guns, the concrete covering pierced. And the really big guns had not yet gone into action.

These weapons arrived on the tenth, together with *Pioniere* deploying heavy mortars, and both the mortars and the 420 millimeter guns went into action on the twelfth, bringing Fort Chaudfontaine, together with Pontisse (the first in line of the left-bank forts), under fire.[6] At about 0730 hours on the thirteenth, a shell penetrated the 210 millimeter howitzer turret of Fort Chaudfontaine and set off one or more internal explosions, and at 1030 hours the fort surrendered, with only seventy-six survivors of a garrison of 408. At 1230 hours, Pontisse surrendered, and so did d'Embourg (at 1930 hours), thus enabling the Germans to take possession of the key chunks of the right bank south of the city.

By now the Germans had free use of the rail lines and roads. For all practical purposes, the guns on all the forts were out of action by 13 August, and in the next forty-eight hours, the Germans battered most of the remaining forts into submission: Fléron (0945 hours on the fourteenth), de Liers (1040 hours on the fourteenth), Boncelles (0730 hours on the fifteenth), and Loncin (1230 hours on the fifteenth). At 1720 hours in the afternoon of the fifteenth, the twenty-third 420 millimeter shell that hit Fort Loncin apparently blew up the magazine, and that was the end of the fort. The two survivors, Forts Flémalle and Hollogne, surrendered early the next morning.[7] Technically, the forts had held out for almost ten days. But this is stretching it considerably: the serious fighting started on the seventh and was over by the fourteenth, and German troops were streaming around the silent forts long before that. That the Liège forts slowed down the advance is a myth.[8]

THE FALL OF NAMUR

At Liège, as one might expect in a situation where troops without combat experience (or even much training) deploy new and untried weapons, the

Germans wasted time and made mistakes. Just how quickly they learned can be seen from what happened at Namur, a *place* defended by nine forts, all dating from 1888–1892, and some thirty-six thousand men. In terms of defenses, Namur was Liège all over again, although smaller. Von Gallwitz, whose troops had been assigned the task of taking Namur, was a gunner. He deployed nothing but heavy weapons: in addition to the usual 150 millimeter howitzers, one battalion of 100 millimeter guns, one battalion of 130 millimeter guns, a whopping five battalions of the 210 millimeter howitzers, a battery of the 420 millimeter guns, and, for the first time, four batteries of the road transportable Austrian 305 millimeter weapons.

The Belgians had also learned. The infantry stayed on and fought, so Namur was partly a siege and partly a series of engagements. Namur lasted only five days. Von Gallwitz's troops opened fire on the evening of the twentieth. On the twenty-fifth, the last of the forts surrendered. There had been no attempts at infantry assaults, German gunners had stood off and simply pounded the forts into submission. But then von Gallwitz had the advantage of an extra two weeks of mobilization time, so he could bring more heavy weapons into play from the first.

What was particularly distressing to the Belgian garrison at Namur was that they had been abandoned and left to shift for themselves. As the British had never planned to land their troops until the twenty-first, the quick collapse of the forts had trumped any help from the BEF. But the French were already there on the other side of the frontier, and French units had reached the Sambre and the Meuse—they could easily have been at Namur in time to mount a serious defense of the position.

There is an old saw to the effect that the side that wins on the battle-field is the side that makes the least mistakes, and the Belgians had made two disastrous ones, first by withdrawing the infantry from the intervals between the forts, and then by doing little demolition work on the trans-portation system. The rail lines down the river from Liège were a demoli-tion team's delight, but only a few of the bridges, causeways, tunnels, and rail junctions were destroyed.

However, the biggest mistake was the one made by the Allies in not quickly moving into Belgium and mounting a defense of the Meuse from the left bank. And for this, the most serious error, there was plenty of blame to go around. The Belgians themselves were initially to blame. Joffre's staff liaison, Lieutenant Colonel Brécard, was in Liège on the fifth, and had reported in on the seventh. On the sixth the Belgians had relayed news to the French that the German attack against the Liège forts had failed, and the attackers had been thrown back ten kilometers, with heavy losses. Two days later, Joffre was being told that German troops attacking Liège were "deprived of supplies and in a bad moral and physical state."[9] The area was in an excellent state of defense, and could hold out for a long time. The French had counted on the fact that the difficulty of taking Liège and Namur was such that the Germans would stay to the south of those strongpoints in their violation of Belgium, and, in the event they didn't, that it would take a great deal of time to reduce the Belgian forts.[10] On the thirteenth, the news from Liège was still good: the forts were still holding on. Incredibly, the news two days later was even more encouraging: the French were in Belgium, and Belgian troops were enjoying great success; the forts would be holding out for a long time to come. It was only on the eighteenth, when observers began to wonder about the absence of any news at all from Belgium, that there was a glimmering of insight.

The key failure was not the failure to recognize that the Germans would move through Belgium, but a wildly optimistic estimate of the capabilities of the defenders. General Fayolle recorded in his diary on 3 August 1914, that "I see the German plan. It is a good one. The principal effort will be to the north"; but in virtually the same breath (four days later), he wrote that he didn't think the German attack developing there could happen quickly, owing to the forts at Liège and Namur.[11] So the French had plenty of time.

Allied propaganda contributed to the false picture. French troops moving slowly up into Belgium were told that the Germans were in terrible shape and had run out of food, and that the Belgians were winning. Wartime propagandists claimed the Germans had twenty-five thousand men killed and wounded in the assault on Fort Barchon alone, and tales quickly circulated, allegedly from eyewitnesses, about human wave attacks by Teutonic hordes driven on by sadistic officers. So the French and British who first encountered the Germans were completely unprepared for what hit them—not waves of men, but waves of howitzer shells: "With us, the worst German weapon was the 5.9 [150 millimeter] howitzer. Whenever a man had withstood the effects of concentrated barrage of 'five nines,' he was never the same afterwards," is how one soldier put it.[12] Instead of a demoralized enemy who had been massacred (eighteen thousand German officers and men were killed in action on the Western Front for the entire month of August), the Allies encountered well-armed and well-led soldiers who were under the impression they were victorious.

To this combination of bad intelligence and wildly erroneous propaganda, a third failure has to be added: the Allies were too slow to get into action. Lanrezac's Fifth Army was mobilized south of the border when the Germans began to attack Liège. Three weeks later he had only gotten a few token battalions to the Sambre. As a result, instead of being able to mount a defense from the shield of a fortified position, the French (and the BEF) would have to fight in the field, against troops who had now undergone three weeks of combat experience, when they had none.

These three components of miscalculation would continue to dog the Allies throughout the war. Their intelligence was always faulty, their propaganda counterproductive to their own cause, and their staff work dilatory. For the next four years, no matter where the theater of operations was, the Allies would always find themselves surprised by their adversaries in one way or another. The Germans were either there first, moved more quickly, or went into action while the Allies were still getting organized. Their metronomes were always set on slow, to appropriate the brilliant metaphor by Marc Bloch.

There was also a general failure to comprehend what was happening on the battlefield. About the same time as the new German heavy guns were obliterating the Allied defenses, artillery experts in London were denying the whole thing. When correspondents for *The Times* spoke of new German guns firing enormous 760-pound shells, their claims were scathingly dismissed by experts writing in *Arms and Explosives,* who demonstrated to everyone's satisfaction that these weapons were a journalistic fantasy, concluding that "the mere idea of loading a 760 pound shot puts a further strain on the imagination."[13] And the war was only three weeks old.

NOTES

1. Marc Bloch, *Strange Defeat: A Statement of Evidence Written in 1940,* trans. Gerard Hopkins (New York: Norton, 1968), 43. Bloch is speaking of May 1940, but his brilliant metaphor is eminently applicable to 1914–1918.

2. In his history of the war, the combat veteran and journalist Jean Galtier-Boissière insists—quite rightly in my view—that the sequence of mobilization indicates ultimate responsibility for starting the war. See *Histoire de la grande guerre* (Paris: Crapouillot, [1932?]), 15–151.

3. According to Henri Bernard, *L'an 14 et la campagne des illusions* (Brussels: La Renaissance du Livre, 1983), 59, there were 234,000 men, with 117,500 in the field army. The author is a professor emeritus of the Belgian École Royale Militaire, and his father was a battalion commander in August 1914 (7) who later became a general. Most of the text is the father's notes, but with useful comments.

4. All the basic data is taken from Colonel A. de Schrÿver [Chef d'État-Major de la 3me Division d'Armée] *La Bataille de Liège (août 1914)* (Liège: Vaillant-Carmanne, 1922), 7–8. In the *Défense de Liège, Namur, Anvers en 1914* (Paris: L. Fournier: 1923), Colonel Robert Normand has useful tables showing the dispositions of forces and time lines: for Liège, 59–63; for Namur, 68–69. The work of Normand, the only trained engineer officer to assess these engagements, is particularly illuminating.

5. The only thorough accounting is that of de Schrÿver, who draws on the official Belgian papers as well as some German records. His analysis of the defenders is on 7–10. See also Normand, esp. 19–59 (Liège), 66–93 (Namur).

6. There are two German accounts of the deployment of these new weapons, both written postwar by men attached to the units involved. For the use of the 250 millimeter mortars by the *Pioniere,* see Theodor Spiess, *Minenwerfer im Grosskampf* (Munich: J. F. Lehmann, 1933), esp. 12–13. For the 420-millimeter guns, the standard account is that of Oberleutnant Schindler in D. R. Schindler, *Eine 42cm Mörser-Batterie im Weltkrieg* (Breslau: Hans Hofmann, 1934). Despite the restrictions suggested in the title, Schindler's collection of eyewitness essays encompasses other heavy weapons as well. There are extensive photographs in both volumes, showing the damage done to key forts, how the weapons were towed, how they were assembled, and typical emplacements.

7. A surprising amount of confusion surrounds the fall of these forts; when Barbara Tuchman summarizes the action there she gets the particulars wrong for every fort. See *The Guns of August* (New York: Macmillan, 1962), esp. 192: "By August 16 eleven of the twelve forts had fallen. Only Fort Loncin still held out." There is a convenient map chronicling the fate of the forts in Arthur Banks, *Military Atlas of the First World War* (London: Heinemann, 1975), 45. The best account is in de Schrÿver 228–52.

8. The general conclusion by French investigators postwar was that the forts slowed the German deployment down by forty-eight hours at most, and possibly not at all. See the comments in Normand, and also in Jean Galtier-Boissière, *Histoire de la grande guerre* (Paris: Crapouillot, [1932], 189–90. The myth of the forts, which began as Allied newspaper propaganda in August 1914, was duly objectified and put into the historical record by eminent writers such as Charles Sarolea in *How Belgium Saved Europe* (London: Heinemann, 1915).

9. The actual words: *"fortement déprimées et dans un mauvais état physique et moral."* Maréchal Joffre, *Mémoires du maréchal Joffre* (Paris: Plon, 1932), 1:244–54.

10. See the comments in Joffre, *Mémoires,* 1:138. Revealingly, he still thought the Belgian Army could be counted on for offensive actions, and apparently had no idea they had retreated toward Antwerp (1:141).

11. Fayolle, *Carnets secrets de la grande guerre,* ed. Henry Contamine (Paris: Plon, 1964), 13, 16.

12. As quoted by Alexander McKee, *Vimy Ridge* (New York: Stein and Day, 1967), 164. Although the remark was made in 1917, it is a perfect illustration of the point: initially, British and French soldiers were unable to differentiate among the various German heavy weapons, and lumped them all together; it was some time before they could tell by the sound what type of gun was firing on them.

13. As quoted by British gunnery expert Ian V. Hogg, *A History of Artillery* (London: Hamlyn, 1974), 125–26.

4

1914: The Battles of the Frontiers

In résumé, the procedure of our adversaries seems to me this: strategically offensive, tactically defensive. Placed behind solid trenches, they let us attack them, and break our efforts with firepower, then counterattack troops exhausted by the losses they have just suffered. Their artillery is perfectly invisible, contrary to what is pretended.
—*General Fayolle, 27 August 1914*[1]

At the same time as the Germans attacked Liège, the two southernmost French armies were launched across the southeastern frontier into Alsace. The French General Staff could afford the luxury: it had only one front to worry about, and plenty of men. The French Army alone had more battalions deployed than the Germans did.[2] It could mount an attack in the south and still have a sizable force ready to deploy into Belgium. Moving into position to the northwest of the Verdun fortifications were the seventeen divisions of the Fifth Army, which had most of France's cavalry, and its senior general, Lanrezac.

Plan 17 had the French armies stacked in the center, straddling the Meuse and the Moselle. If a German attack developed through Belgium, Joffre had plenty of additional troops available to deploy into Belgium. The Colonial Corps of the Fourth Army, for example, was roughly the same distance from Namur as were the Germans. In theory, the Colonial Corps, or any army corps in that position, could move more quickly, since they could use the railroads, while the Germans, in enemy territory, could not.

The problem for the Germans with developing an attack through Belgium was the near continuous belt of forest that dropped down into France and ran parallel to the Meuse, beginning as the Ardennes and ending up as the Argonne. Owing to the fortifications at Verdun, there was only a small area in which to attack along the Meuse. German armies would have to march in an arc to attack on the western side of the forest, since the French General Staff had decided, not without reason, that it was impossible to maneuver a modern army through the dense Argonne. But the arc through which the Germans would have to move meant that the advancing French armies had a shorter distance to travel and could get there first. The German First Army had to march a good two hundred kilometers through Belgium to get to the French frontier at Maubeuge. So the French Fourth and Fifth Armies could either beat the Germans to the scene and control the battle, or they could strike up into Belgium and cut the advancing armies off from their base, since the German Army was simply too small to be able to do both things at once. The Allies had plenty of men, and plenty of men in the right place to stop the German advance on their left wing.

The French General Staff had enough forces at their disposal to block the Germans as they went through Belgium and to mount an attack into Alsace. There was an obvious synergism between the two fronts: once across the Vosges, the French could threaten both Alsace and southwestern Germany, and that is exactly what they tried to do. As we saw in the last chapter, the idea was simple and logical. Liège had provisions to hold out for a month. Siege warfare was a long and protracted business, as the Japanese and Russians had demonstrated earlier. The German assault on the Liège forts had only begun in earnest on 6 August, and the Belgians claimed (indeed claim to this very day) to have repulsed the initial attacks decisively.[3] So on the seventh, the French armies began their attack, penetrating into the modern *département* of the Haut-Rhin.

Initially, this offensive met with some success. At the southernmost end of the border, the French broke through and occupied Alsatian towns—early journalistic reports hinted at an early crossing of the Rhine.[4] But the early advance betrayed a surprising timidity. Far from storming ahead across the mountains in an all-out offensive, French troops moved slowly and cautiously. Before the war, Grandmaison might preach to his chapel of disciples about the importance of the all-out offensive effort, but French officers in the field were having all the problems of command

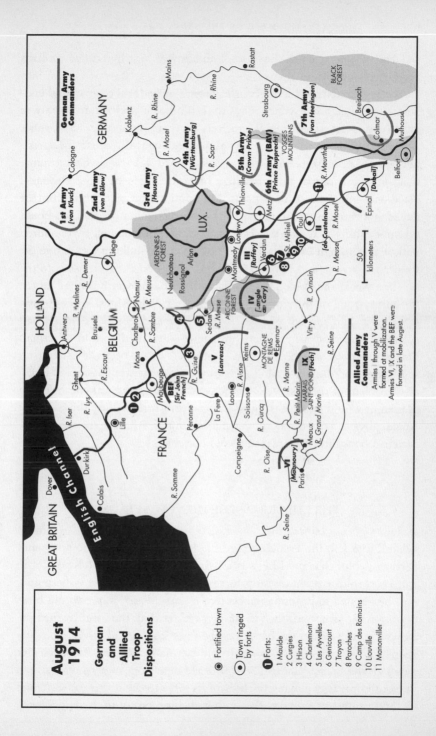

August 1914

German and Allied Troop Dispositions

- ⊚ Fortified town
- ⊙ Town ringed by forts
- ❶ Forts:
  1 Maulde
  2 Curgies
  3 Hirson
  4 Charlemont
  5 Les Ayvelles
  6 Génicourt
  7 Troyon
  8 Paroches
  9 Camp des Romains
  10 Louville
  11 Manonviller

GREAT BRITAIN

English Channel

Dover
Calais
Dunkirk

R. Somme

HOLLAND

Antwerp
Ghent
Bruxels
Lille
R. Lys
R. Escaut
R. Iser
R. Malines
R. Demer

BELGIUM

Liège
Namur
Charleroi
Mons
R. Sambre
R. Meuse

Maubeuge
❶❷
BEF [Sir John French]
❸
R. Guise
La Fère
Péronne
Compiègne

FRANCE

R. Oise
Soissons
Laon
R. Ourcq
VI [Maunoury]
Meaux
Paris
R. Grand Morin
R. Petit Morin
R. Seine
R. Seine

Reims
R. Aisne
MONTAGNE DE REIMS
Épernay
IX [Foch]
MARAIS SAINT GOND
R. Marne
Vitry

V [Lanrezac]

Sedan
❹
❺
R. Meuse
ARDENNE FOREST
IV [Langle de Cary]

Neufchâteau
Rossignol
Arlon
ARDENNES FOREST

LUX.

Montmédy
Longwy
III [Ruffey]
Verdun
❻❼
St. Mihiel
❽
❾❿
R. Meuse
Toul
II [de Castelnau]
R. Mosel
Vitry

Épinal
I [Dubail]
R. Moselle
R. Meurthe
⑪
Belfort

GERMANY

Cologne
Koblenz
R. Rhine
R. Mosel
Mains
Rastatt
R. Rhine

1st Army [von Kluck]
2nd Army [von Bülow]
3rd Army [Hausen]
4th Army [Württemburg]
R. Saar
Thionville
Metz
5th Army [Crown Prince]
6th Army (BAV) [Prince Rupprecht]
VOSGES MOUNTAINS
Strasbourg
7th Army [von Heeringen]
Colmar
Mulhouse
Breisach
BLACK FOREST

German Army Commanders

Allied Army Commanders

Armies I through V were formed at mobilization. Armies VI, X and the BEF were formed in late August.

|————————|
50
kilometers

and control that one might expect of an army of hastily recalled civilians and far too few officers.

Unfortunately, what the French initially seized, they were unable to hold. On the eighth, French troops took Mulhouse and Altkirch, only to lose them to a surprisingly ferocious German counterattack on the eleventh. On the fourteenth, a new attack regained Mulhouse. That, in a nutshell, was the problem. After a week of hard fighting involving something on the order of three quarters of a million men, the French had made only modest territorial gains. Mulhouse was a nice symbol for the public, but the city had no military importance; the key piece of landscape was not Mulhouse, but the Hartmannswillerkopf, a jagged mountain peak that dominated the plains overlooking the city all the way across the Rhine.

In a week, the French had gotten a symbol, the Germans had gotten the cornerstone of their offensive in the West. The Allies, without even realizing it, had run out of time. By the fourteenth, Liège's defenses had collapsed, German armies were streaming south and southeast toward France, Lanrezac's Fifth Army was right where it had been mobilized (still in France), and the BEF hadn't even gotten off the boat. That was the specific problem of the first week of the war. Unfortunately, as the war progressed, it would become the generic problem for the Allies: the Germans would always beat them to the punch; initial Allied gains would be snatched back, and the net result would be chaos.

THE FAILURE OF THE FRENCH ATTACKS

While Liège fell, the French began a leisurely advance to the north and northeast. Not that the BEF was moving any more expeditiously: Joffre had been told a seven-division force would deploy on the twenty-first, now he learned to his unhappiness that a four-division force would be in action on the twenty-sixth. The BEF was faster than that, but by the time they were in position the battle for the forts was already over. The only people moving swiftly so far were the Germans and the Russians. But although the French General Staff still had high hopes for its offensive in the south, it was deploying the bulk of its force to the north and east, and by the twenty-first, the day the Namur shelling began in earnest, French armies were about twenty kilometers inside Belgium, taking up defensive positions along the Sambre (some troops had actually gotten to Namur). The stage was set for a general battle all across the front line, the great decisive battle that everyone had assumed would mark the next war. The Belgians were still fighting at Namur, French armies were trying to break through into Alsace, and advancing into Belgium. So the storm broke all at once, from Rossignol in Belgium on down through the *ballon d'Alsace*. By the twenty-second, the French attacks across the Vosges, which had never made any real progress after those first days, had been thrown all the way back onto French territory, and the Germans had developed their own attack, forcing the French back on the town of Nancy. At the same time, the French had launched a major offensive up into Belgium. The Third and Fourth Armies attacked directly at the pivot of the German advance, going for the German Fourth and Fifth Armies, which were still largely inside Belgium. As proof of just how well positioned the French armies actually were, the Third Army's actual attack was just south of Arlon, and the Fourth Army's was around Neufchâteau. In other words, both attacks were well into southern Belgium, where a decisive victory would smash the pivot of the German Army and abort the movements of the three German armies wheeling through Belgium, as they would quickly be cut off from their lines of supply.

The two French armies totaled twenty divisions, the two German armies twenty-one. The two sides were thus about equal, but the core of the French Fourth Army was the Colonial Corps, ten regiments of the *infanterie coloniale,* France's best-trained and most experienced soldiers.[5] This was France's equivalent of the "professional elite" of the British Expeditionary Force, and, as the numbers make clear, it was a sizable force: In this one battle the French deployed a professional cadre equal to half or more of the BEF.

On 22 August 1914, the colonial infantry attacked south of Neufchâteau, just north of the small village of Rossignol, and was basically annihilated by German artillery. The six colonial infantry regiments engaged (fourteen thousand men at full strength) had 4,577 men killed in action in this one day's fighting: 117 officers are buried in the two military cemeteries at Rossignol, including fourteen captains and five brigadiers. Essentially, there were no officers left. But then with the usually accepted ratio of two wounded soldiers to every soldier killed in action, there were no colonial infantry left for them to command. Losses in the other units engaged—the Fourth Infantry Regiment, the Second Artillery, the Sixth Dragoons, and the Third Chasseurs d'Afrique—were equally bad.[6] Already, words like "decimated" and "annihilated" were beginning to take on their literal meaning. Here were France's best combat units—arguably the best and most experienced troops the Allies had—and in their first day of combat they simply ceased to exist. A few days later, at the other end of the line, in an attack on le Tête de Béhouille, the Thirteenth and Twenty-second Alpine Battalions (*battalions de chasseurs alpins,* or BCA), also elite units (the Twenty-second had been in action in Madagascar), lost half their men and both battalion commanders.[7]

In a combat that involves millions, it is easy to find an isolated massacre of one side or the other, and Allied propagandists wasted no time in finding some. There were places where German units were caught by 75s and massacred as well, as at Mangiennes, north of Verdun.[8] The problem is that on the German side such massacres were the exception: the German Army had eighteen thousand soldiers killed on the Western Front for the whole month. The French had at least one hundred thousand men killed and missing in August, and perhaps even more.[9] France's elite troops were being destroyed in small packets all over the battlefield. Melancholy stone memorials scattered along the Franco-Belgian frontier chronicle those desperate last stands: Brandeville, where the core of the 165th Infantry regiment lies buried; Ethe, the graveyard for the 102nd, 103rd, and 104th Infantry regiments.

A high percentage of these losses were officers and noncommissioned officers. Statistics from any one unit can be misleading, but over the course of the war, French officers suffered proportionally higher casualties than enlisted men, and, making allowances for the differing ways in which command was delegated among the combatants, the same is true for the other powers as well.[10]

Unfortunately, the destruction of the French colonial troops was simply an extreme example of the disaster that overtook French arms, all in the space of one week in August. Two days after the attack in which the Third and Fourth Armies tried to block the pivot of the German advance, Lanrezac's Fifth Army tried to stop the swing north of the pivot, and attacked the German Second and Third in the area to the south and west of Namur. Lanrezac's Fifth Army was intended, together with the BEF (which had finally gotten organized and into action) and the Belgians, to stop a German advance through Belgium. Lanrezac, probably Joffre's best general, had a quarter of a million men in the Fifth Army, including the Thirty-seventh and Thirty-eighth Divisions—more elite colonial troops (like the famous Foreign Legion and *infanterie coloniale*) freshly arrived from North Africa.

The BEF was approximately eighty thousand, and by British reckoning, was the only professional army in the field. Lemann, by pulling his troops out of Liège, had given the Belgians a sizable field army very close to its initial 117,500-man strength, and behind Lille were the fifty thousand-odd soldiers of the French Fourth Reserve Group under General Amade. As the three northernmost German armies only had 403 battalions altogether, the Allies were hardly outnumbered by very much, if at all, as the Germans were now scattered all over central and eastern Belgium. But in fact, the Germans weren't particularly worried about manpower in the West. On the twenty-first, as the Namur forts crumbled, the German General Staff had ordered two army corps to be released to the Eighth Army in East Prussia. Since the Allied armies had never managed to coordinate their efforts, much less combine, the Germans had the Napoleonic luxury of defeating each one in detail, which explains why the same engagement was called by the French the Battle of Guise and by the British, Mons.

This of course reflected the perennial problem of any alliance: how to coordinate actions, and who was theoretically in charge. French, the BEF commander, realized soon enough the precarious position he was in. He had the core of his country's army on the Continent; practically speaking, he had the entire army, and certainly the best part of it. There had been a rather unfortunate tradition of British colonial campaigns opening with the slaughter of the few regular troops sent to the scene, and French had no desire to see the tradition continue. French's problem is easy to understand. Lanrezac's is more difficult to sort out. Joffre had personally gone to Lanrezac's headquarters and tried to bestir him to move on, but the situation was tricky. Joffre had passed him over for the now defunct number-two slot in the Army (it had gone to de Castelnau instead). But the man seemed overwhelmed (a conclusion both Spears, the British liaison, and Joffre reached). So was French, the BEF commander.

Neither he nor Lanrezac hit it off, and neither had any sense of coordinating actions with each other. To make matters worse, both commanders acted as though the Belgians—in whose country they were fighting—

had no army at all, and left them to develop their own plan independently. This was a recipe for disaster, and one was not long in arriving.

The Allies had enough men, but they had entrusted their armies to leaders who, when the crucial moment came, were unable to command. The French and British armies were hardly alone in having this problem. It is endemic in any peacetime army that goes to war. Men who have spent their entire lives in training collapse when the crisis of combat looms near, and officers of great personal courage collapse under the strain of command—or dash off to the front and get killed (nearly a hundred Allied generals were killed during the war).

But the German Army had a built-in system of safeguards: the chief of staff of each unit drew up the orders, not the titular commander, and as long as the right orders were sent out, commanders lower down could execute them. Armies of hundreds of thousands of men weren't going to be directed by generals on horseback waving their sabers and exhorting their troops into combat. The last successful example of this had been Grant at Shiloh—and he had prudently stayed well out of range.

This was precisely what was happening in the East. As the German General Staff had calculated before the war, the Russians were off the mark quickly enough. By the fifteenth, two Russian armies had penetrated into East Prussia, and Germany had a serious war on two fronts. Von Prittwitz, in charge of the German Eighth Army in the East (which as it expanded in the next few weeks came to be known as *Ober-Ost*), was, like French and Lanrezac, on the verge of panic. But the army's chief of staff, a colonel named Hoffmann (a colleague of Ludendorff's) had already assessed the situation and written out the dispositions for the defense.

Von Moltke (who was strangely energetic for an elderly neurasthenic on the verge of a nervous breakdown) promptly—and possibly unfairly—sacked von Prittwitz. He then plucked Ludendorff out of Belgium and sent him off to run the *Ober-Ost* staff. Almost as an afterthought, he had an elderly retiree, von Hindenburg, recalled to active duty and sent to replace von Prittwitz. The sequence suggests which was the more important, but by the time Ludendorff arrived on the scene, Hoffmann's dispositions had largely been carried out by the two elderly but surprisingly spry commanders, von François and von Mackensen. Von Prittwitz, whether he panicked or not, was eminently dispensable.

But in the German scheme, so were all the other army commanders.

As the crown prince records it, von Eichorn, the Inspector General of the peacetime Seventh Army, was actually slated for command of the Fifth Army in 1914. But von Eichorn fell ill, so Kaiser Wilhelm appointed his son instead, investing him with these words: "I have entrusted to you the command of the Fifth Army. Lieutenant-General Schmidt von Knobelsdorf will go with you as chief of staff. What he tells you, you must do."[11] The army commander was not a figurehead, but neither was he the person who made the key decisions.

But in the Allied system, when Lanrezac and French panicked, there was no one on hand to replace them. The BEF had no backup command system, and Lanrezac was too senior for Joffre to feel confident enough to sack him. So the situation drifted. At the crucial juncture, Joffre failed to act and von Moltke acted. Joffre left Lanrezac in place for the next few critical days, and France's last chance to stop the German advance dissolved in a welter of uncoordinated and unplanned border engagements in which the Allies thoughtfully let the Germans choose the when and where. Not surprisingly, German field commanders had the tendency to fight in situations where, owing to a superiority in numbers and position, they were positive of winning. So the Germans were able to use the same tactics that Frederick the Great had first perfected in the 1740s, defeating their enemies in detail before they could combine. Both generals, unwilling to commit their troops to a full-scale battle in which they might lose their armies, tried to husband their resources. It was the classical military dilemma, and resolved in the classical way: instead of losing them all at once, in a great battle that might conceivably have crippled the attackers, they lost them in packets, as the Germans defeated each one in detail.

Unfortunately, the BEF was no better at a withdrawal than it had been at an advance. So on 23 August, the BEF was routed at Mons by elements of the German First Army, while over at Charleroi, on the same day, an outnumbered German force beat the French back into their own country.[12] On the twenty-fifth, the BEF was defeated again at Le Cateau, where the British commander suffered greater casualties than Wellington had at Waterloo, and still lost.[13] Spears, the BEF's liaison with the French Army, summed up the problem facing the Allies perfectly:

I was told of several satisfactory incidents when the French 75s caught the German infantry in fairly close formation and inflicted heavy punishment.... On the other hand, the liaison officers did not

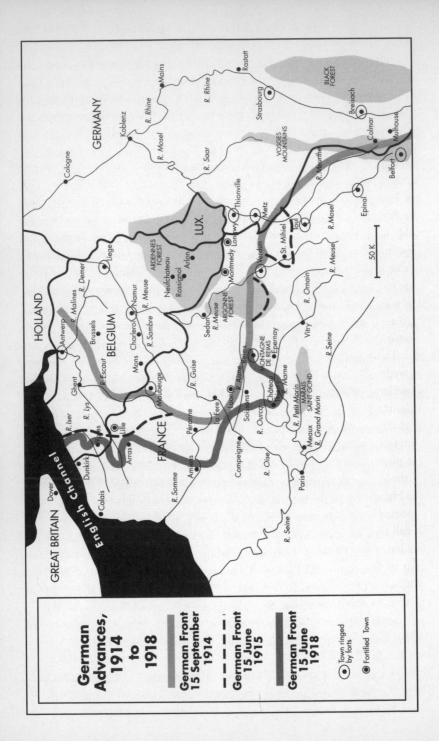

German Advances, 1914 to 1918

disguise the fact that the German heavy howitzers had taken the
French infantry aback.... there was no doubt they were having a most
depressing effect, all the more so that owing to the nature of the
country the French artillery could do little to silence the enemy guns
(143–44).

On the twenty-seventh, there was panic at both the BEF headquarters and
at the French General Staff. According to Spears, the BEF's liaison with
the French, his opposite number (the French liaison to the BEF) believed
the British were completely out of the fight. BEF commanders were being
told to "throw overboard all ammunition and impedimenta not
absolutely required . . . and hustle along" in retreat. The elite BEF did no
better against the Germans than had the crack Colonial Corps. Their
defeat was so decisive that the commander, Sir John French, panicked and
started talking about leaving France altogether.[14] By the time the BEF
retreat stopped, their commander was holding the line along the Seine,
where his men were safely out of harm's way.

The German advance continued to the south. German gunners
moved from Namur to Maubeuge, and began pounding the forts there.
American and British journalists, who were wandering freely around
Belgium, since no one knew exactly who was in charge there, had a brief
field day and actually were able to report the course of the battle. The
American Irwin Cobb saw the destruction at Maubeuge, and reported on
the phenomenal power of the new German heavy guns (ironically, much
of the damage was done by the heavy *Minenwerfer* of the *Pioniere*, but
the big guns seized the popular imagination). The English journalist Fyfe
reported—accurately—that the BEF had been routed in the field and was
in full retreat. It was the last serious reporting of the war. Reported or no,
the bad news continued. By the end of August, the news of the capitulation of the Belgian forts had spread, and the leveling of the Maubeuge
forts created a sort of panic. The whole line of fortifications along the
frontier simply unraveled.

There was no real surprise as to why the Germans were winning. Not
because the Allies were outnumbered, but because they hadn't mastered
the basics of modern warfare. Joffre had noted the same deficiencies in
the prewar maneuvers, as had Percin. The BEF had the same weakness.
Bernard Montgomery's account of what happened to his unit on the
twenty-sixth is emblematic:

The Germans advanced . . . and began shelling us heavily.... The fire was so heavy we had to retire as we had not time to entrench ourselves.... We had to advance through a hail of bullets from rifles and machine-guns and through a perfect storm of shrapnel fire.... the whole air seemed full of bullets and bursting shells.... the whole of the rest of the day we were heavily shelled by the Germans.[15]

As this account makes clear, the advancing Germans were quicker to seize the best ground, and quicker to deploy their artillery in beating off attacks, all against an adversary who obliged them by deploying his men in exactly the way that, as we have seen, Joffre had been so concerned about in 1912. Montgomery's men, part of the Royal Warwickshire Regiment, had seen combat on the Northwest Frontier as recently as 1908. But it apparently made little difference to the outcome.

Meanwhile, in the East, Hoffmann's dispositions succeeded brilliantly. In four days at the end of August, the Russians, who had deployed over three hundred thousand men, were surrounded by the numerically inferior Germans. The tactics were the same as in the West: the Germans defeated the two Russian armies before they could combine. Samsonov, the commander of the Russian Second Army, disappeared, presumably a suicide, and some ninety thousand Russians were taken prisoner. Rennenkampf, the First Army commander, managed to fight his way clear, and by the middle of September had escaped. But as those two armies were the sum total of the offensive capabilities *stavka* had earmarked for the Northwest Front (the front against Germany as opposed to the one against Austria) the Russian steamroller was temporarily laid up for repairs. Russia and Great Britain had both sent their best troops into action, the men with the most combat experience, the core of their regular officer cadre. The losses were irreplaceable. Both empires had millions of men to call up. But who would train them?

An equally serious problem was that the Russians were running out of ammunition. So were the French. And shortly the Germans would begin to feel the pinch as well. But for the Russians the shortages were more acute. Germany, with its enormous industrial capacity, could manufacture all the ammunition it needed for its guns, but Russia was simply unable to keep up with that level of production. For that matter, France and Great Britain were shortly going to be in the same fix: enormous untrained reserves, too few experienced officers to train them (and an inadequate training system), and too few shells for the too few guns, which had to fire many more shells to do the same amount of damage as was being done by their opponents.

So Tannenberg, as Ludendorff and von Hindenburg named Hoffmann's victory, marked the end of the Franco-Russian dream of a crushing joint offensive on two fronts. The Russians would fight desperately for the next two and a half years, and do surprisingly well. But the great dream that had propelled Poincaré to St. Petersburg, of a Franco-Russian march on Berlin, was over, crushed as thoroughly as the illusion that while the Germans were besieging Liège and Namur the French would advance into Alsace and cross the Rhine.

In both cases the Germans had used the same tactics. They had relied on speed to destroy the enemy before he could combine and force a battle of his choosing. Lanrezac kept trying to find a place where he could unpack his artillery and start fighting the set piece battle he wanted to conduct, but he never got the chance. In early September he was sacked, and followed Ruffey into premature retirement. His misfortunes would be repeated over and over again in the next four years of the war.

NOTES

1. Fayolle, *Carnets secrets de la grande guerre,* ed. Henry Contamine (Paris: Plon, 1964), 25–26. On 14 May 1914, Fayolle was at the age limit (sixty-two) for a general of brigade. In 1914, he took command of the 139th Brigade (infantry regiments 226 and 269, plus the 42nd and 44th *Chasseurs* [BCP]), part of the 70th (Reserve) Division. By 14 August he was commanding the division and fought in the battles of Lorraine, then in Artois, where he became, successively, a corps commander and then an army commander. He was made a marshal in 1921 and died in 1928. His secret diary was found in 1942 and published in 1964.

2. The Germans disposed of 86 divisions, broken down into 1,062 battalions of foot soldiers and 502 squadrons of cavalry. The Allies disposed of 96 divisions, broken down into 1,241 battalions of foot soldiers and 532 squadrons of cavalry. Of this total, the BEF contributed 54 battalions, and the Belgian Army, 120. The French Army alone outnumbered the German Army by 1,067 battalions to 1,062 (or maybe only 962). French dispositions and troop strengths: The dispositions for Plan 17 are taken from the official map reproduced in *Inventaire sommaire des archives de la Guerre* Série N: 1872–1919 (Troyes: La Renaissance, 1967), annexe 4. Comparative manpower analyses are to be found in Contamine, *La Revanche,* 200–3, and with a slightly different way of computing it, but with the same totals, in Fernand Gambiez and Martin Suire, *Histoire de la première guerre mondiale* (Paris:

Fayard, 1968), 1.174. Camena d'Almeida, in his authoritative *L'Armée allemande avant et pendant la guerre de 1914–18* (Paris: Berger-Levrault, 1919), gives a lower set of figures for the Germans: 962 battalions of infantry and 486 squadrons of cavalry (146).

3. See the official report of the army commandant, reprinted as *La Guerre de 1914: L'Action de l'armée Belge pour la défense du pays et le respect de sa neutralité: Rapport du commandement de l'armée (Periode du 31 juillet au 31 décembre 1914)* (Paris: Librarie Chapelot, 1915), 13. De Schrÿver, chief of staff of the Belgian 3rd Division, has an extensive account of the early hours of the fighting in *La Bataille de Liège (août 1914)* (Liège: Vaillant-Carmanne, 1922). Most of his text is devoted to what happened before the bombardment: he doesn't even get to August 7 until 205.

4. See, for example, the maps on 25 and 27 of A.J.P. Taylor, *Illustrated History of the First World War* (New York: G.P. Putnam's Sons, 1964). For a more recent example, see the map on 13 of Anthony Livesy, *Great Battles of World War I* (New York: Macmillan, 1989). The map in Cyril Falls, *The Great War* (New York: G.P. Putnam's Sons, 1959), 42, is even more misleading.

5. The *infanterie coloniale* were not, as some historians seem to believe, colonials at all; rather they were the result of a late-nineteenth-century administrative shuffle in which the French Navy's troops, what Americans would call the Marines, were reassigned to the colonial army. It would be more accurate to call them marines; unfortunately, in 1914, the French Navy deployed men into combat on the Western Front, and these troops are sometimes known as marines as well.

6. See also the conclusion of Yves Buffetaut, quoting from *Les Troupes coloniales pendant la guerre 1914–1918, in La Bataille de Verdun, de l'Argonne à la Woëvre* (Tours: Éditions Heimdale, 1990), 5. Figures of the dead taken from the Colonial Infantry Monument at Rossignol. Its two military cemeteries have 1,204 marked graves, while the remains of 2,379 unknowns are buried in the two ossuaries. The figure of 117 officer graves reflects the count of only the identified dead who were buried there.

7. Jean Mabire, *Chasseurs alpins: Des Vosges aux Djebels, 1914–1964* (Paris: Presses de la Cité, 1984), 71–72.

8. See the brief description in Buffetaut, 5–7.

9. For August and September, France had 329,000 men killed in action or missing. The figures have never been broken down more precisely, and there is no figure for the number of wounds cases (a near meaningless figure in any event). See the tables in Michel Huber, *La Population de la France pendant la guerre* (New Haven: Yale University Press, 1931), 420, which closely parallel the figures produced during the war by Abel Ferry, *La Guerre vue d'en bas et d'en haut* (Paris: Grasset, 1920), 120. When Churchill analyzed the official German data that was being worked up in Berlin, he came up with a total of German dead and missing for the first four months of the war that was a third less than France's total for the first two months: *The World Crisis, 1916–1918* (New York: Charles Scribner's Sons, 1927), 1:301. In the one brief period in August after the BEF landed, their admitted casualties were over fourteen thousand, roughly one sixth of the total force engaged.

10. The mortality rate among French officers in combat units was 22 percent, as opposed to 18 percent for their men. For all officers and men, the rates were 19 and 16 percent. See the analysis of the French government data in Huber, 416. The corresponding German figures

are 23 percent for officers and 14 percent for enlisted men. See the discussion in Robert Weldon Whalen, *Bitter Wounds* (Ithaca, N.Y.: Cornell University Press, 1993), 42.

11. Kronprinz Wilhelm, *Meine Erinnerungen aus Deutschlands Heldenkampf* (Berlin: Mittlerer and Son, 1923), 4. It is typical of the level of misunderstanding about the system that in the standard English translation of the crown prince's memoirs, Wilhelm II says, "I have appointed you Commander of the Fifth Army. You're to have as Chief of Staff..." But the German is quite clear: the emperor doesn't say "appointed," he uses the verb *anvertrauen,* which means "to entrust," and he says he's entrusted the command to his son, not that he's made his son the commander. William, Crown Prince of Germany, *My War Experiences* (New York: McBride, 1923), 4. It's a significant difference.

12. Edward Louis Spears, *Liaison 1914: A Narrative of the Great Retreat.* 1st ed. (London: Heinemann, 1930), 176.

13. According to Nigel Hamilton, *Monty: The Making of a General,* 1887–1942 (New York: McGraw Hill, 1981), 80. Hamilton's account of what Montgomery saw is compelling evidence in support of the extent of the disaster that befell the BEF.

14. As related by Brigadier Anthony H. Farrar-Hockley in Peter Young and J.P. Lawford, *History of the British Army* (New York: G.P. Putnam's Sons, 1970), 213. The first quote, relating to Wilson, is from Spears, 247.

15. As recorded by Nigel Hamilton, 76. Similar passages can be found in the accounts of French veterans.

5

1914: The Myth of the Marne

Was there a Battle of the Marne?

—*Marshal Gallieni*[1]

As the August days wore on, the infantry of von Kluck's First Army advanced through France. Their great trek had begun, more or less, on the seventeenth, when the advance units, well to the north and west of Liège, had forced the Belgians back across the rivers, and made a rough arc that turned to the south at Brussels. By the twenty-first, they were on the south side of the capital, on the twenty-fourth they had run over the BEF at Mons, and a day later they were to the south of the forts of Maubeuge.

As a combination of Austrian heavy howitzers and the mortars of the *Pioniere* leveled the forts of Maubeuge, von Kluck's infantry kept moving south. In a little over a week, they had marched about two hundred kilometers, and they were hardly over the frontier. From Maubeuge they marched through Peronne, skirting the edge of the future battlefields of the Somme, and by the thirty-first they were approaching Compiègne.

Although they had much less distance to cover, the men of the German Second and Third Armies were at this point already across the Aisne River and moving through Champagne. The last battle had been on the twenty-ninth, at Guise. When Lanrezac's troops began to fall back, the Germans pressed on, but slowly. The Germans didn't enter Reims, whose forts had apparently never been manned, until 3 September, although the French had pulled out long before.[2]

As one might expect in a war involving so many men spread over such a large front, neither the retreating French nor the advancing Germans were capable of maintaining a solid line as they moved. But for the retreating Allies, the gap was widening with each day, because the BEF, sandwiched between the French Fifth and Sixth Armies, was retreating at a faster rate than the French. If the rates of retreat continued, a big hole would open up to the east of Paris, since the French armies, as they retreated, were shifting to their right, and closing up toward Verdun.

The French, who could see this happening as well as the Germans, began forming up new units to fill the gaps, while Marshal Gallieni, the newly appointed military governor of Paris, was agitating for an army to cover the capital. Two new armies were formed, and the commanders of two of the existing armies were replaced. Ruffey, at Third Army, had gone at the end of August, replaced by the popular (with the Chamber of Deputies) Sarrail. Now it was Lanrezac's turn, and he was sacked on 3 September, to be replaced by Franchet d'Esperey. Firing commanders on the eve of what everyone expected would be a great battle was a move of desperation. Whether good or bad, it put both armies at a disadvantage.

The first of the new armies, the Sixth, was formed up to the north of Paris, under the aging but capable Maunoury. Joffre put Foch in charge of a second new army, the Ninth, which was slotted in to fill the gap that had developed between the Fourth and Fifth Armies. The Fourth Army, like the BEF, had disengaged and retreated much faster than had the Fifth. The French General Staff had plugged that hole, which was the main one, and covered the front of Paris. The BEF was now on the Seine, thirty kilometers or more behind the rough line formed by the French armies to their right. Both sets of commanders saw their opportunities clearly enough, and planned to take advantage of them. The result, which the French would retrospectively roll into a masterful public relations package and call the "Battle of the Marne," was in reality five separate and uncoordinated battles fought over a two-hundred-kilometer section of the front, no one of which was particularly close to (or in fact anywhere near) the Marne River.

EXPLOITING THE GAPS

The Ourcq is a small river that flows into the Marne just below Meaux, a town of about twelve thousand located fifty kilometers north of Paris. As it had come marching down from Maubeuge, it appeared that von Kluck's First Army would advance down the Ourcq and descend on Paris. So the French Sixth Army, supported by the ragtaggle of units that formed Gallieni's Army of Paris, was to the southwest of the town, awaiting their descent. But by the twenty-eighth, von Kluck had seen a new opportunity created by the rapid movement of the BEF to the Seine. The First Army could simply swoop into the gap to the left of the French Fifth Army and roll up the entire French front, crushing it back against the Meuse and the Moselle. Carry the maneuver through quickly enough, and the war would be over, the French armies caught in a bag.

So at Compiègne, some eighty kilometers north of Paris, von Kluck's army had begun to shift to the east. Instead of continuing south and southwest, which would allow them to envelop Paris, they were moving almost due southwest. To Gallieni and Maunoury, this opened up a perfect opportunity for a flank attack.[3] Once von Kluck crossed the Ourcq and then the Marne, there would be no German forces to speak of between Meaux and the Channel. The entire German Army would be south of the Marne River and northeast of Paris. Joffre saw the same opportunity. So did the senior staff of the BEF. If the Sixth Army attacked and pushed in the German flank on the west bank of the Ourcq, and the BEF attacked up along the Marne in the same direction (north), they would take the Germans in the flank, where, as any officer can tell you, an army is at its most vulnerable. Both von Kluck and his adversaries thus aimed to turn the other's flank. The French General Staff counted on the Fifth and Ninth Armies to pin the Germans to the center of the newly developed line, so that Maunoury and the BEF could drive them back. Von Kluck was counting on von Hausen and von Bulow to do the same on his side.

If the original plan had been to drive straight for Paris, someone had forgotten to communicate this to the commanders of the three army groups on the right wing of the German advance: none of them were headed in that direction, and the closest, von Kluck's, had started shifting to its left, and away from the capital, while it was three days march to the north.[4]

Meanwhile, in the Meuse valley north of Verdun, 250 kilometers east of Paris, the German Fourth, Fifth, and Sixth Armies were pursuing an entirely different set of plans. As the French Third Army had retreated southward, it had edged eastward and away from the Fourth Army. So by

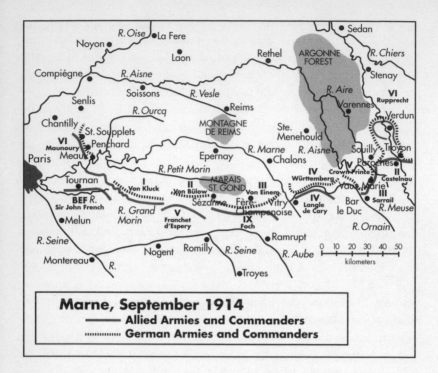

Marne, September 1914
——— Allied Armies and Commanders
·············· German Armies and Commanders

the beginning of September, as the Third Army crossed the Ornain, a small tributary of the Marne runs between Vitry and Bar-le-Duc, a gap had opened up between the two armies, around the village of Revigny. The German Fourth Army aimed to exploit it.

At the same time, the Fifth and Sixth Armies aimed to conduct an operation that would pinch off the entire *place* Verdun. The logic here was simple, and related to the problem the German General Staff had been monitoring nervously for weeks. As time passed and there was no decisive battle, it began to occur to people that there might not be a decisive battle, that the war might continue on in an inconclusive fashion with the French continuing a fighting withdrawal. For the Germans, this posed a major problem, because the bulk of the entire German Army was hundreds of kilometers inside France.

Simple prudence dictated that someone begin to worry about defensive positions, and there was the rub. The best defensive line was the most obvious one: east-west it ran to the north of Reims along the ridges and buttes of Champagne; north-south it ran roughly down the Belgian frontier to the Aisne. But the problem was that the western end of this was entirely up in the air. The Germans had largely stayed east of the Scarpe and the Dender. Any assembled army could break through their exposed right flank, because it was basically unprotected—and it ran for hundreds of kilometers.

The problem with the best defensive position was that it was far to the north—about fifty kilometers north of where the Germans were in early September. But if the Fifth and Sixth Armies could pinch off Verdun, then the Germans would have a solid base from which to extend a defensive line along the Marne—they could stop wherever they liked. The key was Verdun. While von Kluck tried to roll up the French from one flank, and the duke of Württemberg tried it from the other, the two German armies at the end of the line tried to pinch off Verdun.

THE BATTLE OF THE OURCQ

Insofar as there was an engagement called the Battle of the Marne that aimed to break the German flank as the result of a plan hatched by the Allies, the Battle of the Ourcq was that battle. Gallieni and Joffre planned an attack that would begin on the sixth, with Maunoury rolling across the Ourcq. Simultaneously, the BEF and the other armies would try to pin the Germans to their fronts.

The Allied plan went wrong from the start, for two reasons. The first was that Maunoury's Sixth Army was far too weak to mount an effective flank attack. On the fifth, he only had one army corps (the Fourth), four infantry divisions, and one cavalry division. There were plenty of troops in the pipeline, but they weren't north of Paris. None of his troops had seen action, and most of them were from the lower end of the reserve units (which was why they had not yet seen action or had only just been formed up). They were weak in another way as well: the French theory of command saw an army commander as presiding over a set of army corps commanders, who each in turn had divisional commanders under them, with brigades in each division—a neatly symmetrical structure. But Maunoury had a whole mixture, everything from a regular army corps to a brigade of Moroccans, none of whom had ever worked together, run by a staff that had been scavenged the same way the units had been. This was hardly an effective combat force to be entrusted with such a critical mission.

But the Allies assumed that von Kluck had moved off and left himself totally exposed, and that by the fifth, he was by now too far southeast of the Marne to extricate himself. These problems were irrelevant. Which was the second major problem: the Allies simply ignored any consideration of what their adversaries might do. This was a calamitous mistake. Von Kluck had left a capable officer covering his flank. When von Gronau, the commander of the IV Reserve Corps, looked at the situation, he saw the ground favored him. The key area for the Sixth Army's advance was the relatively open ground north of Paris and west of Meaux, a town right on the Ourcq. So von Gronau's men seized the key position there, a surprisingly massive ridge that ran up from Penchard (right outside of Meaux) about eight kilometers in a northwesterly direction toward the village of Saint-Soupplets.

On the sixth, the leading infantry units of the Sixth Army, blundering ahead, ran into the German positions on the ridge. Maunoury's men now discovered what the survivors of the initial attacks in Belgium had learned: instead of standing out in the field and blasting away with their rifles, German infantry dug itself in and watched while its heavy artillery massacred the developing attack. German doctrine had always (since 1905) placed heavy emphasis on digging in. German soldiers were trained to entrench themselves. As a young German infantry commander, Erwin Rommel, recorded in his journal on 7 September 1914, "Our recent experiences indicated but one way of keeping casualties down—the deep trench."[5]

On the Ourcq, what Fayolle had described as the basic strategy of strategic offense, tactical defense paid off handsomely. The French attack, which was supposed to drive in the German flank, was stopped cold. Von Gronau then promptly pulled back, letting the main French attack be delivered against an abandoned position, while his men took up their defenses on a line to the north. This, the opening engagement, was a costly misfire. Far from outflanking the Germans, all the Allies had actually done was to alert the Germans to the fact that they intended to outflank them from the West. Von Kluck's staff saw the problem quickly enough—and they now had the time to rectify it. They shuttled men back to the West, and in two days of fighting broke the Sixth Army completely. Von Kluck's orders of the day for the ninth spoke of the final victory over the French. Given what had happened so far, this was a reasonable assessment of the situation.

THE BATTLE OF LES DEUX MORINS

As von Kluck shifted to the West, von Bulow's army slotted in behind him, engaging the French Fifth Army, and forcing it back still farther, to the Seine. The gap left by von Kluck's shuttle was thus soon occupied by von Bulow. The great hole that was perceived to exist on the east bank of the Marne suddenly closed, and Franchet d'Esperey, now in command discovered to his horror that the BEF were only now on the north bank of the Verre, their center at Tournan, when they should have been (by his reckoning) about twenty kilometers to the northeast.

What this meant was that there was a large hole developing in the Allied line. The original idea had been to exploit the gap caused by von Kluck's shift to the southeast, and cave in his flank. And as von Kluck started shifting troops to cover his flank, he weakened his main force. But as von Kluck developed his forces along the line roughly approximated by the larger of two small streams, the *grand Morin,* the German Second Army moved up along the *petit Morin.*

Provided he was willing to take the risk, von Kluck could destroy the Fifth Army before his flank could be overpowered. And at this point the only force able to move into the gap that had developed as von Kluck had shifted to the southeast was the BEF. Given where the BEF was on the fifth, and the condition of its senior commanders, the Germans believed— correctly—that they could smash through the flank of the French Fifth Army and envelop them before the BEF and Maunoury were able to exploit the gap and the exposed right flank.

French, the BEF commander, was not about to risk what was left of his army in another suicide fight with the Germans. Alone among Allied army commanders, he seems to have possessed some idea of the terrible price that had been paid in August. Three quarters of the men of the BEF division engaged at Le Cateau were casualties. The Germans had simply run over the unit and flattened it. French also seems to have had some inkling of the new warfare. His subordinates—and his superiors—were still keen to fight, but the BEF's commander apparently realized that if the most professional army in the world had been beaten so easily, it was doubtful if anyone else would do much better. His instinct was first to retreat to safety (which he had done) and second to repair his shattered army. His clear preference was to drop out of the fight altogether.

The whole rationale for the participation of the half a dozen–odd divisions of the BEF had been based on Wilson's rather bizarre math, in which six British divisions held the balance of power in a Franco-German war. Since this was clearly off the table, why risk losing the only army his country had? When French confided in the government and complained about the risks, he was told to get back in there and fight. And he did. But in the first weeks of September, he did what any sensible man would do in a like situation—he did as he was told, but he did it very slowly. As Norton Cru observes, apropros of his own countrymen, "if orders had been obeyed to the letter, the whole French army would have been massacred by August 1915."[6] Sir John French was simply ahead of the disobedience curve.

So the most notable feature about the BEF and the Battle of the Marne is that the Germans had already withdrawn by the time they got there, leaving the propagandists to boost a few insignificant skirmishes. But in the fast-growing lexicography of the Great War, where caution equaled incompetence and prudence was cowardice, French was quickly pilloried by his more manly subordinates, who promptly began an extensive campaign to have him replaced. But given what was going on around him, his caution was justified.

THE BATTLE OF MARAIS SAINT-GOND

As their armies had retreated south, the French General Staff had started shifting troops from the First and Second Armies. A new army, the Ninth, was thus fitted into the line between the Fourth and the Fifth. Foch, its commander, had two army corps (the IX and XI) and four stray divisions. His section of the constantly shifting front now lay on the south side of the somewhat misleadingly named Marsh of Saint-Gond, about fifty kilometers due south of Épernay.

Foch assumed the Marsh of Saint-Gond was actually a marsh. Consequently, he tried to attack on the ends, notably around the western end, at Saint-Prix. Foch ran into the same problem Maunoury had run into outside of Meaux: the German infantry had dug in, and the attacking French were decimated. Foch, like most of the Allied commanders, was hardly bothered by heavy casualties. Besides, he had been in action before. He saw sending units into engagements where they would quickly sustain losses of up to 80 percent of their strength as a sort of thinning of the herd. Left to his own devices, he would have continued to attack on the west side of the marsh until he had no more infantry left to send into combat.

But events soon intervened. Someone on the staff of von Hausen, the Saxon commanding the German Third Army, had apparently gone over and looked at the ground, discovering what is plain enough even today: although it has low-lying areas and is intersected by small sluggish streams, the Marais de Saint Gond is not actually a swamp. While Foch tried to attack around the ends, the Germans attacked right through the center and threw him back to the Seine. This attack is notable for having inspired—allegedly—Foch's famous pronouncement of attacking while being surrounded. But this was locking the barn after the horse was stolen. The best face that can be put on the Battle of the Marais de Saint Gond, as the resulting struggle is called, is that on the ninth von Hausen's men had pushed Foch back only past Fère-Champenoise and Mailly, or about fifteen kilometers from the Seine.

Just how far south were the Allies, anyway? Sir John French had installed his headquarters at Melun, a small town on the Seine fifty kilometers southeast of Paris. Franchet d'Espery's headquarters was at Romilly-sur-Seine, which in fact is about fifty kilometers northwest of Troyes. Up until the thirty-first, the French General Staff had been at Vitry-le-François. But it too had moved farther south, first to Bar-sur-Aube and then to Chatillon-sur-Seine, 234 kilometers from Paris. As the French Army prepared to fight for the Seine, the government abandoned Paris entirely and moved to Bordeaux (on 2 September).

The problem was becoming increasingly clear: as the Germans pushed in their front, the French simply retreated farther south. There was no way armies of this size, spread out over hundreds of kilometers, could encircle one another. Nor was there any way an army of that size could be beaten. Frederick the Great, Napoleon, and Grant had been able to thrash their enemies soundly in the field, destroy them so completely they would sue for peace. But the armies in the field in 1914 were too large for this to be possible. Each of France's nine army commanders had a force as large as anything that had been put into the field in the past century. Defeat one and it simply melted away, its place filled up by its neighbors. And so Foch, despite his rhetoric about always attacking at all times and in all conditions, fell back on the Seine just as everyone else was doing.

This cut both ways: even had the BEF energetically closed up the gap and engaged their opponents in some all-out struggle, the Germans could have simply done what von Gronau had done—retreat. Although the theorists in Paris were right—the point of greatest German vulnerability was the exposed right flank—there was little in the practical sense that could be done about it. Maunoury simply lacked the force to push in the flank, and fifty thousand British soldiers would hardly have made much difference. Clearly there were no percentages in this sort of combat for either side. When the Allied plans to outflank the Germans collapsed during the Battle of the Ourcq, the Allies had no real option remaining for offensive action. That was why Foch had retreated like everyone else.

The decisive German effort, however, was far to the East, where there was the possibility of a real solution to the problems of encirclement and withdrawal. At Verdun the line formed to the West by the retreating French hinged with the defensive position along the Franco-German frontier. These troops had been hit hard as well, but were still holding a line which crisscrossed the frontier. If the Germans could force the Third and Fourth Armies back farther, the retreating French would run into the soldiers of the First Army, which was facing Alsace.

The French positions held by those three armies thus resembled an old-fashioned compass. The peak was Verdun, the fixed leg of the Franco-German border positions of the First Army, the movable leg the retreating Third and Fourth Armies. As they retreated farther, the two legs of the compass came closer and closer together. Therefore, the best chance the Germans had lay in the eastern part of the line. If they could force the French back farther, they would have only two choices: surrender or annihilation. That is also why, to be fair to Foch and Franchet d'Espery, if they retreated straight back toward the Seine, rather than being pushed farther east, they were doing reasonably well.

THE BATTLE OF REVIGNY: (1) THE ORNAIN

Thus far, the various engagements of the so-called Battle of the Marne involved surprisingly little fighting. They are battles of maneuver in the classical sense that the eighteenth century knew the term. Both sides were doing more marching than fighting, and in each case one side outmaneuvered the other. Once von Gronau seized the ridge at Penchard before Maunoury got there, the Joffre-Gallieni plan collapsed. Once von Hausen's men realized they could cross the marsh, Foch's position was untenable and he had to withdraw. On the eastern side, however, there was no real room for maneuver, and the two components of the Battle of Revigny were, either singly or collectively, the bloodiest battles the war had yet seen, and the only place where the original idea of a great decisive battle came close to being true.

By 6 September, on the eastern end of the line, from Vitry to Verdun, the French defensive line was unraveling. The German armies on this end, the Fourth, Fifth, and Sixth, basically had two objectives. Elements of the Fifth and Sixth Armies were trying to pinch off the entire Verdun salient just north of Saint-Mihiel. This was the necessary anchor point for any German position along the Marne, but it was a tempting target in itself. At the same time, the German Fourth Army tried to turn the flank of the French Third Army.

At Revigny-sur-Ornain, where the French Third and Fourth Army boundary was, a sizable gap had developed as the Third Army had been pushed back. In the face of German attacks on both sides of the Argonne, Sarrail was folding his front down like a swinging door, with the hinge being at Verdun. By the fifth, the Third Army's front was on the south side of a curved line running from Verdun to Souilly to Revigny, a front of about fifty kilometers, and the French Fifth Army Corps was holding on to the outskirts of the village of Bussy-la-Côte.

As the Germans attempted to widen the line, the French General Staff shifted a new army corps, the XV, over from the East and managed to plug the gap just southwest of Vossincourt. This was on the eighth, and on the night of the ninth, the decisive battle began. The four army groups threw every available man into the fight. If the French line broke, there were no reserves to plug the hole. The closest reinforcements to Sarrail were fighting off the Germans around Nancy. A breakthrough and a whole section of the front (everything from Verdun to Toul) would simply collapse. It would be Tannenberg, but on a much larger scale. Insofar as there was any one engagement under the assemblage of Marne battles that could be said to be decisive, this was it, because by the ninth, the other component of the Battle of Revigny was coming to a climax as well.

THE BATTLE OF REVIGNY: (2) TROYON AND
THE HEIGHTS OF THE MEUSE

The Fifth and Sixth German Armies had a simple aim: pinch off Verdun and its forts, along with most of the Third Army, which was strung out below Verdun. As they advanced to the south, the Germans had simply moved around the forts of Verdun, judging—correctly—that they would be almost impervious to siege and impossible to take with the tactics that had worked in Belgium.[7]

There was a simple reason for this prudence. Most of the twenty Verdun forts had been substantially modernized at the turn of the century. The older carapace of masonry and concrete had been upgraded by using a sort of sandwich in which a layer of sand and rubble lay between the old masonry and the new reinforced concrete. The engineers felt that the resulting structure was basically invulnerable, and as subsequent events would prove, direct hits from 420-millimeter shells had surprisingly little effect on the superstructure.

The French had also realized that the gun turrets of a fort were its most vulnerable point. As the Belgians had discovered, too late, when the guns were wrecked the fort was useless. And near misses from 210 millimeter high-explosive shells could destroy the gun barrels, or even blow rivets out and disable the gun crews inside. So the major Verdun forts all had custom-built disappearing turrets that could be retracted into the carapace, showing only the top sixth of an armored sphere. It would be extremely difficult to put one of these turrets out of commission using conventional artillery fire, and in fact they survived the war largely intact.

The Germans marched around the whole ensemble, and aimed to pinch off the salient at its base, as the main supply line into the *place* Verdun ran up the Meuse Valley. South of the *place,* a string of forts ran down the Meuse to protect that supply line: Gericourt, Paroches, Troyon, Camp du Romains, and Liouville. None of these had been modernized. But they were each positioned on one of the heights overlooking the river valley, and the rough broken ground behind was heavily forested.

This was an area in which the only practical way to move heavy guns was by tractors, and even then the prospects were slim. Moreover, this was one of the only places on the front where the French had deployed their own motorized heavy artillery, 120 millimeter tractor-drawn guns, which had been moved to the heights around Hattonchâtel.[8]

Von Strantz, the Prussian commander, had only two batteries of heavy guns (one of Austrian 305s, and one of motorized 210s), so he chose to concentrate on Fort de Troyon, which was the key. Moreover, it was the only fort he could approach from the back (or elevated) side, since the Germans had successfully broken out of Metz and fought their way across the top of the Woëvre plain. Their opposite numbers in Fifth Army were still trying to break through around Souilly, a small village located below Verdun on the road to Bar-le-Duc (which would subsequently become famous as the *Voie Sacrée* of Verdun).

The resulting battle, properly speaking, should be called First Verdun. But in the aftermath, the French were not anxious to call attention to just how close the Germans had been in those early days in September to pinching off the entire fortified position, and combined both engagements into one battle—Revigny. The only thing keeping the Germans from pinching off Verdun was the string of forts along the river, and the infantry and guns spread out in the intervals. So while Fifth Army tried to push through from the West, von Strantz tried to break the forts.

This unnamed battle showed, for the first—and last—time, the essential correctness of the Séré de Rivières plan. For here along the heights of the Meuse the French had all the ingredients: the forts, manned by proper garrisons of soldiers, regular infantry in the intervals between them, and heavy weapons behind. And in this particular place there was no room for the French to retreat. Moreover, for the first time, the ordinary soldier could see the consequences of failure: everyone knew the forts of the Verdun were to the north, that the lines from the two fronts merged here, and that the loss would be catastrophic to France. So what it all came down to had nothing to do with maneuvering or flanks, or the spirit of the attack, and everything to do with the willingness of the infantry to die defending their country.

The Germans were able to reduce Gericourt and Troyon into heaps of rubble. But the defenders stubbornly fought on from the ruins, and the German infantry attacking Troyon on the eighth was decimated by the French heavy weapons. Troyon was one of the few places where the Germans were massacred as they had been slaughtering the French. So on the ninth, the French were stubbornly hanging on to what was left of de Troyon. Somewhat to their surprise—and distress—the besieging Germans, who felt themselves right on the verge of success, were told to pull back to positions north of Verdun. The same thing happened farther West. Maurice Genevoix, a young lieutenant, was sent off to fetch reinforcements for his regiment (the 106th), which was trying desperately to hang on to its position at the farm of Vaux Marie, south of Souilly. He had been sent because all the other officers were dead. He walked most of the night, only to be told there were no reinforcements. But then, inexplicably, jubilation. The Germans were pulling out. "So," he asked his captain, "this is a great victory?" The answer was equivocal. But the two officers realized quickly enough that if the Germans were withdrawing, they had held.[9]

THE GERMANS BREAK OFF

The reason was simple enough. In Belgium, the German General Staff and von Moltke were becoming concerned. Although there had been a few tactical defeats on both fronts, by the end of the first week in September the Germans had already reeled off an impressive set of territorial gains and inflicted enormous casualties. The exact level of French casualties at this point is conjecture, but, given the numbers for the first two months of the war, the totals for the dead and missing alone must have been close to three hundred thousand men. So roughly one third of France's peacetime army was already dead.

The beefed-up German Eighth Army was in the process of destroying Rennenkampf's First Russian Army, which would mean the end of the Russian offensive effort against Germany, since both of the armies of the Northwest Front had now been destroyed, and the remaining Russian forces in the South were fully engaged with the Austrians. But there was plenty of room to be nervous. Prewar, the *stavka* had never been able to decide who to fight, Austria or Germany. They had compromised—fatally—and decided to fight both. So there were two separate front commands. One, the Northwest, had now been temporarily put out of commission. But the armies of the Southwest Front had simply rolled over the Habsburg armies in Galicia and the Bukovina, and the Austrians were being forced all the way back into the Hungarian plain.

Here again the solution was simple. The German General Staff had a successful operation already in place in the Eighth Army; the sensible thing was to expand into a larger command and expand the German section of the Eastern Front. But this took men and guns. As the war moved into its sixth week, the large reserve manpower pools of both Austria and Germany were beginning to come into play, but it would take months before those men would constitute a major field army.

In the meantime, there was the growing threat in the West. The German General Staff had all its manpower deep in France. Von Kluck could match the steadily growing Sixth Army step for step up the Ourcq and higher. But there was no way the Germans could protect their flank and maintain a front between the Seine and the Marne.

The five German armies in France were at the end of a tenuous line of supply, and Germany did not have the manpower to guard it—nor the horse and train power to keep the armies supplied. The Germans had started the war with more ammunition than anyone else, but they had used it at a prodigious rate—as had everyone else. If the German General Staff wanted to keep its losses at the acceptable level, it needed every shell. Without its firepower advantage, the Germans would have to slug it out in the infantry versus infantry combats that the French and British had wanted to fight since the start of the war. Von Moltke, like Lemann and French, needed to keep his forces intact for the next round.

So von Moltke repeated the same procedure as on the Eastern Front. In August he had sent Ludendorff to take over at the Eighth Army staff in the East. Now he sent the German General Staff's head of intelligence, Lieutenant Colonel Hentsch, down to von Bülow's headquarters to sort out the problem and see what should be done.[10] This was a typical example of how the German staff system worked. Most army chiefs of staff were colonels or below, and there were major German General Staff departments headed by lowly majors.

Joffre had a staff as well, of course, but his staff officers were simply messengers and reporters. Hentsch, like Ludendorff and Hoffmann—who were simply the first in a long series of German General Staff officers dispatched to solve problems during a crisis—had the authority to suggest courses of action. At Liège, Ludendorff hadn't filed a report, he had taken command. And in the East, when he arrived at the Eighth Army, he didn't wait for von Hindenburg to show up, or cable back a suggestion to von Moltke. Instead he consulted with Max Hoffmann, another mere colonel. By the time von Hindenburg got there—by the time Ludendorff himself had arrived—the key decisions had already been made.

Hentsch's course of action subsequently became notorious, so much so that there was a formal court of inquiry. Not surprisingly, it exonerated him completely. All Hentsch did was confer with von Bülow's staff, and the good general himself. The decision, unfortunately, was painfully obvious. The Germans were temporarily masters of the battlefields over which they had been fighting. But they had no supplies, reinforcements were a long way off, and they could easily be outflanked.

To clinch the matter, the offensives on the eastern wing, where German attacks aimed at enveloping Verdun and smashing through the French armies to the West, were having a difficult time of it. Without Verdun, the defensive positions occupied by the German First, Second, and Third Armies were untenable. These were the only trained infantry Germany had, and, unlike Foch, the Germans weren't keen to lose them in a series of futile gestures. So the only sound decision was to retreat back to what was an almost impregnable defensive line north of Reims, regroup, and go on from there. The line would have to be to the north of Reims, because all the positions to the south of the city (and the city itself) are overlooked by the slopes of the Montagne de Reims. But from the high ground to the north of the city, on over to the Argonne, there was an excellent defensive line.

Politically, of course, the decision was a dangerous one, because the Allies did exactly what they should have done under the circumstances. They took all the engagements in early September which occurred along the key two-hundred-kilometer section of the front, and gave them a name—the Battle of the Marne. The use of the singular implied one great battle, and it neatly avoided giving the world the appalling news that most of the fighting had been right on top of Verdun or Paris. Since the Germans had broken off the engagement and retreated back to the north, the Allies announced it as a great victory. Germany had been humbled, the advance had been stopped, and their troops chased halfway back to Belgium.

Allied dispatches spoke of battlefields littered with German dead, and described a frenetic retreat which amounted to almost a panic. All that remained was to throw the demoralized remnants back into Germany. Gallieni, who had a pretty good idea of what had actually happened, was far from convinced. "Was there a Battle of the Marne?" he asked. It was a rhetorical question. Given the legend that he was the architect of the victory, the comment is significant.

On 14 September 1914, Joffre, in his habitually bland and ingenuous style, put it this way:

That day I had the very clear impression that the Germans wanted a new battle on the line they had rested on. In my mind, there was no question of starting a general action that would cost us a lot of losses and would have exhausted all our munitions.[11]

Joffre's remarks conceal as much as they reveal. France was basically out of artillery ammunition. The officer corps, decimated by German fire and his purges, was in no condition to lead, and the infantry had been reduced down to its cadres. When Genevoix looked around him on the night of the tenth, his two companies of infantry had only about twenty men apiece remaining, and not a single officer.

Above and beyond those problems, Joffre's remarks rewrite history in another, more fundamental way. Defeated armies do not immediately turn and attack. The Germans now did just that. Having wheeled about and regrouped, the Germans were ready to fight, and they now had a new supreme commander, von Falkenhayn, who was perceived to have a more aggressive spirit. If this was victory, what would defeat look like? The Allies promptly found out. Gallieni's cynicism was well founded. One week after their great defeat, the Germans went back on the offensive and scored some of the greatest victories of the war.

NOTES

1. As recorded by Jean Galtier-Boissière, *Histoire de la grande guerre* (Paris: Crapouillot, 1932), 240. As Galtier-Boissière points out, Joffre admitted the name was decided upon because the battles fought all in some general way were fought in the Marne Valley. But, as we shall see, this isn't at all true. Even without realizing how much of the fighting was to the East, Galtier-Boissière was still compelled to debunk the myths of the battle, and called his chapter "The Truth About the Marne," (240–46). There are two admirable studies of the Marne: Georges Blond, *La Marne* (Paris: Presses de la Cité, 1963); Robert Asprey, *The First Battle of the Marne* (Philadelphia: Lippincott, 1962).

2. See the invaluable (even though written during wartime and censored) account by Jules Poirier, *Reims* (Paris: Les Étincelles, 1917), 22–25. The part of his narrative dealing with why the forts weren't garrisoned was censored.

3. Once the Marne was turned into a great victory, there was competition as to whose "great" idea it had been to exploit the alleged German gap, the two claimants being Joffre and Gallieni. The answer is that both of them saw the situation. See the definitive account by

Captain P[aul] Lyet, *Joffre et Gallieni à la Marne* (Paris: Berger-Levrault, 1938), esp. 127.

4. There is no hard evidence that von Moltke ever intended a direct march on the capital, other than an exhortatory "order" from Kaiser Wilhelm II; as we shall see in later chapters, no one in the German General Staff paid much attention to such things. See the remarks on how the emperor was systematically isolated and cut off from actual military decisions in Lamar Cecil, *Wilhelm II* (Chapel Hill: University of North Carolina Press, 1996). Evidence to the contrary is simply wartime propaganda.

5. Erwin Rommel, *Infantry Attacks* (first published as *Infanterie Greift an: Erlebnisse und Erfahrungen*) (Mechanicsburg, Pa.: Stackpole Books, 1990). There are excellent accounts of these engagements in Blond and in Asprey.

6. Jean-Norton Cru, *Témoins* (Paris: Les Étincelles, 1929; reprinted 1993), 20.

7. There is a good brief account of this largely unknown battle in Yves Buffetaut, *La Bataille de Verdun, de l'Argonne a la Woëvre* (Tours: Éditions Heimdale, 1990). See also Général J[ean-Joseph] Rouquerol, *Les Hauts-de-Meuse et Saint-Mihiel* (Paris: Payot, 1939).

8. In 1914 France had two batteries of tractor-drawn 120Ls (the only heavy weapons the army possessed in quantity). Their story is a fascinating one, and is recounted in André Duvignac, *Histoire de l'armée motorisée* (Paris: Imprimerie Nationale, 1947).

9. Maurice Genevoix, *Ceux de 14* (Paris: Flammarion, 1950), 61. This quote is from his journal, originally published in 1916 as *Sous Verdun*. His five-volume account of his eight months in combat, in reality one long narrative, was eventually combined into one text with the above title. For some strange reason, the title page suggests *Ceux de 14* is a novel, but this is not at all the case.

10. In the twilight world of "what ifs," the Hentsch mission is notorious; see the sensible remarks by John Keegan, *The First World War* (New York: Knopf, 1999), 120–22.

11. Maréchal Joffre, *Mémoires du maréchal Joffre* (Paris: Plon, 1932), 429.

6

1914: German Offensives After the Marne

*On high, nothing was anticipated, and still at this hour they impro-
vise as best they can.*

—*Colonel Emil Driant*[1]

The Allies had shaped the opening of the war as a three-act play: the battle of the frontiers, the heroic defense of Liège and the wonderful victories of the BEF, followed by victory on the Marne. At the end of the third act, there was a brief intermission: the race to the sea, after which began the stalemate of trench warfare. Unfortunately, the Germans were reading from a different script.

While the French circulated their victory communiqués and the British congratulated themselves on the enormous losses they had inflicted on the enemy, the Germans replaced von Moltke with Erich von Falkenhayn. The conventional portrait of von Moltke: "an elderly man; severe strain would soon expose his chronic unfitness," principally heart trouble and obesity; he was temperamentally unsuited for the supreme command and under its stresses had a nervous breakdown.[2] But the only real evidence suggesting that von Moltke was emotionally unfit comes from Prince von Bülow's *Memoirs,* where it is told third hand: Prince Wedel told von Bülow that an unnamed staff officer had told him that he saw von Moltke in tears.[3]

The evidentiary value of this is dubious, and contradicted by other evidence.[4] At sixty-six, von Moltke was neither particularly old nor older than usual for senior commanders: Von Hindenburg came out of retirement at sixty-six to assume command in the East, and was sixty-nine when he became the chief of staff in 1916; Gallieni was sixty-five in April 1914; Foch, named to the supreme command in the panic of 1918, was nearly sixty-seven. There were plenty of portly generals in 1914: in addition to the notorious case of Joffre, Castelnau, and Pau, there are Allenby, Plumer, Hindenburg, and Currie, the last named being possibly the best Allied general of the war. Lanrezac and French, two of the more fit-looking Allied generals, were well on their way to breakdowns by 20 August, and needed constant reassurance by the rather portly Joffre.

Von Moltke was removed from command for a more basic reason: the German system, which rewarded success and punished failure, held those at the top accountable for the performance of those beneath them. Von Moltke's plan had failed to give the Germans total victory in six weeks; therefore, he was removed and replaced with a man who had different ideas.

Like von Moltke, von Falkenhayn was outside of the central clique of the staff, only more so. Like Joffre, he was a thoroughly political soldier; and, also like Joffre, he had enormous power. Although for propaganda reasons it was pretended that von Moltke was still the chief of staff, von Falkenhayn was not only the real chief but he kept his old position as minister of war.

Von Falkenhayn's actions are those of a man who had realized that the dominant aim of all the combatants before the war, the idea of a great battle of annihilation that would destroy your enemy's armies in the field, was now impossible. The only way to win this war was to persuade your opponents to quit, and in an era of mass armies in the millions, this could be done only by securing what the French had seen as a moral ascendancy on the field of battle. At the level of the ordinary soldier, this meant destroying his will to fight. At the command levels, this meant presenting your opponent with a series of strategic checks, so he would realize his position was hopeless and quit.

Von Falkenhayn took command on 9 September 1914, and his first act was to order a new wave of attacks. These attacks aimed at three objectives, which would stabilize the Western Front and, if successful, force the Allies to confront a series of extremely difficult and potentially exhausting campaigns. The Germans would thus destroy the morale of the Allied troops doing the fighting and give their commanders serious doubts about whether they could win the war. Given the way that the

Allies had propagandized the Battle of the Marne, the mere fact of a massive wave of immediate German attacks would speak for itself. Moreover, the strategic results would be significant. With a few simple offensives, the Germans could virtually guarantee that the Allies would face a long and difficult war.

The first offensive aimed at pinching off the *place fortifiée* Verdun, a rough circle over two hundred kilometers around, from the rest of the front. The *place*, sited almost squarely at the center of the front, controlled the Meuse corridor. The German crown prince, the Fifth Army's nominal commander, had likened the *place* to a postern gate in a castle: from the security of that circle, French armies could sally forth and drive a wedge deep into the German lines. In terms of geography, the riverine plain of the Meuse north of Verdun was the ideal place to mount an offensive, since the relatively flat plain began to broaden out. So the Germans aimed either to seize the position outright or render it unusable as a postern gate.

Von Falkenhayn and the German General Staff also aimed at a second-wave offensive in Belgium. Like Verdun, the port city of Antwerp was a heavily fortified bastion from which Allied troops could strike back into Belgium. It had been designed as the national redoubt, Brussels being regarded as indefensible. In theory, if the Allies attacked both up the Meuse and out of Antwerp, they could sever the German armies from their main lines of supply and end the war.

Then there was the problem of stabilizing the line in Champagne and Artois. As we noted in the last chapter, the German drive south created a vast no-man's-land on the right flank of von Kluck's First Army. When the Germans had withdrawn back to the defensive line north of Reims, they had retired to an almost unbreakable line. But where the line turned to the north, a vast area was vulnerable. Joffre, who could read a map as well as anyone else, had, therefore, urged his army commanders to follow close on the heels of the retreating Germans, and thus prevent them from staking possession of this area.

Unfortunately, the French—who had 329,000 killed or missing in the first two months of the war, or about one fifth of their total mobilization strength in September—were simply in no shape to do more than stagger northward. Nor was the BEF, whose commander had only one aim—to switch positions in the line so his left flank was as close to the Channel as he could manage.

The prize in this maneuver was easy to comprehend: a main railroad line that looped southward from Lille through Cambrai and Saint-Quentin, passing above Reims at Bazancourt, and then dropping down to Saint-Martin-le-Heureux, where it was about midway between Reims and the Argonne. The track then began to curve back to the northeast, terminating in Apremont, on the edge of the Argonne. Before the war, French and Belgian railroad companies had connected this line at key points to the rail lines emanating from Liège. Clearly this was a perfect network for a modern army—provided it could prevent its adversary from cutting it.

There were two keys here. The first was Lille, a major industrial city on the Belgian border, and consequently a rail junction of great importance. The second was in Champagne, where the track crossed the Suippes River, right outside the hamlet of Dontrien. The French had advanced to within ten kilometers of that. Hopefully, an attack through the Argonne, which could be coordinated with an attack in the area of Champagne beside the forest, would shift the German lines farther south, make any penetration of the rail line impossible.

Although Lille had been heavily fortified by Séré de Rivières, in the years before 1914 the fortifications had been neglected. The locals were growing vegetables on the embankments, and part of the fortifications had been turned into a municipal park. Most of the heavy guns had been moved out before the start of the war. Incredibly, the city was basically undefended. The side that got there first would win automatically.

OPERATIONS AROUND VERDUN: SAINT-MIHIEL

The Fifth Army had come dangerously close to cutting off Verdun entirely in early September. Rather than attack the main belt of forts, the Germans had attacked upstream, just above the town of Saint-Mihiel, aiming to cut the *place* off from the rest of the French lines. German commanders felt they had been close to success, close enough to justify a second attack, which would also aim to pinch off the salient. So although von Falkenhayn made this initial attack his personal project, the planning for it was already in place: the Germans simply tried the same strategy a second time.

The attack to the west of Verdun, through the Argonne, would be more or less the same attack as before, but the Germans widened the area to include the entire forty-kilometer stretch of the front between the Meuse and the Moselle Rivers, so the second attack would be on a much larger scale. And since the Germans had retreated to the north of the Reims–Sainte- Menehould–Verdun line, the western attack would have to go through, or come out of, the southernmost part of the Argonne.

Although the area was bigger, the number of troops employed would be fewer. In the Argonne, von Mudra's XVI Army Corps would attack into the forest from the east, while the Infantry Division, on loan from the Fourth Army, would attack from the west. To the east, the III (Bavarian) Army Corps, under Cavalry General Ludwig Freiherr von Gebsattel, together with the Fifth (Prussian) Army Corps and the XIV (Badener) Army Corps, were already in position to attack in the area between the Meuse and the Moselle.

The French General Staff considered the Woëvre Plain impassable on account of the poor nature of its roads, and the same could be said of the Argonne.[3] The Argonne Forest was not only a densely wooded area but the trees covered some extremely rough terrain. Along the right bank of the Meuse, from Verdun on down to just below Saint-Mihiel, the terrain is basically a high rutted ridge, which, then as now, was covered with trees. Below Saint-Mihiel, the ground drops off abruptly. The fort located there, Camp des Romains, controlled not only the approaches to the town (to the northwest) but all the relatively flat ground to the south and southeast, including the left bank of the Meuse. The densely wooded heights run toward the Moselle, but descend quickly into the Woëvre Plain, swampy rolling ground dominated by occasional flat-topped hillocks, which in French, as in English, are called buttes.

If the French General Staff believed the Woëvre was not a likely place for large-scale operations, no one thought the Argonne Forest was suitable either. It was true that in 1792 there had been a battle there (Valmy), but actually Valmy was—even in 1792—well outside of the forest proper. The problem with the Argonne, from a military point of view, was that the dense forest covered a washboarded terrain full of ravines and hills. It is surprisingly rough terrain, and the French, not illogically, assumed that any modern army would stick to the west or east of it. To the east, it was barely twenty kilometers to the first of Verdun's westernmost forts, Bois Bourrus, and the more open rolling ground between was dominated by another series of buttes, a feature that continued on the other side of the Argonne all the way to the north side of Reims.

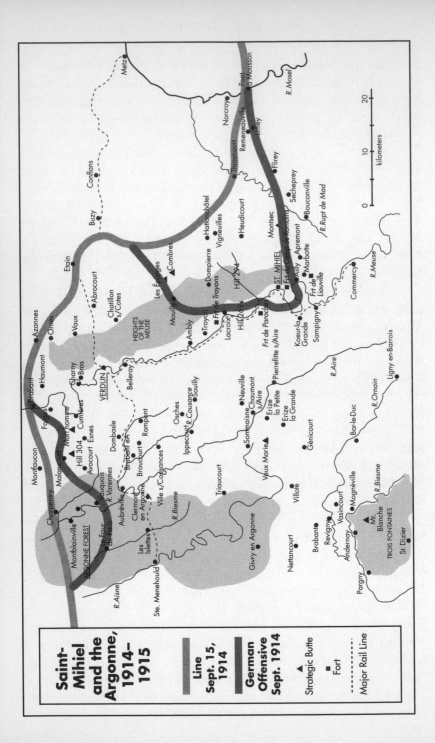

Saint-Mihiel and the Argonne, 1914–1915

Line Sept. 15, 1914

German Offensive Sept. 1914

▲ Strategic Butte

■ Fort

---- Major Rail Line

kilometers
0   10   20

Metz

Pont à Mousson
R. Mosel

Norcroy

Remeneauville
Thiaucourt
Fimey

Flirey

Conflans

Sécheprey
Bouconville
R. Rupt de Mad

Buzy

Hattonchâtel

Vigneulles
Heudicourt

Montsec ▲
Fresne au Camp de Romans
Ailly Apremont
ST. MIHIEL Marbotte
Frt de Camp de Romans
Frt de Liouville

Etain

Combres ●
Dompierre
Hill 294

Commercy
R. Meuse

Abrocourt
Chatillon s/Côtes

Les Éparges ▲
Mouilly
Fresne Troyons
Hill (294)
Lacroix
Frt de Paroche

Ornes ●
Vaux
Azannes

HEIGHTS OF THE MEUSE

Troyon
Ambly

Koeul-la Grande
Frt s/Aire
Sampigny

Charny
Bras

Belleray

Pierrefitte s/Aire
R. Aire

Haumont

Brabant

VERDUN

Cumières

Neuville
Chaumont s/Aire

Bar-le-Duc
R. Ornain

Ligny en-Barrois

Fleury
Mort homme ▲
Hill 304 ▲
Cumières
Esnes
Avocourt

Oches
R. Cousance
Souilly

Sommaisne
Erize la Petite
Erize la Grande

Génicourt

Montfaucon

Malancourt
Dombasle
Brabant en Argonne
Rampont
Ippecourt

Vaux Marie ▲

Chappentry
Vauquois
R. Varennes

Montblainville

Broucourt
Clermont en Argonne
Ville s/Cousances

Triaucourt

Villbie

R. Biesme
Aubréville
Ste Four de Paris

ARGONNE FOREST

Les Islettes

Givry en Argonne

Netancourt

Brabant
Revigny
Vasincourt
Andernay
Mognéville
R. Biesme
Mt. Blanche ▲
TROIS FONTAINES

Ligny en-Barrois

R. Aisne

Ste. Menehould

Pargny
St. Dizier

The roughly three-hundred-meter-high buttes were natural strong-points for the defenders. Accordingly, the French General Staff had allocated only three reserve divisions to the whole eastern flank between the Meuse and the Moselle: the Sixty-Seventh, on the extreme right of the Prussian V Corps, the Seventy-Third, which was opposite the Badeners; holding most of the line between these two was the Seventy-fifth Division, a sadly torn-up outfit that had lost most of its artillery and half of its men repelling the V German Reserve Corps north of Souilly during the Battle of the Marne. In addition, there were the fortress troops manning the forts, Paroches and Troyon above Saint-Mihiel and Camp des Romains below, with Liouville slightly to the south and east of it. To the West, the situation was better, with the II and V Army Corps, but their troops were spread out all over Lorraine, and would take time to get into action.

Unfortunately, time was the one luxury the French would not have. On 19 September, less than a week after the end of the Marne battles, the von Strantz attack began. The three army corps were spread out on a curved line about fifty kilometers long, which ran from just above Pont-à-Mousson to Guissainville, a small town along the Verdun-Metz rail line, with the Bavarians holding about ten kilometers in the middle of the line from north of Thiaucourt to Woël, the V Army Corps to their right, XIV Corps on their left. Basically, once the German advance started, it simply kept on going. The French Seventy-fifth Division simply disappeared, becoming one of the few French divisions never reconstituted after the fighting. Unfortunately, the annihilation of this division meant that the French were unable to take advantage of such natural strongpoints as the butte of Montsec, which so dominated the landscape that the Americans erected their 1918 Saint-Mihiel offensive monument there to commemorate getting it back.

By the night of 22 September, the Bavarians were on a line Loupmont-Narmont, with the eleventh Brigade attacking in the direction of Spada. Just behind their attack and to the left of it, the advancing Prussians installed themselves on the Crête de Combres, the companion peak linked to the butte of Les Éparges. Natural strongpoints that should have held out for weeks—or months—were overrun in a few hours.

The Bavarian advance was being measured not in meters, but in kilometers. From start to finish, they had penetrated over 40 kilometers on a front that had quickly expanded to nearly 8 kilometers. Leaving aside the issue of the strategic strongpoints seized, the total amount of territory gained was about 2,500 square kilometers. By contrast, in five months on the Somme, from July through November 1916, the BEF achieved a maximum penetration less than a third of that, and managed to reconquer less than 154 square kilometers, while the French, directed by General Fayolle (like Pétain a believer in artillery rather than bayonets), penetrated about 12 kilometers into the German lines, and ended up with somewhat under 250 square kilometers of ground.[6]

Measuring success as a function of square miles gained or lost, or of casualties sustained, is a ghastly sort of calculus. However, a comparison of simple acreage gained does make clear the magnitude of these victories, and it suggests that as early as September 1914 at least some German units had begun to understand how breakthroughs could be achieved, and at a reasonably low cost in the lives of German soldiers. The Bavarian success at Saint-Mihiel was not some minor victory. All during the war, the Allies dreamed of *la percée,* the breakthrough. By September 1914 the Bavarians had already done it, and in almost classical fashion: they had attacked in overwhelming force where the French least expected them to attack, and executed their offensive operations so quickly that their objectives had all been seized before the startled French could move up reinforcements and block their offensive gains. Because the advance continued: for the Germans, the best was yet to come.

With the belated arrival of reinforcements French resistance began to stiffen. On 22 September, the French VI Army Corps attacked in the general direction of Les Éparges, while the XVI Army Corps attacked downstream along the left bank of the Moselle. The Eleventh Brigade and the Prussians were unable to take Spada, but by the afternoon of the twenty-fourth, the line was Xivray–Loupmont–Apremont–Saint-Mihiel and the heights overlooking the Meuse and Spada-Maizey. The attack ignored Fort de Troyon, in ruins from the first attack of 6 September, and without most of its guns. It simply filtered around it. Suddenly, German troops were in Saint-Mihiel.

By 25 September the Bavarians had taken the crucial fort of Camp des Romains, the key position on the river. Whoever held this fort had command of the main transportation arteries from the south leading into Verdun, since the railroad, the road, the river, and the shipping canal were all side by side at this point. But the Germans had not simply put themselves in a position to interdict the line by shellfire: their line now extended through the Bois d'Ailly down the hillsides into the town of

Saint-Mihiel, across the river and into the village of Chauvoncourt, thus literally severing the communication links. There were French soldiers in isolated positions holding out all along the line, especially in what was later known as the *tranchée de la soif* in the Bois d'Ailly. The other three forts on the Meuse—Paroches on the left bank, Troyon, just opposite, and Liouville, to the south of Camp des Romains—although in ruins, still held out. But the three attacking army corps had taken all the strategically important ground south of Metz between the Meuse and the Moselle.

What was worse was that Camp des Romains had capitulated in three hours at the cost of twenty-three killed and seventy-four wounded, taken by a combined arms brigade consisting of Bavarian infantry and Prussian *Pioniere,* supported by Austrian 305-millimeter mobile howitzers. The bombardment had been short and intensive. But it was no worse than what Fort de Troyon had experienced. Perhaps the key to the quick capitulation was the use by the *Pioniere* of incendiary devices that prefigured a new weapon, the flamethrower.

Still, given its commanding position (the ruins of the fort are still there for all to see) there is no reason why it should have fallen so easily. Nor is there an easily understandable reason why the French General Staff had left the bulk of the defense of the whole French line between the fort and the Moselle to one weakened reserve division, giving the rest to another reserve division, the Seventy-Third, which was originally formed as a garrison for the fortifications of Toul.[7] Anyone who looked at a map could see that the fort, together with buttes like Montsec, Combres, and Les Éparges, simply dominated the region. In his prewar planning, Joffre had repeatedly talked about the importance of this region as a covering area where French armies could assemble for counter blows against the invaders. Now the Germans had possession of all the best parts. Whoever had them was going to be extremely difficult to dislodge, particularly if the attackers were forced to attack from the south and west. And the Germans had them all, along with the ridged wooded area immediately adjacent to the Moselle, the Bois le Prêtre.

Acreage and names do not, however, convey the magnitude of the victory. The fort Camp des Romains is on a high bluff with commanding views of the countryside across the river and far to the south. This high ground continues along to the east for many kilometers, well past the village of Apremont-sous-les-Forêts, and forms a natural dividing line in the terrain. The only way the ground could be taken back, therefore, involved attacking uphill through a series of densely wooded areas. Troops moving into line for such an attack would be down in the valley, and clearly visible to artillery spotters well before they reached the start line.

The breakthrough at Saint-Mihiel was an enormous success by the standards set by almost all subsequent attacks on either side. A simple explanation of the attack fails utterly to convey the scale of the disaster. At the French military cemetery outside Lironville, where a marker commemorates the limit of the German advance, some 426 of the dead of the 146th, 155th, 167th, 346th, 353rd, and 356th Infantry Regiments are buried.[8] Three hundred fifty of them lie in a common grave, unidentified except for a marker, which attaches them to the Division, the highest proportion of unknown of any cemetery in the area. The seventy-six identified graves mark the colonel of the 146th regiment, Charles Malgouti, who fell on 22 September. The brothers Pidaut are buried in the same grave: Alfred was the commandant of the 357th Regiment, his brother Charles, a captain in the 7th. The casualty list went higher: General Grand d'Esnon, who had commanded the defense of the town of Hattonchâtel, had been killed in action on the morning of 21 September. There had been German losses too, particularly at Spada, but nothing like what had befallen the French. Good soldiers, brave officers, important towns, major strategic pieces of ground, all gone.

In the face of such catastrophes, silence. Clearly there was something seriously wrong, that the French could lose so much so quickly after having supposedly beaten their adversaries so thoroughly. What, exactly, had happened, and why? This was what the president of France himself wanted to know. He was from Sampigny, a town quite literally in the shadow of the Camp des Romains, and knew Saint-Mihiel intimately. Now he was furious, particularly because news that it had fallen came not from the French General Staff liaison, but from the civilian prefect. On Friday, 25 September, he recorded the news.

At the end of the day, I received from the prefect of the Meuse a telegram which filled me with sadness: "Germans masters of Saint-Mihiel and the Fort du camp des romains...."

[Saturday, 26 September] Again, troublingly reticent press communiqués that I give to the Council of ministers. There are no allusions to the capitulation of the Fort du camp des romains.

It is announced that we have retaken Berry-au-Bac and Ribécourt. But it was never admitted that we lost those places. I ask, once more, that we tell the truth. Equally I ask that someone explain to us immediately by whose negligence one of our forts fell so quickly. There where the enemy was entrenched in open country, we were unable to dislodge him, and on the Hauts-de-Meuse, in a position fortified in advance, we were only able to defend ourselves for half of a day.[9]

As is usually the case, those on the receiving end of such disasters rarely explain what they thought they were doing, one reason why the memoirs, reminiscences, and official narratives of the war are often so valueless. If anyone ever told the president why all this had happened, he never recorded it. After the war, the commander of the fort was court-martialed, and then acquitted, in the face of evidence that he had done the best he could.

In 1915, after seeing the ruins of Fort de Troyon (which thus enabled him to envision the ruins of some of the others), Colonel Emil Driant wrote to a friend about his experiences in the first year of the war:

> What a war, my old friend! It surpasses all our imaginations. Seeing the ruins of Fort de Troyon, the effects of the 420 and the 380 [millimeter guns], of these monstrous one ton shells, I am not astonished that they counted on taking Paris within 48 hours. The miracle of the Marne is quite the most extraordinary manifestation of the valor of our race. It is the courage of the common soldiers and the lower ranks, an astonishing contempt of the danger and death that repaired the horrors, the crimes in high places. At the top, nothing was anticipated, and still at this hour they improvise as best they can.[10]

Driant's final sentence—"At the top, nothing was anticipated, and still at this hour they improvise as best they can"—is an apt description of the French command. The question is, why?

There was, of course, the misrepresentation of the Victory of the Marne, a myth that even officers like Driant apparently swallowed, although he should have known better. If the French had won such a great victory, and the Germans were in retreat, the last thing one would expect them to do would be to mount such an aggressive attack. The Allies thus began early to pay the bill for the effectiveness of their own propaganda. Winston Churchill, in writing about the Battle of Verdun, gets right to the heart of the matter: "To the war of slaughter and battles was added that of propaganda and communiqués. In this the French largely had the advantage. They did not cease to proclaim day after day the enormous German losses which attended every assault."[11] The problem, which started early on, was that the French were also the chief victims of the war of communiqués. Here, in the ground between the Meuse and the Moselle, was the first instance. Unfortunately, it would not be the last.

Then there was the speed with which the Germans threw together the second offensive: on Sunday, 13 September, von Strantz's troops had abandoned their attempt to take Fort de Troyon and participated in the general retreat. On the following Sunday, they were back, mounting an attack across the whole front. By the time the two divisions of the French VI Corps were in action, the attack had already seized the key objectives. In theory the VI Corps had plugged a hole around Marbotte, where there could have been a major breakthrough, but anyone who goes over the ground there can see the ingenuousness of the claim. In a war dominated by artillery, there was no point taking the low ground when you already had the high ground overlooking it.

So the German attack was quick in two senses: it was mounted quickly after the initial failure and the general retreat; and, once mounted, it progressed quickly. Similarly, once the Germans discovered Camp des Romains was defended, they put together an attack within twenty-four hours.

Probably the basic reason for having such minimal defenses of the area, in addition to those mentioned previously, was the failure of the officers of the French General Staff to move from the world of precise quantification, the world of maps and organizational charts, to the actual world of combat. On paper, the Seventy-third and Seventy-fifth Divisions should have been able to hold off a German attack until reinforcements could arrive. And, as the records of the graveyards show, those reinforcements arrived and fought. Although outnumbered, the French units had the advantages of the forts along the Meuse to back them up and the advantage of the terrain: on 20 September, key pieces of ground like Montsec were still inside the French lines.

Although French units were obviously handicapped by their lack of the proper weapons needed to beat back such German offensives, the relatively few French officers left by the end of September 1914 simply lacked the training that enabled them to understand the importance of such pieces of ground. Thus Joffre's prewar observations about the ineptitude of the officer corps were correct. The middle of a war is not the best place to fix a structural problem in training.

THE ARGONNE

By 20 September, the French General Staff had other problems besides Saint-Mihiel, as did the French local army commanders. At the same time as the Bavarians were advancing on one wing, the XVI Corps of the Fifth Army launched its own attacks in the Argonne. Earlier, their heavy guns had pounded Fort de Troyon; in the Argonne, using the same heavy artillery, principally 210 millimeter howitzers; Sven Hedin, who saw them firing during the attack, was, strangely enough, even allowed to sketch them.[12]

When the Germans had retreated on 13 September, they had moved back to a line just north of Cuisy and Charpentry, the Fifth Army on the Verdun side of the Argonne, the Fourth Army on the Reims side. The forest was thus a wedge separating the two armies (although they both had troops inside it). On most maps, the Argonne appeared (and indeed still appears) to be a solid, lozenge-shaped mass angling down all the way from Charleville-Mézières to Saint-Dizier, and it was invariably referred to as dense and impassable. But this is misleading: the forest, like the Vosges Mountains, is full of lateral roads, some of which date from the Roman occupation of Gaul.

The central core of the Argonne, a solid block of forest above Sainte-Menehould, had both lateral (east-west) and north-south road links. In the part of the forest below the Autry–Chatel Chéhéry road, which cuts right through the forest, there were three interior north–south road links, all connected at the top by the Varennes–Vienne le Cateau road. Hidden by the dense forest, French troops could in theory infiltrate between the army boundaries and attack the Germans in the flanks. The same thing held true in reverse for the Germans, whose initial advance had already given possession of two of the higher laterals, the one at Grandpré and a lower one at Autry.

On the other hand, just as possession of the lower quadrant of the Saint-Mihiel salient made it impossible for the French to mount any sort of offensive out of Verdun on the right bank of the Meuse, if the Germans seized the eastern border of the Argonne Forest, they would be able to accomplish the same thing for any projected left-bank offensive. This was the same strategy that had led the French engineering officer Séré de Rivières to the construction of the forts: to present the invader with the unpleasant choice between attacking a fortified position head-on or being herded into ground of the defenders' choosing.

If the Germans succeeded on the left bank of the Meuse as they had on the right bank, they would shift the focal point of French operations into Champagne and even farther to the west, where the German lines already commanded the high ground, and where the relatively open terrain across which the attackers would have to move would give any competent officer pause. Essentially, this operation, if successful, would make French offensive operations impossible on the 160-kilometer section of the front that ran from the Moselle to just above Sainte-Menehould. Additionally, it would severely curtail the breakthrough possibilities in the fifty-kilometer section of the front that ran from the western edge of the Argonne to Reims, since if an attack developed it would be moving into a cul-de-sac, with the defenders holding the high ground on either side.

Nor was this the only threat. The main Paris-Reims-Verdun road and rail link began a leisurely northerly curve at Sainte-Menehould, ran through Clermont-en-Argonne and Dombasle, and over to Verdun. In the course of its peregrinations, it looped sharply northward to go through the town of Aubréville. Any serious German advance would mean German gunners could interdict this rail line as well. The Verdun forts would be reduced to a dependence on one country road and a narrow-gauge light rail line that came up from Bar-le-Duc—hardly sufficient to keep France's largest *place fortifiée* in guns and butter.

The worst dreams of the French promptly came true. At roughly the same time as the Bavarians were attacking on the right bank, the Twenty-seventh Division from the Fourth Army attacked from the Reims side, and the XVI Army Corps, under General von Mudra, attacked from the Verdun side. On 22 September, Montblainville fell, and on the twenty-third, Servon and Varennes-en-Argonne itself.

However, compared to the success at Saint-Mihiel, the XVI Corps of the German Fifth Army was having tough going. Heavy weapons were of much less use in a dense forest than in broken ground, so the German advantage in artillery was minimized. But all the same, the Germans (most of whom were from Alsace-Lorraine) successfully gouged out a sizable piece of the Argonne: the front covered nearly thirty kilometers, and in some places the Germans had advanced over two. Considering the terrain—and the later Allied advances during their much heralded offensives all along the line—this was impressive going for a few divisions. Von Mudra's troops chewed off nearly three times as much territory as would Joffre's December offensive in Champagne, twice as much as the May–June Artois attacks in 1915, and at a fraction of the cost to the attackers.

What was more impressive was that, once again, by the time the French reinforcements arrived to halt the German advance, the Germans had the better part of the Varennes-Vienne road, and were trying to break through at the crossroads at Le Four-de-Paris. The success of this attack meant that the critical butte of the Vauquois was now surrounded on three sides by German territory. And the Vauquois was critical for control of the transportation links: observers on the crête could easily spot artillery on the rail lines at the Aubréville curve almost with the naked eye, so the damage was done.[13]

The French were caught off-guard by the force and rapidity of these attacks, but they quickly realized how serious the situation was. Even Joffre, more magisterially, admitted there was a problem:

> The consequences of this German attack were serious. It placed in the enemy's hands at Saint-Mihiel the main road, railway and canal by which Verdun was supplied; near Commercy, it brought the main line under the fire of German guns, and, near Aubréville, the railway running from Châlons to Verdun. Due to this situation, Verdun was no longer supplied except by a single railway . . . a narrow gauge line running from Bar-le-Duc.[14]

Accordingly, he ordered attacks designed to restore the territory to the French. In the words of General Rouquerol (110): "According to General Roques, who had succeeded General Dubail at the head of the First Army, 'The recapture of Saint-Mihiel had become a national priority.'"

ANTWERP AND THE CHANNEL PORTS

Antwerp was the most heavily defended of the three fortified Belgian complexes of 1914, and it had the most modern forts: twelve of its nineteen forts had been built during the period 1907–1910, or well after the recoil revolution, and one of the forts, Bornheim, dated from September 1913.[15] In addition, Antwerp, like Verdun, had numerous small structures (called, variously, *fortins* or *ouvrages*) scattered in the intervals. Antwerp, like Namur and Liège, was heavily gunned: the fortifications had twenty turrets for 120 and 150 millimeter guns, thirty-seven 75-millimeter turrets, and an average of two machine guns per structure.

By this point in September, what was left of the Belgian Army was at Antwerp, a force of six divisions and eighty-seven batallions of artillery. This was much more than a garrison: it was a force large enough to make the threat of Antwerp as a port quite real. The Belgians conducted three separate offensive operations out of Antwerp in September, the last taking place on the twenty-sixth. And, as the siege progressed, Antwerp received reinforcements, British marines and French naval troops under Admiral Ronarc'h.[16]

General von Beseler, who had been given the task of taking Antwerp, had only been given about eighty-five thousand men to do it with. Not only was he outnumbered but his forces were hardly first-line troops. He had the Third Reserve Corps, which contained six reserve infantry regiments and two regiments of *Landwehr*, the so-called Marine Division, which consisted of sailors, three independent brigades of *Landwehr*, and the fourth *Ersatz* division, which consisted of three mixed brigades. *Ersatz* divisions were composed of men who had not been called up for compulsory military service prewar owing to the budget restrictions placed on the army by the Reichstag. Since they had done no military service prewar, they had to be put into newly formed units and given their basic training. By 27 September 1914, these men had perhaps two months of military experience. At the other end of the spectrum, the *Landwehr* consisted of men whose basic training had been decades earlier.

Von Beseler didn't have much in the way of soldiers, but he had an enormous deployment of firepower. The Naval Division alone had three batteries of 305-millimeter howitzers, one battery of 210 millimeter howitzers, one battery of 150 millimeter howitzers, and three batteries of 100

millimeter guns. In addition, von Beseler had two of the monster 420 millimeter guns, as well as four Austrian and two German 305 millimeter
howitzers. He also had engineer units equipped with heavy mortars, as
well as ordinary field artillery.

As might be expected from troops with so little experience, the
Germans made all sorts of costly mistakes. They never managed to seal
off the perimeter of Antwerp sufficiently so that reinforcements went in
and, as the siege came to its inevitable conclusion, most of the Belgian
Army was able to slip out. As the two brigades of British marines arrived
on 6 October, and the siege had technically begun on 27 September, von
Beseler's troops never really mastered the basic principles of siegecraft.

On the other hand, the Belgians had learned something from their
defeats. When Lemann had pulled out his infantry from Liège, he had
given the German artillery observers a free ride. Now the Belgians realized their error. To have any chance of success, the defense of a *place for-
tifiee* required a joint effort involving the garrisons of the forts, infantry
operating in the intervals between the forts, and artillery behind the forts.
Besides, Antwerp was the last defensible Belgian position. So the army
stayed put and von Beseler's troops had to attack each position separately.

Unfortunately for the defenders, the Antwerp forts had not been built
to withstand the shells the German and Austrian heavy weapons were
firing. Fort de Wavre and the *ouvrage* of Dorpvelde fell on 1 October, and
from then on the fortifications surrendered at the rate of one or two a day:
Waelhem, Koningshoyckt, and Lierre on the second, Kessel on the fourth,
Broechem on the seventh. Still, this was slow progress. Von Beseler was
full of plans to speed things up by more aggressive attacks, but he didn't
have the men, and the German General Staff wouldn't give them to him.

In addition to being a port, Antwerp, 126 kilometers from Ypres, was
of course close to the Allied lines, and could have been reinforced. At the
rate of a fortification every day or so, it would take weeks to reduce the
place. So the Allies had plenty of time. But it was the Namur syndrome all
over again, where the garrisons had been left to hold out on their own
while French troops drifted around the frontier a few kilometers away.
Disturbed by the prospect of losing the port, Churchill went to Antwerp to
see for himself what the situation was, and on 4 October, Kitchener
telegraphed that he was organizing a strong relief force of over fifty thousand French soldiers, of which the advance force had already been sent.

But the siege had begun eight days earlier, and the handful of marines (about three thousand) who arrived on the third did little to turn the situation around. By the sixth, the Allies had basically decided that Antwerp was a lost cause. The Field Army evacuated on the seventh, and the population followed it, their desire to flee stimulated by a German ultimatum that unless the place capitulated, they would start shelling the city itself. Exactly what point the prolonged resistance of the city accomplished is curious. The general bombardment began on 8 October 1914, causing the left bank of the Escaut to be evacuated, and Fort Breedonck quickly surrendered. By the ninth, the siege was over, although isolated Belgian garrisons were still holding out while the city was evacuated around them and handed over to the Germans.

None of the projected reinforcements actually arrived, save for the British marines, and these did little fighting. Out of a strength of 3,000 men, there were 32 killed, 189 wounded, 938 prisoners, and 1,500 interned in Holland. Basically the force was wiped out. So was the garrison. In September there had been something under 100,000 men there. Five thousand were taken as prisoners of war, and another 28,000 were interned in Holland. Admiral Ronarc'h's first RFM arrived in what was left of Belgium on 8 October, just in time to engage in a desperate but futile attempt to hold on to Dixmude.

A week later, on the nineteenth, German attacks drove the Allies out of most of the little that was still left of independent Belgium. The remnants of the Belgian Army was penned up behind a small strip of territory on the downstream (French) side of the Yser. The BEF managed, finally, to hang on to a piece of land around Ypres, losing both the city (which was leveled) and what was left of the BEF all at once. Most of the credit for saving the day should go to the engineers who flooded the countryside and thus made the German advance impossible.

At Antwerp the Germans had been far too slow, and not particularly adept; about what one would expect of a patched-together force composed of rusty reservists and brand-new recruits (the troops of the *Ersatz* units), whose military ardor is perhaps best measured by the observation that in a nation where the army was probably the most popular national institution, these were the men who had managed not to do their compulsory service. As inept as von Beseler's mixed force of the raw and the retired was, he had still managed the remarkable feat of forcing the surrender of an opponent who not only outnumbered him but enjoyed uninterrupted communications with the outside.

The Germans found thirteen hundred artillery pieces and nearly a million rounds of ammunition, together with hundreds of trucks. And, of course, the greatest prize of all: Antwerp, arguably the most important port in Europe. In London, Lord Hankey, who like everyone else in the Cabinet was surprised by Antwerp's sudden fall, thought this the worst loss so far.[17]

The large number of internees in Holland and prisoners taken suggests that the Allies were not so much beaten in combat as scared into quitting, and the comments of the survivors make that clear. At first blush, the actual military effects of the heavy guns was less than impressive: in two weeks of shelling the Germans managed to knock out less than half the heavy guns of the forts. But much of the shelling was aimed not at the forts, but at the infantry positions in the intervals.[18] And the psychological impact of the big guns was enormous. Near misses might not destroy a turret, but would pop the rivets on the armor plate loose, with lethal consequences. Few observers or gunners would man a turret after witnessing the gruesome results. The occasional direct hit, which did spectacular damage, apparently left a lasting impression in the collective mind of the garrison. Facing what seemed the near certainty of annihilation—and helpless to fight back—the gunners increasingly opted to surrender.

LILLE

In late September, while the Germans were tidying up the Western Front—and ensuring the war would go on for some time—the French were mounting a series of futile attacks in Artois, trying to dislodge the Germans from their defensive positions along the Aisne, and the BEF was trying to get into position around Ypres.

The BEF was far to the south of Ypres in late September. As they moved northward into Belgium they would, in the scheme of things, occupy Lille, and this was the Allied plan. But by early October the BEF was still trying to get into position. Of the three British army corps, the Second entrained on 4 October, the Third on the seventh—by which time Antwerp had been lost—and the First not until the seventeenth. Not surprisingly, the Germans moved into Lille on the eleventh, thus securing a major prize which, in addition to being one of the major French industrial centers, was the junction of no less than five separate rail lines.

Lille was the final prize of 1914 for the Germans. That it fell not after a long hard fight but owing to a muddle about who was supposed to do what was unfortunate. Doubly so, as the pattern would be repeated several times during the war, notably, but by no means exclusively, at Verdun in 1916.

THE BALANCE

At the start of the war, France and Belgium together had 135 separate forts or fortified positions along the northeastern frontier (or in Belgium) to oppose an attack.[19] By 9 October 1914, only 59 were left, for a loss rate of over 60 percent. More ominously, of the 59 surviving fortifications, 59 had barely been attacked. The German success rate was almost one hundred percent.

The "Race to the Sea," as it was called, was over, and the stalemate of the trenches had begun. The actual events make the term somewhat comic. Antwerp was a port. Since the Allies held Antwerp—and the entire Belgian coast over into France—they were already at the seacoast and had no need to race to get there. The Germans hardly beat them there; on the contrary, they attacked and threw them out. The only race was to Lille, which the Allies lost rather convincingly.

But the phrase captures perfectly the way the Allies successfully twisted the situation around: "a great victory had been won, because we got there first!" Readers of the *New York Times* were left with the impression that the French had retaken Saint-Mihiel in September, and then lost it again in December of 1914.[20]

In any event, readers were invariably told that whatever German accomplishments there were, they had come at a terrible price, an argument that had been developed early on at Liège, and was now almost a reflex response whenever it was hinted that the Germans had done something significant.

The reality was hardly good news for the Allies. The French had 329,000 dead and missing in August and September; in October and November, the figure was 125,000.[21] Not counting the dead and missing officers—who were excluded from the monthly French totals—losses came to 454,000 men for the first four months of the war. By contrast, the German Army on the Western Front had roughly 77,000 soldiers killed during the first four months of the war, and about 123,000 soldiers listed as missing, for a total of about 200,000 men. For every 2 German soldiers dead or missing, the French had lost nearly 5.

During this same period, the BEF had about 44,000 soldiers killed or missing, and the Belgian Army suffered losses of 73,000 men.[22] Not all of these men were dead. A good many of the missing were prisoners of war: thirty-three thousand Belgian soldiers were interned in Holland, for example. However, when the numbers are added up, total Allied losses were well over 570,000 men. It is no exaggeration to say that in the first four months of the war, three Allied soldiers were lost for every German.

This ratio actually understates the imbalance of the exchange. Given that the Belgian Army in August had a total of 234,000 men, that army's losses represent an attrition rate of almost one third. In the military science of this era, losses of a third were taken to mean the unit in question was no longer an effective fighting force. But in reality the situation was much worse than this. Belgium, like Austria-Hungary, had deliberately chosen to train and maintain a small army for reasons of economy. In a prolonged struggle where its territory was intact, it had the potential manpower to field a force of nearly three quarters of a million men, or nearly three times the size of the BEF in early 1915. But by 1 November 1914 the Belgian Field Army had only 75,000 men, and, since most of the country had been occupied by the Germans, no prospects for expansion or even replacement.

The situation for the BEF was, if anything, worse. On 1 November 1914, there were eighty-four infantry battalions in the BEF. A battalion was supposed to have a strength of at least 966 men and 30 officers, or about 1,000 soldiers each. Only nine battalions had a strength of more than 300 men. Churchill, using sources no longer available, reported losses in 1914 as nearly 100,000 dead, wounded, or missing. By the end of 1914, the British Army had lost about half of its effective strength.[23]

The BEF that landed in France in August and September was the best and most experienced body of troops the British Empire was able to field. In August 1914, the regular army was comprised of 182,000 men, with another 138,000 reservists, and the initial expeditionary force, given the breakdown between regulars and reserves, represented a deployment of at least one third of the United Kingdom's regulars and almost one half of its reserves. This was a large percentage of its trained soldiery. Basically the entire expeditionary force of some hundred thousand-odd soldiers was wiped out in those first months, and had to be reconstituted. As a result, even after strenuous recruiting efforts, the strength of the BEF in January 1915 was only 265,000 men.[24]

The true tragedy of the war for the United Kingdom was not simply the loss of what is often called "the first hundred thousand," it was the fact that they were the cadre that was required to train the next hundreds of thousands. The Germans had begun the war with more officers and noncoms than their opponents, and a better training system. Since their losses were lower, they now had more combat veterans to pass on the skills that had been learned. An unhappy equation that leads one to certain gloomy conclusions, conclusions that, unfortunately for the British and the French, were true.

NOTES

1. As quoted by Jacques-Henri Lefebvre, *Verdun, le plus grande bataille de l'histoire,* 10th ed. (Verdun: Éditions du Mémorial, 1993, 27. There is no edition of Driant's letters, but extracts are reprinted both here and, more extensively, in Gaston Jolivet, *Le Colonel Driant* (Paris: Delagrave, 1919).

2. As portrayed by Corelli Barnett, *The Swordbearers: Supreme Command in the First World War* (London: William Morrow, 1963), 36.

3. Fifty pages after Barnett's claim comes his evidence: "a staff officer found Moltke 'sitting hunched up over his table, his face buried in his hands, Moltke looked up and turned a pale and tear-stained face on the officer,'" 86. The incident is found in von Bülow's *Memoirs,* trans. Geoffrey Dunlop (London: G.P. Putnam's Sons, 1931), 2:169.

4. In photographs of him taken on annual maneuvers the year before the war, von Moltke looks remarkably fit; the brief portrait given by Sven Anders Hedin, who visited with him just after he had been sacked, supports the photographic evidence. This incident is in *With the German Armies in the West,* trans. H.G. de Walterstorff (London: J. Lane, 1915), 44–46. Although Hedin was trying to enlist support for the Germans with his account, the account is highly factual and in all other cases corroborated independently.

5. Général J[ean-Joseph] Rouquerol, *Les Hauts de Meuse et Saint-Mihiel* (Paris: Payot, 1939), 31.

6. Calculations based on the maps in Joffre, *Memoirs of Joffre,* trans. Bentley Mott (New York: Harper, 1932), 2:471.

7. Service Historique des Armeés, *Inventaire sommaire des archives de la guerre N 24 and N 25* (Troyes: La Renaissance, 1967), 1:101.

8. Only these last three regiments were part of the Seventy-third Division proper. The 146th Regiment was initially part of the Thirty-ninth Division, Twentieth Army Corps, Second Army. The 155th Regiment was from the Fortieth Division of the Six Army Corps, and thus a part of Third Army.

9. Raymond Poincaré, *Au service de la France* (Paris: Plon, 1931), 5.327–28.

10. As quoted by Jacques-Henri Lefebvre, 27. See note 1.

11. Winston Churchill, *The World Crisis, 1916–1918* (New York: Charles Scribner's Sons, 1927), 1:189.

12. Sven Anders Hedin, *With the German Armies in the West,* trans. H.G. de Walterstorff (London: J. Lane, 1915), 70–75.

13. It is 6.5 kilometers from the Vauquois butte to the Aubréville curve. Then as today the track is hidden by trees. However, steam engines are highly visible, even at night, owing to their exhaust: spotters on the butte would have hardly even needed field glasses to start calling in shots, and by early 1915 the rail line basically ceased operations.

14. Joffre, *Mémoires du maréchal Joffre* (Paris: Plon, 1932), 133.

15. Data taken from Colonel Robert Normand, *Défense de Liège, Namur, Anvers en 1914* (Paris: Fournier, 1923), 111–17.

16. Technically, this was the first rfm, *or regiment des fusiliers marins:* its officers were serving naval officers, and the curiously surnamed Ronarc'h was an actual admiral: the troops were not, as is sometimes assumed, "marines."

17. Lord Hankey, *The Supreme Command* (London: Allen and Unwin, 1961), 200, 207.

18. See the map in Normand, 177.

19. This figure is only for separately named fortifications in the northeast; it does not count those in the interior or in the south, nor does it count the dozens of smaller structures, which the French and the Belgians termed, variously, *ouvrages* or *fortins,* even though many of these were substantial defensive positions.

20. *The New York Times Current History, The European War 2* (January 1915), 798–99, 1011.

21. French data from *Inventaire sommaire des archives de la guerre (N 24 and N25),* annexe 6, corrected for live prisoners of war according to reports made to the Chamber of Deputies as redacted and analyzed in Michel Huber, *La Population de la France pendant la guerre* (New Haven: Yale University Press, 1931), 135. German figures are found in Heeressanitätsinspektion des Reichsministeriums, *Sanitätsbericht über das deutsche Heer im Weltkrieg 1914/18* (Berlin: Reichsministerium, 1935), 3, Tables 155–58.

22. British data from the Official History, corrected for certain omissions and displayed in more elaborate form in Arthur Grahame Butler et al., *The Australian Medical Services in the War of 1914–18* (Melbourne: Australian War Memorial, 1930–43), 2:261. Belgian data from Henri Bernard of the Belgian Military College in *L'An 14 et la campagne des illusions* (Brussels: La Renaissance du Livre, 1983), 149.

23. The battalion-strength figures are from Anthony Farrar-Hockley, *Death of an Army* (New

York: Morrow, 1968), 168–69. In *The World Crisis* (New York: Charles Scribner's Sons, 1927), i.299, Churchill cited the War Office [United Kingdom], *Statistics of the Military Effort of the British Empire During the Great War, 1914–1920* (London: His Majesty's Stationery Office, 1922), 253, for this data. I have not seen those figures in any extant published version, but Churchill's data is within 4 percent of data cited by Butler: 43,685 killed or missing, 55,689 wounded, 78,040 sick. See Butler et al., 2:878 (see note 22).

24. According to the French records summarized by Michel Huber, 115–21 (see note 21).

7

1915: The Struggle for the Buttes—
The Vauquois and Les Éparges

I have reviewed the record of my own regiment. The 18th of March, a heroic folly animated them. Of my company, 250 men set out, twenty men came back; the eighth company was the same. In the German trenches, taken and then abandoned, they found only one dead German....If the wastage continues, the day is very near when the offensive value of our army, already anemic, will be destroyed.

—*Abel Ferry*[1]

Joffre was confident he could drive the Germans out of France within a few months, and said so, to the distress of Colonel Herbillon, his liaison with President Poincaré and Premier Briand.[2] His method was simple: a series of massive attacks all along the line, one after another. There is no better summary of what ensued than the one written by the twenty-year-old Jean Bernier, a corporal in the 117th Regiment in November 1914, a sergeant in January 1915, a lieutenant in October, seriously wounded in December, and declared unfit for active duty:

> The era of *la percée* commenced. For three years, until the sinister offensive of April 16th, 1917, the great chiefs persisted in trying to force the German line, and, during that first winter, without the least organization, the slightest care for the life, the death, the suffering, of their soldiers....

There were the unpardonable offensives of that first winter, the first battle of the Somme in December 1914, of which no word was ever breathed, during which, from Mametz and Carnoy to La Boisselle, regiments hurled themselves each day against the enemy lines, without a canon shot having been fired. Then, in the mud, beneath the rain, in a veritable confiture of corpses, there was the Argonne, les Éparges, the bois d'Ailly, the bois Le Prêtre, about which France knew only lies.[3]

Untangling the sequence of these disastrous campaigns is difficult, because for the year beginning with November 1914, the French had enough men in line to mount simultaneous offensives. By December 1914 there were major operations underway in five separate sections of the front, and some of these overlapped with others begun in 1915.[4] As a result there were always at least two and usually three French offensives going in different sections of the front, while the Germans, usually regarded as passively defending their lines during this period, mounted half a dozen major operations as well.[5]

Any narrative of the fighting, therefore, ends up doing some violence to the chronology. But there is a certain logic to what happened, since the German successes of late September meant that an appreciable section of the front—the two hundred kilometers from the Moselle to the Meuse and up through the Argonne—was basically blocked off to the sort of major offensive effort required to break through the front.

So the key to the westerly end of this section was the Vauquois, a small butte located about midway between the most westerly of the Verdun forts and the Argonne Forest. On the other side of the Meuse is another butte, Les Éparges, which dominates the Woëvre plain to the south and east. The French still had a small slice of the right bank of the Meuse, and as one went downstream to Verdun, the slice widened out, providing a sort of back-door approach into the plain. Les Éparges was the key to the back door: seize it and most of the German positions along the southern heights—the territory seized in the Saint-Mihiel offensive—would become untenable.

This gave the positions an importance out of all proportion to their actual size as military objectives. Once the fighting started there, however, a second factor would ensure that the struggles for the buttes would assume great importance. The infantry division initially at the Vauquois was the Tenth, nicknamed the "Paris" division, since its regiments had their home garrisons in the city. When the fifty-eight-year-old Henri Collignon, former secretary to the President of the Republic, and an officer of the Legion of Honor, volunteered to fight, this was his division.[6] The presence of important figures from Paris, such as Collignon, ensured that the fighting at the Vauquois would receive attention.

In France, elected representatives could serve in the armed forces, retain their seats in the Chamber, and even serve in the government. At Les Éparges, the officer in one of the regiments involved happened not only to be a member of the Chamber of Deputies, and an undersecretary of state, but he also happened to be the nephew of a former premier, Jules Ferry. This was not a good thing for the French General Staff, which wanted to conduct the war in absolute secrecy, divulging only that information it wished to divulge, and exercising control on what little news was released.

THE FIGHT FOR THE VAUQUOIS

There had been a village on the butte of the Vauquois since the Middle Ages. In 1914, there was a sturdy church, a triple row of stone houses, and a main street that ran roughly East-West, since the two small roads up the butte were at each end. On the north side, the slope was such that there were several approaches up to the village. But on the south side, the only access was—and still is—by rather steep paths, so it was a good hike to the top. Like all the villages in this region of France, the houses were solid masonry and stone structures, usually well provided with cellars.

The few remaining stones recognizable as building materials are almost half a meter thick. Contemporary French officers have expressed doubt that even modern heavy weapons would do much damage initially. As one American officer put it: "when the roof and superstructure fall in it makes a nice cushion to protect you if you're in the cellar."[7] In other words, they were natural blockhouses and pillboxes as well as infantry shelters. But nothing indicates that the Eighty-second Regiment put up much resistance, even though the village was a natural fort. Given the French tendency to commemorate the desperate last stands of the war, the absence of markers and plaques suggests the kind of confusion we have already seen during the Bavarian attacks on Saint-Mihiel. There are few if any graves in the cemetery from this early date, evidence of a more concrete kind that this butte, like the ones in the Woëvre, was simply abandoned in a panic by soldiers who had not been given any idea of the importance of the ground they were occupying, and who were facing heavy artillery for the first time.

The Germans lost no time in making their presence known. At the Aubréville curve, the main rail line from Paris into Verdun is six kilometers from the butte. The track itself couldn't be seen from the butte, but the track wasn't the target. An American officer commented: "I wouldn't want to bother the track, I'd wait until I had a nice long train on it." The steam locomotives of 1914, with their distinctive plumes of smoke, were wonderful targets, even at night.

There were intermittent attempts to shunt around the curve, but since by 24 September the Bavarians had severed the only other line into Verdun over at Saint-Mihiel, both the main rail lines into Verdun were gone, the only exception being a narrow-gauge line coming up from Bar-le-Duc, and known as the "Meusien." The only major route into the *place* was a narrow country road. Since in 1914 the Vauquois butte was sitting astride a series of major road intersections, the Germans had a good piece of that as well.

So the French, who never developed either the tactics or the weapons for modern siege work, were going to have to learn the hard way. The butte was not a salient, but a part of a continuous German defensive position. The only way up was the paths up the south side, which was, of course, the steepest of the sides. It dropped down rather abruptly, and then became a long gradual slope down into the plain. It was a natural defensive position, which no soldier in the last three or four hundred years would have wanted to attempt. Nonetheless, the French Army would mount five separate attacks on the butte.

In the last chapter, it was pointed out that the Germans mounted their September Saint-Mihiel and Argonne offensives within a week after the end of the Marne. The French General Staff moved at a more deliberate speed. A month passed after the loss of the butte. On 28 October, the French attacked straight up the south side of the butte, using fourteen companies of infantry from the Forty-sixth Regiment, who went in without artillery support. Unfortunately for the attackers, the defending Germans had artillery and used it. This attack failed, but another was tried the next day. Georges Boucheron, who was there, wrote that the shells from German heavy weapons, *"les grosses marmites boches,"* fell precisely on the irregularly spaced columns of the advancing French: "the groups were struck and soon annihilated."[8]

The decision to attack without artillery was perhaps not as insane as it sounds. Shellfire from the French 75s wasn't going to do much damage to the defenders, and from Boucheron's account, it would appear that the French, rather naively, believed that an attack that came as a surprise might succeed, although how one mounts a surprise attack which has to form up in plain view of the defenders and hike up a hill is hard to fathom. It's also possible that the men who planned the attack simply didn't know all these things. How would they have learned them? In this case it didn't make any difference whether they had mastered the infantry manuals or not: the French had planned only to fight in the open, not how to storm up a three-hundred-meter cliff and seize a bunch of impregnable stone buildings. So the initial blunders are perhaps excusable. The French waited over another month, tried the same approach once more. On 8 December 1914, they attacked for three consecutive days, again with nothing to show for it except casualties.

Right before Christmas, the French General Staff suddenly noticed that the Germans had cut off all the main transportation routes into Verdun. On 23 December 1914, Joffre drew "General Dubail's attention to the situation created by the simultaneous advance of the Germans on the heights of the Meuse and in the Argonne. This advance showed how important were the operations of the French First Army in the Woëvre, and of the Third in the Vauquois district."[9] The delay seems incredible, but unfortunately it would prove all too typical of how the higher levels of the Allied commands managed their crises, always *en retard*. According to the standard intelligence histories of German divisions compiled by the French, and then completed and used by the British and the Americans, Saint-Mihiel didn't even fall until late October, so officially the Allies were only two months behind.[10]

But now that the French General Staff had finally noticed the damage, Joffre's directive meant the next attack would be in force. Planning began in January of 1915, and six weeks later, on 17 February 1915, the attack went in, finally with artillery support. But the French didn't have guns capable of firing large high-explosive shells (Boucheron's *"grosses marmites"*) at the high angles required by positions such as the Vauquois. Instead, they tunneled into the side of the butte and packed it with explosives. The actual attack began with the detonation of mines under the German positions. The first attack relied on the infantry from the Tenth Division, supported by an artillery regiment and a regiment of Territorials (the supposed equivalent of the German *Landwehr*).

At the same time, the Ninth Division would attack that section of the German line that stretched from the butte through the village of Boureuilles and over into the Argonne Forest itself. In addition to the divisional 75 millimeter guns, the French brought up, for the first time, some heavy weapons: a battery of 270 millimeter siege guns and a battery of howitzers, all system deBange guns dating from the 1870s: they had no recoil mechanisms, so the gunners had to reposition the gun after every round. A French artillery officer from the present day, looking at one of these massive pieces of ironwork, thought the crew would be doing well to get off a round every half hour.

Nevertheless, on 17 February, French troops managed to get up the hillside and hang on to the south edge. Unfortunately, although the butte itself was reasonably level, there was a noticeable slight rise as one walked south-north, and the major part of the village was to the north side as well. Once the French got up onto the butte, they had to fight their way into the village. The Germans emerged unscathed from the heavy stone buildings and counterattacked, ejecting the surviving French. The cost: eight hundred men dead, wounded, or missing.

The essential rhythm of all subsequent French attacks, both here and elsewhere throughout the front, had thus been established. After incredible sacrifices, a few survivors of the attacking infantry would claw their way into the ruins of their objective, then hang on for a few hours (or days) while the German artillery blocked their relief and battered them into submission. Meanwhile, down in the valley, the elements of the Ninth Division did even worse. So the French planned another attack.

On 28 February, the Tenth Division attacked the hill again. More artillery support had been promised. André Pézard, a platoon leader in the Forty-sixth Regiment (which had been attacking the butte since late 1914) comments: "With the great day commences a very feeble cannonade. Is that the 'magnificent artillery preparation' of which the colonel spoke?"[11] But the bombardment strengthened, and the French were once again able to get into the village. By the evening of 1 March, the Thirty-first Regiment had secured a hold on the houses closest to the French lines, the Germans holding the ones closest to their lines, as well as the church. That night the Eighty-ninth Regiment was checked in its attempts to secure the remainder of the butte, and the lines stabilized. The cost: three thousand more casualties, or roughly the equivalent of an entire full-strength infantry regiment.

The muddy terrain had frozen, finally, and was covered with snow. The French kept trying. There was an attack on 15 March, and the next day, Henri Collignon, who had volunteered to fight at the age of fifty-eight, was killed as he carried the flag. The French kept on. They attacked again in April to coincide with the grand offensive of the Woëvre, and then again in June as part of the aborted Argonne offensive. But the German defensive line across their side of the butte was beyond the capabilities of the attackers to break. The line across the top of the butte never moved. Essentially, except for a few square meters, it remained the same until the AEF took the Vauquois in 1918.

Getting that toehold on the butte had cost the French the equivalent of an entire infantry division. Officially, between 15 January and 31 March 1915, the French First Army suffered casualties of 27,026 men for its entire front, of which nearly 10,340 were either dead or missing in action; by comparison, the entire BEF suffered total casualties for the same period of 33,678, of which some 9,696 were dead or missing.[12] While a sizable percentage of these losses was suffered in the Argonne fighting, that the futile struggle for the Vauquois accounted for an appreciable percentage of First Army losses has never been disputed.

There was the usual claim that German losses were also heavy, but this is ludicrous, as the accounts of the men who participated in the assaults make abundantly clear: neither Boucheron nor Pézard ever saw the enemy, and their own artillery fire was feeble. Anyone who takes the trouble to walk around what's left of the butte can see why the casualties would be so disproportionate. An attacker would have sustained heavy casualties in 1715, fighting an opponent armed with smoothbore muskets and ordinary cannon. The place would have been easy to defend using bows and arrows. But in 1915, the French government controlled the press: reality was whatever the French General Staff said.

LES ÉPARGES AND THE MASSACRE OF THE INFANTRY

Les Éparges, a 346-meter hillock to the southeast of Verdun, is roughly the companion butte to the Vauquois. But it is larger, higher, and more irregular. There was no village on top, nor does the butte dominate the region as does the Vauquois. The Crête de Combres, which the Germans had also grabbed back on 22 September 1914 during the Bavarian offensive toward Saint-Mihiel, was 340 meters high, and only some 700 meters distant.

The butte is (or was) an irregular kidney shape, and the Bavarians had spent the fall entrenching themselves, with a bastion at each of the three key points of the kidney. From Point X, the east-end bastion, to Point C, the west-end bastion (in the bend of the kidney) there was a double line of trenches. The steepest side of the butte—and the most important—was the one facing back toward the German positions, and the Bavarians had taken advantage of this to tunnel into the butte, building a series of shelters for their infantry, and tunneling all the way up to the trench line itself.

Worse still for the French, the butte of Les Éparges was not an isolated outcropping, as were the majority of the others in the region, from the Vauquois and Montfaucon to the west of Verdun all the way down to Montsec in the Woëvre plain. Not only was flanking fire possible from Combres, but the topography meant that the Germans could filter men and supplies back and forth with relative impunity. At the Vauquois, it was ultimately possible for French gunners to interdict the supply routes to the butte at least some of the time, because the terrain immediately behind (on the German side) was open country. Troops could shelter in the dead angle of the back side, and be safe from French guns, but at some point they had to venture out into the open, and at key points during the March attacks, the French had managed to cut the butte off temporarily with artillery fire. The corresponding approaches to Les Éparges meant that this was not going to happen.

There was also another nasty problem. The Vauquois was originally what in the American Southwest would be called a mesa. It had a surprisingly flat top, albeit one with a noticeable tilt running (unfortunately) downhill to the French side. But the twin peaks of Les Éparges and Combres were terraced slopes, rising out of an extensive three-hundred-meter-high plateau. Once past the three hundred meter line, the attackers were going to be terribly exposed as they worked their way higher along one enormous, exposed slope.

The butte was different strategically as well. The Vauquois was a commanding observation post, one the Germans put to good use. Had the French been able to seize the entire butte, they could, at least in theory, have caused the Germans a great deal of trouble, and they might have been able to secure the reopening of the rail line into Verdun. In any event, at the Vauquois the French needed to regain the butte in order to block German operations. At Les Éparges they needed the butte to secure the only practicable route for an attack into the Woëvre plain: "The possession of Les Éparges and the control of its observatories is indispensable to any offensive envisioned in that sector."[13]

The orders went to take Les Éparges, and the task fell to the VI Corps, composed of the Twelfth and Forty-second Divisions, the latter unit with three battalions of *chasseurs* attached. Although the word *chasseurs* is often taken to mean light infantry, the battalions of *chasseurs* (BCP) were actually closer to heavy infantry: the battalions were oversized units with as many machine guns as an infantry regiment, and thus better equipped to mount an assault.

As on the Vauquois, the attack began with the explosion of a mine, this one on 17 February 1915. The two regiments of the Twenty-fourth Brigade struggled up the slope, finding little ahead of them except shellfire. The initial trenches were empty, because the Bavarians had developed a new defensive tactic. They would abandon the first line of trenches, so that when the French got to them, they found them empty except for a few corpses.[14] Of the two attacking regiments, the 106th took twelve prisoners, the 132nd, eleven.

On 17 February, the French got into the main trench line. On 18 February, the Germans launched six successive counterattacks. Once the French occupied the first line of the Bavarian trenches the German artillery, which had zeroed in the target, annihilated them. Technically, what Lieutenant Maurice Genevoix of the 106th Regiment experienced was shelling that went on for hours, and then, an occasional bullet from somewhere, occasionally a stray enemy soldier, but mostly, the deaths of his comrades.[15] Three days later, the French infantry had been eliminated from the top of the butte. The 106th regiment had three hundred men killed outright, three hundred more missing, and one thousand wounded, or over half of its full strength—if we assume that the regiment was at full strength to begin with. By the standard of any other war, the regiment would have been sent to the rear and retired.

Laboriously, the French assembled more artillery: two rare batteries of the modern short-range 155 millimeter guns, two batteries of the older 120-millimeter weapons, and the usual complement of 75s. On 18 March, the next attack went in, capturing a few hundred meters of trench and a few prisoners. Another attack was ordered, and on 27 March, the French took a few more meters of trench and a few *chasseurs* got all the way to Point X. The Germans again counterattacked, leaving the soldiers hanging on to some eighty meters of the trench line. By now the timetable was up for the general offensive all along the Woëvre plain, which the French would have to deliver without the benefit of the Les Éparges observation posts. So if that was the strategic objective, the attacks had failed completely.

Perversely, the attacks continued, and during the first week of the Woëvre offensive (which began 5 April 1915) French troops got to Point C, the westernmost bastion, only to lose it to a German attack on the eighth. Two days later, troops from the Eighth Regiment of the Forty-Second Division were back clawing away at Point X. But in the face of eighteen separate German attacks against the troops who had gotten onto the top of the butte, the French were never able to solidify their hold on it. And even that achievement faded during the general German attack of 24 April 1915, which effectively ended French hopes of taking back the Woëvre.

The resemblance to the Vauquois is noteworthy, but the scale was bigger. On the west side of Verdun, the battle for the butte had ended up occupying an entire army corps, and French losses had been, very roughly, about two regiments. But at Les Éparges, as the official history admits, the attacks during the first three months of 1915 had absorbed the attention not of an army corps, but of the entire French First Army, which lost the equivalent of an entire division: 2,754 officers and 15,546 men.[16] The 106th Regiment was basically wiped out, along with the 25th Battalion of *chasseurs*, whose troops had actually gotten to Point X. The regiment had lost half of its official strength during the February attacks: it was then patched back together and attacked in March and April as well. Maurice Genevoix, one of the survivors, had a simple title for his narrative of the attack: *La Morte*. Death.

But Les Éparges has considerably more significance than this. As far as propaganda went, the French simply lied to the world about their accomplishments: Les Éparges became a great victory. Their troops had

seized the crête and held it for a few days, and, heroically and unbeliev-
ably, they managed to cling to various bits and pieces of it. So on 10
April, General Herr announced that the French had taken Les Éparges.
This promptly passed into military folklore, and was duly sanctified by
the Michelin Guides: "the Éparges crest, stubbornly held by the enemy
since September 1914, was definitely taken on 6 April [1915] by the
Twelfth Division after more than a month of fiercest fighting."[17] To make
sure the victory stuck, French maps showed the areas as being solidly
French—the actual state of affairs only shows up on the AEF maps of the
September 1918 offensive.

As General Rouquerol observed in 1939, "Never did we chase the
Germans off the heights of Les Éparges which they called the position of
Combres." Anyone who hikes around the top of the butte can easily see
he was right. The French seized a small piece of the top, the Germans held
on to a larger piece at a higher elevation, and the rest was totally unin-
habitable. The price the French troops had paid had no relevance to their
aim.

PATTERNS OF WAR

Although arguably they were the most militarily important of the early
French offensive efforts, the attempts to regain the Vauquois and Les
Éparges were neither the first French offensives post-Marne nor the
largest. But they are of enormous significance for the course of the war. In
effect, they established a curious pattern of combat for the French, one
the Germans would quickly learn to turn to their advantage.

In phase one, the French would lose (or abandon) an area of major
strategic importance. In phase two, they would try one or more unsupported attacks. When these were repulsed with heavy losses, there would
be a third phase: substantial resources of men and equipment would be
dedicated to getting the position back, although the approach would be
exactly the same. Then would come the fourth phase, in which a few survivors would hang on to a small piece of the position, just enough for the
government to declare a victory. Then would come the fifth phase, in
which the combatants would sporadically engage in combat, but without
the basic situation changing: the infantry would be systematically annihi-

lated. The pattern didn't stop until April 1917, when the infantry started to refuse to let themselves be slaughtered.

There were other things about the Vauquois that would prove uncannily prophetic. In their attempt to seize it, the French attacked over and over again, with fatal results for themselves, always with an ever-escalating force. When an attack failed to achieve the objective completely, another attack would be ordered, often delivered by the survivors of the previous assault, and with no discernible change in the situation. By the time the French General Staff had any success at all on the butte, they had tied up one entire army corps, at a time when they only had twenty-seven such units active.

Then there was the slow rhythm of the attacks. Over a month elapsed between when the French lost the butte and the first attack (24 September to 28 October). No real planning went into this attack, nor was there any artillery brought in. So why did it take a month? But then it took three months from the fall of the butte for the French General Staff to start issuing directives, and nearly two more months before the next attack was delivered (23 December to 17 February); it took ten days for a second attack to be mounted (28 February); and the next attacks were separated by intervals of two weeks or more (15 March, 6 April), even though they were all conducted by the same units from the same army corps, using the same divisional staffs and regimental officers.

Of course there are explanations. The most common one, much in use by historians, is that on the 1914 battlefield, commanders lost control early on, communications broke down, it took time to regroup and reorganize. But the Germans could plan and execute attacks and counterattacks quickly enough. As we have seen, the attack on the fort below Saint-Mihiel was put together in twenty-four hours. The Saint-Mihiel offensive occurred within a a week of the official end of the Battle of the Marne. German counterattacks on the buttes came almost immediately after the attack itself.

The French dependence on mines as a substitute for an artillery barrage is another explanation. It took time to dig the tunnels, and the explosives, which were bulky, had to be moved into position by hand. The same holds true for the collection of antique weapons the French depended on for heavy weapons support, which also required a great deal of time to transport and set up. More practically, the French had a near continuous shortage of artillery shells through much of the war. Their peacetime allotment per gun had been far too low, and once the war got started in earnest, they were unable to produce enough. Supposedly, the explosives manufacturers were accustomed to buying the main chemicals (benzol and *toluéne*) they needed for the melinite from Germany, so the war was a slight problem.[19]

But another, equally important explanation lies in the attitudes of the officers charged with leading such attacks, which would be an increasingly significant factor. Mythically, the officers of 1914 are portrayed as sitting far back in some comfortable château while their men are slaughtered. For French and British (and to a much lesser extent, German) staff officers, this was true. But for line officers, those below the rank of major, it wasn't true at all. In absolute terms, officer casualties were over a fourth higher proportionally than were enlisted casualties, and senior German casualties were, if anything, even higher: by 22 August 1914, General von Strantz's (German) V Corps had already lost two of its thirteen *obersts* (colonels), and one of its four majors.[20] The Third (French) Army casualty lists quoted above included 486 officers, of which 204 were counted dead or missing. While no one could doubt either their courage or their willingness to lead their men into combat, it appears that in any one struggle, unit commanders were increasingly unwilling to massacre their men—and themselves—in attempts to do the impossible. As Norton Cru observes, "If orders had always been obeyed to the letter, the whole French Army would have been massacred before August 1915."[21]

Orders weren't ultimately disobeyed, but they could be ignored for a short while, or lost; or a series of excuses could be passed up the line to sympathetic battalion and regimental commanders, who were officers frequently linked together through a variety of bonds (prewar service, home garrison, civilian life, geographical and cultural links, and common battlefield experiences), which were severed above the regimental level. In struggles that were so exclusively being controlled at the regimental, battalion, and even company levels, such factors became important.

MISREPRESENTATIONS OF VICTORY: THE TWILIGHT WAR

The preceding chapter opened with the remark that while the Allies had shaped the opening of the war as a three-act play with a brief intermission, in reality it had five acts. The comparison may seem fanciful, but it points toward an interesting revelation. Both at the Vauquois and Les Éparges, the French, once they had clawed their way to the top and established a toehold there, claimed they had won. The battle is over, the curtain falls, and the viewer's attention is directed to the next scene.

As we shall see, the pattern is remarkably consistent throughout the war, and is hardly limited to these two operations. The result is a distorted view of the sequence of events. Oftentimes, the account of struggles such as those narrated here stops when the action, the dramatic center of the narrative of the war, shifts to another theater, thus leaving the reader with the impression that the fighting simply stopped.

In order to appreciate the true nature of the way the Allies fabricated their accounts of combat, one has only to track what happened in a given theater of operations after the Allies declared themselves victorious. The Vauquois is not only the first case, but in some ways it is the best example of the process, although Les Éparges is a close second.

The point of the struggle may well have disappeared by April 1915, but the struggle only intensified. By early 1916 the combatants had abandoned traditional warfare entirely. Instead, they tunneled into the butte and attempted to blow up the enemy's position from below. The war on the Vauquois became a surrealistic nightmare. On 3 March 1916, the Germans detonated four tons of explosives beneath the French positions. In retaliation, on 23 March the French set off a twelve-ton mine beneath the ruins of the church, still held by the Germans.

The very fact of this explosion is significant. As one might expect in a small French village, the church of the Vauquois was not only the largest and most solid structure on the hill, it was also at the highest elevation of the butte. In other words, one year after the French had supposedly retaken the butte, they still had not been able to dislodge the Germans from what was clearly the key position.[22] As we shall see in succeeding chapters, the majority of the claimed Allied victories were achieved by this same sort of manipulation.

The French blew up the church, turning the highest point into a gigantic crater. Two months later, on 4 May 1916, the Germans set off sixty tons of explosives underneath the French lines at the southeast end of the butte. The resulting crater, thirty meters deep and one hundred meters in diameter, buried 108 French soldiers from the 46th Infantry Regiment, along with an equivalent amount of the French line.

Such explosions were their own undoing. Attacking infantry who descended into this crater and tried to climb up the other side would be massacred as they labored through the loose dirt, which quickly turned to mud. The only real achievement of such mines was to increase the amount of space between the lines, thus ensuring that no infantry assault would be able to sweep the Germans off the butte. The French were never able to shut down the artillery spotters: the main rail line into Verdun from Paris remained closed, and observers on the western end of the Vauquois were still able to look down into the valleys of the Biesme and the Aire, and thus affect the fighting in the Argonne Forest.

By then, as was often the case in the stalemated sections of the front, a direct advance—across the crater line—was impossible. The only way to get the other side off the butte was to blow them off. And in the twilight world of the war on the Vauquois, this is precisely what both sides planned to do. The French talked of setting off three 145-ton mines simultaneously; the Germans, never lacking in wild ideas, thought of blowing off the whole top of the butte. Neither side had the resources to accomplish these tasks. But in the interim, they ignited one thousand metric tons of explosives in 520 underground detonations, the French setting off 664 tons in 320 separate explosions.[23] Although the worst period, in terms of casualties, was the first half of 1915, it is interesting to note that in terms of explosives, the war steadily escalated: fifty-one tons had been set off by February 1916. During the next twelve months, 180 tons; during the final twelve months (March 1917 to March 1918), 431 tons; all of it laboriously moved and loaded by hand. The deadliness and intensity of the struggle only increased with time. If there were fewer casualties, it was simply because the combatants were more skilled, not because their efforts declined.

By 1918, the top of the butte no longer existed. This is not an exaggeration: all that is left today is a sort of rim along the north and south sides. What was the top of the butte now consists of an overlapping set of craters. The butte looks like a sand castle that some obnoxious child trod a path through, pausing occasionally to stomp the ground. On the north side, the remains of the German positions are a grim reminder that the French never actually gained control of their objective, but spent the war grimly hanging on to the south edge.

The remains of the Vauquois are one of the seven demonic wonders of the modern age. Only a few old photographs prove there was once a sturdy village there, that and a few piles of stones along the German lines. Over four thousand soldiers are buried in the French military cemetery of the Vauquois, most from 1914–1915, more than a third of them in a common grave, unidentified.[24] If one is looking for a site that epitomizes this war, the Vauquois comes close to being the archetype.

Unfortunately, the pattern of events there is far from unique. As we shall se, the French continued these futile assaults, which climaxed, in April 1917 with the attack on the ridge of the Chemin des Dames, to the northwest of Reims. The idea of taking a butte or steep ridge remained a fixed idea for the Allies.

NOTES

1. "Mémoire sur les opérations en Woëvre du 5 au 16 avril 1915" as reprinted in Abel Ferry, *La Guerre vue d'en bas et d'en haut* (Paris: Grasset, 1920), 35.

2. His time estimate was six months: Herbillon heard this from President Poincaré. Colonel Herbillon, *Souvenirs d'un officier de liaison pendant la guerre mondiale* (Paris: Tallandier, 1930), 1.116.

3. Jean Bernier, *La Percée* (Paris: Albin Michel, 1920), 46–47. The summary of Bernier's military career is in Jean-Norton Cru, *Témoins* (Paris: Les Étincelles, 1929; reprinted 1943), 572–73. I have used *la percée* instead of "breakthrough," because the French more closely corresponds to the actual concept of a piercing through.

4. To compound the confusion, there is a certain disagreement about what gets enumerated. The four generally accepted named offensives are as follows: First Artois (December 1914), First Champagne (December 1914–March 1915), Second Artois (May–June 1915), Second Champagne (September–November 1915). Operations not numbered but treated as separate engagements: Saint-Mihiel (November–December 1914), Vosges (December 1914–March 1915), Argonne (January–March 1915), Les Éparges (January–February 1915), Woëvre (April 1915), Argonne (May–July 1915), Woëvre (June–July 1915), Vosges (July–August 1915). And, with the exception of First Artois, this enumerates only those operations where French casualties exceeded ten thousand men. See the enumerations in Général M. Daille, *Histoire de la guerre mondiale: Joffre et la guerre d'usure, 1915–1916* (Paris: Payot, 1936).

5. To put the efforts of the BEF in perspective: French casualties for the Woëvre—a campaign few Americans have heard of—were about the same as total BEF casualties for May 1915, the most horrific month of the war for the BEF until July 1916.

6. Information on Henri Collignon taken from the marker erected at the Vauquois. Collignon's age is not as excessive as might appear to the American reader. Half of the

French Army in 1914 was between the ages of twenty-seven and forty-nine, and the age actually went up during the war: in 1918 half of the men mobilized were between the ages of thirty-three and fifty-one.

7. During the course of my fieldwork, I was fortunate to run into many French, American, German, and Canadian officers, who were extremely generous with their professional opinions in these matters, and who, for reasons I hope are obvious, do not wish to be identified.

8. There are two excellent French accounts of these attacks by men who were there. Georges Boucheron served with the 46th Regiment (10th Division) from 3 October 1914 through March 1915, and wrote *L'Assaut: L'Argonne et Vauquois avec la 10e division* (Paris: Perin, 1917). His description of the October attacks is found on 59–80. André Pézard served with the same regiment as an officer commanding the 10th Company, took part in the assaults of February and March 1915, and remained through the great explosions of 1916. See his *Nous autres à Vauquois* (Paris: Renaissance du Livre, 1918; reissued 1974) with corrections and photographs. Some of the more relevant passages are extracted by Yves Buffetaut, whose succinct account of this and subsequent offensives is difficult to surpass: *La Bataille de Verdun, de l'Argonne à la Woëvre* (Tours: Éditions Heimdale, 1990), 31–38.

9. Joffre, *The Personal Memoirs of Joffre, Field Marshal of the French Army,* trans. T. Bentley Mott (New York: Harper, 1932), 2:343.

10. U.S. Army General Staff, Military Intelligence Division, *Histories of the 251 Divisions of the German Army which Participated in the War (1914–1918)* (Washington, D.C.: U.S. Government Printing Office, 1920): "Histories published by French General Headquarters have been used for the years prior to 1918" (7). The error about Saint-Mihiel is on 135. As we shall see, it isn't the only one.

11. Pézard, *Nous autres à Vauquois,* 63.

12. Service Historique, *Armées françaises dans la grande guerre* (Paris: Imprimerie Nationale, 1922), 2:520. BEF figures from War Office [United Kingdom], *Statistics of the Military Effort of the British Empire During the Great War, 1914–1920* (London: His Majesty's Stationery Office, 1922), tables beginning on 253.

13. Gérard Canini, *La Lorraine dans la guerre 14–18* (Nancy: Presses Universitaires, 1984), 82; on-site markers. Général J[ean-Joseph] Rouquerol, *Les Hauts de Meuse et Saint-Mihiel* (Paris: Payot, 1939), 131. Rouquerol also observes that the position had no real value (113). Both to General Rouquerol, writing in 1939, and Yves Buffetaut in 1993, the position had no military value whatever, which unfortunately seems a fair judgment (Buffetaut, 51); see note 8.

14. Historians seem to assume that this device was hit on only late in the war; in reality it was being routinely practiced, as here, by early 1915, and was listed by Lieutenant Ferry as one of the main reasons behind German success in his June 1915 address.

15. Maurice Genevoix, "Les Éparges" in *Ceux de 14* (Paris: Flammarion, 1950), 565–69.

16. *Armées françaises dans la grande guerre,* 2:501; see note 11. Contrary to what is sometimes implied, the French Official History treats losses in surprisingly candid fashion.

17. See, e.g., Michelin Guides, *The Battle of Verdun 1914–1918* (Clermont-Ferrand: Michelin, 1919), 5. The claim has been repeated steadily since then. See the maps in Pétain (from whence most maps come), *La Bataille de Verdun* (Verdun: Fremont, [1931]), 40–41. AEF

maps are in American Battle Monuments Commission, *American Armies and Battlefields in Europe: A History, Guide, and Reference Book* (Washington, D.C.: U.S. Government Printing Office, 1938).

18. Rouquerol, *Les Hauts de Meuse,* 131.

19. Arthur Conte, *Joffre* (Paris: Oliver Orban, 1991), 261.

20. French statistics from Michel Huber, *La Population de la France pendant la guerre* (New Haven: Yale University Press, 1931), 416. The ratio of kia/mia to men mobilized was 186 per thousand for all officers, and 221 per thousand for combat officers. The loss ratio for French combat troops (including all colonial and North African troops) was 175 per thousand.

21. Jean-Norton Cru, *Témoins* (Paris: Les Etincelles, 1929; reprinted 1993), 20. In a passage following, Jean-Norton Cru, who was a combat veteran and a section commander, remarks that there were many instances in which an attack that the staff counted as made never actually took place—yet another reason why I have placed so much importance on fieldwork.

22. Nor is this statement some sleight of hand. Few maps of the butte are extant, but they clearly show that the French had only a small slice of the south end; a small concrete model of the butte, which shows both craters and trench lines, is located at the south stairs, and makes the point as well.

23. Information taken from the plaques located on the battlefield. See also the table in Canini, 80; see note 12.

24. Officially, 4,368, according to the new cemetery plaques. My count was 3,890, including 1,970 in the ossuary, of whom 284 were identified, leaving 1,686 unknowns. Almost all the dead were 1914 and 1915. The Michelin Guide, in an attempt to minimize the losses, omits the ossuary totals and confines itself to named individual graves. Yves Buffetaut (94–95) says 2,400 in tombs and 1,972 in the ossuaries, for a total of 4,372.

8

1915: Champagne and the Woëvre

*At the General Headquarters they tell me: "Things are going well; in
the Argonne, Success."*

*At Army Headquarters they tell me: "We are advancing, but with dif-
ficulty."*

*At Corps Headquarters, General Gérard tells me: "We are losing
hundreds of meters a month; the Germans are slowly devouring
us, and the letters our soldiers write home are discouraging."*

—*President Poincaré*[1]

As the struggle for the buttes slipped into the spring, the French High
Command apparently realized they had to mount the offensive operations
for which the reconquest of the Vauquois and Les Éparges had supposedly been the necessary prelude. To the West, in Champagne-Argonne, the
French had little choice. As we have seen, the Germans had begun attacking in both sectors at the end of September, and in response the French
embarked on a slippery slope that led to the first major Allied offensive of
the war, First Champagne.

First Champagne, which began in December 1914, at the same time
that the attacks on the buttes were under way, had as its chief aim the
attempt to clear the Germans out of the low ridges that stretched from
the edge of the Argonne over toward Reims. In September 1914, the
Germans had stabilized their lines in this part of Champagne, so that the
front was well to the south of the critical lateral rail line and roughly
parallel to the old Roman road, which ran from Reims to Verdun.

In December the French tried to break through the section of the German line between (roughly) Souain and Ville-sur-Tourbe, a position about thirty kilometers east of Reims and thirty kilometers south of the Aisne. This is, relatively speaking, much flatter country than the Argonne or the Meuse. There are no real buttes or hillocks, and no natural position equivalent to the ridge of the Chemin des Dames northwest of Reims.

But flat is a relative term in military topography. The ground is like a snapshot of the deep ocean, one long, low, ridged wave of earth succeeding another. And the folds between the ridges are considerable. The ridge of Massiges isn't much of a hill compared to the bluff occupied by the fort of camp des Romains south of Saint-Mihiel, or to the Vauquois. But it is part of an extensive rise in the ground to the west of the Argonne, and there is (and was) no way to get around it. The only military option was the same as with the Vauquois: up and over, and that meant a direct assault across ground that no competent officer would want to attempt. "I certainly wouldn't want to have to fight across this without armor" is the usual comment by the soldiers of the 1990s.

Incredibly, First Champagne went on until March 1915. Its ostensible aim was to outflank the German positions in the Argonne. In three months the French managed to slice off a roughly rectangular piece of the line about one thousand meters by eight thousand meters, hardly enough to force the Germans to retreat. The cost came to a staggering one hundred thousand casualties (about what German losses were for the whole Western Front) and two enormous cemeteries: Massiges-Minaucourt and Souain, between them, contain almost one half of the French dead buried in Champagne.[2] In March the French General Staff wound down First Champagne in favor of a more promising target to the east: the Woëvre.

THE BATTLE OF THE WOËVRE

It will be remembered that the loss of the Saint-Mihiel salient was an enormous setback for the French: it severed the main transportation links into Verdun and made offensive operations out of the *place* Verdun impossible. In November and December 1914 the French had attacked to the north of Saint-Mihiel, trying to secure the wedge of ground they still had on the right bank. Those attacks had led to the assault on Les

Éparges, the possession of which would hopefully ensure the success of the larger offensive. By the end of March, the French hadn't actually gotten possession of the butte, but they pressed ahead with their offensive plans regardless.

Few have heard of the Battle of the Woëvre, for reasons that will shortly become clear. However, despite its obscurity, it was intended to be a major operation. The planned front for the attack, which was set for 5 April 1915, was eighty kilometers, which makes the battle one of the largest of the war as far as acreage goes.[3] The French committed thirteen infantry divisions and the First Cavalry Corps, and with what was for France in 1915 a major investment in heavy artillery. In August 1914, the French Army had gone to war with only 304 pieces of heavy artillery. By January 1915, the army had less than seven hundred heavy guns in service, and the French General Staff allocated half of them, 360 heavy weapons, for the offensive, and over nine hundred 75-millimeter guns.[4]

For the time, it was an impressive commitment. Unfortunately, it wasn't nearly enough to accomplish the job using the tactics to which the Allies had resorted. In August 1918, when the AEF finally got the salient back, Pershing committed over 3,000 artillery pieces, 1,400 planes, 267 tanks, and 660,000 men to the offensive.[5] On the other side of the Meuse, in their Argonne operations, the Germans committed as much or more effective firepower to support an offensive that involved one brigade of infantry.

As the guns, so the troops: the regiments of the VI Corps had already been badly mauled at Les Éparges in February. The VIII Corps, whose soldiers had been holding on in the bois d'Ailly outside Saint-Mihiel, had lost half its combat strength in the final months of 1914, and in October there apparently had been disciplinary problems with one of its divisions, the 16th.[6]

On the German side, the troops were the same units that had captured the ground in September 1914: the Third Bavarian and Fifth Prussian Army Corps, reinforced by the Fifth *Landwehr,* the Thirty-third Reserve, and the Eighth, Tenth, and guards *Ersatz* divisions.[7] Only the divisions of the Bavarian and Prussian corps were regular army divisions, although the Thirty-third Reserve Division was unusually well equipped with heavy artillery. Given the disparity between the modern guns and the antiques the French were using, it had almost as much firepower as the French attacking force. Like the Fifth *Landwehr,* they had been fighting around Les Éparges since November 1914.

The attack was supposed to be a surprise. Most senior participants, however, discovered to their chagrin that the date and location of the attack were common knowledge in Paris. One brigade commander, to his horror, was greeted by a member of the Senate with the comment, "Good! You're preparing to reduce the Saint-Mihiel salient!"[8] So it seems safe to assume the Germans knew as well.

The Germans clearly expected the offensive: right before the attack, the 121st Division was added to the far eastern end of their defensive line. This was one of the new divisions the Germans were forming by the expedient of eliminating the fourth infantry regiment from each division. Since a second machine gun company had been added to each regiment, the new, smaller division now had fifty percent more machine guns than before, and in each new division, there were fewer field guns but greater numbers of the more effective howitzer.[9] As 1915 progressed all German divisions would be remodeled in this fashion, as the German General Staff traded manpower for firepower.

April was a bad month to mount an offensive in the swampy ground of the Woëvre. And April 1915 was exceptionally nasty: the French encountered heavy rains, which turned the plain to mud, fog, and, incredibly, snow. Either to effect a surprise, or because the weather hampered artillery spotting, the attack of 5 April went in without much artillery preparation, an inadvertent repeat of the initial Vauquois attacks. Not surprisingly, the attack was a complete failure. In the lower elevations, the troops found that the area between the two lines was a lake. In the higher elevations, German artillery fire broke up the attacks before they began.

To the north of Les Éparges, the Forty-third Regiment, attacking into the Bois de Pareid, lost thirty-four officers and 511 men in a few hours. But all the attacks were completely checked. The French attacked again on the eighth, and this attack failed as well.

The only success was that, as related in the last chapter, the *chasseurs* had gotten a piece of the crest of Les Éparges by 9 April, and the Bavarians had been unable to throw them off. Unfortunately, the military value of this achievement, was nil: the Germans still had possession of the part of the crest that overlooked the Woëvre plain, and their artillery, directed by spotters on the crest, continued to pound away at the French. But for purposes of morale, or because he actually believed something had been accomplished, General Herr, commanding the VI Corps, promptly announced that the French had reconquered Les Éparges.

As we have seen, this was untrue; obviously it was an attempt to salvage the Woëvre offensive, which so far had achieved nothing at all. General Dubail, in overall command, knew exactly what to do. He sent out a new order: the troops would change their methods, and continue the attacks by what he called a "methodical progression" rather than an intense assault. In other words, since all element of surprise had been lost, the attacks would go in only after sufficient artillery preparation, and would have more limited objectives.

Having been stopped at the northern end of the line, in a curious change of direction, the French now attempted to take the most formidable of the positions the Germans held in the Saint-Mihiel salient, the wooded heights between Saint-Mihiel and Apremont. In one of the most disturbing and brilliantly written accounts of combat to emerge from the war, an account that reads like a piece of modern fiction rather than sober reporting, Sergeant Paul Cazin records the results:

> My company had to take a trench. We had been told it was at seventy meters: it was more than two hundred. It was necessary to crawl and keep still: all the world was up and screaming. My half platoon held the left. I had six men around me when I reached the German wire, between eight and nine o'clock in the evening.
>
> I stepped over their bodies, the next morning, about four o'clock.[10]

Cazin's account of their fate makes clear just how horrific the fighting in this war was, as well as the disorientation of the narrator:

> I found the first pantless, as if claws had scratched his trousers off. His buttocks exposed, cut back and forth as though by a butcher's knife. The second hung whole on a bush, his head balancing on the end of the highest branch, like the head of a dead sparrow. The others were rolled into a porridge of mud and blood. I didn't look at them. I returned on all fours, my blanket around my neck and my packs up under my chest. When I caught sight of the stones of our trenches, I straightened up and I cried out. I was pulled in by the legs and was given cold coffee and rum to drink. The slopes were covered in haze.

What have we done? We have gone on ahead under the shrapnel, lost, decimated, from the very first hundred meters. All the officers down.

The French General Staff counted this disaster as a modest success, since the infantry actually got a few meters of trench.

Elsewhere, the French gained a few square meters of ground here and there and captured eight hundred German soldiers. From 26 March to 30 April, they had lost 65,200 officers and men, or roughly the same as the total losses sustained by the BEF in May 1915. Total German losses for the entire Western Front during the same period were slightly over eighty thousand officers and men.[11]

ITALY AND ARTOIS: THE TRIUMPH OF WISHFUL THINKING

The French General Staff, undaunted by the loss of sixty or seventy thousand soldiers, promptly turned its attentions elsewhere. The plan was simple. The French and British together would attack in Artois, and this attack would be given a boost by the entry of Italy into the war against Austria-Hungary. It would be a sort of one-two punch administered from both sides, and the two German empires would simply implode.

The French General Staff based this plan on three key assumptions: by May 1915, they would have more men on the Western Front than the Germans; the Germans had suffered heavy losses and were in sad shape; the Austro-Hungarian Empire was on the verge of collapse and needed only a good push. Unfortunately, all three assumptions were erroneous.

The French General Staff's intelligence estimates were wildly inaccurate. The Allies believed that on the Western Front they had fourteen men for every eleven Germans. In reality, the French had 2,132,000 men while the Germans had 2,181,918.[12] The Belgians and British together hardly came to another half a million. In May 1915 the Allies had no numerical superiority to speak of.

To make matters worse, the French General Staff was still counting men, as though the war would be decided by soldiers blasting away at each other with bolt-action rifles. As German divisions got smaller, this was seen as proof that Germany was running out of men; but in terms of firepower—which was the important measure—the divisions were becoming more and more powerful, as machine guns replaced rifles and the standard field gun was replaced by howitzers firing explosive payloads three times as deadly as the guns they replaced.

Firepower was the real measure, and in the spring of 1915 the Allies were worse in every way than their opponents. Eight months into the war, they still had many fewer heavy weapons than the Germans had when the war had begun, and hardly any of the indispensable modern howitzers were in service: in June 1915 the army had only seventy-eight examples of the new 105 millimeter howitzer, which had been in the planning stages for years.[13] Prewar, the French had counted on the 75 millimeter field gun to fulfill all their artillery needs. It was hardly the best gun for the kind of warfare they had been forced into, but by May 1915 French artillery units had only about three 75s for every four they should have had.

The second problem was that the Germans were far from being beaten. In April 1915, the Germans launched what might be termed a spoiling offensive in Artois. Considered on its own, it was only a moderate success: the Germans chewed off a small piece of territory around Ypres, and terrified their opponents by (for the first time) using poison gas. The BEF's defense of Ypres had by now reduced the town, which had no particular military value to begin with, to a heap of rubble. But since the BEF still hung on to the ruins, the German attack was judged a miserable failure—although compared to Woëvre and First Champagne, it was a smashing success. Nevertheless, the Allies were supremely confident. The failure of the German offensive meant theirs would be a success. Once begun, it would continue on as Italy entered the war, and that would be it. Counting on Italy, then, was the third major mistake in the planning.

But the significance of the German offensive in Artois lay not in its tactical success. The Germans had begun to realize that the best way to deal with Allied offensive operations was to launch a preemptive attack of their own. It was only necessary to shift the front a few thousand meters for the rigid Allied offensive plans to be completely disrupted. Their heavy guns would then have to be moved, or new targets found for them. New objectives had to be found for the infantry, and, if the attack caused heavy losses, new units had to be deployed and trained. All of this took time.

The Italian card was the perfect example of how the Allies pursued grand strategies at the expense of the details. The grand strategy was sensible enough: clearly it would take more than France, Great Britain, and Russia to defeat Germany. On paper, Italy had a sizable military and a modern fleet. Moreover, it had a common border with Austria-Hungary that was almost the length of the Western Front. One good push and the empire would collapse. Italy would supply the final push needed. The German General Staff would have to strip the Western Front of men to prevent the two German empires from imploding.

The problem with this assumption about Italy lay in the startling neglect of details. The first detail was the geography of the proposed theater of operations. The Austro-Italian frontier between Lake Garda and the Adriatic was a ragged ellipsoid squashed at the ends so it almost resembled three sides of a rectangle. But the two longest legs, running roughly from Lake Garda in a northeasterly direction up to the source of the Piave River and then looping slowly back to the southeast toward the source of the Isonzo River, were entirely alpine. Basically the frontier demarcated the end of the alps and the beginning of the transition to fertile plains of the regions of Friuli–Venezia Giulia, Veneto, and Lombardy.

The only part of the front that offered any possibilities for a big offensive of the sort London and Paris were counting on was on the eastern side (now Slovenia), where there is a valley, or gap, between the Julian Alps and the Karst (Corso), whose most northeasterly portion forms a sort of massive outcropping between the Gulf of Panzano and the valley. From the Italian side, the opening is surprisingly small—about five kilometers wide. It is deceptive in another way: after about twenty kilometers the valley closes up, hemmed in by mountains on both sides.

The Austrian frontier on this side was well out into the plain, running very roughly twelve kilometers to the east of the Isonzo River. But the river anchored a natural defensive line, with rugged mountains right behind it. The obvious thing to do in defense was to construct defenses on a line parallel to the river, and this is what the Austrians had done. The prewar Baedeker described the Karst as "an inhospitable and dreary plain, strewn with blocks of limestone . . . the surface intersected with gorges, and partly covered with underwood and loose stones; and numerous funnel shaped cavities are observed in the rocks. The fierce Northwest wind which often prevails here has been known to overthrow loaded wagons."[14] Yet this was where the Italians would have to fight.

The Italian Army's general staff, the *Commando Supremo* (CS) had no particular offensive plans for a war with the Habsburg Empire, and, as a logical result, following the French model, it had no heavy artillery to speak of. It was difficult to envision how the Italians—or any army of the period—could mount a successful offensive over such terrain.

The Allied answer to this was quite simple. They were convinced that Austria-Hungary was teetering on the verge of collapse and needed only a good hard shove to send it over the edge. The empire's ethnic minorities were thought to be on the verge of a revolt, so the army was simply impotent. Impotent, small, and backward: Austria-Hungary, which had a population of roughly fifty million people, and was thus nearly a fifth more populous than France, maintained a military barely two-thirds the size of France. The peacetime army of the Habsburgs was hardly larger than Serbia's, and in 1914, the empire went to war with fewer battalions than it had possessed in the war with Prussia half a century earlier.

During the initial months of the war, that was good news for the Allies. But by the spring of 1915, demography was coming into play. With fifty million people, Austria-Hungary could sustain a large army (larger than France's, as it turned out), and indeed was doing so. Prewar, the army had been both small and poorly equipped. But this was more a function of lack of funds than of anything else. The army lacked the money to buy modern artillery, but the empire had the factories at hand to make the guns required, and the engineers to design them. No army in the world had heavy guns as advanced as the Skoda-Porsche 305 millimeter weapons that had smashed the Franco-Belgian forts in 1914.

So as the war progressed, the empire had more soldiers with more and better guns than when the war started. The Allies of course believed that these soldiers wouldn't fight. But this was a gross misreading of the citizenry. Fighting Russia was one thing; the Imperial and Royal Army perpetually worried about the reliability of its Slavic units in action against other Slavs. That was hardly the case with Italy, the one country the Austrians had beaten soundly (by their reckoning) twice in the previous century. Ironically, Italy's entry into the war simplified the empire's problems: its Slavic soldiers fought on to the bitter end against the Italians.[15]

But in early May 1915, if someone had told an officer on the Allied staff that there would be a dozen separate battles of the Isonzo over the next two years, and that the British and the French would end up by siphoning off their own resources to keep Italy in the war, the officer would have laughed in his face.

So the Allies began their part of what they believed would be the knockout blow. First Artois started in May and ran through June. BEF casualties for May 1915 came to 65,000 men. French casualties in Second Artois, which was declared officially over on 15 June, came to 102,500 men. Both General Daille and the French Army's own historians compute German losses in Artois for the first half of 1915 at around fifty thousand men, which includes the "failed" April offensive. In April the German Army had 11,606 men killed, and in May the figure was 16,859—for the entire Western Front. From the Allied perspective, this was hardly the way to win a war of attrition. The Allies gained some ground. Most of it was ground the Germans had thoughtfully taken up in April, and could thus easily afford to lose.

On 23 May 1915, or right in the middle of Second Artois, Italy, having been suitably bribed by the Allies with the promise of a sizable chunk of the Habsburg Empire, entered the war against the ally of its former ally. Obviously, this was too late to be of much help on the Western Front. The Austrian General Staff in Vienna had pretty much figured out at the end of April (when the Italians signed the secret treaty with the Allies) that war was coming, and had begun shifting the few spare resources it had over to the frontier. But this was a slow process: for the first month of the war the Italians had an enormous advantage in men, outnumbering the defenders by over two to one.

But Cadorna, the Italian commander, was the same cautious, slow-moving officer of the sort who had dawdled in August 1914 during the French attacks into the Alsace. His offensive didn't begin until 23 June, a week after First Artois had been called off. The Austrians were still outnumbered about two to one, but they had a month to prepare. The Italian Army was in even worse shape than the French when it came to officers and training: Italian troops in 1915, like French troops in 1914, had plenty of zeal, but they made all the same mistakes the Allies had made at the start of the war.

Unfortunately for the Italians, there were two major differences between June 1915 and August 1914. In August 1914, there were no German soldiers under the age of seventy-five who had actually been in combat. In June 1915, the Austro-Hungarian Army had been fighting desperately for ten months: an army of survivors was also an army of veterans. In August and September of 1914, the Germans had been forced to fight out in the open, on foreign soil. The soldiers of the Imperial and

Royal Army were on their own territory, and fortified territory at that. Not surprisingly, Italian casualties were horrifying, the gains nonexistent. First Isonzo, as it was called, was aborted in July. Its main accomplishment had been to give the soldiers of the Imperial and Royal Army a major boost in morale.

This was hardly the anticipated outcome. But the French remained supremely confident. True, except for the "conquest" of Les Éparges the Allies had no real gains during the first half of 1915. But British and French intelligence remained convinced that the Germans had been thoroughly smashed, with losses so severe the army would soon be scraping the bottom of the barrel to keep its ranks filled.

The British, who had essentially lost their original force for a second time in 1915, concentrated on rebuilding their shattered army. The French General Staff simply switched its attention to someplace else, and planned major efforts for the near future: the Vosges in July, the Argonne as soon as possible, and, the biggest of all, a fall offensive in Champagne. By then—they believed—the Italians would certainly have destroyed the Austrians, and one great push would end the war. The Woëvre promptly disappeared into the memory hole, as Orwell would later call it. After all, the French flag was on the crest of Les Éparges. Official French maps showed the area between Saint-Mihiel and Apremont as being French, a fiction that has been maintained ever since.[16] Underneath the fiction, a disturbing reality: in the first half of 1915, there were twenty-two Allied casualties for every nine German.

THE AFTERMATH OF THE WOËVRE

Officially, the fighting between the Meuse and the Moselle was over. But the Bavarians kept on grinding away throughout the summer, picking up a piece of ground here, a stretch of trench line there. Small-scale tactics, and hardly worthy of notice—except for the losses: according to the Official History, the First Army lost 106 officers and 7,300 men in the Tranchée de Calonne alone, and sixty-two officers and 3,692 men, "among them seven hundred prisoners," in the fighting around the Bois le Prêtre in June 1915.[17] The numbers began to add up. Abel Ferry, who as a member of the Chamber as well as a serving officer, had multiple sources of information, duly toted up the losses, calculating them to be over 120,000 men.[18]

As on the Vauquois, the war between the two rivers had its own strange life, which went on regardless of strategy or even common sense. Beneath the butte of Les Éparges, the French and the Germans continued to dig. On 11 July 1915, the French set off an explosion beneath Point X, which was the end of the blockhouse there. But the French were unable to exploit the success: the attacking infantry were wiped out by artillery fire. On 15 September, the Germans set off their own mine, and a month later, another, effectively erasing a big chunk of the French positions on the butte.

No matter how much was blown up, nor how many offensives were planned, the French were completely unable to shift the line of the Saint-Mihiel salient. Basically, in September of 1918, they were exactly where they had been in September of 1914.

But the German Fifth Army's limited resources had already been shifted to the extreme ends of its sector of the front. And with good reason. Down in the Vosges, a junior *Jäger* captain was applying what had been learned at Liège to the new warfare of the trenches, and over in the Argonne, a virtually unknown sexagenarian engineering general was developing a new offensive tactic that would turn the Argonne into even more of a nightmare than it already was.

THE GERMANS IN THE ARGONNE:
NEW TECHNOLOGY AND NEW TACTICS

The Argonne was a much different kind of struggle from elsewhere on the front. Everywhere else, intensive combat was a sporadic event, at least during the first part of the war. But in the Argonne, the fighting was continuous from late August 1914 until late September 1915. Boucheron, who had been in the Vauquois assaults, after enumerating the names of the places inside the forest, observes that "each of those names recalls, not a combat, but a series of combats. An arduous and incessant struggle . . . The Argonne was a true sector of the war, never at peace, always at struggle."[19] But the most intense part of it occurred in the summer of 1915, when in a bloody repeat of what had happened in April in Artois, a devastating German offensive ripped into a planned French offensive.

The roughness of the terrain also makes the Argonne unusual. The heavily forested hills had traditionally been the kind of landscape that European armies liked to avoid. As the attacking Germans quickly learned, their artillery superiority was of little use, owing to the density of the trees. Of course, by the end of the war, when most of the extant photographs were taken, the battle zones really did look like moonscapes. But this was in 1918, after the AEF offensives of September of that year. It took a surprisingly long time for all of the trees of a forest to be destroyed, a fact that was true from the Argonne all the way down through the Vosges.[20]

The Argonne front by itself was approximately the same size as the section held by the BEF in 1915.[21] There were stretches in Lorraine with open fields, but the heavily forested, rugged landscape of the Argonne was duplicated on the right bank of the RFV, while the ridges that led from the Argonne to the Meuse were also heavily forested, as were most elevations of the Vosges.

Trees posed unique problems for the armies of 1914. Wherever possible, of course, gunners liked to set their batteries up so that the position was screened by trees. Given the rather primitive nature of aerial reconnaissance, a small wooded area could provide excellent cover, even during the winter, and the guns could be aimed up through the branches. Provided, of course, we are talking about guns with a high enough angle of fire, which the majority of French weapons didn't have. Then a site on the edge of a forest, so the guns were firing out across an open field, was the best choice.

The problem began, however, when the shell tried to descend through the tree canopy at the other end, and its descent was obstructed—temporarily—by branches and trunks. The result was minimal accuracy. Shells went off course, plunged deep into the wet ground, or burst too high in the air. The ideal ending for a shell is to explode either right on contact with the target, or directly above it. In the former case, it would destroy the target itself, while in the latter, the blast would destroy the people beneath.

However, the main problem was that it was impossible to observe where the shell actually fell. Indirect fire was totally dependent on gunner-observer coordination: the observers providing continuous feedback on the initial shots. The realistic objective was one long, one short, and then a rapid-fire barrage right on the target. But when the shell exploded beneath the tree canopy, it was next to impossible to spot it accurately. And even if the impact was observed, it was quite possible that the fall had been deflected, and the observer's correction would walk the gunners away from, rather than into, their target.

Heavily wooded areas were problematic for machine gunners as well. For their weapons to be effective, they needed large unimpeded spaces for the weapon to traverse with its fire. So the Argonne appeared to be an area where the German advantages in matériel, especially in artillery, would be largely offset by the terrain, while the French had plenty of *chasseurs* relative to the Germans, as well as the various kinds of colonial troops whose experiences fighting in broken country, where small-unit tactics were the norm, should stand them in good stead.

And it was true that initially the Germans had tough going. In their initial offensive of 23 September 1914, the Germans had taken a reasonable piece of the forest.[22] But by the twenty-eighth, French resistance had stiffened, and then, on 2 October, the French began their own attacks, the success of which created a kind of salient into the German line, centered around Bagatelle and Saint Hubert.

The commander of the German XVI Corps was General von Mudra, an engineer. He had been governor of Metz before the war, the home garrison of the XVI Corps (which was thus largely composed of ethnic Germans from Alsace and Lorraine), and the head of the *Pioniere*. He was sixty-three years old, which seems suitably mature; however, the former chief of the corps, Marshal von Haesler, a veteran of 1870 and an octagenarian, had accompanied his old army corps into combat in case the youthful von Mudra wasn't up to scratch.

But von Mudra, like his counterparts to the east, Generals von Strantz and Freiherr von Gebsattel, was an officer of the first order, while the XVI Corps had historically been lavishly equipped with artillery. As early as 1900 it had four field artillery regiments and two heavy artillery regiments, and, as would be expected of an engineering officer's command, it was well equipped with weapons that subsequently became household words, but which in 1914 the Allies regarded as still in the gadget category: flamethrowers, mortars, grenades, and gas shells.

Von Mudra was one of the few German commanders the French habitually referred to by name, and the only German field commander Joffre mentions in his memoirs, while Boucheron begins his recollections of the Argonne fighting by singling him out. Initially, he was only the commander of the XVI Army Corps, which was based in Metz, where he had been the military governor. But after the first wave of operations in September, his responsibilities were expanded to include the whole of the Argonne, and the XVI Corps became a sort of ad hoc task force that grew in size and firepower.

As soon as von Mudra had moved his phone lines and headquarters farther into the Argonne, he directed another attack, which began on 4 October 1914. It was notable for being the first engagement of the war in which the Germans used everything in their arsenal: in addition to the 210 millimeter howitzers already used in the September attacks, which were normally part of corps artillery, von Mudra added a new and extremely effective weapon, the *Minenwerfer,* known to subsequent generations simply as mortars. The infantry and the engineers used hand grenades and flamethrowers.[23] As the Allies would discover with tanks, the use of a new weapon did not automatically mean success. The Germans had tough going, and it wasn't until the thirteenth that they had taken off the first line of trenches.

Von Mudra had objected to this offensive. Despite the new weapons, it was a costly operation. So on 13 October, he was formally put in charge of the whole sector. At his disposal he had three infantry divisions: the Thirty-third and Thirty-fourth from the XVI Corps plus the Twenty-seventh Division (on loan from the Fourth Army), Fifth and Sixth *Jäger,* three regiments of *Landwehr,* an extra three battalions (twelve companies) of *Pioniere,* and eight regiments of artillery.

Von Mudra's tactics were simple. A small section of the front was selected as the target. There was a massive artillery bombardment, but one of a very short duration, conducted by very heavy weapons. The effect was like dropping one enormous shell on the enemy positions. Then, a mixed force of engineers and infantry infiltrated into the pulverized position, followed by groups of infantry and machine gunners. When the new light mortar came into production, mortar crews followed along.[24]

These tactics took time to develop, and at first they were conducted on an even smaller scale. Thus on 1 December 1914, five companies of infantry from the Twenty-seventh Division grabbed three lines of trenches and took twenty-one prisoners, at the cost of six dead and thirteen wounded. In November and December, there were nine such attacks.

On 7 January 1915, another attack in the Ravin des Meurissons advanced over a kilometer and captured eight hundred prisoners, a major achievement only when one considers that there were almost as many live French prisoners as there were German attackers.

On 29 January 1915, there was another, somewhat bigger attack toward the Ravin de Dieusson. The French lost about three thousand men, roughly three times the casualties suffered by the attacking Germans. In the first three months of 1915, fighting mostly in the Argonne, the French Third Army lost nearly thirty thousand men.

No description, however, can make clear the desperate nature of the struggle. In the December fighting, the Fourth Regiment of the Foreign Legion (the Garibaldiens), was essentially wiped out, and the Garibaldi brothers, nephews of the famous Italian, killed. On 7 January 1915, General Gouraud, commanding the Tenth Division, and an officer much admired by his men, was wounded and replaced at the *Fille Morte*.[25] Von Mudra's men continued through the forest, accumulating a string of impressive-sounding place-names. On 8 January 1915, they had taken the Crête of the Haute-Chevauchée. On the nineteenth, Saint-Hubert and then the Fontaine de Madame. On 4 February, the Bagatelle. On the tenth, Marie-Thérèse, and on the sixteenth, they were at the small hamlet of Le-Four-de-Paris. No one place was significant, perhaps, but the string was impressive, and, in fact, the ruins of Le-Four-de-Paris mark the end of the central core of the forest. One more push and the Germans would be out into the clear. French morale fell precipitously.

These small methodical advances solved the other problems as well: there was no need to accumulate a mass of reserve troops, no need to move guns after each lunge. The area attacked was always within range. And since there was no particular reason to attack any one spot, each attack could be delivered as a surprise: it was difficult to forecast and the preparations for it would leave no aerial intelligence footprint.

It was Joffre who has been credited with the word *grignotage:* "gnawing." But it was von Mudra who was doing the gnawing. And he was destroying the French in the process. As Lieutenant Jean-Marie Carré, attached to the staff of the Fourth Division, put it: "we lost, in four months, a little over eight hundred meters on the average. But we lost the Fourth Division."[26] Joffre was beside himself. He had always had his doubts about the Third Army's commander, Sarrail, who was prodded to take control, and to assert the superiority of the French troops over their adversaries. Sarrail, duly prodded, promised a great offensive in July.

But von Mudra had prepared a nasty surprise. In May 1915, he met with von Falkenhayn, who, as always, was concerned about unnecessary losses. The result was that von Mudra was able to put his ideas into play in earnest. The operations in January and February had been only dress rehearsals. Now the real attacks began, a whole series. For the first, launched on 20 June, the Germans had assembled an arsenal of heavy weapons. In addition to the usual seventy-six field guns and twenty-six 105 millimeter howitzers, von Mudra deployed seventeen modern heavy guns in the 100 to 150 millimeter range, ten of the 210-millimeter howitzers, and another ten guns of even larger size. As infantry support, there were forty heavy and medium *Minenwerfer.*

This doesn't sound like much of an arsenal when compared to offensives like the Woëvre or Champagne, where the French deployed weapons in the low thousands. But this is misleading. The French arsenal was deployed in support of attacks of two hundred thousand men spread out on a wide front aiming for a breakthrough. Von Mudra's arsenal was in support of an attack conducted on the ground by a few thousand soldiers, a brigade or even less, in an attack aimed at a few thousand meters of the line outside the village of Binarville.

As usual, Von Mudra was employing the newest technology he could get. Although at Ypres in April the Germans had used gas, they had released it from cylinders, hoping it would float toward the Allied lines, but the 20 June attack was the first in which gas shells were used as part of an artillery barrage.

Ten days later, another massive attack. There were fewer of the light field guns, but now there were no less than thirty of the big 210 millimeter howitzers. In addition to its *Minenwerfer* and flamethrowers, von Mudra's attackers were armed with thirty-six thousand (of the then new) hand grenades. All this for a two-kilometer front in which the attack would again consist of a brigade. By 2 July, the Germans had captured the Bagatelle.

Joffre was deeply worried about events in the Argonne, where, as he admits in his memoirs, the Germans always seemed to have the upper hand. He ordered the French to mount a major offensive in the Argonne, and it was scheduled for 13 July. Precisely ten days after the capture of the Bagatelle, on 12 July, von Mudra delivered another hammer blow. The Germans lost 525 dead and 1,838 men were wounded. In return, they captured 3,688 French soldiers and counted over 2,000 dead left on the battlefield. And, of course, more territory was gained.

Incredibly, the French attack still went in on the fourteenth, and was stopped cold in the face of German gas attacks. The first colonial brigade fought its way back into the Ravin de Dieusson, only to be rejected with nearly three thousand casualties, over half its nominal strength. Joffre promptly sacked Sarrail, a decision that won Joffre no friends either in the government, where Sarrail was extremely well connected, or in the Chamber, where he was well liked. As a consolation prize, Sarrail was sent to command the great Allied invasion force in Salonika, which in September 1916, with a strength of nearly a quarter of a million men, would distinguish itself by being thrashed by the Bulgarians.

Von Mudra's system was munitions intensive. So far, he had only been given the resources to keep hacking away in a fairly small area. Every battle was a victory, but the French had the luxury (still) of being able to lose men in the thousands in the Argonne while planning major offensives elsewhere. And this is what happened. In September, the Germans began diverting resources back for the anticipated Allied offensives of Second Champagne.

It is customary to speak of these theaters as being entirely separate, but von Mudra's theater of operations in the Argonne was contiguous with the Champagne front. As the French attacked there, von Mudra's efforts had to be stopped and the guns directed to his right. In late September, he was able to mount one more operation before the resources had to be switched. On 15 September, the French lost hill 213 and the bastion of Marie-Thérèse. On the twenty-seventh, von Mudra's last attack went in, and seized yet another piece of ground, the Fille Morte, for the last time.

Practically speaking, the French had lost the Argonne, which doomed in advance the chances of Second Champagne. By seizing so much of the forest, von Mudra was forcing the French to attack across the rolling country on both sides of Reims, where, as on the Somme, they would be attacking uphill against prepared positions over terrain that was ideal for artillery spotters.

Not surprisingly, Second Champagne was a gloomy repeat of the Woëvre. The French General Staff persisted in the offensive, which went on through November. Pétain, who had worked his way up from an obscure colonel slated for retirement to an army commander, protested at the continued massacre. As Serrigny, Pétain's adjutant, remarked, "Champagne had serious consequences: it caused thousands of men to be murdered and it deceived the public," who were led to believe that the few hectares of ground gouged out represented yet another French victory.[27] Pétain's unwillingness to let the men under his command be massacred confirmed the suspicions the more offensive-minded officers in the French General Staff already had: he lacked the requisite desire to win at all costs.

The attacking French deepened the curves in the German lines to the west of Tahure, all the way over to the surviving Reims fort, Pompelle. In June the line had been mostly straight, now it was a series of sinuous curves. But the key points were all still German, the total territory gained under sixty square kilometers. And the gains had come at a terrible cost. The French lost nearly two hundred thousand men, including over thirty thousand soldiers killed outright. In the adjacent Franco-British offensive, sometimes known as Third Artois, the BEF lost nearly a hundred thousand. The Germans, taken aback by the suicidal nature of the attack, also lost heavily, but their total casualties were—once again—about half of those sustained by the Allies.[28] By now the only claim the Allies could advance was that they were killing many more Germans than the Germans were killing French and British.

From the German side, the lesson seemed clear enough. It was much better to control the battlefield through offensive operations than to endure these massive kamikaze attacks. So the value of the Argonne offensives went far beyond territory gained and casualties inflicted. In terms of territory, von Mudra had sliced off, at a minimal cost, more ground than any of the Champagne offensives would get. Ferry's estimate was that the French had lost about eighty thousand men (his total for the killed, the wounded, and the missing) in the Argonne, not counting the Vauquois), and this seems about right: the eight French cemeteries in the Argonne contain about thirty-six thousand French soldiers.[29]

German losses were about a fourth of that.[30] Above all, von Mudra was destroying French morale. Because every attack was a success. Some of them were less successful than others, but with each the Germans took and held strongpoints the French believed to be important, inflicting heavy casualties in the process. Insofar as there was a simple key to the German Army's success on the battlefield, this was it. In what was basically a year of combat on both sides of the Meuse, the French were unable to take a single important position and hold on to it for more than a few days, if that. On the contrary, when the Germans attacked, they were invariably successful, and at an alarmingly low cost to themselves. During 1915, about 390,000 Allied soldiers were killed in France and Flanders; the German Medical Services reported 114,000 German soldiers killed on the Western Front.[31]

NOTES

1. In a conversation with Abel Jules Ferry, who recorded it. See his *Les Carnets secrets d'Abel Ferry 1914–1918* (Paris: Grasset, 1957), 35.

2. There were 93,432 according to Général Daille's abstraction of the official data in Général M. Daille, *Histoire de la guerre mondiale: Joffre et la guerre d'usure, 1915–1916* (Paris: Payot, 1936), 2:89. Cemetery data taken from on-site markers: buried in eighteen cemeteries in Champagne are 111,659 French soldiers—21,064 at Massiges and 30,743 at Souain. By no means are all of these graves from First Champagne. German data for the spring of 1915 taken from Heeressanitätsinspektion des Reichsministeriums, *Sanitätsbericht über das deutsche Heer im Weltkrieg 1914/18* (Berlin: Reichsministerium, 1935), 3, Table 148. The best account of the fighting there is Louis Guiral, *"Je les grignote..." Champagne 1914–1915* (Paris: Hachette, 1965).

3. The front from the Verdun-Etain road to where it crossed the Mosel above Pont-à-Mousson is almost exactly ninety-six kilometers, but the upper end of this line, about eight kilometers, was apparently not part of the offensive. The Somme was less than fifty kilometers of front.

4. Including four batteries of 120-millimeter Longs, four batteries of 120-millimeter Shorts, and 155-millimeter Rimailho guns. Data on artillery strength comes from Daille, 2:41, 110, 179. See also Joffre, *The Personal Memoirs of Joffre, Field Marshal of the French Army,* trans. T. Bentley Mott (New York: Harper, 1932), 2:343–44; Général J[ean-Joseph] Rouquerol, *Les Hauts de Meuse et Saint-Mihiel* (Paris: Payot, 1939), 119.

5. Figures from Pershing, who also has an excellent description of the problems: *My Experiences in the World War* (New York: Stokes, 1931), 2: 260–61.

6. Gérard Canini, *La Lorraine dans la guerre 14–18* (Nancy: Presses Universitaires, 1984), 84.

7. It will be recalled that the *Landwehr* was the third and next to lowest level of German soldiery, while the term *ersatz* denoted units composed of service-age males who had not completed their military service prior to the war.

8. Yves Buffetaut in *La Bataille de Verdun, de l'Argonne à la Woëvre* (Tours: Éditions Heimdale, 1990), 46.

9. The best discussion of this new structure is in Pierre Joseph Camena d'Almeida, *L'Armée allemande avant et pendant la guerre de 1914–18* (Paris: Berger-Levrault, 1919), 208–19. Allied intelligence, optimistic as always, saw this as proof the Germans were desperate for men. For details on how the Germans formed more divisions, see Eugene Carrias, *L'Armée allemande: Son histoire, son organisation, sa tactique* (Paris: Berger-Levrault, 1938), 101–6.

10. Paul Cazin, *L'Humaniste à la guerre: hauts de Meuse, 1915* (Paris: Librarie Plon, 1920), 117–26.

11. German data from *Sanitätsbericht über das deutsche Heer im Weltkrieg 1914/18*, 3, Table 148. Allied intelligence frequently used such data to mislead the respective high commands, confusing German losses for the entire Western Front (and oftentimes, for all fronts) with the losses in one specific theater of operations.

12. Mott, 2:354.

13. In July 1914 the War Office gave British officers the impression this weapon was being phased into French divisions as the standard howitzer. The figure of seventy-eight guns in service is from Daille (179); there is little debate about the deficiencies of French artillery in quantity and quality. See the scathing analysis by Général [Firmin Émile] Gascouin, *L'Evolution de l'artillerie pendant la guerre* (Paris: Flammarion, 1920) — his comments on the 105-millimeter gun are on 32.

14. Karl Baedeker, *Austria Including Hungary, Transylvania, Dalmatia, and Bosnia* (Leipzig: Karl Baedeker, 1896), 198.

15. A conclusion supported by Ludendorff, who generally had nothing good to say about his allies. See the conclusions in Gunther Rottenberg's *The Army of Francis Joseph* (West Lafayette, Ind.: Purdue University Press, 1976), 187–89 (see 187 note 2 for the Ludendorff quote).

16. The only historian to notice this discrepancy on the French maps is Jacques-Henri Lefebvre, *Verdun, le plus grande bataille de l'histoire*. 10th ed. (Verdun: Éditions du Mémorial, 1993 [1960]), 24–25, 168.

17. Service Historique, *Armées françaises dans la grande guerre* (Paris: Imprimerie Nationale, 1922) 3:209–12.

18. In a report Ferry made to the Cabinet in 1916; he listed the casualties by theater or objective, but did not add them up (53–54).

19. Georges Boucheron, *L'Assaut: L'Argonne et Vauquois avec le 10e division:* (Paris: Perrin, 1917), 95–96.

20. There are numerous photographs that show the existence of large forested areas even as late as July 1915, e.g., in the 1974 edition of André Pézard's *Nous autres à Vauquois,* photograph 24, of the ancient Roman road through the forest, reveals a landscape on 14 July 1915 that looks remarkably like it does today. So does photograph 23, simply labeled "Argonne."

21. By January 1915, the front had stabilized to a measured length of 773 kilometers, of which roughly 170 looped around Verdun from the Moselle over to the western edge of the Argonne, and another 180 kilometers across Lorraine and then down the Vosges to Belfort. The BEF held 5 percent of that line, or 40 kilometers. The straight-line-as-a-crow-flies distance from the edge of the RFV to the western edge of the Argonne is over sixty kilometers. Figures from Senate [France] Report 633:186, as summarized by Huber, 112. See also Ferry, 167–170.

22. The only account of the Argonne battles of 1914–1915 in English is J.M. Scammel's redaction of some rather propagandistic French sources, "The Argonne 1914 and 1918," *Infantry Journal* (October 1929) 354–61. Scammel is apparently unaware of what happened after 12 September 1914, as his account stops there. The best short account is in Buffetaut 31–36.

The most comprehensive treatments are Général J[ean-Joseph] Rouquerol, *La Guerre en Argonne* (Paris: Fayolle, 1931) and a very early monograph by Bernhard Kellermann, *Der Krieg im Argonnerwald* (Berlin: Juliius Bard, 1916).

23. The flamethrower in the accepted sense of the term wasn't used until February 1915 at Malancourt, north of Verdun. Eyewitnesses seem to be talking about some sort of incendiary device used by the *Pioniere,* a larger and more cumbersome unit that is referred to briefly in Paul Heinrici, *Das Ehrenbuch der Deutschen Pioniere* (Berlin: Wilhelm Rolf, [1931]), 516.

24. The medium *Minenwerfer,* a 170 millimeter weapon, tossed twelve kilograms of high explosive out to distances of about nine hundred meters, and was a fairly heavy weapon for men to lug around, although it could certainly be carried by its gunners. The new 76-millimeter light mortar delivered only about a kilo of explosive, but it was much easier to transport, and represented the first true infantry weapon.

25. A marker a few meters south of the monument at the *Haute-Chevauchée* marks the spot. Gouraud is interred in the Navarin ossuary in Champagne, along with ten thousand other French soldiers.

26. Jean-Marie Carré, *Histoire d'une division de couverture* (Paris: La Renaissance du Livre, 1919), 186.

27. [Colonel] Bernard Serrigny, *Trente ans avec Pétain* (Paris: Plon, 1959), 41.

28. There is a surprisingly blunt discussion of this in the *Armées françaises dans la grande guerre,* 3:541–42. Interestingly enough, in this section the writers compare—rather slyly— the actual figures with the estimates made during the war, accepting the estimates given not by their own intelligence service but by the official German historians, and those figures are used in this paragraph.

29. Technically, the eight cemeteries contain 35,902 remains, but the ossuary of La Gruerie supposedly contains 10,000 of these, and one learns to be suspicious of ossuaries with 10,000 remains (or in the case of Verdun, with 100,000 remains). By contrast, about 17,000 soldiers are buried in the fifteen Meuse cemeteries, about 112,000 in the eighteen Champagne graveyards, and another 56,000 in the twenty-one cemeteries of Verdun.

30. As German cemeteries were consolidated from wide areas, comparisons are difficult. However, the sum total of all German war dead buried on the left bank of the Meuse through the Argonne—including the consolidated cemetery of Servon-Melzicourt, which includes about six thousand remains removed from Champagne, and Brieulles, mostly devoted to Verdun dead—comes to only thirty-four thousand remains, a figure that is all-inclusive through 1918.

31. British data from the Official History, corrected for certain omissions and displayed in more elaborate form in Arthur Grahame Butler et al., *The Australian Medical Services in the War of 1914–18* (Melbourne: Australian War Memorial, 1930–43), 2:261. French data from Service Historiques des Armeés, *Inventaire sommaire des archives de la guerre* (N 24 and N 25) (Troyes: La Renaissance, 1967), annexe 6, corrected for live prisoners of war according to reports made to the Chamber of Deputies as redacted and analyzed in Michel Huber, *La Population de la France pendant la guerre* (New Haven: Yale University Press, 1931), 135. German figures are found in *Sanitätsbericht über das deutsche Heer im Weltkrieg 1914/18,* 3: Tables 155–58.

9

1915: The War in the Vosges

In tiny little attacks, partial attacks, attacks made solely for the communiqués, *three or four hundred thousand men were lost . . . Hartmannswillerkopf cost us, without a meter of trench being taken, fifteen thousand men.*

—Abel Ferry.[1]

[4 January 1916] Council of Defense: The necessity of bringing to an end isolated operations like those at Hartmannswiller, and wasting the lives of our men.

—Marshal Gallieni.[2]

In January, the French General Staff decided on an offensive in the Lower Vosges that would clear the mostly Bavarian *Landwehr* out of the mountains entirely and enable the French to threaten the whole plain of the Rhine. On each side of the river there is a pleasantly flat plain that is in places almost thirty kilometers wide, and then a range of mountains running roughly parallel to the river itself, known on the French side as the Vosges, and on the German side as the Schwarzwald. After 1870, the Franco-German border ran basically down the middle of the mountain chain, and when the war broke out, both sides attacked across into each other's territory. Although the Vosges are not particularly high (the highest peak is only 1,424 meters), they are rough forested country of the sort that armies had traditionally stayed away from—like the Argonne Forest.

But they were not impassable. Geologically, the Vosges Mountains form two distinct masses, with a valley between them, the Bruche, which runs from Saint-Dié to Strasbourg, and thus penetrates right through the chain. The southern stretch, from the Bruche down toward Switzerland, is higher and rougher, but it too has passes which work their way almost completely through the mountains. Like the Bruche, these were named after the small mountain streams which thread their way through each valley. Although neither the Lauch (Guebwiller) nor the Thur (Mulhouse) penetrates as far as the Fecht (which emerges outside Colmar), each one allows relatively easy access to the plain from French territory on the western side of the mountains. The Bruche was the best avenue through, but after 1870, the Germans placed two forts at the Strasbourg end, close to the town of Mutzig, and a ring of forts around Strasbourg itself. The French had never planned an offensive which involved siege warfare, nor, as we have seen, had they developed the heavy artillery needed. So an attack along the Bruche was not feasible.

The other easy access was via the Belfort Gap, down at the southern end of the Alsatian plain. An attack up through the Gap was in theory much more promising, and this was more or less what the French had done in August 1914. Although the Strasbourg forts were an obstacle, an army operating in the southern end of the Alsace would cause the Germans enormous difficulty. At the very least, it would tie down large numbers of soldiers, because this section of the Rhine is scarcely an insurmountable obstacle. Then, too, the reconquest of the southern part of Alsace all by itself would have been an enormous morale booster for the Allies—one sound reason why it had been in the initial French General Staff plan.

The problem was that the Germans controlled most of the mountain peaks that ran alongside the plain: spotters could call in artillery fire and destroy any army as it deployed across the plain, well before it could come into action. The next step in the logic was simple enough: if the French could seize these peaks themselves, they could do the same thing in reverse. The solution was to ignore the valleys, and seize the peaks, which the Germans could use as artillery spotting posts.

Although the initial attacks in August had failed miserably, both Joffre and the French General Staff felt the basic plan was sound. The more so since as the Germans shuffled troops around the various theaters, the French General Staff felt—accurately enough—that the German line in the Vosges was essentially being held by units of *Landwehr*. The potential existed for a classic mismatch, since France in 1914 had the largest alpine infantry force in the world. Moreover, the mountainous terrain meant that the Germans would have great difficulty in deploying their heavy guns, which the Allies had come to realize gave them a terrific advantage everywhere else.

So by December, the French General Staff had regrouped the survivors of the twelve alpine battalions (the *battailions de chasseurs alpins,* or BCA) and assembled them in the Vosges. Together with their combined reserve and territorial battalions, this came to a sizable force. Technically it was only thirty-seven battalions, but this is to misstate the case considerably.[3] In 1914, an ordinary French infantry battalion had a wartime strength of nine hundred officers and men and two machine guns. The battalions of *chasseurs alpins* had a wartime strength of sixteen hundred men and six machine guns. Although often called "light" infantry, these battalions had the same firepower as a regular infantry regiment. Additionally, the BCA, as mountain troops, had their own attached light artillery.

The BCA had another advantage as well. They had been the only units from the metropolitan army (as opposed to the colonial army) to see combat; half of the BCA had been in campaigns in Madagascar, Morocco, or Tunisia. Moreover, in the French Army, the most promising officers were routinely attached to the battalions of *chasseurs* during their early years. Pétain had started out with them, and so had Colonel Driant. This traditional flow ensured that these units received special attention from the French General Staff; in return, much was expected of them. So far, the expectations had been met. In late September and October 1914, for example, the Sixth and Twenty-fourth BCA had distinguished themselves around Montfaucon in the vain efforts to stop von Mudra's attacks into the Argonne. So it seemed reasonable that three divisions of France's best troops, fighting on ground they had trained to fight on, would be able to dominate the theater of operations, particularly given their opposition.

The French thus began to concentrate their alpinists in the Vosges, forming them into larger units. The Forty-seventh and Sixty-sixth Divisions consisted of eighteen battalions of alpine troops, while the Fifty-seventh Division consisted of six reserve regiments drawn from the immediate area. In January Joffre approved a three-division offensive that would begin on the nineteenth and capture the whole section of the line that ran from the Hartmannswillerkopf, which the *chasseurs* called HWK, to the Lingekopf. The BCA had already made a promising start for this

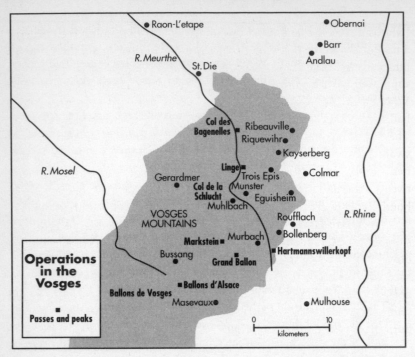

Operations
in the
Vosges

■

Passes and peaks

offensive. In November 1914, they had pushed the *Landwehr* off a 956-meter mountain peak on the southern end of the Vosges, known as the Hartmannswillerkopf, and so the struggle began.[4]

Although HWK isn't the tallest of the peaks in this area, its roughly triangular summit juts out some five hundred meters into the Alsatian plain, and from the far eastern end there are spectacular views across the Rhine into Germany.[5] In theory, observers out on the end could call artillery fire in on an enormous region. Had the French planned an attack up through the plain from Belfort, heavy artillery controlled from HWK could have destroyed any advance before the troops ever closed with the defenders. Assuming the French had been able to hold onto Mulhouse, which they briefly took in August 1914, and assuming the Germans had then mounted an attack along the plain to get it back, the same thing would have been true.

The French attack was set for 19 January 1915. Once again, the Germans moved first. By the twenty-second, supported by fire from the dreaded *Minenwerfer,* the heavy infantry mortars that were still new on the battlefield, they had pushed the French off the crest of HWK.[6] Joffre (who is strangely silent about this in his extensive memoirs) then ordered a new attack in the direction of the town of Münster. Again the Germans attacked first. On 22 February, four regiments of Bavarian *Landwehr*, supported by heavy artillery, drove the French back all across the line. When the attack was stopped, on the twenty-fourth, the *chasseurs* alone had lost 33 officers and 1,519 men, the equivalent of an entire battalion. The Bavarians—mostly *Landwehr* and reserve units—had taken a huge swathe of territory—more than was gained in the Champagne-Artois battles. In the first four months of 1915, the French Seventh Army had over twenty thousand casualties in the Vosges and managed to take only seven hundred prisoners. The French General Staff planned more attacks.

The top of HWK is a rough triangle about five hundred meters long, sloping down gradually as it juts out onto the plain, and then terracing down into it in easy stages. As at Les Éparges, the Germans had plenty of access routes to the top, and the insufficiency of French artillery in high-angle plunging fire meant that the infantry defending the position could set up camp at the base of the peak with impunity—and, as pictures taken during this period testify, they did.

On what was then the French side, the hill is a 14 percent grade with a slope of about five hundred meters. HWK was a terrible position to be attacking, even worse than the Vauquois: the base line for the bottom of HWK is also the bottom of another equally steep hillside. So the attacking troops, having climbed up to a nine-hundred-meter-high ridge, faced the prospect of advancing down a 10 percent slope of about five hundred meters, then fighting their way up the 14 percent grade to the crest of the HWK. The symbolism of this descent into the abyss was hardly lost on the French; when Sergeant Bernardin went down into position the first time he recorded some very unpleasant feelings.

> I go like an animal driven to the abbatoir....we meet the wounded, all BCA . . . in an uninterrupted procession, with haggard faces.
> "Ah! you go down there too," they say. "A beautiful slaughter-house!"
> Such are the encouragements that follow us in our descent, while already some shells come to flay the woods....[7]

And when the survivors finally reached the crest of the HWK, the first sight that greeted their eyes as they staggered over the crest was a sort of concrete flight deck—a surprisingly dense array of blockhouses, concrete and stone shelters, and stone- and masonry-lined trenches that could be destroyed only by accurate heavy artillery fire using the kinds of guns the French still didn't have. In the meantime, German mortars at the back of the crest could drop their shells down onto the attackers with impunity.

Unlike HWK, the Lingekopf is part of a trio of peaks that form a roughly straight line. From southeast to northeast, these are the Bärrenkopf (980 meters), the Schratzmännele (1,010 meters), and the Lingekopf (983 meters). Here, too, the French faced the prospect of a series of uphill battles. In some respects it posed a substantially worse problem: from their concrete and stone-lined trenches on the crête of the Lingekopf, the defending Germans could look down a long relatively flat slope, which the French would have to climb to reach the crest. Both positions are still largely intact, so the basic problem is easy to grasp. The buttes, even today, would represent a formidable task for an army. An attack on any of these positions was essentially a suicide mission.

Nonetheless, after the failure of their initial effort, the French kept on. In June they managed to stabilize their line. Another major offensive was planned, making use of a new division, the 129th, which had four battalions of the BCA (the entire class of 1915), two infantry regiments, and, finally, some heavy guns. On 20 July, the French launched a direct assault on all three positions. Theoretically, the BCA had gotten to the tops on the twentieth, but were ejected, so another attack was ordered in on the twenty-second, but with the same results. On the twenty-sixth and twenty-seventh, the French launched new attacks, and this time the Bärrenkopf was temporarily occupied.

On the twenty-ninth, another attack tried to fight its way up the slope to the positions on the Lingekopf. This was the most well-constructed of the positions, and the attackers were mostly massacred as they tried to fight their way up to the German wire. On 17 August, the French launched an attack that went on for ten days, and gave them temporary possession of the crest of the Schratzmännele.

Officially, the French had taken a piece of each peak, and this was touted as another victory both during the war and immediately after, with the 1920 Michelin Guide for the Vosges claiming that the French had won, or anyway, the Germans had been defeated.[8] And in a theater of the war about which there was never any real reportage on the actions, the tendency has been to leave it at that. The Michelin breaks off its narrative at the end of the ten-day offensive in August, leaving the impression that the French were the masters of the site.

The crête of Le Linge has been preserved as a memorial, and anyone who visits it can see for himself that here, as at HWK, the German positions, which dominate the ridge and the surrounding area, were never seriously breached. The limits of the French advance are marked by a series of melancholy crosses—the remains of French soldiers found when the site was cleared in the 1970s. In the first few days of fighting, the French lost one thousand men, mostly alpine troops, close to the strength of an entire battalion. For the period from 20 July to 20 August, they lost a staggering ten thousand men, again, mostly alpine troops.[9] The only results were a partial hold on the top of the Schratzmännele and the peak of the HWK. Given the need for concrete success, these partial achievements, like that of Les Éparges, were touted as victories, while, as usual, German losses were said to be heavy.

The war continued. The few heavy guns the French had were moved to support the second Champagne and Artois offensives in September 1915, and the decimated alpine units were left to hang on to their gains. On 31 August, the Germans, never slow to react to French movements, began to apply the lessons of the Argonne. The First Brigade of Bavarian *Landwehr*, strengthened by the Fourteenth *Jäger* Battalion and the *Garde-Schützen* battalion, promptly attacked and reclaimed whatever ground had been lost. In an assault that combined conventional shells with gas, grenades with rifles, they took most of the main section of the Lingekopf that the French had won in August. On 9 September, another attack, this one accompanied by an attack at HWK as well as the neighboring Bärrenkopf. In addition to gas, the Germans used flamethrowers, methodically reducing the French positions. All that remained from the gains of the summer offensive was a piece on the summit of the Schratzmännele. On 12 October, the penultimate German attack began, which reclaimed the rest of the summit.

There was no chance of further action around the Lingekopf, but the French persisted, switching their attention to HWK, where they still had a foothold on the crête. Thus on 21 December 1915, began the debacle that so roused Ferry and Gallieni to protest: the last French offensive apparently ran into a developing German attack, as had been the case in the Argonne in July. The accounts of the survivors are vague. But in the two weeks following the twenty-first, the French lost fifteen thousand men (which agrees with Ferry's calculations) including General Serret, commander of the Sixty-sixth (alpine) Division, and any chance of remaining on the crête.

What was worse was the percentage of men lost. By their own accounting, half of the troops engaged on the Hartmannswillerkopf in December were casualties, a proportion that seems true of earlier struggles there as well. This was bad even by the terrifying standards of les Éparges. What made it worse was that the German troops doing most of the fighting were *Landwehr*, while their opponents were elite. The French were not only losing vastly more men in these exchanges, but they were losing men from their best units, in areas where they should have won.

And so the campaigns of 1915 wound down to one final massacre of what remained of France's best troops:

> Two steps farther, a wounded man, nearly naked to his waist, sits in the frozen rain, "I am cold!" he moans through chattering teeth.... As we go up, cadavers make themselves more numerous. On a section of barbed wire that has been cut by hand, I count a cluster of ten dead. While approaching the top, two captains of the 14th BCA, recognizable by their beautiful black tunics trimmed in gold....
>
> Everywhere are the dead and even some injured, most of the cadavers have been covered with canvas until the stretcher bearers have the time to collect and bury them. One of these sad packets lies on the parapet in front of where we take up our position. However here the canvas quivers and emits a plaintive cry.
>
> "But he isn't dead!" I say to the soldier who watches from across the gap.
>
> "Not yet. But the Major said it was useless to evacuate him, he was f——. He's been like that for forty-eight hours...."[10]

Surprisingly, one of the first instincts of any soldier is to try to help a fallen comrade, despite the danger to himself. The refusal of soldiers to give aid to one of their own is a dangerous sign. Gallieni was right to be so concerned about what was happening in these mountains. The French Army was not simply wasting away physically, it was wasting away morally.

TACTICS

The German General Staff devoted one whole section, the *Nachrichten-Abteilung,* to the analysis of enemy armies.[11] None of the Allied powers had made any serious effort to study the German Army: well into 1916 the BEF had no one studying German artillery, for example. And the absolute censorship placed on journalists and reporters ensured that the only news passed on was the news the government wanted people to hear.

Unfortunately, the propaganda for the general public turned out to be the same information being used by the planners themselves. American officers in 1918 reading the Franco-British intelligence appreciation of the Sixth Bavarian division, for example, would have learned that it attacked Saint-Mihiel on 27 September 1914, and that these attacks continued through October. In the real world, Saint-Mihiel had been overrun on the twenty-third. In the world of Allied military intelligence, it hadn't been taken until the end of October—if then.[12] The 6th *Landwehr* Division, which had basically run the French off the mountain peaks in early 1915, was solemnly declared to be a fourth-rate unit capable only of holding some quiet sector of the front. So it isn't at all surprising that the innovations in the Vosges on the part of the Germans went unnoticed—as they had in the Argonne. This gave the Germans the luxury of developing new tactics (to go with their new weapons) in peace.

Initially, the Germans had stumbled into combined arms tactics as a result of the need to neutralize the French and Belgian fortifications. In the Argonne, von Mudra, an ex-*Pioniere* and former inspector general of that branch of the service, had carried the siege tactics one step farther, and applied them to trench warfare. But as an ex-*Pioniere,* he naturally thought in terms of high-explosive and heavy weapons. So his infantry assaults in the Argonne were based around the application of enormous amounts of high explosive delivered by an array of high trajectory weapons.

The Germans, of course, were perfectly aware that this was solving only part of the problem. As long as the infantry were still armed with bolt-action rifles there wasn't much they could do when they ran into small fortified points (or even well-dug trenches) except call for help. And, as any infantryman can vouch for, at ground level, precision delivery of high explosives is an oxymoron. Already the Germans had developed (or rather redeveloped) hand grenades. German assault troops in the Argonne were scuttling along the ground carrying spades and sacks of grenades early on. But grenades were far from being the complete solution.

As early as February 1915, the *Pioniere* had mounted a local attack at Malancourt (north of Verdun) using flamethrowers developed by a Captain Redemann, who had come to his new trade from the Leipzig fire brigade. The flamethrower *Abteilung* was initially composed of volunteers, and proved so successful that the use of flamethrowers spread rapidly through the army, being routinely issued to the *Pioniere* companies attached to the infantry.[13] So the *Pioniere* as they spread throughout the army, took with them grenades, flamethrowers, three sorts of mortars, and, of course, their expertise with explosives—this last being the only area where the British and French had a similar level of expertise.

That was one approach, and it worked well. But elsewhere there was the idea of an approach that was not so dependent on precision-guided explosives. The test bed for these ideas was the German equivalent of the *chasseurs*. In the German Army, the *Jäger* went back to the same period as the *chasseurs*, to a time when there was demand for elite troops armed with rifles (as opposed to muskets). The long-barreled rifle of the 1750s was the hunter's gun par excellence, so the first specialist troops were recruited from the ranks of hunters—and the two words, *Jäger* and *chasseurs*, mean just that: hunters.

In the French Army, these units proliferated. But in the German Army, there were only eighteen battalions of *Jäger*, which were consequently more of an elite force. The composition was the same: each *Jäger* battalion had the firepower of an infantry regiment, and about half the manpower. The greater firepower had meant initially that these battalions were attached to cavalry divisions—and were thus the forerunners of the famous *Panzer Grenadiere* of the next war. But the Germans quickly saw that cavalry were of little use, and the battalions were used in two ways.

In the Vosges, they were used to stiffen the *Landwehr* and an even lower category of soldier, the *Landsturm*. These were troops thought to be good only for static defense. But German Army doctrine demanded an active defense. So the *Jäger* became the first generation of storm troops, infantry able to mount countering attacks that would throw the decimated attacking force back to its own lines. And the Vosges was the ideal theater for experiments. So the Fifth Army, nominally in charge of this end of the front, authorized the premier *Jäger* battalion, the *Garde-Schützen,* to develop new offensive tactics.[14]

The first of these had arisen almost spontaneously, at the end of 1914, when units of the *Garde-Schützen* decided to take a section of the trenches at HKW by infiltrating from each end of the trenches, rather than trying a direct assault. The Vosges positions were a great stimulant for innovation because the terrain was too rough to allow the easy movement of heavy weapons. So von Mudra's techniques simply wouldn't work. But the *Garde-Schützen* had some enterprising captains and majors, and on 30 December 1914 they mounted an extremely successful attack that ejected the French at minimal cost.

Colonel Bauer, the German General Staff's siege warfare expert, had also been fiddling with the idea of giving the infantry a light gun of 37 millimeters. Krupp had developed one, and a special unit had been formed to try it out. The commander of the unit, Major Calsow, was never able to exploit the gun properly, and in August he was sacked and replaced by a *Garde-Schützen* captain named Rohr, who—not coincidentally—had been one of the officers involved in the December operation. The resulting unit was a sort of hybrid of *Jäger* and *Pioniere*, because Rohr had a machine gun platoon, a mortar platoon, and a flamethrower platoon, as well as a lot of infantry, who were increasingly grenadiers rather than riflemen; that is to say, they no longer paid much attention to the rifle as an offensive weapon.[15]

The German General Staff's intentions were to use *Sturmbattalion Rohr* as a test bed for developing the new basic infantry unit. Already, as firepower per unit increased, they saw that infantry divisions would be run at the battalion, rather than the brigade, level. But the testing involved combat, and Rohr's men, along with the *Garde-Schützen* (still working on their own tactics), were the key players in all the successful German assaults in the Vosges. Thus the BCA were the first Allied troops to encounter what would subsequently be called "storm troops" or "assault troops" operating almost entirely as independent infantry.

In 1915, the German General Staff was sponsoring several different approaches to combat, and personnel were shifting from one side of the front to the other, cross-fertilizing the new tactics. Consider the example of the young infantry officer Erwin Rommel, who started the war as an officer in the 124th Infantry Regiment, which was part of the VIII Army Corps.[16] The VIII Corps was part of the Fifth Army, and Rommel fought in the Argonne beginning with von Mudra's September 1914 offensive until the end of 1915. Then he was transferred to a new alpine unit being formed, the *Königliche Württembergische Gebirgsbattalion*. The first active-duty assignment of the newly formed battalion: the Vosges, where Rommel was until October 1916, when the unit was shipped out to Rumania and fought in the Carpathians.

In other words, it was in the Vosges that these revolutionary new ideas of combat were mostly developed and refined, by men who promptly turned around and passed them on to other units. By December 1915, Rohr and his men were training other soldiers.[17] His first class consisted of officers from the Twelfth *Landwehr* Division. The new tactics were being spread like a virus.

The importance of this is quite simple. Infantry units, once they have tasted the benefits of superior firepower, will not easily be persuaded to go back to the rifle and the bayonet, and particularly not in positional warfare. Those boundaries had traditionally been regarded as sacrosanct. The infantry by definition consisted of men with rifles. Only the artillery had guns. And this model was well established. In the British Army, for example, machine gunners were part of the Machine Gun Corps. When mortars were (finally) introduced, they were the provenance of a new body of troops.

The result was to proliferate low-level commands. The Germans had begun the war with the realization that ad hoc task forces would integrate the various branches of the army into one unified strike force. By March 1915, they were well down the road to the idea of simply giving the infantry more firepower and letting them go about their task on their own. At the next level up, the Germans were systematically increasing the firepower of their infantry at the division level. Before the war the gospel had been that reserve divisions had only a fraction of the artillery of regular divisions, and hence were much less potent. By 1916 it would be possible to find German reserve divisions whose heavy artillery complement was the same as entire Allied army groups. For example, the Twenty-sixth and Twenty-seventh Reserve Divisions both had seventeen batteries of heavy weapons, in addition to their complement of field guns.[18] And, of course, the important thing was not just the number (and kind) of weapon, it was the level of control.

Troops so equipped were infinitely more dangerous than any infantry had ever been. In the Vosges, the French lost more than vital territory and their best troops. Conceptually, they lost the war, by failing to grasp that the nature of combat had been changed dramatically, and irrevocably.

When, in February 1916, the Germans hit Verdun using the next generation of these tactics, they would prove unstoppable.

Not coincidentally, when the AEF disembarked in France, they were trained by the remnants of the French Alpine troops. Although at the higher levels of command the infantry were still seen as the infantry of old, the survivors of the alpine battalions had seen firsthand what the costs of this myopia were on the battlefield. Though Pershing was appalled to discover that the French had given up on the rifle and the bayonet, it was the Alpine training that was probably responsible for the relatively small mortality rate of about eighty-five thousand dead out of the million Americans sent into combat in 1918. (The Italians on the Western Front, during the same period, and fighting in the same theaters, with only forty thousand men in combat, had nine thousand of them killed.)[19]

NOTES

1. Abel Ferry, *La Guerre vue d'en bas et d'en haut* (Paris: Grasset, 1920), 54. Italics are Ferry's.

2. [Général] Joseph-Simon Gallieni, *Les Carnets de Gallieni,* publiés par son fils Gaëtan Gallieni, notes de P.B. Gheusi (Paris: Albin Michel, 1932), 245–46.

3. The regular or active BCA were numbered 6, 7, 11, 12, 13, 14, 22, 23, 24, 27, 28, and 30. The reason for this was that originally each BCA unit was actually a battalion of *chasseurs à pied* (BCP). So the "missing" battalions in the BCA numbering scheme represented the BCP. The reserve BCA were numbered by adding 40 to the BCA numbers, except that there was the BCA 32 in addition to 46, 47, 51, 52, 53, 54, 62, 63, 64, 67, 68, and 70. The territorial BCA were numbered 102, 106, 107, 114, 115, 116, 120, and 121. See the discussion in Jean Mabire, *Chasseurs alpins: Des Vosges aux Djebels, 1914–1964* (Paris: Presses de la Cité, 1984), 96–98.

4. French propaganda from 1870 to 1918 made much of the Frenchness of Alsace, while the Germans made much of its Germanic character. The reality is that the Alsatians were the Alsatians. They spoke, and still speak, a dialect of German, and their place names reflect this. In the anti-German fervor of the times, the Hartmannswillerkopf was referred to as Vieil Armand. The men who fought there referred to Hartmannswillerkopf as HWK (French) or HW (German). As Bonnet de La Tour, a lieutenant in the BCA 13, observed: "Never did anyone employ that stupid word Vieil-Armand." As quoted by Mabire, 105.

5. HWK may well be the best preserved battlefield in the world: almost every German trench and concrete shelter is still intact. It is possible to hike to the crest, walk out into the German positions, and look across the Rhine into Germany. The enormous shell holes at the base of the slope were made by the *Minenwerfer*.

6. A marker on the far eastern end of the crête of HWK makes this claim.

7. As recorded by Armand Durlewanger in *Sites militaires en Alsace* (Strasbourg: Éditions la Nuée Bleue, 1991), 20.

8. Michelin, *L'Alsace et les combats des Vosges (1914–1918)*. (Clermont-Ferrand: Michelin, 1920), 2:39.

9. See the maps and general comments in the Michelin guide, esp. 1.37–42. The most detailed discussion is in Armand Durlewanger, *Le Linge 1915* (Colmar: S.A.E.P Ingersheim, 1980), 14–20. There are some interesting albeit overly enthusiastic accounts in Mabire. To give Mabire his due, he speaks of the July attacks by the alpine troops as being a massacre. The French official history isn't much kinder.

10. Extract from a letter Sergeant J.A. Bernardin wrote to his family in July 1915, as recorded by Durlewanger in *Sites militaires*, 20.

11. Confusingly, IIIb was sometimes called the *Geheimer Nachrichtendienst*, and this section, commanded by Major Nicolai, is often erroneously identified simply as the *Nachrichtendienst*. Apparently the Germans were confused as well; eventually they renamed Major Rauch's *Nachrichten-abteilung* the *Abteilung Fremde Heere*. See the organizational chart (Anlage 1) in vol. 11 of the Official German History: Reichsarchiv, *Der Weltkrieg* (Berlin: Mittlerer and Sons, 1931).

12. U.S. Army General Staff, Military Intelligence Division, *Histories of the 251 Divisions of the German Army which Participated in the War (1914–1918)*. (Washington, D.C.: U.S. Government Printing Office, 1920). The same document as used by the British; despite the title, in reality "histories published by French General Headquarters have been used for the years prior to 1918" (7).

13. See the chapter in Paul Heinrici, *Das Ehrenbuch der Deutschen Pioniere* (Berlin: Wilhelm Rolf, [1931]), 516–24. The flamethrower troops were melded into the Third Guards *Pioniere*, which (in a rather ghastly coincidence) was known as the *Totenkopf* Battalion. See also the excellent discussion in Bruce I. Gudmundsson, *Stormtroop Tactics: Innovation in the German Army, 1914–1918* (New York: Praeger, 1989), 33–50.

14. The *Garde-Schützen* battalion was unnumbered, and referred to by name; in addition, there were 14 battalions of *Jäger*, numbered 1 through 14, and two Bavarian battalions, numbered 1 and 2. The proliferation of German units with the same number was one reason the Allies never were able to keep track of them.

15. As a defensive weapon to be used against infantry in a counterattack it was still heavily used. The point is that the rifle was becoming one weapon among many, not *the* weapon.

16. Service data taken from David Fraser, *Knight's Cross* (New York: HarperCollins, 1993), 23–45.

17. The history of the Rohr detachment is in Heinrici, 558–62. There is a widespread myth that these tactics were either developed in the East and brought over by von Hutier for the 1918 offensives, or were copied from the theories of Laffargue. Not so. See the extensive discussion in Gudmundsson, appendix C.

18. Data from Pierre Joseph Camena d'Almeida, *L'Armée allemande avant et pendant la guerre de 1914–18* (Paris: Berger-Levrault, 1919), 284.

19. Data on the little known Italian Expeditionary Force, which fought in Champagne-Ardennes from April to November 1918, comes from information at the main Italian military cemetery, in Bligny, France. It has long been an article of faith in official U.S. publications that the army only had 50,510 men killed in France, and that the Marines had another 2,457 dead. But these figures are disingenuous to the point of dishonesty. In the eight military cemeteries in Europe, 85,252 American remains were buried (including memorials for 4,452 whose remains were "never recovered or identified"), so 85,000 seems the most accurate figure for comparative purposes.

10

1915: Allied and German Plans and Goals

Nothing is more dangerous in war than theoreticians.

—*Colonel Serrigny.*[1]

And so 1915 came to a gloomy close with the failure of the grand French offensives in Champagne and Artois, the collapse of Serbia, and bad news from the Balkans and the Eastern Front. The only concrete achievement was a string of government press releases alleging the recapture of obscure pieces of French real estate such as Hartmannswillerkopf, Les Éparges, and the Vauquois, together with a few hectares of meaningless ground in the Champagne and Artois.

The French General Staff professed to believe that German losses were astronomical, that by the end of January 1915, the Germans had already lost almost two million men, and that the Germans would shortly run out of troops altogether—as they had already run out of trained men.[2] Kitchener assured the Cabinet in February that the Germans were running out of men and in a "few months" would "have exhausted their reserves."[3] The following month the French data was published in the *New York Times,* and was widely accepted. The resulting calculus was impressive. Edgar Crammond estimated casualties for the first twelve months of the war as being nine hundred thousand Germans dead and only four hundred thousand French.[4] The American general Greene's figure was six hundred thousand Germans to four hundred thousand Allied.[5] English newspapers carried estimates in July 1915 giving German casualties at three and a half million men.[6] Seven months later, on 25

January 1916, Colonel Repington, who in his position as *The Times* military correspondent knew everyone, soberly recorded the same estimate, given to him by the Dutch ex-Minister of War, Coleyn.[7]

The press and the staffs believed the same thing. The information the Allies leaked to the press and that appeared in March 1915, was the same information Kitchener was telling the Cabinet in February. Joffre was no different from the British. He believed that the French were gaining a numerical superiority. In addition to the enumeration of fantastic German losses, French intelligence kept on claiming that the Germans were shifting more and more troops to the East to prop up the situation there. This initial misimpression had been one of the reasons for his insistence on the post-September 1914 attacks. By January 1915, Joffre realized his initial information had been mistaken, but the realism was only temporary. In short order French intelligence was busy shuffling German troops eastward once more, and Joffre, forgetting their earlier blunders, believed them.

The Allies had always hoped the Russians would put so much pressure on the Germans that they would evacuate France, or would be driven out of it more easily, and insiders in the government were initially delighted by the news of great Russian successes. As the winter set in, those hopes faded, to be replaced by new sets of fantasies: Serbia, Italy, Turkey, and, finally, Rumania. But the fantasy that German resources were dwindling was persistent. Joffre believed that by May 1915, he would have a decisive superiority: there would be only 1,113 battalions of Germans to 1,794 Allied battalions (1,384 French, 330 BEF, 80 Belgian), and in August he was told that three more divisions had been moved East.[8] So he reckoned on his offensives meeting with success.

As we have seen in the previous chapters, they did not, but the figures Joffre quoted are intriguing. They suggest what the basic Allied problem was. First, the figures are wrong. They grossly understate the size of the German Army on the Western Front. The figure of 1,113 battalions is only a 15 percent increase from the initial infantry deployment, whereas we know from the monthly reports of the medical services that the average ration strength of the German Army on the Western Front had increased by almost 40 percent from August and September 1914. By March 1915, the average strength, which had been hovering around 1.5 million men, broke the two million mark, and in May 1915, it was 2.1 million, while French forces totaled only 2,132,000 men.[9] Although the Allies always had more men in the West during this period than the

Germans did, they never had the superiority they thought they had, which is one reason for their repeated failures.

Given their conviction that the Germans had heavy losses, the Allies easily fell into the trap of misinterpreting two other key bits of data. The German Army controlled by *Ober-Ost,* the German Command on the Eastern Front, was growing almost exponentially. By September 1914, there were ninety-seven divisions in the West and thirty in the East; by the end of December, there were only 101 divisions in the West and forty-six in the East; by May 1915 there were 106 divisions in the West and sixty-four in the East.[10] It was not until the end of 1915 that the trends shifted, with 114 divisions West, forty-seven East, and eleven in the Balkans—the third front von Moltke had written about before the war.

The Allies saw the transfers to the East as confirming their belief that the West was being weakened. Upon being questioned, they explained this by claiming the Germans were simply lowering their standards—drafting older, younger, and less fit men. The French had run nearly 85 percent of their pool through some sort of military service, while the British, who had tried to fill out their armies by voluntary enlistment, promptly ran into shortages in key strategic industries where the workers were, ironically, more apt to join up. Their own experiences led them to misinterpret the evidence. But since less than half of all eligible German males had actually been conscripted, and only about a fifth of all Austro-Hungarian males, the two powers had, relative to the Allies, an enormous manpower pool on which to draw.

A more ominous piece of information was also twisted around. From the start of the war (or even before) the German General Staff had substituted firepower for manpower. Early on, the experiences led them to the conclusion that the more guns the men had, the less men were needed. So in 1915 the Germans began to reconfigure their basic units. The prewar four-regiment infantry division disappeared, to be replaced by a three-regiment division of three battalions each. This meant fewer infantry per division, and the Allies seized on this shift as a sign that the Germans were running out of men, and thus cannibalizing their units.

But the new divisions had more machine guns (in the first year of the war, the number of machine guns in service quadrupled) and more howitzers; increasingly, the heavy weapons were assigned downward to the divisional level, and the new light infantry mortar came into use. With their increased firepower, the new smaller divisions were more potent than their ancestors, and easier to manage.

The switch to the three-regiment division had another important benefit. It meant the disappearance of the brigade, and hence the elimination of an entire layer of command. Even though the regimental affiliations were still maintained, the regiment was rapidly ceasing to become the basic tactical unit, which was now the battalion.[11] As command decentralized, the army became an even more potent fighting force. On the offensive, units were combined into the ad hoc groups that would become the famous *Sturm Abteilungen,* or storm troops. On the defensive, company commanders would operate with more and more autonomy. Already by the middle of 1915 they had the authority to pull back from their positions during heavy bombardments—only to return in force in time to massacre the advancing infantry.

The Allies thus calculated erroneously on two different levels. At one level, that of manpower estimates, they interpreted the data to mean that the Germans were getting steadily weaker, when in fact they were getting steadily stronger. At another level, the increasing German reliance on battalions meant that the Allies had more and more difficulty determining the actual strength (and losses) of the forces arrayed against them in any one sector of the front. Since they were fixated on divisions and brigades, they interpreted the presence of a battalion to mean the presence of the larger unit, when in reality it meant nothing of the sort.

These Allied errors help to explain moves that otherwise seem preposterous. If the model Joffre had been given was right, then a combined offensive on a massive scale would probably succeed. It would be particularly sure of success if it was synchronized with activities on the other fronts, since the Allied model basically assumed that the only way the Germans were coping with offensives was by shuttling troops back and forth. If the enemy was this weak, then the entry of another country into the war, even a marginal one like Rumania, might be the last straw. An army of half a million men, even badly trained and equipped, might simply overpower the already overextended German and Austrian troops.

Finally, an enemy so weakened was hardly going to be able to mount any major offensive: he simply lacked the manpower that the Allied commanders believed was necessary, and there was no point during the war when they realized the truth—that the German superiority in applied firepower was such that they simply didn't need overwhelming numerical superiority to mount operations. In that respect, Antwerp was typical. English and American critics of the Allied efforts there had opined that even outnumbered two to one the Allies should have done better—but in reality the besieged somewhat outnumbered the besiegers.

Then again, the Allies were not simply counting wrong, they were counting the wrong things. The constant lament that runs through all personal accounts by combat veterans is not that the Allies were outnumbered, but that they were outgunned. Again and again, they encountered the phenomenon of the empty battlefield. It didn't make any difference how many British infantrymen there were, given the German superiority in firepower. So long as the Germans maintained their superiority in modern artillery, any French attacks would be costly failures.

On paper, the Allied situation was improving. The French deployed twice as many heavy guns in 1915 as they had at the start of the war. But the statistics are misleading. Most of the "new" heavy weapons were mechanical-recoil weapons designed by deBange in the mid-1870s, on cobbled-together mountings, and weighed nearly four metric tons.[12] In addition to 300 of these antiques, the French had brought back into service 870 examples of the guns that their 75 had replaced. And since the field gun deBange had designed in 1878 was a 90-millimeter weapon, it, together with a 95-millimeter deBange design from 1888, was now listed as though it was "heavy" artillery, while their more powerful modern replacement, the 75, was considered to be field artillery.

On paper, then, the French situation was enormously better than it looked in the field. Nor was the situation with respect to the famous 75 encouraging: in May 1915, the French Army should have had 4,170 75-millimeter field guns in service. But they had only 3,365, which was why the obsolete weapons were pressed into service to make up the deficit. Nor were guns the whole problem. In the firepower of the battalions themselves—mortars, machine guns, hand grenades, flamethrowers—the French were also far behind. The first primitive modern mortars had seen action in April of 1915, and by the fall they were deployed in reasonable numbers, but the 58-millimeter mortar was in every way inferior to its German counterparts, particularly to the new 76-millimeter light *Minenwerfer* the Germans were now deploying in quantity.

Since the French General Staff remained oblivious both to the actual numbers and to the German superiority in weapons and tactics, the Allies thought it obvious that one massive blow would knock the Germans out of France. Certainly if the French General Staff's estimates were anywhere near being true, the German Army would soon be exhausted. So from

Joffre's point of view, all that remained was one final blow, and the crucial task was to get the British to fight. By the end of 1915, they had over a million men in France, all penned up behind a front that was smaller than the front around Verdun.[13] If they could be persuaded to mount a major offensive synchronized with the French, and in the same place, they could break the German front, force a massive retreat.

As far as strategy and tactics went, the choices were simple. Joffre and the French General Staff, like their British colleagues, had only one concept of attack, the *coup de bélier,* the massive blow of the battering ram, which would break the front open and run the Germans out of France (a claim Joffre was still making in public as late as the fall of 1915).

JOFFRE'S GREAT IDEA

Joffre's idea was sound. Given the Allied problems, only a massive offense had any chance of success. As long as the offensives were limited to one or more theaters, the Germans, with their greater mobility and firepower, could shuttle resources around and shut each one down sequentially. In 1915, the only real achievement of most Allied offensives had been to force the Germans to shut down their own offensive operations.

But if the offensive was massive enough, it would suck in resources and overload the defense. It wouldn't make much difference how slow moving and cumbrous it was, it would be so massive that it would smash through the line. Moreover, it was a concept that was technically feasible. Civilians and a few military experts might fantasize about some new technology that would enable a breakthrough, but, in 1915, the internal combustion engine was too underpowered to be the basis for much more than towing heavy guns and moving supplies: when, in 1916 and 1917, the British and French deployed their newly developed tanks, the overwhelming majority of them either never cleared the lines or were destroyed or abandoned on the field of battle. A not unsurprising statistic, given the absurd power-to-weight ratio of the machines, which were so slow that German infantry could disable them with mortar fire, and were often so lightly armored that ordinary armor-piercing bullets went right through them. Besides, the Allies needed to win the war in 1916, not in 1917 (when the French believed, rather sensibly, that a battlefield capable vehicle might be in production). But as 1916 began, all the Allies had going for them were a great arsenal of antiques.

The French problem, particularly after the debacle of 1914, was that France lacked the manpower to mount such an offensive on its own. For Joffre's plan to work, it required a major British force. Essentially, that meant waiting until the summer of 1916. In 1914, the BEF had landed 118,000 men. By the end of the year, most of these men were casualties. So the buildup was slow: over a quarter of a million by January of 1915, a little over half a million by July, and finally, by January of 1916, the BEF was projected to be over a million men. If all went as planned, by the summer of 1916, there would be a million and a half. The Allies would then so outnumber the Germans that they could easily smash through their line. The key, in other words, was a massive coordinated offensive. The obvious spot was the Somme. The problem was that there was no way the Allies could get this offensive under way until the middle of the summer.

THE WORRIES OF GENERAL GALLIENI

Not everyone was as sanguine as Joffre. General Gallieni, who had become minister of war in October of 1915, sarcastically recorded his reactions in his secret diary.

[10 November] . . . at the Council of Ministers. Discussions confused, as always.

11 November. Council. Always words, never decisions. Poincaré, Briand, Bourgeous, Doumergues talk constantly, and about everything. Nothing is resolved.

18 November. At the Chamber of Deputies. Interminable bickering.... In the evening, great measures of reorganization indicated by Boucabeille: the French General Staff is a machine whose motor doesn't work.

[22 December] The French General Staff, always incorrigible, lives in an atmosphere of unreality.[14]

It isn't too difficult to see what must have been in the back of the minister of war's mind. In 1919, it was revealed that France had suffered 2,478,000 casualties by the end of 1915, of which 941,000 were either dead or missing.[15] In public, the government didn't admit there were any casualties at all, but an approximation of the true figures wasn't too difficult to obtain. By October 1916, Ferry had computed them in a report made to the Cabinet. His data was almost the same as the postwar accounting: German fatalities were running at about half the Allied total.[16]

While Poincaré and the ministers talked and Ferry researched, Gallieni worried. Here were his worries at the end of 1916.

> 16 December. In the morning, Council of Ministers, discussion about Joffre and the trenches. Worry about the next German attack. At certain points, the defensive fortifications are not prepared. The matter is grave. Must do what is necessary towards Verdun and Toul....The first line to be carved out, but hardly anyone about. At 1,500 to 2,000 meters, neither the second line, nor the troops (231–32).

So on the sixteenth, Gallieni wrote to Joffre expressing his concern about the defensive positions: "In particular, and notably in the regions of the Meurthe, of Toul, and of Verdun, the complex of trenches are not complete as is the case over a large section of the front" (234).

Gallieni had to write to his senior general, because Joffre had sealed off the "zone of the armies" from prying eyes. Not simply journalists and those irritating foreigners, but the representatives of the government itself. The only way someone like Poincaré could visit the front was with Joffre himself, who treated any attempt by a government official to visit on his own without proper guidance as a vote of no confidence in himself and reacted with appropriate violence. The French General Staff might not be able to handle the Germans, but they could certainly handle their fellow countrymen in the government, the press, and visiting foreigners.

The trigger was a letter from Emil Driant, a lieutenant colonel in the *chasseurs*. In one of the greater ironies of the war, Driant's *chasseurs* (the Fifty-sixth and Fifty-ninth), stationed in the Bois des Caures, would be the first French soldiers overrun in the German attack on Verdun, and Driant's last stand and martyrdom there would become a major French legend, no less so for being real. But in the fall of 1915, Driant was simply another deputy who was also a serving officer (and a well-known writer) taking advantage of his dual citizenship to complain outside of channels. Moreover, to add insult to injury, he was Boulanger's son-in-law. Like Abel Ferry, who was Jules Ferry's nephew (and also a serving officer), he was thus controversial by definition. And, also like Ferry, he was making himself obnoxious with his claims that the French General Staff didn't know what it was doing.

So Joffre responded by complaining he couldn't run a war if people in the army were going to go around him and complain about things, taking advantage of their position as members of the Chamber. Liddell Hart subsequently made this part of Joffre's response famous as the archetype of the enraged bureaucrat.[17] However, Gallieni, near the end of his life, had not been made minister of war simply because he was a distinguished soldier. No Frenchman could rise to senior rank in the army before 1914 without having an acute set of political antennae. Nor is there any evidence that Gallieni was particularly in awe of Joffre: witnesses record him as speaking to him like a captain addressing a cadet.

And now, as minister of war, he forced Joffre to come out of the closet about Verdun, to put in writing what the situation actually was. Here is the key part of the response. Joffre said, flatly, that in the areas mentioned by Gallieni,

> There exist three or four successive defensive positions, finished or on the road to completion. The organization is, for the whole ensemble, greatly better and more complete than that of our adversaries.... In conclusion, I consider that nothing justifies the fears you have expressed in the name of the government in your dispatch of 16 December [1915] (235–36).

So nothing justified Gallieni's fears. The minister of war had his chief commander on the spot because if the defenses weren't there (and everyone except the French General Staff knew they weren't), then Joffre either was lying to the government, or he didn't know what was happening at the front, because he had been to the Verdun front twelve times during 1915. In fact, Joffre visited it as late as 19 February 1916.[18]

Which may account for the politesse of Gallieni's response. On 21 December, Gallieni, with the approval of the council, sent Joffre a letter expressing its unequivocal support: "The Government is full of confidence in you,"... assuming that the facts are as you stated in your letter (238). But that went unspoken. And Joffre, who trusted his staff, and to whom it apparently never occurred that things were otherwise than the way they were represented to him, confident that if things weren't fine at Verdun he would have noticed it on his periodic tours of inspection, went back to planning the great offensive in which the BEF would eject the Germans from France.

Gallieni, who, unfortunately for France, only had five months to live, went back to worrying.

> [20 December] Wastage everywhere at the front. Wastage of men. Useless fatigue . . . Wastage of guns and cartridges. In sum, nothing is ordered for the front (234).

> [29 December] Council. Haig. Always indecision. Affair at Hartmannswillerkopf (242).

> [30 December] Morning, Council of Ministers: increase production of heavy artillery, force production of the 105, decrease that of the 75 (243).

> [4 January 1916] Council of Defense.... Necessity of bringing to term isolated operations of the genre of the Hartmannswiller, and the squandering of the lives of our men.... (245–46).

Whether Gallieni and the government recognized the tactical pattern or the disturbing nature of the exchanges, they could recognize the fact that instead of weakening and getting worse, the Germans seemed to be getting better. And over and above that was the question that anyone with even a shred of military experience could ask: had the French General Staff lost its collective mind? What was the point of continuing these futile attacks in which France's elite troops were being massacred? What would happen if the Germans attacked somewhere else on the same scale as in the Argonne? In *La Percée,* Jean Bernier observed that "Joffre pleased himself by the sound of snorting 'I gnaw at them,' and threw, or let be thrown against the strands of wire and the German machine guns the best of the French blood."[19] By the end of 1915, Joffre's nibbling and gnawing had an unexpected twist: the government was beginning to smell a rat, the minister of war most of all.

THE SECRET

Gallieni shared with Joffre a certain disdain for the soldier-parliamentarians of the Third Republic, and a man like Driant was suspect in any event: in his writings he aspired to military competence. But in any event, the defenses, unlike claims about victory, were concrete—both literally and figuratively. The question of Verdun's readiness—unreadiness would perhaps be a better word—was a scandal of the first order. But in one sense, it was beside the point.

What the French General Staff had done, on 5 August 1915, was to reclassify Verdun in such a way as to take away its autonomy. It was no longer *a place forte*, administered by a military governor who reported directly to the High Command, but the *Region Fortifiée de Verdun*, subordinate to the local army group commander. The new commander of Verdun, General Herr, now reported to the commander of the Center Army Group, General Dubail. The troops of the garrison were now combined and assigned to infantry divisions, and one of Dubail's first orders was for the removal of supplies and equipment from Verdun.

The August decree made it clear that the original concept had been discarded. The fourth article begins by saying that "the defense of territory depends exclusively on armies in the field," and that "it is therefore more useful to employ the troops of the *places* in the execution of works at the front," while the fifth article begins with the ominous phrase "the disarmament of the *places*."[20]

On 4 October 1915, orders were issued detailing what to do in the case of an enemy breakthrough. The solution: blow up everything that could be destroyed, and to that end high explosives were shipped in and plans were drawn up detailing what was to be done. Embarrassingly, exact copies of those same maps turned up in the pockets of German officers during the February offensive, enabling them to find their way about and also to dismantle the explosive charges. And also providing pretty conclusive proof that there wasn't much going on in the French Army of any importance that the German Army didn't know about.[21]

Militarily, the French General Staff decision was sensible. The only fort the Germans had failed to take was Troyon, now an unusable pile of rubble sitting on the right bank of the Meuse. Politically, it was a decision France couldn't afford. But in any event, the French General Staff simply lied to the government. As late as 15 February 1916, Colonel Herbillon,

Joffre's liaison with the government, was assuaging their fears. This conversation is fascinating, not least because Herbillon records it himself.

> "General de Castelnau," I tell them, "visited the RFV and in particular the northern front, that seems more especially targeted by a German attack. He has pointed out work to complete the system of defense.... he has been satisfied with what he saw and thought that it will be able to hold."
>
> "This attack is certain?" the president asks me.
>
> "Everything warns us of that . . . I do not doubt we therefore will have a rude shock to undergo."
>
> "Will it hold?" asks Briand.
>
> "I believe so, but it is necessary not to have illusions here, and I believe it very likely our first lines will be taken. We will stop them after that, as they stopped us in Champagne, but it is necessary to avoid panic when parts of our lines are yielded on the first day."
>
> "So ultimately, finally, they won't take Verdun?"
>
> "No. General Joffre himself has attended to this for a long time. He has taken measures, brought troops closer in and ordered heavy artillery in considerable numbers, but there is no need to hide the fact that that part will be rough."
>
> "The essential is that they will not seize Verdun! It would be a disaster."[22]

Neither Briand nor Poincaré was a neophyte. Government functionaries had been lying to them for years, and both of them get right to the bottom line: "Will it hold . . . so in the last analysis the Germans won't get it?"

THE GERMAN PLAN

By contrast with the Allies, von Falkenhayn, the overall German commander, had managed his resources well enough during the first sixteen months of the war. Even the most visually challenged among the Allied staffs could see the results. A combined Austro-German-Bulgarian force had destroyed Serbia so completely that the debris of the Serbian Army had to be taken offshore to Corfu by French naval vessels. On the Eastern Front, the *Ober-Ost* had smashed the Russians back all along the line.

Contrary to the Allied predictions of immediate gloom and doom for the Habsburg Empire in the event of a war, Austro-Hungarian armies were keeping the Italians at bay along the frontier, and bearing a heavy burden in the East as well. The Bulgarians, who had supplied almost half the manpower for the Serbian offensive, were keeping a growing Anglo-French force penned up in Greece. Aided by a few German officers, Turkey, the "Sick Man of Europe," was giving the British major problems in Gallipoli and Palestine. Germany's three allies were more than holding up their end of the table.

But holding one's own was hardly the same thing as winning. The Allies still had plenty of men—and, what was worse, plenty of confidence. Even the pessimists believed it was simply a matter of time, better organization, more ammunition, the right kind of guns. And since they had simply been lied to from the start about the course of the war thus far, the populations of France and Great Britain were confident of victory.

A curious sort of gap thus began to emerge. Not the gap between the reality of the battlefield and the myths the Allies spun about it, nor the gap between the casualty rates of the two sides, but one more basic and fundamental to the nature of warfare. Simply put, it was the growing gulf between what the German Army was actually doing, and what the Allies assumed it was doing.

We have already seen a glimpse of this with the crushing of the Belgian forts. Not understanding the nature of the tactics and weapons the Germans deployed, the Allies moved from error to error. They first assumed that the forts were being besieged using the same mid-nineteenth-century techniques they would have employed. As the news worsened, they decided it was all because of human wave attacks, and then, finally, as the news began to trickle back, they decided it was all entirely owing to the new super-heavy guns.

But that was simply the tip of the iceberg. By the end of 1915 the German General Staff had come to some fundamental decisions about modern warfare, decisions that would change how the war was conducted. Decisions and actions that the Allies never really understood. Consequently, as the war progressed, they moved further and further away from any comprehension of what their opponents were doing, what their aims were, and how they set about carrying them out.

In a memorable passage in his memoirs, Lloyd George caustically noted how the Allies spun every engagement into a victory, minimized every setback, and generally painted a picture of a war that bore no relationship to the real one.[23] His unspoken point was that the British and the French General Staff simply lied to their governments about what was going on. This may well be true, but it is more probable that the military misrepresented what was going on because they completely failed to grasp what was happening. Even when they saw the situation, they misread it.

GOALS AND OBJECTIVES

To put it somewhat differently, the Allies were unable to grasp the difference between a goal and an objective. Joffre, for example, had a laudable goal: to run the Germans out of France. And he had a plan: pick a point where the French and British armies butted against one another and attack. What would then happen was fuzzy. The Allied soldiers would break through the German lines, the front would collapse, and the Germans would retreat all the way back to Germany. This breakthrough was simply the idea of the great battle translated into positional warfare. The Germans would either be annihilated or they would be forced to retreat.

The reason the Germans had done this well so far was that they had defined their goal (win the war) by constructing a set of objectives, tangible accomplishments that could be easily measured, and which would move them toward their goal, step by step. The best way to win the war was to beat France on French territory. That meant going through Belgium. In order to move into France through Belgium, the Franco-Belgian fortifications had to be neutralized or destroyed, and quickly enough so that the Allied armies would be caught off-guard and unable to carry the war into Germany.

The Allies had only the general aim of ending the war by beating the Germans somewhere, anywhere, in any way they could. But the German General Staff had concentrated on a series of objectives—concrete and realizable accomplishments that would fit into a plan that would result in their getting to their goal of either winning the war outright, or, at the least, not losing it. The path to both goals, one being the fallback target, was the same.

Germany's conduct of the war in the first six weeks had been remarkably consistent with the objective of hitting the Allies so hard during that period that they would either lose it outright or only be able to continue the war under the most adverse of circumstances. Prewar, von Moltke had lobbied for ammunition reserves using the argument that it would be a long war, not a short one. The first priority, if either of these goals was to be realized, was the preservation of the German Army in the field. In other words, if the choice was between the probability of fatally weakening the army on the chance of a great victory, or preserving it intact for a long war, the correct decision was preservation. That was why the German General Staff had ordered a withdrawal in September 1914. The decision to withdraw was the concrete and practical execution of an action that would allow Germany to achieve its goals, and without which the goal could not possibly be attained.

A second goal, which arose from the ultimate one—one von Schlieffen had never understood—was to insulate the population from the war, so that Germany would be willing to continue it. War, as von Clausewitz had rather pedantically remarked, is simply an extension of politics by other means. Among other things, this meant ensuring there was a political base allowing the war to be continued. So three objectives had to be met: low casualty rates, protection of Alsace, and protection of East Prussia.

In September 1914 von Falkenhayn had turned to the next logical set of objectives. On the Western Front, the way to break through the German lines lay in an offensive coming out of the areas shielded by the Verdun fortifications and rolling up the Meuse. The reason was simple: rail lines. The German position had been carefully chosen so that key rail lines ran laterally, that is, behind the general path of the position, roughly paralleling it. Coincidentally, the point at which the rail lines ran the closest to the front happened to be the riverine plain of the Meuse to the north of Verdun.

So the Germans had pinched off the supply routes into the fortified area, and, by seizing the territory around Saint-Mihiel, they blocked any offensive from developing: German gunners could rake the whole area with fire, preventing troops from detraining and deploying north.

The other critical area was the Belgian coast. By seizing Antwerp and the Channel ports, the German General Staff made German naval operations, and particularly submarine operations, a credible threat. Moreover, they made a blockade a practical impossibility. Finally, by seizing Lille, the Germans gave themselves control over the northern rail network—and forced the Allies to engage in a series of roundabout shuttles. As a result of Lille, the British and the French were more or less forced to run the war in the West as two separate fronts.

Clearly, since all of these things had actually happened, the Germans were quite successful at achieving their goals. And, given the extent to which the Allies were surprised by them, it is fair to say that the British and French completely failed to understand their importance. The pattern had continued through 1915. The significance of von Mudra gnawing his way through the Argonne was that the forest was a great barrier between the relatively open ground both to the west (in Champagne) and the east (the area on the left bank of the Meuse). Possession of the Argonne forced the French to attack in Champagne-Artois, where basically they were forced to attack uphill over open ground against heavily entrenched German positions that had been established at higher elevations.

There was another, less tangible but equally important, objective: what the French called (to use the English equivalent) the moral ascendancy. It was what Grandmaison—who was not nearly as crazy as he was later made out to be—had been talking about before the war, and it was the only part of the theory that Foch apparently ever grasped. Joffre grasped it as well, and even his usually imperturbable persona worried about its loss: the point of the Argonne and the Vosges was that they formed a pattern in which the Germans asserted their moral ascendancy on the field of battle: they controlled the rhythm, dictated the outcome, and boosted the morale of their troops.

THE NEXT OBJECTIVES

Alone of the commanding generals, von Falkenhayn had demonstrated both that he had a proficient army and that he knew how to use it. The decision facing him was what to do next. Joffre—and the Allied staffs—were still framing victory as a goal that could be accomplished only by a great battle in which the Germans would be defeated; a big hole would be punched through their lines, and the resulting breakthrough would destroy their military capabilities. When Joffre predicted he would drive the Germans from France, this was what he meant. The projected offen-

sive on the Somme, in which an enormous British army would partici-
pate, was how the goal would be accomplished, now that the French realized they themselves lacked the resources to break through on their own.

But so far this goal was unrealizable. During 1915, the French had
hardly been able to take the first line of German trenches. Failing to
attain their goal, they failed utterly. By contrast, von Mudra's offensives
in the Argonne had consisted of a series of small manageable tasks, the
successful accomplishment of which ensured a steady progress toward
his goal. Moreover, by focusing on highly specific targets, the Germans
developed specific means to achieve them: the element of surprise, quick
bombardments, the deployment of specially trained troops. French (and
British) troops were still attacking with fixed bayonets and most of their
gear. German troops were carrying sacks of grenades and bundles of
shovels.

But the more von Falkenhayn considered the events of the war, however, the more he saw that the battle the French were aiming at, whether it
was called a classic battle of annihilation, or a breakthrough (*la percée*, as
the French termed it), was impossible.

> Moreover, the lessons to be deduced from the failures of our enemy's
> mass attacks are decisive against any imitation of their battle meth-
> ods. Attempts at a mass break-through, even with an extreme accu-
> mulation of men and matériel, cannot be regarded as holding out
> prospects of success against a well armed enemy whose morale is
> sound and who is not seriously inferior in numbers.[24]

Whereas Joffre thought that all you needed was a bigger hammer, von
Falkenhayn realized that no hammer was big enough. Whether Fayolle
and Pétain had figured this out at the end of 1915 or not, based on what
they said and wrote later on, they certainly had come to exactly the same
conclusion by early 1917.[25]

This was a revolutionary conclusion. In a few sentences, von
Falkenhayn was throwing the military wisdom of the previous centuries
into the trash bin. It might be argued that this was what Churchill (and
later Lloyd George) was lobbying for with his ideas about alternative theaters of action. But alternative theaters of action would simply reduplicate
the same situation: as weak as Austria was, even with having to fight on
two fronts, it was still able to keep Italy from a breakthrough on the

Isonzo. As the months (and years) passed, the Allies would try to solve this problem by piling on more resources. But as von Falkenhayn realized, unless one side was seriously, deeply, inferior both in numbers and in morale, the breakthrough would never happen.

If von Falkenhayn was right, then Joffre's one great idea of a gigantic joint offensive could never be made to work. How then to win the war? France, von Falkenhayn observed in December of 1915, was still hanging on, despite losses that German commanders found horrifying. But those losses simply proved his point. The front will collapse only when "it is clear to the eyes of the French people that, militarily, they have nothing to hope for. Then will their limit [of endurance] be surpassed."[26] By the "limit of their endurance," von Falkenhayn meant not the endurance of the military, but of the population at large. The way to win the war was not to destroy the French Army, but to destroy the will of its population to continue the war. As von Falkenhayn wrote, in December of 1915, the theaters of Paris reopened.

Fair enough, one might say, but so what? Von Moltke the Elder had learned that lesson in 1870: he had destroyed the French Army and taken Napoleon III prisoner, and the French had fought on from Paris for months. If a breakthrough was impossible, what was the alternative?

As the French attacks foundered, the propagandists, stimulated by Allied intelligence, came up with a new and somewhat grisly alternative. It was a never questioned assumption that the Germans were losing two or three or four times as many men as the Allies were, so, therefore, they would eventually run out of troops. Some analysts pegged this to happen at the end of 1915. The French called this rather ludicrous idea the *guerre d'usure*, or war of attrition. As a sergeant in the BEF would subsequently put it, this was the idea that the "abstruse science of war consists in killing more of the enemy than he kills of you, so that whatever its losses—agreeable doctrine—the numerically preponderant side can always win, as it were, by one wicket."[27]

Although the BEF would subsequently elevate this to grand strategy, Abel Ferry was quite right to dismiss it—in the summer of 1915—as "a journalistic formula, not a military one (35). If von Falkenhayn was right, then the British claim that developed during 1917 that the way to win was to destroy lots and lots of Germans, a claim studiously being pushed by the Allies all during 1915, was wrong as well. Armies could sustain serious reverses and heavy losses and still continue to fight.

But von Falkenhayn thought he had found an alternative. Throughout the first sixteen months of the war, the French had exhibited not merely an admirable tenacity and heroic endurance. They had also demonstrated a surprising literalness in their formulation of military objectives, a literalness that had surprised the Germans as much as it perturbed Gallieni. Given the resources of French gunners in 1915, places like the Vauquois and the Lingekopf were basically impregnable.

Hurling masses of infantry against such positions was insane. And yet, as Norton Cru—himself a veteran of the war—remarked, "none of these people were crazy."[28] The stubbornness with which successive attacks went in while the bodies piled up is horrifying. In a way, it is even more horrifying than the subsequent massacres endured by the British infantry in 1916 and 1917, simply because so much of those losses happened all at once, as in the first day on the Somme, when the BEF had nearly sixty thousand casualties.

Whatever the reason, the facts were that the French went after minor objectives with suicidal determination. At almost precisely the same time as von Falkenhayn was putting his strategic musings on paper, Gallieni was writing about how to stop disasters like Hartmannswillerkopf. So the logical question was this: if France was willing to kill off all its alpine troops in a vain attempt to get back a couple of small mountain peaks in the Vosges, which were of use only in the unlikely event of a great offensive there, to what lengths would they go to try to get back something of real importance?

A rhetorical question, and von Falkenhayn answered it. If they were given an objective that the French realized was really important, "the French leadership would fight to the last man to get it back."[29] Based on how they had conducted operations so far, this was certainly true enough. Von Falkenhayn was simply putting the two sides of the formula together. The French would quit only when they finally realized their military impotence.

But this was not a goal, because von Falkenhayn embodied it in a specific place. Places that France could not afford to lose. "If they try to fight for them, whether they are actually in our possession or not, they will destroy themselves militarily. But if they don't try to fight for them, and they fall into our hands, the effect on French morale will be"—and here he used a word, *Ungeheuer*, which means "frightful, ghastly, horrific," as well as "enormous, huge, monstrous."[30]

The trick, of course, was to find just such an objective. And here, too, von Falkenhayn thought he had the answer: Verdun. The largest and most modern set of fortifications in the world. The sector of the front occupied by the fortified region of Verdun was 112 kilometers—nearly as much as the entire stretch held by the BEF. Prewar, even as the French General Staff had stealthily decamped from places like Reims and Lille— to the consternation of political leaders like Jaurès—they had pumped resources into Verdun. Most of the twenty-odd major forts had been rebuilt or modernized. Special retractable turrets had been added, so that the guns were impervious to shelling, and the main forts were capable of withstanding direct hits from the largest guns anyone dreamed could be built.

In the popular mind, Verdun was impregnable. And, as we have seen, France's two senior statesmen, seasoned politicians who had spent decades decoding the utterances of the bureaucrats of the Third Republic, had been repeatedly assured that the defenses were impervious. Joffre had even put it in writing.

So, clearly, Verdun met von Falkenhayn's objective, which he formulated precisely, if awkwardly: "directly behind the French section of the front are strong points, the possession of which the French leadership would fight to the last man." In setting this down, von Falkenhayn had used the plural: strongpoints, the twenty-odd forts surrounding the city. Verdun itself was an indefensible town located in a sort of bowl-shaped depression. By the end of 1915 it was largely a ghost town, and had no military value whatsoever. In fact, the main forts were a good distance— about five kilometers—from the city, and another ten or so from the actual lines themselves. A not unimportant fact: when Herbillon had reassured the government that the Germans would at most get into the first lines of the defense, he had obviously excluded the forts themselves, since no fort was anywhere near the actual front line. The implication is thus clear enough. Von Falkenhayn planned to go after the forts, as these constituted the defenses. When Briand and Poincaré were asking if Verdun could hold, they didn't mean the city, which had no defenses at all, but the fortified positions that surrounded the city.

Thus far, well and good, but von Falkenhayn's plan makes sense only if one condition is met: the Germans could easily mount a credible threat against the forts with the resources they had. And in fact, he specified this quite plainly: "this objective can be met with the limited means we have at our disposal." A not unimportant point. *Ober-Ost* was rapacious in its demands for troops and guns, and, post-Tannenberg, von Hindenburg and Ludendorff, who had been built up as a pair of military geniuses of the first rank, had been steadily claiming that the war could be won in the East.

That they hadn't won already—they claimed—was because they were being starved of support. Von Moltke the Elder had always claimed that it was stupid to attack West; instead the Germans should go East. So the *Ober-Ost* position resonated with a respectable school of thought in the staff, which was anyway not enthusiastic about von Falkenhayn, who, it was thought, owed his position entirely to his abilities as a courtier and was not a full-fledged, card-carrying member of the German General Staff.

Practically speaking, of course, the problem was the one von Moltke the Younger had gloomily foreseen. Germany was fighting a war on three fronts, and simply lacked the resources to do so. Throughout 1915, von Falkenhayn had tried to resolve this problem behind the scenes, trying to get Russia to quit the war. That had failed. So, too, the attempt to keep Italy out of it. So although the Germans had won in the Balkans, which should have theoretically reduced their commitments, they had Italy to reckon with, as well as the possibility of some sort of reignition of the war in the Balkans by the Allies, who were trying to get Rumania in, and had basically occupied Greece and were forcing its government to enter the war on their side.

In all this, von Falkenhayn had two trump cards. The first was the support of the emperor. Wilhelm II had no direct control over the course of the war. Before it had started, he had made such a nuisance of himself at maneuvers that von Moltke had ejected him. Von Falkenhayn kept him distracted, placated, and at arm's length. As one of Wilhelm's better biographers remarks, "The Kaiser's ignorance of the true nature of the struggle in which Germany was engaged was profound and his utility to the military leaders quite limited."[31] He had no more control over the actual course of the war than the pope. But the emperor did have one important duty: according to the constitution he was technically the supreme commander, and, therefore, he had to concur before any senior appointments could be made—or unmade. And the emperor, not without reason, hated Ludendorff, who had been lobbying for the job since September of 1914.

Von Falkenhayn had a second trump card, one he kept carefully hidden. The Germans knew what a good many French officers either knew or suspected, and what Driant had charged: the Verdun forts had largely been abandoned.[32] So long as it had a certain element of surprise, an attack delivered against the forts would most probably succeed, simply because there were so few resources allocated to the defense. In other words, von Falkenhayn was hoping to pull off the same trick that had worked in 1914. The Germans had grabbed Saint-Mihiel before the French could react, and then, at Les Éparges and in the Battle of the Woëvre, let them massacre themselves in an attempt to get it back. Given their losses, and the continued disasters of command, there had to be a breaking point.

Besides, how could Verdun be defended? Both the supply routes in were blocked. Something could be done by the road coming up from the south through Bar-le-Duc, but it would be a formidable task. It was always vaguely possible the French might quit the war entirely if faced with a disaster of enough magnitude. Their resources were hardly infinite, and the BEF was building up at a snail's pace.

An attack on Verdun offered another important advantage. The attack could go in during February, there would be a good bit of daylight, and the ground would be frozen. By the time the low-lying areas began to thaw and turn to mud, the weather would be going against the French, who would then have to make some hard choices. France lacked the manpower to mount two major offensives at once. They would either have to cancel one or, more probably, hedge, and lose both.

The sort of attack envisioned required enormous amounts of ammunition. It also required a great deal of digging. In high-combat zones, the Germans entrenched with a vengeance. Entrenchment is a misnomer. They built encampments out of concrete, sunk into the ground and layered with earth. When shelled, the infantry went to cover. When the shelling stopped, they climbed back out and massacred the attackers, who often were killed before they even got to the (unbroken) wire.

If the bombardment was particularly intense, the defenders simply withdrew, and then threw the exhausted first and second waves out of the positions they had so laboriously reached. So for the Germans, attack and defense were inextricably intertwined. Aided by the presence of the hundreds of thousands of *Pioniere*, who fought alongside them, the Germans were constantly working on their positions. Even today the German lines are easy to find: the trenches have long since eroded, trees grow out of the shell holes, which are partially filled with undergrowth—but the bunkers are all still there. In some places there are whole bunker cities of stone and concrete.[33]

This incessant activity posed the French aerial reconnaissance teams a bit of a problem. By October of 1915, work had begun in earnest on the German side of the lines around Verdun, and by late December and early January, French aerial reconnaissance was picking up the new infrastructure that had been built.[34] Their problem: was it offensive or defensive? It was impossible to tell from the air, or indeed from the ground, since the same shelters could be used for both. But the French were seriously worried by early December.

Even Joffre was concerned, although he didn't admit it. By the late fall, the steady flow of weaponry out of Verdun, which had been going on since its demotion in August of 1915 from a *place forte* to the Region Fortifiée de Verdun, had begun to reverse, proof that the French General Staff was worried. In August of 1915, right before the famous decree, the RFV deployed 828 guns of all sizes, of which 468 were field guns and the remainder heavy weapons. By late November, the number of medium guns had dropped from 332 to 225, but the number of field guns available had begun to increase, as the French moved more infantry units into the Verdun sector. By February of 1916, the Verdun front was rather better defended than is usually made out.[35] But, as we have seen, so was Liège.

NOTES

1. [Colonel] Bernard Serrigny, *Trente ans avec Pétain* (Paris: Plon, 1959), 56.

2. *New York Times Current History, The European War* (New York: 1917), 3.246.

3. According to Lloyd George: *War Memoirs* (London: Odhams, 1938), 1:545.

4. *New York Times Current History,* 5.321.

5. Ibid., 5.255.

6. Ibid. 4.1042–43.

7. Charles à Court Repington, *The First World War 1914–1918, Personal Experiences of Colonel Repington* (London: Constable, 1920), 1:112.

8. *The Personal Memoirs of Joffre, Field Marshal of the French Army,* trans. T. Bentley Mott (New York: Harper, 1932), 2:354.

9. Figures for the average strength by month for the Western Front, the *Iststärke,* are found in the Heeressanitätsinspektion des Reichsministeriums, *Sanitätsbericht über das deutsche Heer im Weltkrieg 1914/18* (Berlin: Reichsministerium, 1935), Tables 147–50 (3:140–43).

For French figures, see General Daille, *Histoire de la guerre mondiale: Joffre et la guerre d'usure, 1915–1916* [vol.2] (Paris: Payot, 1936), 110.

10. See the extensive analysis in Général Edmond Buat, *L'Armée allemande pendant la guerre de 1914–18* (Paris: Chapelot, 1920).

11. See the comments of Hugo Freytag-Loringhoven, *Deductions from the World War* (New York: G.P. Putnam's Sons, 1918), 141. In *The World Crisis, 1916–1918* (New York: Charles Scribner's Sons, 1927), 1.268, Winston Churchill makes the same point.

12. Daille, 41; See the discussion of French heavy artillery in Général [Firmin Émile] Gascouin, *L'évolution de l'artillerie pendant la guerre* (Paris: Flammarion, 1920), 25–34. French sources are unanimous in their negative analysis of French heavy artillery.

13. According to Huber's analysis of French reports, by January 1916, the BEF had 1,119,000 men in France and was holding down 96 kilometers of front, or 15 percent of the total line. The RFV was over 110 kilometers of the front. Michel Huber, *La Population de la France pendant la guerre* (New Haven: Yale University Press, 1931), 115–21.

14. [Général] Joseph-Simon Gallieni, *Les Carnets de Gallieni,* publiés par son fils Gaëtan Gallieni, notes de P.B. Gheusi (Paris: Albin Michel, 1932), 217–39.

15. Huber, 420. The same figures can be found in Abel Ferry, *La Guerre vue d'en bas et d'en haut* (Paris: B. Grasset, 1920), 120–26.

16. For Ferry's computations, see 120–26. Those figures are used in preference to later computations for the precise reason that they were computed during the war from information available to government officials.

17. See the discussion in Jacques-Henri Lefebvre, *Verdun la plus grande bataille de l'histoire.* 10th ed. (Verdun: Éditions du mémorial 1993), who quotes Liddell Hart at length (22–26). The standard discussion in English is in Alistair Horne, *The Price of Glory: Verdun, 1916* (New York: St. Martin's, 1963), 61–62, who, like Liddell Hart (whom he quotes), uses a somewhat scrambled translation of Driant's letter of 22 August 1915 to Paul Deschanel, president of the Senate. See the version used by Lefebvre (48), which is basically a reprint of the letter quoted (in its entirety) by Gaston Jolivet in *Le Colonel Driant* (Paris: Delagrave, 1919).

18. According to Raymond Recouly, *Joffre* (New York: Appleton, 1931), 263–64.

19. Jean Bernier, *La Percée* (Paris: Albin Michel, 1920), 46.

20. As quoted by Lefevbre, 56. In his excellent popular book on Verdun, Georges Blond has an excellent summary of the thinking behind this decree: *Verdun,* trans. Francis Frenaye (New York: Macmillan, 1964), 24–25.

21. Or in the BEF. As we have already seen, the number of instances in which the Germans either struck first or pulled back, spoiling the Allied attack, are far too numerous to be a coincidence.

22. Colonel Herbillon, *Souvenirs d'un officier de liaison pendant le guerre mondial* (Paris: Tallandier, 1930), 1:243.

23. The passage quoted in the introduction to this book; see Lloyd George, 2:1313.

24. Erich von Falkenhayn, *The German General Staff and its Decisions 1914–1916,* no transla-

tor given (New York: Dodd, Mead, 1920), 243. Other passages are my translation. Gregor Dallas, in *At the Heart of a Tiger: Clemenceau and His World, 1841–1929* (New York: Carroll and Graf, 1993), judges Von Falkenhayn's letter to Wilhelm II to be one of the most important documents of the war (487); unfortunately, the key passages are usually taken out of context and the translation everyone relies on is quite poor, the result being it is also the most misunderstood.

25. Fayolle had figured this out as early as June 1915. See the entries in *Carnets secrets de la grande guerre*, ed. Henry Contamine (Paris: Plon, 1964), 78, 109.

26. Erich von Falkenhayn, *Die Oberste Heeresleitung 1914–1916* (Berlin: Mittlerer, 1920), 181.

27. As quoted by Malcolm Brown, *The Imperial War Museum Book of the Somme* (London: Sidgwick and Jackson, 1996), xxi.

28. Jean-Norton Cru, *Témoins* (Paris: Les Étincelles, 1929; reprinted 1993), 15.

29. The whole sentence: "Behind the French lines there are many strong points, for possession of which the French leadership would fight to the last man to hang on to." Falkenhayn 181–82.

30. Literally "the effect of morale in France will be ghastly." The word he uses is *Ungeheuer*. The idea that von Falkenhayn was proposing to embark on a war of attrition rests partly on a misreading (and mistranslation) of his letter and partly on a misunderstanding of the war itself—the idea of a war of attrition had already been floating around for some time in 1915, as previous chapters have made clear. Besides, if the German General Staff thought they could win the war by piling up bodies, all they had to do was stay on the same course. No competent professional soldier would make that argument.

31. Lamar Cecil, *Wilhelm II* (Chapel Hill, N.C.: University of North Carolina Press, 1996), 2:212. The generally accepted idea that von Falkenhayn was writing this letter to get approval for the offensive is clearly nonsensical—in any event work had been going on for some time when the letter was written. As Kitchen has pointed out, the Kaiser's erratic pre-war behavior (caused by birth injuries) had already "convinced the vast majority of the generals that the Kaiser was not capable of playing a decisive part in any future war." Martin Kitchen, *The German Officer Corps, 1890–1914* (Oxford: Clarendon, 1968), 19–20.

32. The extent to which the German General Staff knew all about the problems of the RFV is discussed at length by Colonel [Paul] Rocolle, "Preliminaires de la bataille de Verdun," *Revue historique des armées*, 1975 2.4: 29–58; esp. 49–57.

33. One of the largest is some 1,200 meters off the road which runs from Varennes-en-Argonne to the ruins of Le-Four-de-Paris and then on into Clermont-en-Argonne. It is so well known to the locals that it even appears on the large-scale Michelin maps.

34. See General Becker's summary of rail construction in Lefebvre (65); the discussion of the aerial photos is in Charles Paquet, *Dans l'attende de la ruée: Verdun (janvier–février 1916)* (Paris: Berger-Levrault, 1928).

35. For Verdun artillery strengths, see the annexes in Alain Denizot, *Verdun, 1914–1916* (Paris: Éditiones Latines, 1996), 266–67—some of the totals are wrong, and German gun sizes are misrepresented. Although it is often claimed that the sector was empty of infantry, this isn't true either. In February, Verdun was held by three army corps, with a fourth

detraining, along with two independent divisions. See the extensive discussion in Général M. Daille, *Histoire de la guerre mondiale: Joffre et la guerre d'usure, 1915–1916* (Paris: Payot, 1936), 2:298–99, which gives the same figures as the more elaborate accounting in Jules Poirier, *La bataille de Verdun, 21 février–18 décembre 1916* (Paris: Chiron, 1922), 50–59.

11

1916: Verdun, an Unfinished Victory

*Things are going quite well for the French at Verdun and they are not
the least bit anxious about it.... It is part of our policy to let the
Germans beat themselves to death against the stone wall....The
Germans have lost enormously and they can't afford to.*
        —*Bernard Montgomery, in a letter dated March 1916.*

*My views on the fighting at Verdun were not in any way in accor-
dance with the true facts.*
        —*Montgomery's postwar annotation of the March 1916 letter*[1]

At Verdun, the German Fifth Army had assembled an impressive arsenal: 246 150 millimeter howitzers, 140 of the extremely effective 210 millimeter howitzers, and thirty of the super heavy guns in sizes greater than
280 millimeters, for a total of eight hundred pieces, none of them the relatively ineffectual 77 millimeter field gun.[2] This at a time when, according
to Joffre's own (rather charitable) estimates the entire French Army possessed only sixteen weapons in the super-heavy category.[3] Technically the
French had more weapons in the Verdun sector of the front than the
Germans did, but the figure of 943 guns is quite misleading. Of the guns,
564, nearly three-fifths, were field guns of less than 95 millimeters, and
only 312 of those field guns were modern long-recoil 75s. The two guns
the French had in the greatest numbers, the 90 millimeter field gun and
the 120 millimeter Long, were mechanical-recoil weapons built in the late
1870s. Most of the 279 heavier weapons deployed were mechanical-

recoil weapons designed by DeBange and cast in 1878, and all of them lacked ammunition and shelters.

The point of this overwhelming superiority in firepower was to pulverize the enemy's defenses. Not simply the initial trench lines, but the entire defensive position, in depth, preventing reinforcements from being brought in to repel the attackers. The initial bombardment was short. It began at seven on the morning of 21 February 1916, and continued through the late afternoon.

By the standards of later artillery barrages, when the Allies pounded away for days on end, it was short. But the duration of a bombardment, like counting the number of guns, is a misleading indicator. In terms of real throw weight of high explosive—the only measure that counts—the German bombardment at Verdun was hardly going to be equaled any time soon.[4]

For the first time, a major offensive was coordinated with airpower, used in three ways that would subsequently become more or less standard in warfare: air superiority over the theater through overwhelming numbers, which in turn enabled bombing and artillery spotting. This last was done in two different ways. Six artillery observation units of airplanes (*Artillerie Flieger Abteilungen*) were employed, in addition to seven balloon units deploying fourteen observation balloons (*Feld-luftschiffer Abteilungen*).[5] The difference between the two types of artillery spotting was that the balloons were tethered over German positions, enabling the observers to look down into the other side from a relatively stable platform, while the airplane could cover the entire battlefield. For this system to work it demanded air superiority, and aircraft were pulled in from elsewhere so that the balloons and observers could be protected: the initial complement was sixty-odd planes in ten *Feldflieger Abteilungen*. With this much observation power, the initial barrage could be short. New targets could be acquired and destroyed as the battle continued.

This much had been done before, although hardly on this scale.[6] What was new came with the inclusion of two of the Army's five strategic air squadrons (*Kampfgeschwader der Deutsch Oberste Heeresleitung,* or *Kagohls*), *Kagohls* I and II, usually described as the elite of the German Air Service, reinforced by two additional squadrons (*Kampfstaffeln,* or *Kastas*). Each *Kasta* consisted of six aircraft, and as *Kagohl* consisted of six *Kasta*, the air over the RFV was flooded with aircraft, and during the first week of the offensive they dropped 4,500 kilograms of bombs on targets the guns couldn't reach. As the bombs in use at this time apparently weighed about twelve kilograms, and weight was at a premium on the planes of the era, these totals represented a great many sorties. Twelve-kilogram bombs seem rather puny, but when it is considered that very few artillery shells in use carried even half that much in the way of an explosive payload, the effect was far from negligible. The planes in use in 1916 had the sort of aerodynamics that made extremely slow low-level flying quite feasible: under those conditions, bombs dropped from the air could be surprisingly accurate.[7]

In the popular view, once the bombardment lifted, waves of heavily encumbered infantry struggled out of their trenches and advanced in waves across no-man's-land, where they were mowed down by the machine guns of the defender, or they tumbled into the trenches and fought at bayonet point, or they found nothing but bodies. In 1915, the French had experienced all three. The Fifth Army, prodded by the innovations that had been steadily introduced in 1915 in both the Vosges and the Argonne, had developed a different form of attack, what would eventually be tagged as "storm troop" tactics. Small clumps of infantry and *Pioniere* would make their way cautiously through the rubble. Instead of bayonets, they used grenades and flamethrowers. Machine gun units and teams pulling the newly deployed light mortar followed along behind. The regular infantry came last, to occupy the ground.[8] The "wave" of the attack was more like an action of infiltration.

The other feature of these new tactics was repetition. In the Argonne offensives, von Mudra would pound a section, take it, then pound another section, and take it. A series of hammer blows. In the Argonne, his resources were insufficient to keep up a steady pounding, so there were intervals between attacks. But now Fifth Army was lavishly supplied, so each day there was another attack, and the Germans sliced off another section. The first week at Verdun was the prototype: each day saw another slice cut off. No one slice was very large, or very important, but the momentum it generated was difficult to stop. Almost exactly a year before the Verdun offensive began, General Sarrail had described this method to Colonel Herbillon. "The Germans have seized, in the Argonne, the *supériorité morale*. They conquer parcels of terrain where the loss or gain is of minimal importance, but their operations permit them to conserve a moral ascendancy."[9]

THE OFFENSIVE ON THE RIGHT BANK

Initially, the main thrust of the German attack was the twelve-kilometer upper corner of the Verdun sector, the section between the Meuse and an imaginary line drawn between the villages of Azannes (in German hands) and Beaumont on the French side. This section was defended by two divisions of the French XXX Corps, while a third division held the right-hand side of the sector, all the way down to the Verdun-Etain road). There were plenty of troops farther back as reserves, but the barrage prevented them from deploying. So the six German divisions (and an independent brigade) simply obliterated the dazed attackers. In the course of these first days of the offensive, these divisions were wiped out.

A massive bombardment on the twenty-first lifted in the late afternoon and the Germans sliced off a very small twelve-hundred-meter-deep section of the front. Small, but it encompassed most of the first line of the left-hand sector of the front, a defensive line that ran from Brabant on the Meuse through the village of Haumont and then through the Bois des Caures. At the end of the first day there was some confusion about the extent to which the attacking troops had actually gotten through this first line, but by the evening of the twenty-second, they were well clear both of Haumont and of the Bois des Caures, which was essentially the limit of any projected attack. At that point, new troops moving up would throw the advancing Germans back out of the first line.

Instead, at the end of the twenty-third, the Germans had pushed farther south, this time mostly on the eastern side of the sector, where the first line consisted of the positions running from the village of Ornes, up through Herbebois, and then through the Bois de Ville (which was essentially an extension of the Bois des Caures. By the evening of the twenty-third, only the part of the line around Ornes was still intact. The Germans had essentially taken a two- to three-kilometer slice out of the top of the RFV, so that the line, which on the twenty-first had been a semicircle with a jagged crown at the apex, was now a slightly curved line running from just above Samogneux to just above Ornes.

In the Argonne, von Mudra's attacks had proceeded in this same fashion—but after a few days of biting off small slices, his offensives had stopped because of shortages of ammunition and fresh troops. Whereas here, at Verdun, by the evening of 24 February, the Germans simply kept right on without a break. In fact, the advance on this, the third day of the

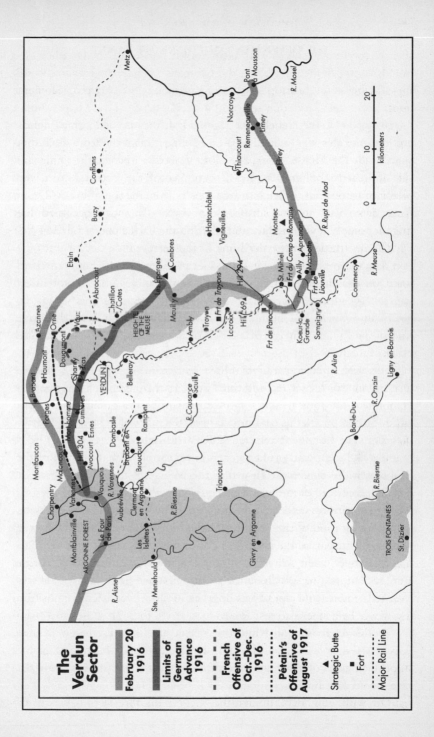

The Verdun Sector

	February 20 1916
	Limits of German Advance 1916
-----	**French Offensive of Oct.–Dec. 1916**
— · — · —	**Pétain's Offensive of August 1917**
▲	Strategic Butte
■	Fort
----	Major Rail Line

kilometers

0   10   20

Metz
Pont de Mousson
Norcroy
Remeneauville
Thiaucourt
Jamey
Flirey
R. Mosel
Conflans
Hattonchâtel
Vigneulles
Montsec
Frt du Camp de Romaine
Apremont
R. Rupt de Mad
Buzy
Combres
St. Mihiel
Ailly
Marbotte
Frt de Liouville
Commercy
R. Meuse
Etain
Les Éparges
Hill 294
Abrocourt
Chatillon /-Cotes
Mouilly
Frt de Troyans
Hill 269
Frt de Panoche
Koeur-la-Grande
Sampigny
Azennes
Orne
Vaux
HEIGHTS OF THE MEUSE
Troyen
Lccroix
Ambly
Haumont
Douaumont
Bezonvaux
Belleroy
R. Aire
Le-Baoni
Sharny
Tavas
VERDUN
Scully
R. Causarce
Forges
Marre
Cumieres
Dombasle
Rambnt
Montfaucon
Malancourt
Esnes
Brabant en A
Broucourt
R. Ornain
Ligny en-Barrois
Charpentry
Hill 304
Avocourt
Bar-le-Duc
R. Biesme
Vauquois
Varennes
R. Varennes
Aubréville
Clermont en Argonne
Triaucourt
Montblainville
Le Four de Paris
ARGONNE FOREST
Les Islettes
R. Biesme
Givry en Argonne
TROIS FONTAINES
St. Dizier
R. Aisne
Ste. Menehould

offensive, went over twice as far as any of the previous days. On the westernmost sector of the right bank, the Germans ran past the French second line, which was the position based on Samogneux, hill 344, and Marmont Farm.

In late 1915, the French had decided that they needed a third defensive line, and this was defined as a line running from the Côte de Talou, right beside the Meuse, along the Côte de Poivre and then through hill 378 and on to Bezonvaux. By the evening of the twenty-fourth, the Germans were about twelve hundred meters from the top of hill 378, and about twice that distance from Bezonvaux. They had occupied the approaches to the Talou ridge, and were on the back slope of hill 344.

The penetration of the third line of the defense didn't occur until the next day, the twenty-fifth, when the Germans pushed the line in around Fort Douaumont. Although the ruins of the town held on, the fort itself was taken, and the Germans went past the ruins of the village of Bezonvaux, which had been the eastern anchor of the third defensive position and the northwestern anchor of the second line for the eastern sector of the front.

This was, of course, a grave blow. As Bezonvaux had been a double anchor point for the second and third lines, Fort Douaumont was the center point of the fourth (and final) defensive line the French had established. To compound this calamity, late on the night of the twenty-fourth, an order had been sent out from RFV headquarters (General Order Number Eighteen) calling for a general evacuation of that portion of the southeastern Verdun sector known as the Woëvre.[10]

The effect of this order, when coupled with the collapse of the key defensive positions, can easily be imagined. The (mostly) *Landwehr* units surged forward, advancing at what in this war was great rapidity. By the evening of the twenty-sixth, the Thirtieth *Landwehr* Brigade had advanced over eight kilometers, and by the twenty-seventh, as the Germans stopped to stabilize their positions, the French had lost everything to the north and east of Les Éparges, and the new defensive position that would be delineated was alongside the road that ran southward from Eix through Chatillon and Haudromont and then into Fresne-en-Woëvre (which was now in German hands), a piece as large or larger than the total Allied gains on the Somme later in the year—and this was only the sixth day of the offensive.

The advancing Germans had now come up abreast of a westward

loop in the Meuse, the portion of the river between Vachereauville and Champneuville. The loop is dominated by the Côte de Talou, a 280-meter ridge, which, as it goes inland, rises to become hill 344. The next ridge to the southeast, which also dominates the riverine plain, is the Côte de Poivre. The only other geographical feature of any importance remaining on the right bank was the Côte de Froidterre, a skinny ridge aimed directly at Verdun, and an L-shaped ridge on which there were three forts (Souville, Michel, Belleville).

By the night of the twenty-fifth, the westward portion of the line, the sector assigned to the VII (German) Reserve Corps, was lagging behind the central portion. Two reserve regiments held a line solidly to the south of the ruins of Bezonvaux, while on their right, two regiments were encamped around Fort Douaumont, and two more were on the north side of Douaumont village. On the twenty-sixth, troops from the Twenty-first and Twenty-fifth Divisions, which had been positioned on the south side of the ruins of Louvemont and atop the Côte de Poivre, launched an attack aimed at securing the westernmost side of the line. Simultaneously, the Reserve Division attacked in the direction of Vacherauville, with an eye to consolidating the positions on the Talou ridge.

In the next six months the Germans mounted offensive operations on the right bank that secured more ground and netted them some important successes—the capture of Fort Vaux being the most spectacular. However, by 28 February 1916, hardly a week after the offensive had begun, 90 percent of the territory the Germans would ultimately possess on the right bank was firmly in their possession.

As far as casualties go, French records lump the whole period from the twenty-first through the tenth of March (in some systems, the fifteenth) together, which means that casualties in the left-bank operations, started on the sixth, were included as well. However, clearly the vast majority of the losses during the initial period were sustained on the right bank. In the first five days of the fighting, the French had losses of 681 killed, 3,186 wounded, and 19,593 missing, this last an unusually high figure, given the number of identified dead.[11] As such figures suggest, the defending French units were simply obliterated. Although casualties in the two German reserve divisions, which had borne the brunt of the initial fighting, eventually became heavy enough, in these first days the losses were relatively light: for the period running through 20 April 1916, fatalities for both divisions came only to 1,426, with the missing listed as 358.[12]

Through 10 March 1916, French casualty figures came to 6,399 killed, 21,407 wounded, and 17,961 missing, for total casualties of 45,767; in the totals for the next week (the fifteenth), these figures changed enormously: 7,957 killed, 37,983 wound cases, and 33,508 missing, for a total of 69,448. The total strength of the *region fortifiée* Verdun was about 130,000 men on the eve of the battle; nearly three fifths of the force had been put out of action in the first two weeks. The Germans had cut off a swath of territory on the right bank between ten and thirteen kilometers deep, and stretching from above Les Éparges to the Meuse.

THE LEFT BANK OFFENSIVES OF 1916

The initial offensive had been directed at the forts on the right bank of the Meuse, above the city. In February 1916, the front line on the left bank— between the Meuse and Avocourt—was shaped like a floppy straw hat set at an angle on an imaginary head. The high point was at the Meuse, just opposite the village of Brabant. The crown of the hat was a northwesterly bulge between the villages of Bethincourt and Malancourt, which was about five kilometers across and about three kilometers deep. Roughly four kilometers back from the line was what might reasonably be called a double-humped ridge. The easternmost hump was a 260-meter-high lozenge-shaped plateau covered with trees, known since time immemorial as Le Morte Homme. Observers there could see across the river plain and on to the reverse slope of the Côte de Talou, and thus the argument that as the Germans advanced on the right bank, the left bank became more and more of a concern, since two kilometers to the south of Le Morte Homme was another tree-covered ridge, the Bois Bourrus. The forts of the northwestern sector of Verdun were located on the reverse slope. Observers on Le Morte Homme could direct artillery fire from the guns sheltered by the ridge of the Bois Bourrus. Although observers in the forts along the southerly ridge had some lines of sight into the German advance on the other side of the riverine plain, the key position was Le Morte Homme, as observers there had a fine view of the terrain on the other side of the river.

Although ridge is a convenient term, in reality the ridge is two distinct segments with a marked valley between, which is where the village of Bethincourt was located in 1916. Immediately to the left of the valley is a very broad-based hill, 304, which, as its name suggests, is 304 meters high. Or was in 1916: by 1918 it was only 290 meters high. This hill is connected to an irregular mass of raised ground; indeed at this point the whole area is about 280 meters above sea level. The hill commands the lower ground between Le Morte Homme and the ridge of Bois Bourrus, a valley about twelve kilometers long and seven across.

The Germans began by attacking the easternmost part of the line, that is, they ignored the bulge, and attacked along the five-kilometer strip that ran from the Meuse to Bethincourt. After a bombardment on 6 March, which French observers thought as heavy as the one that started the offensive, three German reserve divisions moved the line forward so that the Bethincourt-Malancourt bulge was now an obvious salient. By the fourteenth, the Germans, in three attacks, had pushed all the way to Le Morte Homme and were in fact in possession of the end facing the river, their line being anchored outside of the village of Cumières.

The second phase of the offensive began on the twentieth, when the Eleventh Reserve Division, reinforced by a brigade, whacked off the top of the bulge in two attacks. The first (20–22 March 1916) basically caved in the western base of the salient (the part from Avocourt to Malincourt), while the second (28–30 March) took the village itself. The Germans had now taken all of the original bulge in the line. Additionally, through their coup of the twentieth, they had possession of the western approaches to hill 304, which meant that the French defenders were holding a line that was beginning to curve back in on itself.

On 4 April 1916, the Twelfth and Twenty-second Reserve Divisions launched another round of attacks on the eastern end, in which they seized the whole top of Le Morte Homme, while on the twenty-first, the Eleventh Reserve Division attacked across the remnants of the bulge (the new one created by the March offensives) and sliced that off as well. The line was now a more or less straight one, which ran from the end of the Bois d'Avocourt to just outside of the village of Cumières.

The French were now reduced to the upstream side of the ridge itself. In May the Germans launched three more attacks, using troops from three newly deployed divisions. The initial attacks (4–8 May) aimed at driving through to the top of hill 304; a second attack (18–21 May) aimed to pinch off the ends of the hill. A final offensive, which began on the twenty-fourth, caved in the right (Meuse-ward) side of the line. The Germans now had everything except the peaks of the two hills. But, as was the case with the earlier peaks, the portion the French had control of had no real value except as propaganda, since the Germans had occupied the Meuse-ward portion of the plateau in March.

Although starting in May the French had made determined counterattacks, and these continued through August, the Germans held on to a large section of ground for about a year and a half, until Pétain's August 1917 offensive forced them off the heights of the ridge. Even after that, the Germans retained all the initial French positions in the territory between the two hills and the original front lines until September of 1918.

The left bank was the only area of operations in which the Fifth Army was forced to mount direct frontal assaults of the type the Allies mounted all throughout the war: attacking divisions had to fight their way uphill across ground that alternated between marsh and woods. The total casualty list came to fifty-six thousand, although these figures take the fighting well into July. Almost exactly one out of every five casualties sustained was owing to the left-bank fighting. French casualties, although not separated out, were probably about the same—which for the Second Army was certainly a distinct improvement. The Germans ended up with a slice of the Verdun front that was roughly twelve kilometers wide and five kilometers deep, as a result of an offensive operation conducted by forces that never totaled more than three divisions at any one time.

Pétain always thought that the German left-bank offensive would have been successful had it been delivered earlier, before he had set up the defense. The crown prince felt that the offensive should have been stopped much earlier, blamed his chief of staff (von Knobelsdorf) for basically going behind his back and over his head to German General Staff, and ultimately (in August) had him sacked.

While fifty-six thousand casualties (killed, wounded, and missing) for sixty or seventy square kilometers seems far too high a price to pay— regardless of the value of the territory conquered—the BEF had more casualties in these same three categories in less than twenty-four hours on the first day of the Somme and achieved nothing whatsoever. The slice the Germans got on the left bank is about the same as the territory gained in the Allied Second Champagne and Second and Third Artois, it had infinitely more military value, and it was gained at a fraction of the cost in manpower.

THE THIRD SERIES OF ATTACKS: APRIL THROUGH AUGUST

The March attacks are often called the Battle of the Wings, because most of the fighting occurred on either side of the initial attack point, with the fighting in the months that followed being termed the "Battle of Attrition." Although it is true that their initial attacks, which encompassed roughly the space of a month, were the ones that won the greater part of all the ground seized and held through 1916 and on into the fall of 1917, it is misleading to see the German attacks as being indecisive or for minimal gains.

In planning the Verdun offensive, the German General Staff had undoubtedly been aware that once summer arrived, they could expect Allied offensive operations to commence on many different fronts, including the Western. One of the great attractions of Verdun was that it was a place ideally suited to von Mudra's style of offensive, and could be conducted economically in terms of manpower. The German General Staff basically had no reserves. Once an offensive began somewhere else, it could be stemmed only by the diversion of resources. So far the Germans had been able to use their still substantial superiority in firepower to compensate. But the guns, like the men, would have to be diverted when the next offensive began. Moreover, the situation in the summer of 1916 looked to be much worse than in 1915. Germany could look forward to a BEF close to the size of the initial deployment of the French Army in 1914, and both the Italians and the Russians still had plenty of fight left in them. Anyone could pinpoint the most favorable month for operations to begin: June, when the ground had dried out from the spring thaw (or rains), and when the hours of daylight were at a maximum.

Nor did it take a military genius to figure out that when pressed hard on the Western Front, the Allies would scream loudly for help from elsewhere. Consequently, a German offensive that started in February (and was already two weeks late owing to the weather) had only about three months to achieve any major goals. After that, the best that could be hoped for would be that as the French resorted to their customary attack-at-any-cost behavior in an attempt to gain back the lost ground, they, too, would lack the resources to stage a massive offensive. But in any event the clock was running, and as the weeks went by, and the spring set in, the German General Staff became increasingly less parsimonious with resources, in an attempt to preempt or at least cripple the coming offensives.

Subsequently, this would be interpreted as desperation, but it made good sense. All the more so because the French were slow in falling back on their traditional response. When April arrived and the French General Staff found itself—somewhat to its collective surprise and relief—still hanging on to the last line of the Verdun defenses, an immediate campaign began to force Pétain to go over to the offensive. On 8 April 1916, he received a rather peremptory telegram from the High Command urging him to begin "a vigorous and powerful offensive to be executed with only the briefest delay."[13] Given the situation during the first week of April, the timing of the telegram was exquisite. Far from being able to go over to the offensive, French troops were hardly able to contain the steady advances of their opponents. On the seventh, the Germans had bitten off the top of the left-bank salient, the whole area between Haucourt and Bethincourt, including most of the villages themselves. In fact, the French had abandoned the latter rather than lose men in a hopeless defense.

After 1 May 1916, when Pétain was kicked upstairs to relieve him of direct command over the Verdun operations, and replaced by the more suitably offensive-minded Nivelle, these suicidal offensive operations started in earnest. German attempts to force a closure before the offensives began and French attempts to mount a countering offensive substantially complicated the course of the battle. Rather than being the carefully scripted affair that von Mudra's offensives had been, it became much more opportunistic. On the one hand, the Germans sought to profit by French counterattacks, while on the other, they systematically went after the key points in the line.

On the left bank, the Germans continued with their April offensive, and by 3 May, they had basically eliminated the northeastwardly thrusting bulge in the French lines. As this happened, a new bulge began to emerge. To the northeast of the village of Spinne, in the Bois d'Avocourt, the Bavarians began to work their way around hill 304, just as the main force established itself on the crest. On the other end of the line, by the Meuse, the Germans seized what was left of the village of Cumières. By 29 May, they were well to the south of the ruins, and the French were hanging on to the highest part of the reverse slope of Le Morte Homme.

As far as artillery spotting goes, the military value of the high ground positions the French had held on the left bank had been nil for some time, and by the end of May the positions served no purpose at all. The portion of ground the French struggled so desperately to keep, and fought to regain, is (or was in 1916) actually forty meters lower than the portion the Germans had already taken. Similarly, the French possession of the actual crest of 304, although it sounded good on paper, was in reality of hardly any value now.

On the right bank, there were two distinctly different types of operations. In a series of discrete operations, the Germans expanded their control over the areas around Fort Douaumont and essentially surrounded Fort Vaux, their eventual objective being Fort Souville, which was the last thing standing between them and the town itself. The distances involved are greater than is usually assumed: at the beginning of March the nearest German positions were about three kilometers from Fort Vaux and about four kilometers from Fort Souville.

On 8 March the V Reserve Corps began a carefully planned offensive that by the nineteenth had pushed them through the village of Vaux and up against the fort, while their neighbors on the right extended the area around Fort Douaumont. Although this last was insignificant in terms of territory, it was of great tactical significance: any French attack aimed at recovering the fort would effectively be charging down a dead-end alley, with the fort itself being the end of the alleyway (in May the French found this out the hard way). At the same time, the Germans opened up the left end of the line, pushing forward along the Etain-Verdun rail line, operations that opened up the possibility of encircling the ruins of Damloup and setting up an attack against Fort Tavannes.

These very careful operations, which were directed by von Mudra himself, were simply the preparation for the next offensive. But von Mudra's gnawing paid off. On 2 June, Fort Vaux was stormed by *Pioniere*, who used satchels of grenades to destroy embrasures left untouched by the heavy shelling, and pickaxes to break through the debris blocking some of the entryways and the heavily damaged gun turret (which had taken a direct hit from a 420 millimeter shell). Commandant Raynal, the irascible commander of the fort's garrison (five hundred men plus about a hundred stragglers) held on for six days, while the German engineers blocked the air vents, and with flamethrowers—a weapon that had been operational since February 1915—they forced their way deep into the fort. On 8 June 1916, with no reinforcements—and no water—Raynal surrendered.

In the next few weeks (until 12 July), the Germans systematically developed a large salient on the right bank. The northwestern end was anchored at Thiaumont; the southeasterly corner was anchored on a natural outcropping called Le Nez de Souville, on the southern edge of the Bois Fumin, in front of Vaux. The salient bulged out at each end, one end, the northwesterly, heading toward the ouvrage of Froidterre, the other, much larger, enveloping the ruins of the village of Fleury. This final offensive was spearheaded by the newly formed *Alpenkorps,* and to their left the Germans pushed out a smaller bulge from Fort Vaux.

The period from 23 June to 12 July was possibly the most critical in the battle. In terms of territory gained, this was the biggest slice on the right bank since the end of February: at the center the *Alpenkorps* advanced about three kilometers over a front of about the same length. Not a great deal, but at this point the Germans didn't need to advance a great deal: they were already hitting the downward slopes going into the town proper. The next step seems equally clear: a thrust along the rail line down into the city itself, while the wings enveloped the final defensive position. On paper, there was still a line of forts, anchored by Souville. But Fort Souville, which had never been upgraded from its early years, was at this point an ungarrisoned ruin temporarily occupied by lost infantry, and the older forts on either side, Tavannes and Belleville, were also in ruins.

THE FRENCH RESPONSE

In April, Mangin, the general commanding the Fifth Division, had suggested a plan to recapture Fort Douaumont, which was clearly a high priority, and he estimated it would take four divisions. In May the plan was approved, although with only two divisions. Mangin's apologists suggest this is the reason for its failure. However, after the March efforts around Douaumont, the whole area was like a giant one-way trap. Even a brief look at the map makes clear that an attack aimed straight at the fort would be difficult. Moreover, the Germans, who at this stage still had much more effective firepower than the French did, were already showing the way with their offensive against Fort Vaux—isolate the fortification, not storm it head on.

But this is exactly what happened. On 22 May, troops from the French Fifth and Thirty-sixth Divisions stormed the fort, after what observing officers felt was the most well-coordinated artillery barrage they had yet seen. The day got off to a good start with the loss of six German observation balloons, and the advancing French were on the top of the fort in eleven minutes. The problem was that this was hardly a good place to be in the middle of a battle. In fact, it was more or less like climbing to the top of the mast before the ship slides under the water and you drown. Although a counterattack was launched the next day, it failed. German infantry mopped up the survivors, and by seven the next evening (the twenty-third) everyone else had surrendered. Mangin's superior officer, General Lebrun, ordered him to attack yet again; this was apparently too much even for Mangin, who refused, since his division was essentially now destroyed, having lost 130 officers and 5,507 men in five days.[14]

It's very difficult to see how this operation had any hope of success. Not only did the infantry basically have to mount an assault into a cul-de-sac, with German positions on three sides of them, but there is no record of any provisions having been made for what they would do when they got to the fort itself. Apparently the plan was based on the assumption that the French artillery would simply punch holes in the fort, and the infantry would find the defenders dazed and unable to mount a defense from the ruins.

This reflects a rather curious confidence in the power of heavy artillery. One that the German commanders obviously didn't share, even though at this stage their artillery was still bigger and better coordinated than the guns of their opponents. On 21 February, the Germans had sent out small advance parties, a combination of patrols and reconnaissance in force, ascertaining how bad the damage to the French positions had been. But, having spent the first part of the war mounting assaults without any effective artillery support, officers like Mangin apparently believed that its mere existence would solve all their problems.

In early June, as the situation around and inside Fort Vaux worsened, General Nivelle, who had replaced Pétain as the overall commander for the Verdun front, ordered an attack to rescue the fort. Four companies of infantry, specially equipped with scaling ladders, were to conduct the attack, which went in on 6 June. But much the same conditions now prevailed around Fort Vaux as at Douaumont. When the attacking troops were slaughtered, Nivelle proposed a second attack, in which a brigade would be pulled from the left bank, trucked across the river, and then thrown immediately into action.

When the Germans began eating away at the right bank in late June, Mangin—by now promoted to command of an army corps—simply ordered counterattacks with no apparent concern for losses or results. On 15 July, Mangin ordered the 37th Division to retake Fleury, which had been taken by the *Alpenkorps* the week before. This attack was such a disaster that on the eighteenth, Pétain, as commander of the center group of armies, and thus technically still in charge of Verdun, stepped in and stopped all further attacks except in cases where he was assured the preparations had been adequate.

So far the French had behaved exactly as von Falkenhayn had wanted them to, and, despite Pétain's calm, sensible leadership, there were plenty of signs that the French Army was cracking. In fact, a great deal of the German success was a result of French bungling. Chronologically, the first was General Order Eighteen, which signaled an evacuation of the Woëvre, and was received by the divisions involved just before midnight on 24 February 1916.[15] The next day, for reasons that have never been explained, General Balfourier, who had before him an order prescribing that the right bank was to be held position by position, refused to transmit this new order. As a result, the whole southeastern area of the sector, generally known as the Woëvre plain, was simply abandoned, together with about 5 percent of Verdun's heavy weapons.

Nor is there any valid reason why it shouldn't have been held. The opposing German forces south of the Verdun-Etain road consisted of one cavalry brigade and five *Landwehr* regiments. The area had been bombarded, but some of the shelling was misdirected—although some of the abandoned guns had already been destroyed, the French could certainly have held their ground here. The evacuation of the Woëvre was a costly mistake, clear proof that the French Army was still infected with the same disease that had cost it so dearly in 1914, when fortified positions (Lille) and strategic sections of ground (the Vauquois, the butte of Montsec) had been abandoned almost without a shot being fired.

Similarly, the fall of Fort Douaumont was also the result of another muddle. If the position was going to be held, the forts should have been garrisoned. Even stripped of their weapons, they were formidable shelters. Douaumont could have provided a secure shelter for a battalion of infantry at least. Moreover, the one turret-mounted gun had not been removed and was still working. But the occupants of the fort consisted of fifty-seven Territorials, commanded by a noncommissioned officer, Chenot. Incredibly, this was still the complement of the fort four days after the attack had begun.

As a result, when cautiously probing German units approached the fort, it was silent, and the infantry and *Pioniere* more or less broke into it. The upshot of it all: nineteen German soldiers led by a lieutenant rounded up the fifty-seven French defenders (who, according to one story, were incredulous to find they outnumbered their captors), and Douaumont, the strongest and most modern of the forts, the largest concrete structure in the world, which turned out to be impervious to the heaviest shells, fell into German hands on the afternoon of 25 February 1916.

Such blunders were not limited to the chaotic period of the initial attack. On 4 September 1916, there was a terrible accident in the Tavannes rail tunnel. Since the rail line going toward Étain was unusable, the tunnel was used as combination aid station and shelter, with electricity being supplied by gasoline engines. The tunnel was a mixture of men, explosives, and gasoline. The wires carrying the electricity weren't insulated. The Tavannes tunnel was a disaster waiting to happen, and when it did, somewhere between five and six hundred men died.

While this incident is hardly in the same category as the others, it suggests a lack of order in the French Army. The Germans were routinely castigated for their ferocious discipline, obsession with detail, and overzealous punctiliousness about minutiae. More sober observers spoke of the Germans as being "well organized."[16] But in a well-organized and properly run army such things as the Tavannes tunnel disaster don't happen. That they were still continuing in the French Army in the summer and fall of 1916 is both an indictment of its administration and an ominous portent of its future.

However, the worst of the disasters is still to be mentioned. When the Germans began their left-bank offensive, they attacked the zone closest to the river first. Having secured a good portion of it, they then switched their troops over to the far end of the RFV, and attacked the area leading up to hill 304. The French positions from there to Avocourt were probably the best organized in the RFV. By rights, the defenders (the Twenty-ninth Infantry Division) should have given the Germans a very rough time.

Supposedly, the defenders were fatigued, worn out by the fighting, and in a surprise attack on 20 April, the Eleventh Bavarians simply caught them off-guard and in two hours captured the whole position, taking the defenders prisoner in the process. A final telephone call from one headquarters said not a shot had been fired. A court of inquiry after the war established that they had surrendered their positions without a fight, although whether they did so out of treason or defeatism, as is often charged—and as more recent researchers believe—or simply panicked when they found themselves in a bad situation, no one really knows.[17]

Ironically, the less well known the calamity, the more catastrophic it was. The fall of Douaumont has generated the most attention. General Rouquerol, commander of the Sixteenth Infantry Division, termed it a disaster "equivalent to the loss of one hundred thousand men."[18] It had been the keystone for the fourth and last defensive line on the right bank. Without it, it was only a matter of time before the other forts fell as well. However, the evacuation of the Woëvre was a worse disaster. For the German defensive line established in August of 1916, the fort was useless, and when the French mounted an offensive in November, they abandoned it without a fight.

But the section of the Woëvre that the French abandoned in a panic, and which wasn't taken back until September 1918, was a serious check. Before February 1916, the Allies, operating out of this section of ground, could have threatened to pinch off the Saint-Mihiel salient at its base and drive deep into German-held territory, as indeed they had attempted in April 1915. But once the Germans had seized it, the only way the salient could be reduced was by a direct frontal assault up and across the heights of the Meuse, an operation entirely beyond the resources of the French and the British. In the long run, the loss of the Woëvre was probably almost as big a disaster as the original loss of the salient had been in 1914.

But the collapse of the Avocourt–hill 304 position on 20 March 1916 was probably the gravest moment of the battle, and despite French attempts to put a good face on what happened, the actual events that led to the collapse, in which two regiments of infantry in strong defensive positions simply quit, clearly prefigured the national nightmare of April 1917, in which the entire army basically refused to go forward.

Actually, the situation on the left bank in April 1916 was much worse. There is a substantial difference between refusing to execute suicidal orders for an attack—or delaying the execution of those orders as far as possible—and surrendering your positions to the enemy. The former was endemic to the French Army and probably to other armies as well. The latter is treason. It suggests an army on the verge of cracking. So do the other problems: this far into the war, the French should have at the very least been able to avoid such disasters as the evacuation of the Woëvre and the garrisoning of Douaumont—and it is precisely this sort of confusion that demoralizes the ordinary soldier.

AFTERMATH

The French, always quick to blow the whistle and signal the end to a battle if they could claim a propaganda victory, deliberately stretched this one out until the end of the year. But as the German offensive wound down in July, and the French attacks didn't begin until late October, this is simply another attempt to spin the outcome of the battle. By any reasonable standard, the Germans had won at the point they wound down their offensive, and it took the French months even to make a partial attack. Nor had German losses been such as to make Verdun a Pyrrhic victory. On the contrary, when compared to the earlier battles in Champagne and Artois—and to the subsequent fighting on the Somme— losses were much less than is usually supposed. Over the course of the fighting, 71,504 German soldiers were either killed outright, died of wounds, or were listed as missing. French losses in the same categories came to 160,000.[19]

The German victory was incomplete, but that was no fault of the officers and men of Fifth Army. The victory was incomplete because the Germans were forced to switch their resources elsewhere to counter the most serious threats they had faced in two years of warfare, not because they had been stopped by French arms at the gates to the city.

NOTES

1. As quoted by Nigel Hamilton, *Monty: The Making of a General, 187–1942* (New York: McGraw Hill, 1981), 103.

2. French and German artillery figures all taken from Alain Denizot, *Verdun, 1914–1916* (Paris: Éditiones Latines, 1996), Annexe 2 (French) and 3 (German).

3. *The Personal Memoirs of Joffre, Field Marshal of the French Army,* trans. T. Bentley Mott (New York: Harper, 1932), 2:597.

4. See the discussions of Allied artillery problems in chapters 12 and 14: the Allies still had very few long-recoil high-trajectory guns in calibers over 175 millimeters: the British barrage on the Somme had mostly been conducted by standard field guns firing shrapnel.

5. Even though Henry Corda observed that *"les enseignements tactiques le plus important de la bataille de Verdun concernent l'artillerie et l'aéronautique"* in *La Bataille de Verdun, 1916: Ses enseignements et ses consequences: conferences faites en 1921 aux sociéte d'officiers suisses* (Paris: Gauthier-Villars, 1921), 35, no one ever talks about the role airpower played. There is the briefest of accounts in Alex Imrie's *Pictorial History of the German Army Air Service* (London: Allan, 1971), 30–33; the data supplied here is taken from him.

6. Although standard histories of the subject, such as Robin Higham's *Air Power: A Concise History* (New York: St. Martin's, 1972), imply that that "in 1914, the major European powers each fielded about fifty aircraft" (13) this is hardly the case. In 1914 the Germans (and the French) both deployed heavier-than-air machines in the low hundreds, their use primarily reconnaissance. German gunners depended heavily on air-based observers for spotting targets. See the excellent monograph in Imrie's misleadingly titled *Pictorial History of the German Army Air Service.*

7. By January 1918, the German Army Air Service was dropping 2,000-kilogram bombs, of which 710 were dropped by the war's end. Paradoxically, the biplanes of this era were better suited to these tasks than their faster and more powerful successors, owing to their ability to "loiter" over a target.

8. The best account of this stage of the fighting is in Georges Blond, *Verdun,* trans. Francis Frenaye (New York: Macmillan, 1964), esp. 58–65. The standard repository of Verdun data is Jacques-Henri Lefebvre, *Verdun, la plus grande bataille de l'histoire.* 10th ed. (Verdun: Éditions du Mémorial, [1993]), who has lengthy quotes from eyewitnesses (without evaluating their reliability), and there is a succinct account of the opening disasters in Pétain, *Le Bataille de Verdun* (Verdun: Fremont, [1931]). I have not found the German studies of the battle to add much to the early French accounts, although Werth, who looked at the German casualty figures, was as far as I know the first analyst to point out that the figures for the missing included prisoners and deserters. See German Werth, *Verdun: Die Schlacht und der Mythos* (Bergische Gladbach, Germany: Gustav Lübbe Verlag, 1979), 386–87. For many years the basic English language account of Verdun has been Alistair Horne's brilliantly written and deeply flawed *The Price of Glory: Verdun, 1916* (New York: St. Martin's, 1963). As the present chapter makes clear, Horne's arguments are hardly supported by the facts.

9. Colonel Herbillon, *Souvenirs d'un officier de liaison pendant la guerre mondiale* (Paris: Tallandier, 1930), 1:106.

10. See the discussion in Lefebvre, who terms this a "criminal fault" (108–9).

11. French weekly figures are all taken from *Service Historique Tome IV*, vol. 1: 294, 649, 650, 651, 652.

12. Heeressanitätsinspektion des Reichsministeriums, *Sanitätsbericht über das deutsche Heer im Weltkrieg 1914/18*, 3 vols. (Berlin: Reichsministerium, 1935), 2:646.

13. As quoted by Yves Buffetaut in *La Bataille de Verdun, de l'Argonne à la Woëvre* (Tours: Éditions Heimdale, 1990), 72. No one else refers quite so explicitly to this telegram.

14. Figures from Blond, 165. It's generally assumed that Allied units in these situations were at their theoretical strength. This was hardly likely. So 5,600 casualties is not 45 percent but more like 65 percent, and in this short a period, there would be no reinforcements to replace the casualties.

15. The only extensive discussion is in Lefebvre (108–11), although there is a brief summary of the situation in Jules Poirier, *La Bataille de Verdun, 21 février–18 décembre 1916* (Paris: Chiron, 1922), 108–9.

16. A direct translation of the expression *"bien organisée"*; interestingly, in June of 1994, a French grounds supervisor at the cemetery of St. Thomas en Argonne used the same phrase in a conversation in which he was describing the administration of German military cemeteries versus his own.

17. Stephan Ryan, in his excellent and well-researched, *Pétain the Soldier* (Cranbury, N.J.: Barnes, 1969), argues that it was as a result of negotiations between the two sides, which is to say, treason, probably brought about by defeatism (93–94). Buffetaut argues it was panic (71).

18. As quoted by Lefebvre (119). This seems an exaggeration, although in some senses, as we shall see, he was right.

19. German casualty data taken from on-site markers currently posted at the German military cemeteries for Verdun. Postwar casualty estimates went into the millions, usually owing to the writer confusing total casualties—which would include the wounded—with the figures for the dead and the missing; and with some analysts then taking those totals and assuming that "losses" meant deaths. See the discussion in Yves Buffetaut (90) and in Werth (387). In November 1916, Abel Ferry reported total French losses (dead and missing) of 148,930 to the government, which suggests that French internal accounting of casualties was reasonably accurate. His report is contained in *La Guerre vue d'en bas et d'en haut* (Paris: Grasset, 1920), 132. Both Churchill and A.J.P. Taylor had noticed that the Germans lost fewer men than the French, but most writers ignored them: the idea of Verdun as "the most senseless episode in a war not distinguished for sense anywhere," as Taylor puts it, was simply too strong. See Winston Churchill, *The World Crisis, 1916–1918* (New York: Charles Scribner's Sons, 1927), 1:90; A.J.P. Taylor, *Illustrated History of the First World War* (New York: G.P. Putnam's Sons, 1964), 123.

12

1916: Massacre on the Somme

*I thought of the Crimea today, and of what another French officer
said then of the English—"It is magnificent, but it isn't war."*
—*French artillery observer on the Somme*[1]

At the end of 1915, Joffre had gotten the British to agree to a major
combined offensive. The blow would be massive, as Joffre and the French
General Staff argued that the only way to beat the Germans was to punch
an enormous hole in their lines, creating a rupture that could not be
sealed off. Ironically, at the same time, von Falkenhayn and the German
General Staff had come to the conclusion that such a breakthrough was
impossible: the areas were too vast, the armies involved too big. The
Napoleonic concept of a battle of annihilation, von Moltke's idea of a
great encirclement after the fashion of Hannibal, both were impossible
maneuvers for ending a modern war.

As we have seen, the Allies were far behind their adversaries both in
the application and integration of technology on the battlefield and in
their strategic thinking. But as the bitter spring of 1916 wore on, the
basics seemed irrelevant. The French were getting desperate for relief at
Verdun. At the end of May, the Allies met to finalize the joint offensive.
Haig wanted to attack in August. Joffre, although in most respects as out
of touch as Haig with the fortunes of the war on the battlefield, at least
could look disaster in the face: the offensive would have to be mounted in
July. By August, at their rate of progress, the Germans would have sliced
off the entire Verdun sector of the front. Haig, who was spoiling for the

battle that would break the Germans and make his reputation, agreed, since there was no real reason to wait for August, and a good many reasons for an earlier date.

There was only one place on the front where there could be a combined offensive. Just north of the Somme River, the newly expanded British section of the front butted up on the French one. This in itself was a major concession forced on the BEF. Haig wanted his left flank on the Channel, and he wanted enough troops in the line so that there was no possibility of the Germans breaking through and cutting him off from his line of retreat.

So in January of 1915 a BEF of 265,000 men was holding down 40 kilometers of a 715-kilometer front. By January 1916, 1.119 million British soldiers were holding down 96 kilometers of a 646-kilometer front. Naturally, this was a sore point with the French, who were beginning to wonder why it was that the BEF required nearly as many troops to hold down a small portion of the front as they did to hold down the entire front. But there was little chance of Haig moving very far, so the French General Staff went for the area where the two armies bordered.

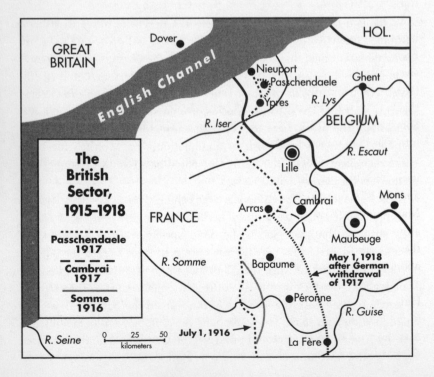

THE PROBLEMS

The junction point was unfortunate. It would have been difficult to have found a worse theater of operations on the entire front. The Somme at this point, just to the east of Amiens, was a muddy turgid stream whose serpentine loops continued over to the west of the small town of Peronne, converting much of the adjacent ground into a bog. In 1916 the front dropped down a few kilometers to the east of the town of Albert. But the Germans, who found no profit in camping out in a swamp, had established their positions on the higher and drier ground to the east. Outside of Albert, the front made a sharp right turn, and then dropped, forming a surprisingly regular line from just northeast of the village of Maricourt to just to the west of the village of Chaulnes.

The dogleg in the line meant that as the offensive progressed, the internal defense line for the Germans would be constricting, while the combination of bog and river running through the area meant that the offensive would be operating on either side of a trough of mud and water. It would thus have no elbow room to expand even if it broke through.

The area between Albert and Peronne was thickly infested with villages and hamlets, and although no town was of any size, and most had been hamlets of a few hundred people, the BEF's projected offensive sweep would force its soldiers to fight their way through somewhere over twenty villages, which posed exceptional difficulties for the infantry of this era. Much of the area not urbanized was forest. So basically, the Somme offensive called for the Allies to attack out of a swamp and up into a heavily forested urban area.

The natural boundary between the two armies was the Somme River itself. However, the BEF had thoughtfully left the swamps to the French, and the BEF boundary ran roughly parallel to the river from the front at Maricourt back to the southwest in the general direction of Bray. So although the combined section of the front was about thirty kilometers, the section occupied by each army was much less: the British stretch was about twelve kilometers, the French stretch about seventeen or so.

This was far too small a front for the classical breakthrough that Haig and Joffre dreamed of to be feasible. Successful offensives either had to be mounted over much larger sections (Saint-Mihiel, Verdun, the Austrian and Russian offensives of 1916), or over much smaller ones (as the Fifth Army had established in 1915). This is hardly a criticism made in hindsight. General Fayolle, who would prove, ironically, as the French Sixth Army commander, the only commander to achieve any success on the Somme, had said this a year earlier, in June 1915.

> In this positional warfare, it is not sufficient to open up a breach, it must be a hole of at least twenty kilometers, without that it is impossible to expand to the right and left. It has to be made with one army and so that another one can pass through. It is not easy.[2]

In other words, if the hole punched through the line was too small, the attacking troops would not have enough room to pass the new troops through the lines and create the rupture. Churchill had hit on this as well, although his reasoning was somewhat different: "Unless a gap of at least twenty miles can be opened, no large force can be put through."[3]

The troops had no real objective other than the abstract one of a breakthrough. Haig's definition of a breakthrough was reaching the small and insignificant village of Bapaume, which lay eighteen kilometers from the front lines, down a ruler-straight road from Albert. Suppose the breakthrough didn't materialize. What would have been accomplished by the offensive? The Somme was a completely worthless piece of territory.

There was no town of any importance whatsoever there, because there were no rail junctions, no important roads, no strategic passes of buttes. The Pozières ridge, which dominated the dogleg, commanded the ground between the Somme and the Ancre (another muddy little stream that had turned everything into a swamp), but it had little significance for the positions to the northeast. In 1900, Bapaume, Haig's breakthrough objective, was a village of less than three thousand people. Today is has thirty-five hundred people, and it never had any military importance whatsoever: "What are Bapaume and Peronne, even if we are likely to take them?" Churchill fumed.[4]

This was von Falkenhayn's analysis turned on its head. Instead of attacking positions that the defense couldn't afford to lose permanently, the Allies automatically gave the Germans the invaluable option of mounting the nastiest sort of defense possible, one where the defenders try to extract a high price in lives for each strongpoint—only to give it up and fall back to the next one.

But the French were desperate, and this was the only area where an attack could be mounted. The English—who, like the French General

Staff were convinced that the Germans were at the end of their tether in terms of men—felt that for the first time in the war, the Allies would have a decisive advantage in artillery. The barrage would go on for days, demolishing the German entrenchments, destroying the dreaded wire, and eliminating the German infantry and artillery. Then the Allied divisions would simply punch through the debris and round up the prisoners.

As May became June, the dependence on heavy guns became more and more important, because the vast sixty-division force had been reduced considerably. Instead of twenty-five divisions, the BEF would deploy only eighteen, divided between the Fourth and Fifth Armies. The initial French idea of forty divisions had vanished completely, to be replaced by two French armies, the Sixth and the Tenth, with less than a dozen divisions. However, the French artillery component was much heftier than the British. Basically, the BEF had one heavy howitzer for every forty meters of the front, and the French had twice that many.' Insofar as the Allies had any real success on the Somme, it was achieved by Fayolle's Sixth Army. By the time the offensive was finally called off, the French had taken over twice as much ground as the BEF and suffered one quarter the losses.

The German Second Army, which was defending this sector, had only seven divisions, and everything had been stripped to the bone to support the Verdun operations. In this one area Joffre's calculations were exact: an offensive by nearly forty divisions would force the Germans to wind down Verdun, or scale it back, whether there was a breakthrough or not. The catch was that the offensive would have to succeed in the first few days, because otherwise the German General Staff would start switching reinforcements over and the defenses would stiffen, assuming the Germans had any reinforcements to shift. That was the other leg of the tripod on which the hopes of the BEF rested. The Germans lacked the manpower to reinforce, heavy guns would smash the defenses and enable a breakthrough, and the mass of the attacking infantry would penetrate the lines.

It was not only the Allied estimates of German manpower that were fantasies. Unfortunately, the other two elements were shaky as well. Although the British were on the threshold of entering their second year of war on the Continent, they had still not mastered the basic lessons. A month before the Somme was scheduled to begin, James Noel Birch, the BEF's newly appointed artillery expert, discovered that "there was not even a list of the guns in France in the office [at GHQ]....There was no department to collect the technical expertise of other nations and nobody watched the tactical development of artillery."[6]

Not surprisingly, there wasn't any tactical development to speak of. So on the Somme, the artillery was still operating on the assumption that shrapnel shells could cut barbed wire and high-explosive shells couldn't. The only gun the British had in any quantity on the Somme was the eighteen-pounder, which comprised three out of every five guns used on the Somme. The eighteen-pounder, an 84-millimeter weapon inferior in every respect to the French 75, suffered from all the same disadvantages on the battlefield: it fired too small an explosive round at too flat a trajectory to do serious damage to entrenched positions.

Not only was this the main weapon in use on the Somme, but three out of every four shells fired by this gun were shrapnel, and almost one third of the high-explosive shells fired by British gunners failed to explode.[7] On close examination, the great barrage was a myth. When the infantry began their attack, they found that the German wire was largely untouched and the German defenders largely unscathed.

The gunners were firing the wrong shells, and the infantry were trained in the wrong tactics. In Germany, where the Reichstag never appropriated enough money for training, the army had been forced to become more efficient in its basic training. In the United Kingdom, with its traditions of a volunteer army, there had never been any pressure forcing the military to train efficiently, or any agency questioning whether the training was related to the task at hand.

As a result, the infantry was poorly trained to operate under the conditions that prevailed on the modern battlefield, and the military seemed to think its recruits were too dense to learn anything other than the simplest of maneuvers. Two years into the war, the British still saw the infantry as men with bayonets stuck in their rifles; consequently much attention was paid to marksmanship and bayonet drill, and very little to real firepower. Even when the soldiers were introduced to such new weapons as grenades, the instruction gave them no clear idea how to use them. "Having crossed No-Man's Land..." began one manual on grenades.

Tactically, the idea of the infantry assault was simple. The infantry would climb out of the trenches and advance across to the other side in a series of long continuous rows, each rifleman carrying with him twenty kilograms of supplies. This, of course, was in and of itself disastrous. French infantry had been abandoning their packs (and carrying only the bare essentials) since early 1915. It was difficult enough to get through the cratered moonscape of no-man's-land intact, much less carrying twenty kilograms.

THE FIRST PHASE

Clearly, advancing in long rows at a walk was suicidal, but that was the plan. On 1 July 1916, the British infantry—all one hundred thousand of them—climbed out of their trenches in four distinct waves, and began to advance across to the other side. The German machine gunners, unscathed by the bombardment, could hardly believe their eyes. In two years of fighting, they had never seen anything like it. As one German who was there wrote: "We were surprised to see them walking. We had never seen that before....When we started to fire we just had to load and reload. They went down in their hundreds. We didn't have to aim, we just fired into them."[8]

Such tactics had hardly even been seen in August 1914, and by this time in the war, the French had abandoned them completely. Captain (later General) Edward Spears, the BEF's liaison with the French, observed both armies attacking on the Somme, and his observations make clear why the French were so much more successful than his own army.

I remember well an incident during the Somme which illustrates how much we had to learn from them in this respect. A joint attack by the French and British had been ordered....The French had already adopted the self-contained platoon as a unit. Tiny groups, taking every advantage of cover, swarmed forward....

Meanwhile, on the left, long lines of British infantry, at a few yards interval and in perfect order, were slowly advancing. Wave after wave sprang forward from the trenches, joining in the parade, for that is what it looked like. And they provided magnificent targets....

The British were soon enveloped in clouds of bursting shells. It looked as if they were advancing through the flames of hell. At times whole portions of the advance disappeared, and when the thick clouds of smoke were dispelled and the greatly thinned lines were once more revealed, they were seen to be far fewer, but still plodding over the deeply scarred and difficult ground at the same even pace.[9]

The British had squandered 1915, producing an army that relied on tactics that would hardly have won them battlefield success in the Crimean War.

British casualties for the first day of fighting on the Somme came to 57,470 officers and men, of which 19,240 were killed, so roughly half of the infantry committed were casualties in the first day of action. By contrast, only 23,628 German soldiers were killed on the entire Western Front for the whole month of July. British deaths in this one day exceeded German figures for such combat-intensive months of the war as August 1914 and April 1915.

At the end of the day, the BEF had chewed off a small piece of ground south of the Albert-Bapaume road, just north of Fricourt. Below Fricourt, where the front made a dogleg to the south, the French had pushed through to the village of Hardecourt, and the British troops on their left had pushed northward, carrying Mametz and Montauban—all penetrations measured in meters rather than kilometers.

Initially, the British commanders were optimistic. But by the fifth, Haig had begun to realize that the first push had failed to break through. Another was planned for the following week, but already the Allies now rationalized the outcome of the battle. It had never been intended to be a breakthrough, rather it was to be a wearing down of the enemy by killing his soldiers in great numbers.

The Germans knew an attack was coming. Conditions on the Somme were so unfavorable, however, that the German General Staff hoped that an extremely aggressive initial defense would bring a halt to operations there. In other words, if the Allies saw nothing to be gained after the initial attacks, they would quit, and not let their men be slaughtered to no avail. Curiously, the German Staff was assuming that there was a learning curve, and that after Second Champagne in the fall of 1915, the Allies had learned when to call off offensive operations.

When it became obvious that the BEF would attack using the same kamikaze methods as the French had used in Champagne a year earlier, von Falkenhayn promptly sacked the Second Army's chief of staff, replacing him with Colonel Lossberg, an expert on defensive operations. He brought with him the mandate to ensure that the defenders used the standard procedures that had been used by all German troops to the east of Reims since early 1915. Henceforth, the defenders would trade territory for lives.

So the Allied territorial gains of July and August, as minimal as they were, were more the result of deliberate defensive tactics rather than their own offensive accomplishments. Despite the mounting bill, the offensive ground on through July and August. Why? By now the Germans had closed Verdun down as an offensive operation. So that part of the objective was fulfilled. The breakthrough clearly was not going to occur—what was the logic in continuing?

The main reason was the fantasy the Allies had about German losses. Haig, for example, convinced that the Germans had no reserves, believed one more push would shatter their lines completely. As the battle wore on into August and September there was the hope that the concurrent offensives in Italy and southeastern Europe would contribute to the strain, and the front would collapse.

But whatever the reason, Haig now seemed possessed by the same ailment that had smitten the French General Staff in Champagne a year earlier. He decided—on the basis of no hard evidence—that the Germans were on the ropes, and continued the offensive. By September, he had a new and secret weapon at his disposal, and, despite the objections of all concerned, decided to use it. On 14 September 1916, the BEF deployed the first tanks.

THE SECOND PHASE: TANKS

The British thought of the tank as a peculiarly, even uniquely, British idea, and postwar armored enthusiasts went even further, claiming that tanks were both a testimony to Britain's (unique) ingenuity and an indictment of a fossilized military. Neither was true. The French and the Russians had been working on the concept for some time. Actually, the Russians were ahead of everyone when it came to the basic idea, as the Russian Army concluded early on that only a tracked vehicle offered any real combat capability, and the Army of the Northwestern Front had a prototype based on the plans of the engineer Porokovskikov constructed in January of 1915.[10] By late 1915 the French were developing tanks on their own, and the Germans, who had less need to develop a weapon to break through the enemy lines, soon followed suit.

Nonetheless, by September 1916, the British had forty-nine tanks ready to go into action. Only thirty-two actually made it to the start line on the British side, and only nine made it across to the German lines and accomplished anything.[11] The idea, of course, was sound enough. A vehicle moving on tracks was capable of traversing much rougher ground than a wheeled vehicle, as it could climb greater elevations. As the area of the track in contact with the ground at any one time was enormously greater than anything on wheels, a tracked vehicle could navigate far softer ground than a wheeled vehicle. Sufficiently armored to escape harm, the crew of the tank would destroy the enemy machine gun positions that had escaped the artillery barrage, and crush the hated barbed wire, so that the infantry could get through the line. If enough tanks could be deployed all at once, they would simply sweep through the enemy position and crush it.

But this unfortunately was a fantasy like the one in which the Allied barrage would so destroy the German positions that the infantry would have no opposition. And the two were incompatible in execution. No tank commander of today would try to navigate across the cratered landscape of the Somme or Verdun—or any of the other battlefields of this war. If the ground is soft enough, a tracked vehicle will bog down in it. If the crater is deep enough, the slope will be too steep for the vehicle to climb out of it. If the crater is wide enough, the vehicle will fall into it.

In 1916, tanks could only cross trenches or craters of less than two meters, and only one of the early tanks, the one designed by Renault, could surmount an angled slope of even forty-five degrees. Unfortunately, the large-caliber shells that the Allies were increasingly relying on to destroy German positions made craters too large and too deep for a tank to cross or climb out of, and the intensive shelling of the first trench line and the barbed wire in front of it created a natural tank trap, forcing the commanders to navigate their way slowly around the various obstacles and craters. In the process, they became vulnerable to enemy fire, since their speed was extremely low.

The British Mark I through V tank was an almost unusable vehicle, and for a very simple reason. In 1915 (and indeed throughout the war), no one had yet designed an engine powerful enough to propel a vehicle of almost thirty tons at anything more than a leisurely walk. Initially, the best the British or the French could come up with was an engine of one hundred horsepower, which was just about sufficient to move tanks Mark I through V along at a leisurely six kilometers an hour on relatively level ground.[12] Just how far off this figure was from the optimal is best revealed by making a simple comparison. The American M4A4 Sherman tank weighed thirty-six tons and had a 430 horsepower engine, while the Russian T34 weighed the same and had a five hundred horsepower diesel.[13] The German Mark III, one of the better designs of the 1930s, weighed only twenty-five tons and had a three hundred horsepower engine. As a result, all three tanks were capable of cross-country speeds of very close to twenty kilometers an hour.

Speed was important. An object the size of a garage, moving at the speed of a leisurely walk, is an easy target to hit. Once German soldiers got over their immediate panic at this new weapon, they discovered it was easy to destroy. Given the limitations of engine performance, the first tanks had only minimal armor, so one of the other main assumptions— that the tank would be impervious to infantry fire—turned out to be as false as the one about performance across no-man's-land. Given the size of the battlefield a tank had to traverse, and the speed with which it was moving, it could be put out of action even by mortar fire.

The Germans would learn all this quickly enough. But in the short run, they hardly needed to; mechanical unreliability accomplished their task for them. By the next tank attack, on the twenty-fifth, at Thiepval, 70 percent of the tanks deployed failed to clear their own lines. The birth of the tank was hardly auspicious. Apologists for armor would later claim that the whole problem was that tanks were employed on the wrong terrain and in insufficient numbers. Had they been deployed in the right conditions, and in masses, they would have been a decisive breakthrough weapon. The record in 1917 and 1918 suggests otherwise: basically between half and two thirds of the tanks deployed would be out of action in twenty-four hours, and, within forty-eight hours, the number available would be roughly one quarter to one third of the original force.[14]

THE BALANCE

After the failure of the new weapon to produce the great breakthrough, the Somme deteriorated into a repeat of Second Champagne. The French and the British fought doggedly on through November, when the whole operation was finally wound down. In five months, they took a roughly rectangular section of territory of possibly four hundred square kilometers, a very small piece in proportion to what the Germans had achieved at Verdun.

But the important thing in measuring territory is not acreage but its actual military value. The left bank at Verdun, for example, was valuable territory. In order to mount operations on either side of the ridge, the French had to reclaim the ridge itself. This, of course, illustrates the crucial difference between the two sides. The Germans picked their objectives carefully, and went for the ones that had serious military value. The Allies simply picked a spot on the line and tried to break it open. It was always possible to claim there was the possibility of a rupture, or a breakthrough. But there was never any practical value to what was taken in case the offensive didn't score a major success. So on the Somme, the importance of the ground seized was, alas, nil.

There had been no breakthrough, and the ground had been gained at a staggering cost. The BEF ran up appalling casualties. From the first day of fighting, the British claimed to be winning. But even Colonel Repington, the military correspondent for *The Times*, and a fanatical supporter of the British military, had doubts. On 6 July, he met with Haig's intelligence chief, and recorded in his diary that "Charteris says we had lost fifty-five thousand men, and put down the German losses at seventy-five thousand, which I did not believe. He is going to say officially that the Germans have lost sixty thousand and says that I can safely say fifty thousand."[15]

Haig himself admitted to Repington on the sixteenth that he had lost over a hundred thousand men, but by the end of July the British had already begun to spin the figures; Robertson, the chief of the British General Staff, told Repington on 4 August that the British had lost 150,000 men, which was "certainly very heavy, but that sixty thousand of these had happened on the first day, and that we now had not lost lately more than twenty thousand a week," which apparently canceled out the damage (1:298). While admitting that British casualties had been heavy, Robertson took refuge in the idea that the Germans had been hit even harder: "The enemy had suffered 750,000 casualties in the course of the past two months on all fronts," he told Repington in this same conversation on the fourth.

This was disingenuous in the extreme: both fronts in June and July 1916 included two months at Verdun and two months of desperate fighting in the East. Moreover, as Repington thoughtfully pointed out, the three quarters of a million figure also included "382,000 mainly Austrian prisoners," which the British could scarcely take any credit for, since there were no Austrians fighting the BEF.

In their initial reporting, the armies of all three nations aggregated the various types of casualties together, producing a figure that included the dead, the missing, and the wounded. As we noted in the introduction, such figures are extremely imprecise: only the numbers for soldiers actually killed (and to lesser extent, missing) are reliable indicators. However, in the case of the Somme, these gross totals are the only good indicators we have.

The standard British estimate of their own losses, which emerged during the fighting, is 498,054 casualties of all types, including the wounded, but as this figure apparently omits the "diversionary" offensives to the north, most notably the Aubreville Ridge, it may well be too low. French losses for the Sixth and Tenth Armies fighting on the Somme came to about 204,000 men, for an Allied total of 704,000 casualties (dead, missing, and wounded).[16] On the German side, the *Reichsarchiv* tabulations for casualties of all kinds sustained during the fighting for sixty-nine separate divisions comes to 237,159 casualties of all types, which is very close to what the official Australian historian, Bean, initially calculated.[17]

These figures, as they are for casualties of all types—wounded, missing, prisoners, and the dead—are inherently problematic, and are displayed simply to make it clear why it was so necessary for Allied intelligence to estimate German casualties as being 600,000 or more. Here is a better comparison. In 1916, almost exactly 150,000 British and 268,000 French soldiers were killed, for a total of 418,000 Allied dead. During 1916, 143,000 German soldiers were killed in action on the entire Western Front fighting both the French and the British.[18]

If the Germans were considerably more efficient at killing their enemies than the Allies were, the data suggests that the French were considerably more efficient than the British. On the Somme, Fayolle's French soldiers had taken a rough parallelogram of ground coming to almost 250 square kilometers. They had thus gained over twice as much ground at about half the cost in lives, most of it taken up during the first few days in July. This was noted at the time, and by the middle of October, Lloyd George was already invoking the comparison and asking the pointed question, "How it is that our losses are so much heavier than those of the French?"[19]

But by then, as we have seen, the spin on the casualties had already started, with the claim that the Germans were being mowed down in heaps. Instead of the objective of a breakthrough, the new objective was to win the war of attrition by killing lots of Germans, and from the end of July on all the figures produced by the British supported this idea.

Having sustained five hundred thousand casualties in the battle, the British analysts were under a great compulsion to believe that losses were at least equal. So, on 2 December 1916, when Repington interviewed Yarde-Buller at British General Staff in London, he was told that the "most careful estimates make the German casualties 670,000 at Verdun and 600,000 on the Somme" (1:402).

Although Churchill, the War Office statisticians, the official Australian historian, and a score of other experts have demonstrated the absurdity of these claims, the postwar fight over these figures became so bitter—and the BEF's apologists so vicious in their attacks on anyone who actually looked at the data—that to this day most people believe that either the hyped-up figure is true or the amount is in dispute, and even the most distinguished British military historians tiptoe delicately around the problem.

This is not to say that the Somme was not a nasty struggle for the German Second Army. On top of Verdun, Rumania, Italy, and the Eastern Front, the German General Staff could ill afford to have 140,000 men killed on the Western Front, and the strain of maintaining the lines there, when coupled with the stresses in the East and at Verdun, pushed the German Army to the breaking point.

But the BEF could hardly afford to lose over a third of its effective strength either. Although in the popular mythology the massacre on the Somme was the massacre of the poorly trained new recruits whose military worth many professional officers deprecated, this wasn't in fact the case. On the contrary, what was particularly bad about the losses—from a purely military point of view—was the massacre of some of the BEF's best troops as the fighting went on. In the fight to take Pozières ridge, for example, the three Australian divisions engaged had launched nineteen separate attacks in forty-five days and had taken twenty-six thousand casualties. No one doubted that the Australians—along with the

Canadians—were the BEF's best troops, even if they were colonials.[20] Even the most cynical and chauvinistic British officer had to concede that heavy Australian losses were bad news, if only because there weren't all that many Australian troops to begin with. Haig had proposed to use half a million men to win the war outright. Instead, he had generated nearly that many casualties.

NOTES

1. As remembered by Edward Louis Spears, *Liaison 1914: A Narrative of the Great Retreat.* 1st ed. (London: Heinemann, 1930), 110.

2. Maréchal Fayolle, *Carnets secrets de la grande guerre,* ed. Henry Contamine (Paris: Plon, 1964), 109.

3. Churchill memorandum of 1 August 1917, as quoted by John Laffin, *British Bunglers and Butchers of World War One,* 91.

4. Ibid.

5. Tim Travers, *The Killing Ground: The British Army, the Western Front, and the Emergence of Modern Warfare, 1900–1918* (London: Unwin Hyman, 1990), 161.

6. Birch to Ivor Maxse, as quoted in Denis Winter, *Haig's Command* (New York: Viking, 1991), 60.

7. Figures on numbers of eighteen-pounders, percentage of shrapnel fired, and percentage of dud shells all in Martin Middlebrook, *The First Day on the Somme* (New York: Norton, 1972), 258–59. Recent British analysts are unanimous in pointing out that most of the shells fired were shrapnel, and completely unsuitable for cutting wire or destroying concrete emplacements. See the discussion of shrapnel in Travers, 161. The complete disorganization of the BEF artillery is discussed in Winter, 59–62.

8. As quoted by Laffin, 68. The Somme is probably the most described and written about battle of the war. By far the most exhaustive account is Middlebrook's somewhat mistitled *The First Day on the Somme.* In addition to the discussions in Winter, Travers, and Laffin, see also Lynn Macdonald, *The Somme* (London: Michael Joseph, 1983). Keegan's early discussion in *The Face of Battle* (New York: Viking, 1976) remains one of the best short accounts.

9. This account is by Spears (109–10), and parallels the account by another officer who also witnessed both armies in action, Colonel Head. See the quotation cited by Winter, 64.

10. See the summary in John Milsom, *Russian Tanks* (London: Leventhal, 1970), 11–12.

11. Like every other detail about the Somme, the actual numbers are in dispute—but not the general outlines. The best discussion is in James Cary, *Tanks and Armor in Modern Warfare* (New York: Franklin Watts, 1966), whose figures are on 33; these are different from those given by Holger M. Herwig, *The First World War* (London: Arnold, 1997), 202, while Travers, who doesn't discuss tanks specifically, seems to be reading from a different script.

12. Ricardo had developed an engine specifically for British tanks, which developed 150 horse-power at angles up to thirty-five degrees: the first of these engines was ordered in January 1917 and the vehicles with the new engine did not appear until the end of 1917. See the discussion in Duncan Crow, ed. *AFV's of World War One* (Windsor: Profile, 1970), 100–2.

13. The main source for tank data is the Aberdeen Proving Ground's *Tank Data*, ed. E.J. Hoffschmidt and W.H. Tantum (Old Greenwich, Conn.: WE Press, 1969); their early figures, especially for ground pressure, are erroneous, and should be corrected by the extensive data in Crow.

14. For example, when on 8 August the BEF began with "more than 450 [tanks] on the first day, there were about 150 left on the second day and 85 on the third." Data from Peter Beale's misleadingly titled *Death by Design: The Fate of British Tank Crews in the Second World War* (Gloucestershire, England: Sutton, 1998), 19.

15. Charles à Court Repington, The *First World War 1914–1918, Personal Experiences of Colonel Repington* (London: Constable, 1920), 1:259.

16. *Service historique, Armées françaises dans la grande guerre* (Paris: Imprimerie Nationale, 1922) Tome IV, vol. 2, appendix 2, 522–23.

17. German data in *Reichsarchiv*, 10, Anlage 3: "Zur Schlacht an der Somme 1916." See the discussion of Bean's figures—and Bean's bitter criticisms of the BEF—in Laffin. Bean's later estimates, notably in his one-volume redaction of the Australian history, are much closer to the British official position. See Charles Edwin Woodrow Bean, *Anzac to Amiens, A Shorter History of the Australian Fighting Services in the First World War*. 5th ed. (Canberra: Australian War Memorial, 1968).

18. British data from the Official History, corrected for omissions, is in Arthur Grahame Butler et al., *The Australian Medical Services in the War of 1914–18* (Melbourne: Australian War Memorial, 1930–43), 2:261. French data from Service Historiques des Armeés, *Inventaire sommaire des archives de la guerre (N 24 and N 25)* (Troyes: La Renaissance, 1967), annexe 6, corrected for live prisoners of war according to reports made to the Chamber of Deputies as redacted and analyzed in Michel Huber, *La Population de la France pendant la guerre* (New Haven: Yale University Press, 1931), 135. German figures are found in Heeressanitätsinspektion des Reichsministeriums, *Sanitätsbericht über das deutsche Heer im Weltkrieg 1914/18* (Berlin: Reichsministerium, 1935), 3, tables 155–58.

19. As reported by George Allardice Riddell in *Lord Riddell's War Diary, 1914–1918* (London: Nicholson and Watson, 1933), 216. Although Lloyd George did not become Prime Minister until 7 December 1916, he had been minister of war since June of that year, and minister for munitions for the years previous—he was clearly in a position to know what was going on if anyone was.

20. Elite units like the Royal Welch were hit hard as well: a third of the men in Robert Graves's battalion were casualties before they even got into action. At the end of their spell in action in July, there were only eighty survivors from his entire battalion. See his description in *Good-Bye to All That* (New York: Blue Ribbon, 1930), 258–63.

13

1916: Rumania and Other Catastrophes

Rumania may be the turning point of the campaign. If the Germans fail there it will be the greatest disaster inflicted upon them. Afterwards it will only be a question of time. But should Germany succeed, I hesitate to think what the effect will be on the fortunes of our campaign....and yet no one seems to have thought it his particular duty to prepare a plan . . . and this is the third year of a campaign which has seen so many muddles of the same sort....

—*Lloyd George*[1]

Ironically, despite the twin disasters of Verdun and the Somme, what really brought about the most decisive changes in the conduct of the war—and on both sides—was Rumania's entry into the war, and the German reaction to it. Lloyd George saw the situation perfectly: Rumania's entry brought about major changes in German strategy, and as he foresaw, the German victory there ensured that the war would go on for years. But the road from Verdun and the Somme to Rumania—and back, since 1916 ended with the recapture of Douaumont—is a twisted one that involves all the other theaters of the war.

The genesis of the situation was prewar, when the French had enthusiastically allied themselves with the Russians, seeing Russia's great military power as a counterbalance against Germany. At the start of the war, the French had counted on the Russians to bail them out in the West by forcing the Germans to turn their resources to the East. That hadn't worked particularly well, but the principle seemed sound enough. So the

Allies persuaded (which is to say, shamelessly bribed) Italy to enter the war as well. Italy's entry into the war was from the start a mixed blessing, but in the spring of 1915 it looked quite promising, and at the end of the year, with Serbia occupied and the debris of the Serbian Army stranded in the Adriatic, dependent on Allied naval charity, the Allies looked around for another partner. Calculating everything by the gross, the Allies decided that since Rumania had a total military of nearly three quarters of a million men, and since Austria-Hungary was reeling on the verge of collapse, the entry into the war of hundreds of thousands of Rumanians would be the straw that broke the camel's back.

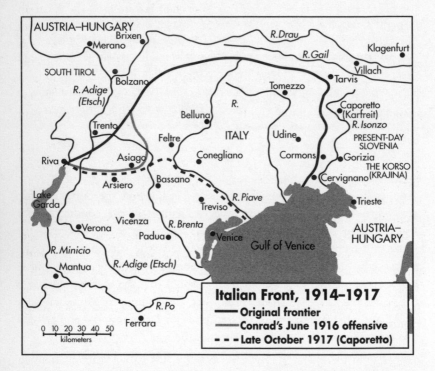

Italian Front, 1914–1917
—— **Original frontier**
—— **Conrad's June 1916 offensive**
- - - **Late October 1917 (Caporetto)**

BREAKTHROUGH IN THE TYROL

Curiously, it was what happened in Italy that set events in motion. In April 1915 the Allies had bribed Italy to enter the war against Austria-Hungary, believing that the empire was on the verge of collapse and a good push would send it over the edge. But in June, the Italians had found out to their horror that even after the disasters of 1914 on the Russian Front the Habsburg armies were hardly on their last legs. In most respects the Imperial and Royal Army of 1916 was stronger still.

Strong enough that the Austrian General Staff in Vienna, still presided over by Conrad von Hötzendorf, was itching to mount its own major offensive. After the Battle of Lake Naroch of March 1916, the Russian armies of the Northwest had shot their last bolt, so the Austrian General Staff, concluding the chances of a new major Russian offensive in the East were slim, planned a major attack against the Italians. This was sensible enough in terms of tactics. The only place where there was any real chance of a breakthrough was in the Isonzo valley, on the far eastern end of Friuli-Venezia Giulia (modern Slovenia). So the Italian supreme command had concentrated all its efforts there: basically the entire Italian Army was in this one small section of Italy.[2]

But Austria had a southern border in the alps, and the Austrian General Staff's plan was to attack out of the area just to the southeast of present-day Trento, on the far western end of the frontier by Lake Garda. A breakthrough there would sever the province of Friuli–Venezia Giulia from Veneto and the rest of Italy. Once the attack broke through the Italian defensive line, which was in the alps, the Italians would be retreating downhill, and the next decent defensive position was far to the south. Even if the attack was only partially successful, it would pose such a threat to the left flank of the Italians on the Isonzo that they would either have to pull back or divert their efforts to the northwestern sector of the frontier.

A reasonable plan, and indeed, with variations, it was basically what happened in October 1917, when a combined Austro-German offensive broke the entire Italian Front open (the misnamed Battle of Caporetto). The problem in the spring of 1916 was that, because the German General Staff had no men to spare, the Austrians would have to mount the operation entirely on their own, and that meant stripping the Eastern Front. The Germans weren't at all happy about this plan: if the offensive bogged down, or if the Russians did mount offensive operations, the critical reserves needed to halt their advance would be in Italy—a long way off.

Nevertheless, on 15 May 1916, the Austrians mounted a major offensive, which, although delayed by the weather, ended up by coincidence nicely in synch with German offensive efforts at Verdun. In thirty days, more or less, Habsburg troops smashed through from fifteen to twenty kilometers on a broad front of about fifty kilometers, capturing Asiago and Arsiero, both key towns in the Italian defensive system (Arsiero was basically the gateway to the plains below).

The Allied situation was grim. By the middle of June, the offensive was slowing down in the face of Italian reinforcements, but Italy was teetering on the brink of disaster. Italy's entrance into the war, which had been planned for the sole purpose of draining off Austro-German resources, was now moving in the contrary direction. The reverse flow (of Allied troops into Italy) had not yet begun, but the danger signals were there. The Habsburg Army was supposed to be in even worse shape than the German one, certainly in no condition to mount a major offensive. Now it was perilously close to smashing Italy out of the war. But once again, the Russians came to the rescue with a grand offensive in the East, and by the start of the Somme, Habsburg troops had been driven back from their forward positions around Arsiero and Asiago, and had to content themselves with having pushed the front forward about ten kilometers on average. Considering the gains the French and British had made so far—and would make in the future—this was a major success. But the breakthrough had failed.

RUSSIA'S LAST GASP

The Russian offensive was largely in response to the French General Staff's desperate calls for help as the pressure on Verdun mounted—and as the Italians were being thrown back. In theory, the Russians had been given a golden opportunity. *Ober-Ost* was hoarding its resources in the North, claiming no troops could be spared. And Austro-Hungarian troops were holding down roughly 450 kilometers of the Russian Front, beginning about seventy kilometers south of Pinsk and running all the way down to the Rumanian frontier, with the southern end anchored

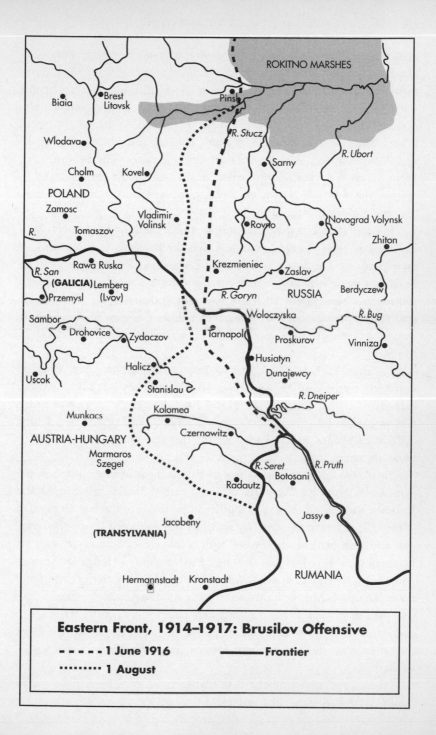

Eastern Front, 1914–1917: Brusilov Offensive

- – – – 1 June 1916 ——— Frontier
- ·········· 1 August

about thirty kilometers east of Czernowitz, the main city of the Bukovina. Holding this section of the front, from north to south, were the Fourth, First, and Second Armies, Army Group A (South), and, for the whole Carpathian front and the Bukovina, Seventh Army, whose headquarters was at Kolomea. Opposing them were the armies of the Southwestern Front, commanded by Brusilov, the only Russian and, along with Fayolle and Pétain, the only Allied general of any real talent. The Southwestern Front matched the Habsburg portion of the line almost perfectly, and to oppose the five Austrian armies, Brusilov had the Eighth, Eleventh, Seventh, and Ninth Russian Armies.

In order to mount their Italian operations, the Austrian General Staff had used all their reserves, assuming that the Russians would simply sit there passively. The area held by Seventh Army had been the worst hit. So Brusilov saw clearly enough that a major offensive would break through somewhere, because the Austrians had moved their reserves to Italy. He also saw, quite clearly, what Haig had failed to comprehend: The only way for an offensive to break through was to mount operations on a large front.

Lacking the heavy weapons to pound through the line, Brusilov opted for a simple all along the line attack, thus depriving the Austrian defenders of what they needed most—time. So Brusilov's tactical grasp was as good as his strategic grasp, and his timing was perfect. On 4 June 1916, the Russians attacked all along the front, and immediately began to break through.

Breakthrough in this sense has to be qualified. In sheer distance, the gains were impressive. When the offensive stalled out, in early August, the Russians had moved the entire southern two thirds of the line an average of fifty kilometers to the west. By anyone's standards this was a phenomenal achievement. But they were still about eighty kilometers east of Lemberg (now Lvov) which, although a major Austro-Hungarian strongpoint in the defense of Galicia, was in itself a long way to the east of any major objective. Although this was clearly not the Austro-German defensive plan in June of 1916, the defenders could just as easily trade space and territory on one front as on the other. The only thing that varied was the scale: instead of one or two kilometers in the West, it was ten or twenty.

The exception was in the Seventh Army sector. There, the Russian Ninth Army had smashed completely through the Bukovina, advancing well over one hundred kilometers, occupying Czernowitz (and also Kolomea, the Austrian Seventh Army HQ), gouging out a huge chunk of territory (a rough quadrilateral about 180 kilometers wide and 120 deep). By the time the drive was controlled, the Habsburg armies were holding out along the ridges of the Carpathians, which formed a natural barrier shielding prosperous and developed Transylvania. Obviously, the Austrian General Staff had to break off its Trentino offensive, so it is no exaggeration to say that Brusilov had saved Italy.

Most Russians thought the cost far too high: the armies of the Southwestern Front lost roughly one million men, so it wasn't much consolation to Brusilov that the Austrians had lost heavily as well, with, as noted in the last chapter, well over three hundred thousand prisoners alone. Because there was a moral cost as well: when the offensive stalled, Russia's offensive capabilities stalled as well. The armies of the Northwestern Front had already exhausted themselves at Lake Naroch. Now, Russia had no more offensive capabilities left; after August 1916, there would be nothing more than a few token jabs at the Germans.

But the success of the Brusilov offensive set in motion a complicated chain of events. In those first weeks of June the Austrians saw success right before their eyes in the Tyrol. Arsiero and Asiago were far behind the Italian lines: it was as though the BEF had stormed through to Saint-Quentin or Lille, or the French had managed to take Laon or Vouziers—all places far enough back from the front that they might as well have been on the moon, as far as the Allies went. To have to break off such a success was maddening.

It was also technically difficult to move the reinforcements, since the men and guns in the Dolomites needed to be shipped some fourteen hundred kilometers across the empire. So the Austrians had to appeal to the Germans for help in staunching the hemorrhage of the Southern Front, which meant that Ludendorff and von Hindenburg claimed—with perfect justification—that it was impossible for them to send reinforcements to the Western Front once the Battle of the Somme began, owing to the near collapse—which, of course, they exaggerated—of the Eastern Front. This controversy brought to a head the debate in the German General Staff about East versus West.

Way back in the years before von Schlieffen, von Moltke the Elder had counseled a German strategy of defense in the West, offense in the East. Given the geography of Prussia-Brandenburg, and the historic emigrations and dispersals in that direction, the idea of expanding into the East always had a certain appeal, whether in things military or political. Von Hindenburg and Ludendorff were Easterners in all three senses of the word. They had both been born in Posen (now Poznań, Poland) and so were East Prussians. They had served almost exclusively on the Eastern Front, and, as their postwar careers made clear, they were men whose politics disposed them to German expansionism.

Theirs was, of course, but one of the competing beliefs in the army, but they had a major advantage: from September 1914 on, it seemed as though the Eastern Front had been nothing but one long chain of great victories and successes. Von Hindenburg, who looked (and talked) like everyone's grandfather, had another advantage: he was a tailor-made hero and warlord, while Ludendorff, whether or not he possessed any great military acumen, was, like Foch, a master politician and tireless self-promoter. As a result, right from the start in 1914 they were able to horde their resources, so that the German General Staff and von Falkenhayn were not really running the entire war, only the part of it on the Western Front. So when the Austrians collapsed, instead of shuttling men south, Ludendorff and von Hindenburg took the opportunity to demand there be a unified command over the entire war, suggesting themselves as the logical candidates.[3]

As a result, the German General Staff was forced to pull troops out of Verdun and send them eastward. At the start of May there were 125 divisions on the Western Front, and 47 divisions on the Eastern Front (counting the two in the Balkans). By June the proportion had changed to 122:51 divisions; by early July, 124:54; by August, 119:64 divisions.[4] In other words, Brusilov's offensive operations had drained thirteen German divisions from the Western Front.

The number seems small, but at Verdun the Germans simply didn't deploy that many troops. For example, there were only thirteen divisions involved in all of the left–bank offensive operations (and only three or four of these were in line at any one time). Fayolle's successes on the Somme had been achieved with even less. Had the divisions used up in the East been shifted to Verdun, the Germans could have doubled their manpower. This is an oversimplification, of course, but it does give an idea of the impact the rapid succession of the Trentino offensive and the Brusilov offensive had on the Western Front. As the summer wore on, von Falkenhayn's position began to unravel. The German General Staff had the resources to contain the Somme and keep the pressure on at Verdun, but not enough to accomplish both those tasks and bail out the Austrians. As if trying to juggle resources on three fronts wasn't enough, the Germans and the Austrians now found themselves facing a new enemy and a new front: Rumania in the southern Carpathians.

THE RUMANIAN TEMPTATION

The Rumanians had been following the war with interest, trying to figure out how they could benefit from it. As the example of Serbia had shown, there was no profit in tangling with the Austro-German-Bulgarian triad unless you had serious Allied support, and the Rumanians were less than enthusiastic about their nearest potential supporter, Russia. For Rumania to be persuaded to enter the war, the bribe would have to be substantial.

The Allied analysis of German losses led them to the conclusion that Germany was on the verge of collapse. With their astronomical losses at Verdun and the Somme, the army was on the verge of imploding. In fact the standard explanation of why the Germans had attacked at Verdun was that they knew they were at the end of their rope. As an article in the supposedly objective and independent *New York Times* put it:

> Germany's manpower is dwindling. There can be no question of that. The available number is much less than that of the allies, and unless Germany can inflict losses on her enemies out of all proportion to those which she herself sustains in the process, sooner or later she will be worn out. This is merely a matter of arithmetic.[5]

And since equally authoritative estimates in the newspapers assured readers that German casualties were three times the French ones, clearly the country was standing with one foot over an open grave. The estimates, ludicrously wide of the mark, were widely believed at the time, from top to bottom, and most particularly inside the Allied governments.

And thus the importance of Rumania. Verdun was Germany's lastditch offensive. If it failed, Germany would collapse. How could it be made to collapse faster? Clearly only so much could be expected from Russia at this point. But Rumania had a sizable army. The Allies believed that the country had a standing army of 590,000 men and available reserves of 380,000: on paper a formidable force. In reality, Rumania had twenty infantry divisions, two cavalry divisions, and three additional infantry divisions in formation, a force smaller than the Allies estimated, but still well in excess of half a million men.[6] Austria was on the verge of collapse; Germany couldn't fight the war on its own; Rumania would be the straw that broke the camel's back. If the Central Powers had been as enfeebled in the summer of 1916 as British and French intelligence insisted they were, the Rumanian gambit would have worked. So, unlike all the other Allied ventures (Palestine and Arabia, East Africa, Gallipoli, Greece), this one was coldly rational.

It was also completely immoral. Despite all the talk about its backward decrepitude, the Habsburg Empire inspired a sense of envy in its neighbors not seen since the wars of the seventeenth century, when everyone acted as though it was perfectly acceptable to attack another country if it had what you wanted. So the Allies simply auctioned it off. They had bought Italy's entrance into the war by (secretly) promising key bits of the Habsburg Empire adjacent to Italy. Before the end of the war, nearly ten thousand Italian soldiers would be killed fighting in Champagne and the Argonne alongside the French, so that Italy would have the historically Austrian southern Tirol.[7]

The king of Rumania was, of course, a Hohenzollern. However, Rumania was a newly formed nation with a great grievance against Austria-Hungary, which it regarded as the occupier of Ardeal (Transylvania, known to the Hungarians as Érdély and the Germans as Siebenbürgen). The Rumanians claimed Ardeal was the core of historic Rumania, since, largely because of the stability and tolerance the area enjoyed, it had a majority of ethnic Rumanians.[8] So it was easy for the Allies to bribe Rumania to get involved: All they had to do was to promise them Ardeal. Like the Serbians, whose fanatical quest for territorial aggrandizement had started the war, Rumanians dreamed of a Greater Rumania.

That is not to say that Rumania did not have a claim, only that it was one that should have been discussed by the peoples who lived there—as indeed Wilson wanted. But by the time Wilson enunciated his points, the Allies had already decided the fates of enormous numbers of people, handing them over to countries whose services the British and the French needed in the war. Italy's bribe had been Trieste and the South Tirol. Serbia, whose expansionist aims had triggered the war, would be suitably rewarded for its pains by being given Croatia, Bosnia, Slovenia, and part of Hungary (the Vovojdna). Now Rumania would be given Transylvania. In no case would the inhabitants of these areas be allowed to decide what their fate was; they were simply handed over. In order to bring Rumania into the war, the Allies not only appealed to that nation's greed, they then sweetened the deal by making promises of military support, which they ultimately did not keep and probably had no intention of keeping.

Once Rumania declared war, General Sarrail, who commanded an Allied army of twenty-three divisions encamped at Salonika, would begin offensive operations out of Greece. Sarrail's force was being used to pressure the Greeks into entering the war. The king of Greece felt like the king of Belgium—and said so, being unable to comprehend why it was wrong for the Germans to commandeer Belgium and acceptable for the French and British to commandeer Greece.[9] But Greece had an army, and General Sarrail would prod it into action.

So the Allies would attack into Bulgaria from Greece, thus forcing the Bulgarians to keep far to the south of their common border with Rumania, and enabling the Rumanian Army to concentrate on an invasion into Ardeal. Simultaneously, the Russians would begin offensive operations in the Carpathians. Three Russian divisions would move into northern Rumania to help exploit the breakthrough, and more would follow if needed. Russia would supply Rumania with three hundred tons of supplies a day, and the Black Sea Fleet would be available to support operations and counter any Austrian naval forces using the Danube. And finally someone in the French government dispatched a military mission to Bucharest to help bring the army up to par.

In addition to toppling Austria-Hungary, the Allies would smash Bulgaria, which would stopper the German supply route to Turkey and bring an end to the fighting in the Middle East, as well as justify the Allied presence in Greece, where Bulgarian troops had been blocking General Sarrail's army since debarkation. Bulgaria, like Turkey, was able to put a surprisingly tough army into the field. So the Germans and the Austrians had a surprisingly formidable ally, and Bulgaria's importance in the Rumanian endgame would soon become all too apparent.

With Bulgaria out of the way, the Rumanians could smash through southeastern Hungary, an option that made a good deal of sense as well. As we have seen, in the summer of 1916 the Austrians were already stretched to the breaking point. On top of losses on the Isonzo, they had been badly mauled by the Brusilov offensive. There was no way the

Austrian General Staff could assemble half a million men and get them into Ardeal before the Rumanians had seized it. But if they didn't, the whole eastern portion of the empire would be vulnerable. This was a blow that might well knock Austria out of the war. So the German General Staff would have no choice but to shuttle men East.

The Allies, of course, figured that the German High Command simply didn't have half a million high command spare German soldiers to send to the East any more than the Austrians did. So this would put the Germans in a double bind. Move the men East, and risk the Somme turning into a decisive breakthrough battle of the sort Joffre had planned for. Keep them West, lose Austria's food supply and risk losing Austria altogether. The prize was tempting, and the Allies kept dangling it in front of the Rumanians. Finally, they succumbed to the temptation, and on 27 August 1916, declared war.

THE FALL OF VON FALKENHAYN

Rumania's entry into the war provoked a major change in the German General Staff. The first casualty was not Austria-Hungary, but von Falkenhayn. All through the summer, von Falkenhayn had maintained his composure (more or less), insisting that the Allied offensive on the Somme would self-destruct, and that his efforts at Verdun would end the war in a few months. German General Staff planners were more pessimistic. When Lossberg was sent to take over the Second Army as chief of staff, he had tried to exact a promise that offensive operations at Verdun would stop entirely. They slowly wound down, but the Allies, in defiance of basic military principles, simply kept on mounting attacks on the Somme. Meanwhile, there was the Austro-Russian fiasco.

Von Falkenhayn had never been a popular commander: the General Staff clique disliked him intensely because he hadn't been a member of their fraternity and worked his way up on "merit," but had played politics. The Easterners, headed by the dynamic duo of von Hindenburg and Ludendorff, were convinced they could do much better than von Falkenhayn, and made sure everyone knew. So he was in a precarious position of being unable to withstand even the slightest of setbacks, and the overextended armies of the summer of 1916 certainly constituted a setback. Moreover, France still hadn't collapsed.

Von Falkenhayn, like Haig and Joffre and Pershing, owed his appointment to his political rather than his military abilities. One of the main assets he had brought to the job in September of 1914, besides a good track record running the War Ministry, was that he could handle the emperor. Von Falkenhayn's only real ally was Wilhelm II.

Anyone who wanted to get rid of von Falkenhayn, for reasons good or bad, had to get the emperor to agree, and to sign the order. Bad news for Ludendorff, whom Wilhelm II hated, with von Hindenburg a close second. The feeling was mutual: as von Moltke the Younger's chief of operations prewar, Ludendorff had advised him that the best way to get along with their ruler and supreme warlord was to tell him nothing at all about what was being done. In this sense, France and Germany had contrasting problems: Joffre soldiered on because no one could agree on who to replace him with; von Falkenhayn stayed on because the only logical successor was someone the emperor couldn't stand.

Wilhelm had been kept at arm's length from matters military, and fed a steady diet of cheery news. But he was as capable as Lloyd George of reading between the lines and realizing that things were not going according to plan; Rumania's declaration of war was deeply upsetting. He had been resisting the Easterners for years (the dynamic duo had begun lobbying for supreme command in September 1914). Wilhelm II was not without a certain insight, and his instincts about the two were probably right: once they seized the reins of power, they would not willingly relinquish it, and, like Haig, would become so powerful inside the government that it would be next to impossible to show them the door should they fail. If Wilhelm doubted their abilities, he was right.

But Rumania was, in this one case, the straw that broke the camel's back. The day after the declaration of war, von Falkenhayn "resigned," and von Hindenburg took his place, with Ludendorff given effective control of the army.[10] As a sort of bitter joke, von Falkenhayn was given command of the Ninth Army, and charged with destroying Rumania.

Tactically, as we have already seen, most of the changes ascribed to Ludendorff had already been implemented by someone else before he moved West. German tactics continued on their same evolutionary line as before. Where the changes came in—and almost immediately—was in the overall strategy. As we have seen, in September troops began shifting to the East, and this reflected Ludendorff's determination to end the war there. Instead of a balancing act, in which the German General Staff tried to handle all three theaters of war, now the priorities were to smash each adversary in turn. Rumania would be merely the first.

In his new role as de facto supreme warlord, Ludendorff had an unexpected advantage: the Allies had miscalculated the practicalities of the Rumanian intervention on every level. In their obsession with quantification, they had neglected the importance of actual leadership. Having lied to themselves about how badly they were doing on the Western Front, they generalized from their own failures to form a completely false picture of modern warfare.

THE DESTRUCTION OF RUMANIA

Ardeal was a region with its own historic identity and a large German minority. Resistance to the Habsburgs over the centuries hardly meant that the natives would welcome the Rumanians with open arms, particularly since the Rumanian army's habits of occupation resembled those of the Mongol horde more than a modern army.[11] The natives had fought the Turks for centuries, and more recently, in vain contests to win their independence, they had battled both the Austrians and the Russians.

Von Straussenburg, the Austrian local commander, rallied local militia, convalescing soldiers, regular army units sent to the area for refitting, together with the police (the *Feldgendarmerie*), and put up a surprisingly stout defense.[12] Three weeks into September, the Rumanians were still trying to fight their way out of southeastern Transylvania, and had failed to get much farther than Hermannstadt (present-day Sibiu). The delay was fatal for Rumania, and fatal for Allied hopes.

Because the German General Staff, which had been brooding about Rumania's possible entry into the war for some months, already had a plan developed to counter the threat. Von Mackensen, the elderly German commander in the Balkans, attacked out of Bulgaria almost immediately, using a force composed almost exclusively of Bulgarians and Turks. Although most of the border between the two countries was the Danube, about four fifths of the way along the frontier, the river makes an abrupt turn to the north, leaving a wedge-shaped section of Rumania with an ordinary land frontier. This was the country's most vulnerable spot, because the Danube delta in the north meant that the only serious deep-sea port, then and now, is at Constanta, in the vulnerable section to the east and south of the river.

The Rumanians were aware of this, and at key points had built fortifications to block any offensive. One of these forts, Turtukai, the Rumanian commander alleged to the press, would be Rumania's Verdun. A day later, on 6 September 1916, the fort had fallen, with hardly a shot being fired, and von Mackensen's patched-together army was spreading out into Rumania. The Allied plan had collapsed completely in ten days.

This, of course, was not supposed to happen. Sarrail's army in the south was supposed to stop the Bulgarians from doing precisely this by attacking on their own. General Sarrail, who now had over twenty divisions of French, British, and Italian troops, plus a Greek Army corps, was the French commander in the Argonne whose offensives the Germans had repeatedly finessed by attacking first. Joffre claimed he was absolutely incompetent, and sacked him. But Sarrail had a sizable following in the Chamber, the whole affair ended in interminable wrangling, and he was packed off to the Balkans, where he proved that Joffre did occasionally have an insight into the problems of command.

The Allied advance never got started, which was hardly surprising, given the roughness of the terrain and the lack of any road system. But in any event, the Greek soldiers involved, sensibly enough, immediately opted out of a war that they perceived as both futile and ludicrous, and promptly surrendered to the Bulgarians.

Faced with an invasion from the south, and the potential loss of their only seaport, the Rumanians had to make some hard choices: put everything into an attack into Transylvania, or try to eject von Mackensen from the Dobricia (or Dobrudje), as this part of the country is called. Although the actual decision is usually thought of as wrong, it's difficult to see what real options the Rumanians had at this point. So they tried to mount operations in both directions, a plan for which they lacked the resources. From the point of view of the Rumanians, things had gone disastrously wrong from the start.

But to France and Great Britain, the Rumanian campaign looked more promising. The German General Staff and Austrian General Staff were going to have to send troops to Transylvania, and if the Allied analysis of casualties was correct, diversion of the forces needed would cause the Western Front to collapse. Confident, the Allies pounded away on the Somme: the only way the Germans could ship men East was to pull them from the West. Von Falkenhayn, the new theater commander, arrived in Transylvania on 18 September 1916, bringing with him the nucleus of a sizable Austro-German force, subsequently known as the Ninth Army. On 27 August, the German General Staff had shipped off seven infantry divisions. In September the Third Guards Division and another five divisions. In October came another regular installment: the Alpine Corps and another five divisions. Still more units followed in November: the Seventh Guards Division and four more regular divisions. Not all of these went to Rumania, but since by the end of August the Russians had basically collapsed as far as offensive operations were concerned, the movement East was dictated by Rumanian operations.

Despite assurances of the British High Command (the IGS) in London that the Carpathians were impassable if defended, by the middle of November the Germans had broken through the passes and were in Walachia, and Bucharest fell on 6 December 1916. The remnants of Rumania's armies and government were penned up behind the Seret, by Moldova, the only city of any size still remaining in their hands, ironically, being Jassy, the cradle of that peculiarly Rumanian blend of apocalyptic religious nationalism and anti-Semitism which would so disfigure the country's psyche postwar. Never to be outdone by the facts of the case, in late November the Allies approved a master plan of operations for 1917, which called for Bulgaria to be put out of action by a Russo-Rumanian force operating in the north and an Allied army operating out of Salonika.

About 150,000 Rumanian soldiers had been taken prisoners of war, and the dead and the wounded were roughly 200,000 men. There was hardly any Rumanian Army left by January 1917. Nor was much left to arm them with: the invading armies claimed they had captured 350,000 rifles and 350 pieces of artillery. Where would this new Rumanian Army come from? "Free" Rumania was now a small piece of Moldavia. Who would equip an army even if one were found? The Russians? They hardly had enough rifles for their own troops.

THE END OF THE YEAR AND THE RISE OF NIVELLE

Lloyd George grimly concluded that the war would go on for a long time. The Allied governments, desperate after the fall disasters, were now clutching at straws. By October 1916, there was a growing concern within the French and British governments about the progress of the war. The obvious collapse of the Rumanian enterprise was the catalyst. The success of the Allied plan had been predicated on heavy German losses, that would make it impossible for them to prop up the collapsing front without imperiling their position in the West. Clearly this hadn't happened.

In Paris, Abel Ferry hit on an obvious answer: the estimates of the French General Staff as to German casualties were far too high. Ferry did his own calculations, beginning with the inflammatory assumption that the official German casualty figures (which the Germans were still publishing in their newspapers) were reasonably accurate estimates. He padded these figures to allow for what he considered to be possible Germanic obfuscation, and came up with a truly horrific conclusion: "the figures for French and German losses are very near."[13] The reason this was horrifying was that his analysis implied that the Germans were hardly losing any more men than the French were—and yet they were fighting the Russians and the BEF as well. When he pursued the differences between the figures derived from his estimates and the figures of the French General Staff, he found the difference to be well over half a million men. The obvious conclusion—which Ferry didn't hesitate to draw—was that the difference explained why the Germans had been able to find an extra half a million men to shuttle off to Rumania (132). And since the French General Staff admitted that it had lost at least two hundred thousand men dead or missing as a result of Verdun and the Somme, the balance was hardly in France's favor.

Ironically, seen from London, the French appeared to have great military expertise. Although the official line was that the Somme had been a success, it was on grounds quite different from those envisioned at the planning conferences of 1915 and 1916. It had not escaped notice in London that the French offensive on the Somme had been considerably more successful than the operations of the BEF. On 1 October 1916, someone asked the obvious question. Why?[14] As with any bureaucracy, there was no lack of reasons why, and the Cabinet in London was fatally handicapped by its lack of any solid base among the military. Neither government felt strong enough to sack its top general outright: both resorted to bureaucratic maneuvering.

Moreover, Lloyd George and his colleagues in the Cabinet (he wouldn't become prime minister until 7 December 1916, but had been minister of war since late June) were beginning to realize that the British General Staff's understanding of the war was minimal. Rumania bought this home. Ironically, the French and British civilian governments probably had better sources of information about how things were going in Rumania than they did on the Western Front. In the Balkans, they could rely on diplomatic channels as well as private ones. In France the two armies had the entire front sealed off and their control over the news there was more absolute than in October 1914.

Obviously, the Allies needed new leadership. Key players in both the French and the British governments were beginning to realize that the new leader had to have new powers: he had to be the actual overall commander of the armies in France. So far, as Charles Dupuis wrote in a memorandum of 16 October 1916, the conduct of the war had been characterized by an "absolute absence of coordination."[15] It was no good having agencies and individuals reporting to a supreme council composed of "eminent men totally ignorant of warfare." That was why the results were out of all proportion to the effort expended. The Dupuis document was an incisive statement of the troubles to date, and it outlined sensible solutions. But now that Gallieni was dead, where would the man come from to implement them?

In France, the Joffre clique was desperate to keep out Pétain. The stated reason was that he was too negative, too pessimistic. The actual reason was his popularity with the troops and his contempt for the staff and the overall direction of the war effort. Joffre had pushed Nivelle, who had taken over at Verdun from Pétain in May 1916, as he felt Nivelle had the proper offensive spirit that Pétain lacked. As we saw in the eleventh chapter, Nivelle's offensive spirit consisted of ordering up attack after attack until there were literally no more attackers, and then asking for more. In the fall of 1916, the French Army needed a leader with more offensive spirit about as much as they needed more red pants (the army had begun changing to the horizon blue uniform in late 1915). But Nivelle, like Haig, Foch, and Ludendorff, was a tireless self-promoter. And, unlike them, he was an utterly charming officer who spoke fluent English. And now, to add to his credentials as the man who had really saved Verdun, Nivelle planned an offensive operation that would recapture all the ground lost.

This attack, which began in October 1916, could hardly have been better timed to boost Nivelle's career. Using the method developed by Pétain of an intensive and meticulously planned bombardment—and using the troops Pétain had trained—the French planned to pulverize the area between the Côte du Poivre and the battery of Laufée, one of the only French strongpoints not in German hands. Then a three-division assault on a front of about seven kilometers would take back both of the major forts.

The attack began on the twenty-fourth, and by the next day, the French had taken both Douaumont and Vaux. Mangin, directing the attack, planned another one, and by 15 December, the French had gotten back a rough semicircle stretching from Louvemont on the northwest, over to Bezonvaux and then back down to Vaux. Nivelle was the man of the hour, who had reversed the disasters of Verdun. Joffre was kicked upstairs to a fictitious post of supreme commander, and Nivelle was given his job, with the clear understanding that the British would follow alongside and do what he wanted.

Although admitting that the Germans had not yet cracked, the British General Staff claimed that German morale was badly shaken, and the Allies now had the moral ascendancy, and their manpower superiority was increasing day by day. Up through early October, the song of the day had been numbers. Now clearly something was seriously wrong in the Allied reckoning, because here it was October 1916, the Germans were holding on all along the line, and they had mysteriously come up with enough troops to smash Rumania. There was an obvious question to ask at this point: Where had all the extra Germans come from?

Lloyd George, ever the devil's advocate, asked for proof. Like Ferry in France, this string of Allied pseudo-victories and alleged German catastrophes had made him suspicious of the claims he was hearing. He recorded that the British Army's proof that the Germans were losing their grip on the Western Front was that "several German divisions had fled from the Western Front to the East. Why? Not because they were beaten but because they felt they could hold their own in the West with 74 fewer battalions. What a commentary on the smashing triumphs of the Somme!" (1.539) Lloyd George looked past the claims at the figures themselves, noting that the great Allied superiority in manpower was totally a function of Russia and Rumania. Even if one played the war strictly by the numbers, the figures were hardly reassuring.

But France's sleight of hand about Verdun even got past Lloyd George.

In fact, it went right past everyone. In the first instance, what Nivelle and Mangin had got back was hardly the sum total of what the Germans had gained. They still had all their territory on the left bank, which meant that any great advance on the right bank was impossible: German gunners could fire into the French advance on the right bank from their newly won positions just as easily as the French had been able to do against the Germans earlier. As we shall see in the next chapter, the French didn't make any real gains at Verdun until August 1917 under Pétain.

Recapturing the forts was hardly much of a military victory, as the Germans had abandoned them both at the start of the offensive. Ominously, the Germans on the right bank had simply given the Allies a taste of a new German defensive tactic: strategic withdrawal, the same technique that they had begun to use on the Somme. This imposed an ever greater strain on the Allies, as it forced them to mount successive attacks over ground destroyed by previous offensive efforts.

So Nivelle's great offensive at Verdun would hardly survive much scrutiny. Nivelle, jubilant, proclaimed that he had found the formula for the breaking of the German lines, and the Allied leadership, desperate, was unable to see through the public relations fog that surrounded Nivelle's achievements.

And the government needed to act. On 7 December 1916, Briand's government survived a vote of no confidence 344 to 160. So on 13 December 1916, Nivelle was made the supreme commander, and Joffre given a purely ceremonial role. On the twenty-sixth, Joffre, no fool when it came to political infighting, resigned. The Nivelle era had begun. It would be short and costly.

NOTES

1. David Lloyd George, *War Memoirs,* new ed. (London: Odhams, 1938), 1:549.

2. In the discussions that follow, although I differ greatly with many of his conclusions, I am deeply indebted to Norman Stone's brilliant analysis: *The Eastern Front 1914–1917* (New York: Charles Scribner's Sons, 1975), and also to Gunther E. Rothenburg's uniformly excellent *The Army of Francis-Joseph* (West Lafayette, Ind.: Purdue University Press, 1976).

3. Stone sees straight through the various apologias: "If, to cut them down to size, the Austrians and von Falkenhayn were defeated, so much the better for Ludendorff" (258). In *The German High Command at War: Hindenburg and Ludendorff Conduct World War I* (New

York: Morrow, 1991), Robert Asprey entitles his thirteenth chapter "The War Against Falkenhayn" (151–60).

4. Data from the tables in Général Edmond Buat, *L'Armée allemande pendant la guerre de 1914–18* (Paris: Chapelot, 1920).

5. *New York Times, European History 7* (April–June 1916), 45.

6. The higher figures are taken from Sir William Robertson's memorandum to the British Cabinet, as reprinted by Lloyd George, 1.538. The divisional breakdown given here is the one used by the U.S. Army in staff college lectures in 1944, as reprinted by *Relevance* 1.2 (Fall 1996).

7. Seventy-odd years later, even though there are precious few people left who remember when they lived under the black and yellow Habsburg flag, the most commonly seen bumper sticker in this part of Italy is *"Ich bin ein Südtiroler."*

8. Later propaganda claims give the impression that Transylvania was mostly Rumanian, but the actual proportion of Rumanians was a little under 60 percent. See the discussion in such basic tourist guides of the period as Karl Baedeker, *Austria* (Leipzig: Karl Baedeker, 1896) 393–94. Propagandists juggled this proportion by acting as though Transylvania consisted only of Hungarians and Rumanians, in which case the Rumanians outnumbered the majority by roughly 2:1. But this sleight of hand omitted all the Saxons, Jews, Armenians, and Gypsies, as well as overlooking the fundamental reason why—in modern history—the number of Rumanians in Ardeal had increased (political and economic conditions there were so much better than across the mountains).

9. See the discussion, together with the king's remarks, in H.C. Peterson, *Propaganda for War: The Campaign Against American Neutrality, 1914–1917* (Norman, Okla.: University of Oklahoma Press, 1939), 45.

10. The bizarre title he assumed usually passes without comment, but in retrospect it is probably the tipoff that Ludendorff was already unbalanced. Post-1918, after his pretentiousness and eccentric politics had alienated his former colleagues, the National Socialist government tried to soothe him by making him a field marshal, but he declined, having already awarded himself an even more bizarre title of his own making. See the discussion in D.J. Goodspeed, *Ludendorff: Soldier, Dictator, Revolutionary* (London: Rupert Hart-Davis, 1966), 246. The interpretation of this by Roger Parkinson in *Ludendorff: Tormented Warrior* (London: Hodder and Stoughton, 1978) is more sympathetic (224–25); however, there is no question that Ludendorff began to develop serious emotional and mental problems.

11. See the scathing comments of the American Army's representative in Budapest postwar, Major General Harry Hill Bandholtz, whose private diary for 1919–1920 was published posthumously as *An Undiplomatic Diary* (New York: Columbia University Press, 1933).

12. In addition to the U.S. Army narrative cited above, there are excellent brief accounts of the Rumanian campaign in Rothenburg, 187–200; Stone, 270ff.; and from a somewhat different perspective, see D. von Wienskowski, *Falkenhayn* (Berlin: Sigismund, 1937).

13. Abel Ferry, *La Guerre vue d'en bas et d'en haut* (Paris: Grasset, 1920), 129.

14. As recorded in George Allardice Riddell, *Lord Riddell's War Diary, 1914–1918* (London: Nicholson and Watson, 1933), 213.

15. As quoted by [Colonel] Bernard Serrigny, *Trente ans avec Pétain* (Paris: Plon, 1959), 129–32.

14

1917: The Allies Play Their Last Hand

Most of the earlier plans of the British High Command . . . particularly the Battle of the Somme, had been criticized as lacking any proper strategical objective.

—*Lord Hankey*[1]

Evening. Sadness. Two causes: the mentality of Foch . . . and the absence of any grand perspective at the top. What is the plan for 1917?

—*General Fayolle*[2]

Lloyd George, in looking over the British estimates of manpower, had noted that the Allied superiority was totally a function of Russia and Rumania.[3] By January of 1917, Rumania had to be subtracted from the list. A month later, the Tsar had abdicated, and Russia became a major question mark. Curiously enough, although the Russian northern armies had stopped offensive operations after Lake Naroch in March of 1916, and Brusilov's Southwestern Front had wound down operations in August of the same year, both sides continued to regard Russia as a major combatant, despite the obvious evidence to the contrary.

Ludendorff and von Hindenburg were resolved to smash Russia permanently, and to gain as much new territory as they could in the process. Although there was a sinister political underside to this, there was also rational economics at work. In 1913, Russia had been the world's largest exporter of grain. If the Central Powers had enough Russian wheat and Rumanian oil, they could fight a war indefinitely:

Military conquests in the East meant the war could go on forever in the West.[4]

In November of 1916, another joint Allied conference at Chantilly, which echoed the one of 1915, allowed Nivelle to set forth his plan for a second joint offensive. Someone had noticed that the Somme was not a good place to conduct offensive operations, and by November 1916 the terrain was obviously in atrocious condition. So Nivelle proposed to attack on either side of the slight westward bulge the German line formed as it curved to the southwest below Arras, and then slowly curved back to the east just above Reims. The two attacking forces would catch the bulge between them and eliminate it. The resulting rupture would be enormous, and it would knock the Germans right out of the war.

Nivelle of course had the formula for success, which he had developed at Verdun.[5] An overwhelming concentration of heavy artillery would smash the defending positions, and the infantry would simply walk in and occupy them. It had worked at Verdun; it would work here on a larger scale. Additionally, Nivelle had two other trump cards to play. The French had been constructing tanks, and would have hundreds of them to put into action in April, as would the BEF. Moreover the Allies continued with their fantasy that the Germans, already on the ropes and suffering heavy losses, had now lost the will to fight as well.

This was the thinking that led the Allies to dump Wilson's December Peace Proposal. Wilson had tried to end the war by serving as a mediator, and had asked each side to indicate its terms. The Germans, who not unreasonably felt they were winning, replied by insisting on what might be termed the status quo ante plus: Everything to be as it had been in 1914 with a new set of rules for Belgium, Serbia suitably chastised, and reparations made. The Allies responded by demanding the dismemberment of Germany and Austria, and then blamed German arrogance for scuttling the process. The French and English staked everything on the success of the Nivelle offensive.

THE APRIL 1917 OFFENSIVE

As Fayolle had grimly noted in his diary, this was the last card the Allies had to play, and it was being risked on an offensive where he estimated the chance of success to be less than three in four. It was also yet another example of complete disregard for the terrain. The land to the northwest of Reims is dominated by the ridge of the Chemin des Dames, which the Germans had been fortifying since 1914, but this ridge is connected with others, and the approaches are crammed with deep ravines and gulleys. An attack on the positions there would be another Vauquois, except on a much larger scale. The defenders would be able to see the attack developing, as their spotters could look for kilometers into French territory. Nor was the territory around Arras much better.

The justification was that the Allies could, if successful, pinch off the bulge in the line. In picking two widely separated points, Nivelle was returning to the older tactics of 1915, and had thus discarded Joffre's one sound idea: for a combined offensive to be successful, the Allies had to attack side by side, because only that way would they have the manpower to rupture the line on a broad front and make a big enough hole in it.

The only justification for Nivelle's plan was the belief at the top that the Germans were on the ropes. The most obvious evidence was turned on its head to sustain this thesis. For example, the Germans were creating whole new divisions at a rapid pace: six in the spring of 1916, thirty-one in the fall, and thirteen in January 1917.[6] This process, as we pointed out earlier, had begun in 1915, when the Germans abandoned the two-brigade/four-regiment structure and went to a three-regiment system in which the battalion increasingly became the basic tactical unit. The Allies explained this process away as cannibalization: new divisions were being formed only at the price of breaking up existing ones, and they pointed to the downsizing of the infantry component as proof.

It was true that reducing the infantry component allowed the formation of more divisions (and made sure that each new unit had a cadre of veterans as well), but the Allies totally overlooked the huge increase in firepower for these new units: each of the new divisions had a complement of 150-millimeter howitzers (guns that prewar had been distributed only at the army corps level), and the number of machine guns per battalion was essentially what it had been prewar for each regiment. In key areas such as mortars, the Germans had an advantage of two or three to one.[7]

In March came a development that, although subject to contradictory interpretations, should have forced the aborting of the offensive. The Germans abruptly downsized the front, withdrawing from the bulge so that the new front line ran to the northeast of Bapaume, dropping down behind the Somme battlefield entirely. The advantage to the Germans was that the new line was shorter, it took less troops to defend, they had established serious defensive positions on the new line, and, last but not least, it made Nivelle's projected offensive gratuitous. There was now no salient to pinch off. Moreover, the way the new lines ran, Allied break-throughs at either end of the former bulge, where the offensives were scheduled, would promptly run into a new defensive line, which they would have to batter through.

This too was interpreted as evidence clinching the growing weakness of the German Army—they lacked the manpower to hold the longer front, and so were forced to economize. In reality it was simply a continu-ation on a grander scale of something the Germans had been doing since the Battle of the Ourcq in September 1914—a retreat to a more tactically advantageous position to deal with the anticipated enemy attack.

At this stage, Lloyd George, who had only become prime minister on 7 December 1916, still trusted the French. Their performance on the Somme, which he could compare with the BEF's, suggested they had some glimmering of how to fight the war. But the French leadership was about to change. Briand had squeaked through a no-confidence vote in December, and on 17 March 1917, his government fell, after Lyautey, the minister of war, refused to answer questions put to him by the increas-ingly restive Chamber. Briand was replaced by Ribot, and Painlevé, the new minister of war, was disturbed enough about the situation to call a meeting to discuss the planned offensive.

Although the government and its ministers had changed, neither the outgoing nor incoming civilians at the War Ministry were happy with Nivelle's grandiose scheme for a great breakthrough. In a sadly memo-rable phrase, Lyautey had observed that it was the sort of thing that might have been "dreamed up by the army of the Duchess of Gerolstein," and Painlevé saw clearly enough that Nivelle was going back to the tactics of Champagne-Artois.[8] Like Lloyd George, he had his own sources of information: after the fall of Joffre, the links among the various military cliques and the Chamber began to multiply, and the news Painlevé was receiving was disturbing, the most distressing item being that, once again, everyone in Paris knew the when and where of the projected offensive.[9] But Nivelle had been enthusiastically endorsed by the government in December 1916, and thus far there had been nothing on the battlefield indicating their enthusiasm had been misplaced. So Painlevé took the unusual step of interviewing the three army group commanders (Micheler, Pétain, and Franchet d'Esperey).

This was a dangerous step, tantamount to withdrawing confidence in Nivelle as commander. Moreover, all three generals were unenthusiastic. But Painlevé, experienced politician that he was, knew exactly what to do. He called a meeting. Nivelle assured the members of the government who were there (including Ribot and Maginot) that his offensive would smash through the lines and end the war in a few days. Faced with this level of assurance, Painlevé temporarily backed down. The British were polled as well. Robertson and Haig, who had now managed to run British casualties on the Western Front in 1916 to just over the million-man mark, still convinced they were winning the war through attrition and destroying the enemy's will to fight, were all set to attack.

Painlevé's apparent capitulation was only the first step. There were now men in the army who were truly desperate. They saw that Nivelle was going to destroy the last army France had on the heights above Reims. Someone had to stop him, and they lobbied the War Ministry once more. Painlevé decided to have another meeting. The army commanders would be present as well as the civilians, and it would all be thrashed out in proper parliamentary fashion. Nivelle again promised everyone in the room that the offensive would succeed, but he made an important concession. If, within two days, it had not broken through, it would be called off. There would be no Second Champagne or the Somme.

Argued down, Painlevé took a step that bespeaks either the utter desperation that had descended on him or reveals him to be a bureaucrat of the first order. He turned to the army commanders, knowing their negative opinions, and forced them to choose between openly undercutting their superior or letting their soldiers be massacred. Not surprisingly, they waffled. Except for Pétain, who now let those assembled have it with both barrels. No breakthrough was possible, he said, echoing what Fayolle and von Falkenhayn had already figured out. And, in any event, the army was now too weak to accomplish it, as it lacked the half a million or so fresh troops required to exploit the opening.[10]

But Nivelle had a trump card. He threatened to quit. He had been put in power by the government, given the task of winning the war, and this was how he proposed to do it. Officially, the planned offensive was still on track, and the British were mesmerized by Nivelle's fluent command of their language. To call it off would mean the end of the Ribot government. Still worse, it would mean putting Pétain in charge. As de Gaulle would later remark, you could tell the situation was bad when Pétain was brought in. So now all the indecision and weakness, the maneuvering and squabbling of France's tangled and inept politicians, came to a head. Better to clutch at straws. Besides, Nivelle promised success.

The offensive was left to develop, the only real reservation being the clear understanding of everyone present that if the breakthrough was not achieved immediately, within the first forty-eight hours, the operation would be aborted. So the second and last major Franco-British offensive, which would be the final throw of their armies in any unassisted and independent attempt to win the war, went through because of bureaucratic inertia, a failure of political will, and someone threatening to quit his job.

The reason everyone was so pessimistic about the attack Nivelle was proposing was that he was aiming to take what was essentially a long sinuous ridge that dominated the French lines. The position the Germans held on the Chemin des Dames was radically different from their positions on the Somme or in the rest of Champagne. Instead of isolated pieces of high ground, the Chemin was one continuous ridge, with a steep slope down to the French lines. But there was a comparison, and an ominous one: the Chemin des Dames was basically like the Vauquois and Les Éparges, only bigger. And the defenders had been digging themselves in for thirty months.

It was totally unlike the right bank at Verdun, where the ground was so chewed up that the Germans had been unable to construct serious defensive positions around the forts. Their real defensive positions were well behind the forts, and when attacked they promptly retreated to them. So Nivelle mistakenly assumed that success against defenders with no prepared defenses meant success against defenders in well-prepared defenses. Moreover, after July 1916, the Germans had withdrawn their air force from Verdun, as they desperately needed the planes elsewhere. But on the Chemin des Dames, the Germans had almost complete command of the air.[11]

Once again the Allied bombardment was, seen from the Allied lines, formidable. Unlike British gunners on the Somme, the French gunners were using high-explosive shells. But the majority of the French guns fired in too flat a trajectory over too short a range. The only effective weapon here, as on the heights of the Meuse to the east, was a howitzer, a gun with a very high angle of fire that could drop a heavy payload of high explosive down at such a steep angle that it would penetrate into the shelters. Although the new Schneider 155 millimeter howitzer had begun to enter service in reasonable numbers, the majority of the heavy guns in use were older weapons, and field guns and antiques from the 1870s were not sufficiently effective to prepare the ground for a successful infantry advance.

As a result, the preparatory barrage went on for a week, churning up the ground over which the troops had to advance and allowing the German defenders ample time to sight their guns on holes in the wire. When, on the morning of 16 April 1917, the infantry attack on the ridge developed, forward observers were stupefied to hear what was, under the circumstances, the worst sound that could be imagined: German machine guns, soon drowned out by the fire from all the German heavy weapons that the French had failed to destroy. So the battle was lost in a few hours. The infantry at first thought they were being fired on by their own gunners by mistake, and there was an almost immediate sense of panic that set in. On the Somme, the BEF commanders had been told to expect heavy casualties—although obviously not at the level they experienced—but the French thought they had long passed the days of the massacre of the infantry. Ironically, although at the highest levels of the army the generals had no confidence in the offensive at all, the infantry had believed what they had been told.

Ordinary soldiers had also put a great deal of faith in Mangin, a colonial officer. Like Nivelle, he had demonstrated his talents at Verdun, where his allegedly brilliant victory on the right bank erased any memories of how he had destroyed his entire division in an amateurish counterattack around Fort Vaux in May. A year later the core of his attack force consisted of roughly twenty-five thousand Senegalese *tirailleurs,* who would attack at the key point in the line, around the Hurtebise farm, and then break through to Laon. By now the prewar cadre of the colonial army was mostly dead, but the mystique lived on, and in a peculiar way that is difficult to explain rationally, the presence of these colonial troops from Africa had a powerful effect on the other troops.[12]

Unfortunately, this worked in both directions. On the sixteenth, the rain had already turned to sleet, and was shortly going to turn to snow.

The Senegalese had no experience in freezing weather. Half frozen, unable to keep their guns in working order, they were massacred by German artillery and machine gunners, and broke. Of the ten thousand in the initial assault, six thousand were casualties.[13] Therein lay the actual horror of the Chemin des Dames: not the numbers of casualties in absolute terms, but the proportions of those engaged. The soldiers—and their officers—expected better.

Nivelle and his staff were not so foolish as to believe that their artillery would be completely successful. They had counted on the new French tanks to more than compensate for any shortfalls in the barrage. The French had been furious at Haig in September for unleashing his armor too soon, since everyone agreed that the only proper way to deploy tanks was in large masses. On the sixteenth, the French deployed 121 of their new Schneider tanks. In theory, the French tank was a much better design than the British: it weighed only about half what the British tanks weighed, and was armed with a 75 millimeter gun.[14]

The results, however, were disastrous. By nightfall, eighty-one of the vehicles were out of action; ominously, fifty-two of those were the result of German antitank tactics. As the French only had two hundred Schneiders in working order when the battle had begun, the idea of a massive tank deployment collapsed almost immediately. The French tanks were still too heavy and too underpowered to be able to survive on the battlefield, no matter how many were deployed.

Of course, it didn't help that the Germans had been given seven months to ponder the problem. Not only were they designing their own tanks (which would appear in due time) but they now had the measure of what defensive tactics worked: objects nearly three meters high and two meters wide moving along at a maximum speed of six kilometers an hour—about a brisk walking pace—made wonderful targets. As an added bonus for the infantry, the gasoline tanks of the Schneider were placed where they were easily ignited by hostile fire, while the armor, like those on the first British tanks, was too thin to withstand the new armor-piercing bullets.

On 5 May 1917 there was a second attempt on the ridge, and another tank attack, this one with forty-six tanks in three separate groups, including a company of the new Saint-Chamond tanks. The Saint-Chamond, which had been built solely by the state arsenal to prove it was better at tank design than the private firm of Schneider, rapidly proved itself a disaster: of the sixteen Saint-Chamonds, only nine made it out of their own lines, and of those only three survived. The plain of Juvincourt, where the tank force deployed, was an enormous rolling plain three kilometers deep, dominated by German positions on two sides. German gunners had ample time to hit their targets. The plain of Juvincourt became the cemetery of the French tank force.

That the French were still attacking three weeks later was a surprise, since Nivelle had assured the entire government that the attack would be called off within forty-eight hours if there was no breakthrough. But despite the lack of progress, Nivelle was determined to keep on, adjustments had been made, progress was announced, and the offensive was not stopped until the ninth, when it was painfully clear that there was no conceivable set of circumstances under which a breakthrough could be foreseen. In those three weeks, the French had at least thirty thousand men killed in action. A simple comparison: in three months of fighting on the Somme the death toll had been slightly over fifty thousand.[15] The army had expected a victory and gotten a massacre.

Meanwhile, around Arras, Haig had begun a series of offensive operations that were very hard to reconcile with the idea of a great breakthrough, and in fact, Haig's ideas seemed to be to continue grinding away at the Germans on the basis of the by now Holy Writ that prevailed in the BEF and in the General Staff in London, to the effect that the Germans were a beaten force and their losses were far higher than those of the Allies.

There was then neither the pangs of reality nor the inconvenience of cooperating with the perfidious French to mar British operations. The offensive actually began a week before the French one, on the ninth, when the Canadians captured the Vimy ridge, just to the northwest of Arras. Tanks were employed there as well, but few if any actually made it to the enemy lines—if anything the BEF's breakdown rate was worse than the French one.[16]

The capture of Vimy Ridge was an impressive accomplishment, but the army commanders were unable to follow it up properly. The Canadians and the ANZAC troops (Australians and New Zealanders) were the best soldiers the BEF had in 1917. If it was humanly possible for them to take an objective, they would succeed, regardless of the cost, and around Arras they did, taking and seizing the ground around Bullecourt. But the Australians had ten thousand casualties at Bullecourt; the overseas troops incurred a disproportionate share of the thirty thousand dead and missing the BEF lost during this battle. Vimy Ridge became the grave-yard of the Canadian forces, just as the Vosges was the graveyard of the French alpine troops.[17]

There was an ominous undercurrent here. At the Somme, the Australians and the Canadians had been in the vanguard of the heaviest fighting, and most of the real gains there from late July were won by their sacrifice. Now the same pattern was repeating itself at Arras. But there were only so many of these troops, and when they were gone, or their will shattered, Haig would have no real offensive capabilities left.

PÉTAIN AND THE MUTINY

A weak civilian government and a thoroughly captive military enabled Haig to keep on bashing away as long as he liked. Such was not the case in France, where the agreement had been that if the offensive did not pro-duce immediate results, it would be aborted. Nivelle, backed by Poincaré, simply ignored the agreement and proposed to continue the fight.

Nivelle's offensive unraveled in a surprising way. When Nivelle went to Micheler and demanded yet another attack—in the face both of the agreement and the evidence of the battlefield—Micheler not only refused, he started screaming at his commander in chief. Below Micheler, there were complaints being made directly to the ministers and the Chamber by senior officers. The mutiny began at the top, with senior commanders actively refusing to follow orders and pleading with their civilian counter-parts to intervene.

Someone had to go. Given the opposition of the army commanders and the minister of war, the choice was obvious. Nivelle was summarily dismissed, to be replaced by Pétain. Finally—as von Falkenhayn had pre-dicted—the army had reached its breaking point. And not only the French. Birdwood, the ANZAC I Corps commander, met personally with the survivors of the Fourth Australian Division, which had lost at least half of its strength at Arras, and revealed to them how he had tried to get the plans changed.[18]

Any form of disobedience in an army is serious. In the BEF, even crit-icisms of a superior officer were taken seriously. So Birdwood's behavior was extreme. So was the behavior of the French officers who succeeded in replacing Nivelle and stopping his offensive. As the actions of the officers make clear, it was not so much a mutiny as the refusal to destroy their nation's fighting capacity by continuing the suicidal attacks that had been the norm so far.

And now another mutiny broke out, more or less spontaneously, all over the army. Not a mutiny in the normal sense of the word: the French term, which translates well enough into English as "collective indiscipline," is actually rather accurate. In the vast majority of the 250 cases (which involved sixty-eight divisions, less than half the army), the soldiers obeyed their own officers, and held their positions. There was no question of the front being abandoned. The soldiers—and their officers—behaved as though the war was going to be continued. They mostly stayed in their positions and defended them—not that much defense was necessary, as the Germans saw little need to mount attacks on an adversary who could be counted on to destroy himself.

Nor was there much in the way of retribution—if the records are to be believed. Although the number of soldiers finally executed as a result of the "collective indiscipline," about fifty, may well be too low, only seven hundred French soldiers were executed during the entire war. In fact, three British soldiers were tried and given the death penalty for every two French ones (despite the image of strict Prussian discipline, capital convictions and executions in the German Army during the war were hardly a tenth of the British or French figures).[19]

Pétain, who succeeded Nivelle almost one year to the day after he himself had been removed from command at Verdun, was faced not with a problem of "discipline," but of dealing with the soldiers and remediating their grievances.[20] These were numerous and legitimate. By comparison with their allies and enemies, French soldiers were badly fed, badly doctored, wretchedly housed, and poorly treated. By now everyone realized that they had also been badly led.

The difficulty lay not in how to solve the problems the men faced, but in recognizing there were actually legitimate grounds for complaint within the army. Nivelle himself blamed the failure of the government to deal with civilian discontent and political agitation, while the government blamed Nivelle. Pétain, who held them both responsible, went about solving the problems. The solutions were simple, and in many cases (the lack of mobile field kitchens to give the troops hot meals) went back to governmental penuriousness before the war. By August 1917, or less than three months after the mutiny and the failure of Nivelle's offensive, Pétain had the French Army in good enough shape to mount a major offensive.

The men of the BEF had as much cause as the French to demand change. That they did not is probably because the BEF itself had been so thoroughly destroyed in 1914 and 1915. For the first years of the war, the BEF had been a volunteer force, and as there had been no service obligation in the United Kingdom, the new recruits were unfamiliar with the military: it took time to realize that its ways were not simply different, but inept.

But the changes brought about by British incompetence in the long run were worse than those the French suffered. In Pétain, the French soldier had a leader he felt understood his plight and who had pledged to end the mindless attacks. The leadership of the BEF never changed. When Pershing got to France, Clemenceau observed to him that Great Britain was finished as world power. Not merely because of the "immense drain" of the fighting, but because "the experience of her Colonial troops in the war will make their people more independent and she will lose her control over them."[21] Birdwood's apology to his Australians was thus not simply an act of insubordination; it marked the end of the British Empire as its leaders had known it, and as they assumed it would exist indefinitely.

THE PÉTAIN OFFENSIVES OF 1917

Nivelle's fall offensive at Verdun had been hailed as the restoration of the ground conquered by the Germans. Even the usually skeptical Lloyd George had bought into "these two brilliant victories," as he termed the recapture of the forts.[22] But at the end of 1916, the Germans still held about four fifths of the territory they had seized earlier in the year, and they held about half of it as late as September 1918. It wasn't until September 1918 that the AEF finally broke through the last of the German positions on the left bank, and in October the French were still encamped along some of the original German lines on the right bank.[23] The difference between what remained and what Nivelle had taken back is one measure of the success of Pétain's newly re-formed French Army.[24]

In an attempt both to restore the army's morale and imbue it with new tactics, Pétain planned an offensive designed to throw the Germans back to their 21 February 1916 start lines. This was not a small operation, being five times as large as Nivelle's October operation at Verdun, and larger even than the Somme. Pétain deployed sixteen divisions on both banks of the Meuse. But the number of infantry divisions tells only part of the story: there were nearly twice as many gunners deployed as infantry, and the bombardment went on for six days, with some of the newly minted 400 millimeter super-heavy guns zeroed in on the left–bank defenses, which were pulverized—infiltrating French infantry found mostly corpses.[25]

A list of the corps objectives makes pretty clear just how far the Germans had actually gotten from their 1916 start line, as well as where they still were. On the left bank, the XIII Corps had as its goal hill 304, and the XVI Corps had the neighboring ridge of Le Morte Homme. On the right bank, the XV Corps was slated to recapture the Côte de Talou and hill 344, while the XXII Corps targeted the Bois de Fosses, Bois la Chaume, and the Bois des Caurières. By and large, as a result of the careful planning, and Pétain's reliance on the by now traditional German tactic of heavy firepower, the offensive was a success. Although it did not throw the Germans back to, or past, their original lines of 1915–16, it stabilized the left bank and regained a significant piece of the right bank ground lost in 1916, including what might be called the two grand prizes: the twin humped ridge of hill 304—Le Morte Homme on the left bank and the tactically dominant Côte de Talou on the Right.

There was nothing radical about Pétain's ideas, which were in fact very close to von Mudra's, and may be summed up in Pétain's aphorism "Fire conquers, infantry occupies." Infantry assaults should be delivered only against positions where the defenses have been almost completely destroyed by shellfire, and in such conditions that there is no possibility of an immediate counterattack. Given France's resources in 1917, Pétain felt that a breakthrough was impossible: the most that could be done was to mount small local offensives that would restore morale and establish a French moral ascendancy on the battlefield.

Unlike all the other Allied senior officers, Pétain's background was in the infantry. He understood the folly of suicidal struggles across noman's-land in an attempt to conquer half-empty trenches at bayonet point. Following the German model, Pétain broke off the offense when the defense began to stiffen—the point at which, in the traditional Allied model, commanders would pour in more and more troops, trying to exploit a largely mythical breach in the line, a tactic that resulted in a simple slaughter. It is worth pausing here for a moment to appreciate the enormity of this accomplishment, which may be summarized easily enough: the war had been going on for three years, and this was the first time a large-scale French offensive had ever succeeded in taking and holding objectives of any importance.

On 21 October 1917, Pétain launched another highly symbolic offensive, this one an affair of half a dozen divisions that aimed at the recapturing of the Malmaison fort on the ridge of the Chemin des Dames, where the infantry had been massacred during the Nivelle offensive. This time, finally, there was a tank attack (sixty-eight Schneiders and Saint-Chaumonds) that was coordinated with the infantry and the artillery. Although only twenty tanks managed to accomplish their mission and return (twenty-four never made it past the start line and nineteen were left on the field of battle), the offensive itself was a success, and a foretaste of what could be accomplished with careful planning.

With those offensives (and a smaller one of less significance), and by making long overdue improvements to the conditions under which the ordinary soldier labored, Pétain restored a great measure of confidence to French troops. More important for the average soldier was that French casualties under Pétain in 1917 were roughly half what they had been under Nivelle in the last months of 1916.[26]

Since the government had already announced to the world—and to its allies—that this territory had been reconquered at the end of 1916, Pétain and the newly renovated army were both deprived of their fair share of the praise they were so justly due. This was an excellent example of how lying about the war boomeranged. From August 1917 on, the one thing France needed most was what Pétain's troops had given them, to dispel the illusion that their army had been beaten in the field or was in revolt. But there was no turning back now. The only option was to maintain the official version of what was happening.

THE DEATH OF THE BEF

The BEF and the Imperial General Staff in London had been fixated on operations in Flanders. Some evidence suggests that while agreeing to the joint offensive on the Somme, Haig had actually envisioned it as a sort of diversionary operation to cloak another greater effort around Ypres.[27] Throughout 1916 and well into 1917, however, the British government had repeatedly insisted on a unified effort, and since Joffre had stuck to his one great idea, Haig had been forced to go along. Nivelle's ascendance had coincided with Lloyd George becoming the prime minister, and Lloyd George was even keener on joint efforts than were the French.

But as Nivelle's offensive collapsed, the British found themselves facing a serious crisis. As an island, the country was completely dependent on control of the sea. Prewar, the navy—which hatched strategy independent of the army—had contemplated a blockade as the means of beating Germany, and when the war broke out, the British had simply ignored the requirements and conventions of maritime law to try to strangle Germany. The Germans had fought back, their weapon of choice being the submarine. For a new and hardly ever before used weapon, the submarine was remarkably successful. In 1916, the British calculated they had lost 1,231,867 gross tons of shipping, and had only managed to build 630,000 tons. By the end of April 1917, however, according to Lloyd George's figures, they had already lost 1,343,378 tons (1.709).

But now, of course, they needed the ships more than ever. America had entered the war (on 6 April 1917), and could be counted on—hopefully—to supply the manpower needed to win it. But not if the shipping losses continued, since there would be no shipping available (or left) to transport the American military to France. This empowered Haig, who now aimed at a major offensive that would break out of the Ypres position and roll up the whole Belgian coast, thus regaining the Channel ports and stopping the German menace to British shipping.

The area around Ypres was, therefore, to be the springboard for a great BEF offensive that would sweep the coast and break the Germans. The British had been working on this front for years, and on 7 June 1917, announced the opening of their campaign by detonating nineteen mines underneath the Messines Ridge, which dominated the line to the south of Ypres, and allowed the Germans to control the lowlands to the north.

The resulting explosion was heard in London, and ANZAC troops (along with British and Irish divisions) stormed what was left of the ridge. The mines had been set off at three in the morning. By nine what was left of the ridge was in British hands. Supposedly ten thousand German soldiers simply disappeared, and Messines was acclaimed as a great—albeit local—victory.

Underneath was a more disturbing reality. Ten thousand is almost exactly the figure for total German dead in June 1917 on the entire Western Front, and by all accounts there was a week of hard fighting to come after 7 June, since the German Fourth Army counterattacked almost immediately. Even more ominously, it appears that the Germans had already evacuated the ridge four days before the mines were set off. The explosions were so enormous that there were dazed German soldiers wandering around the battlefield as the BEF attacked, but the British were simply experiencing the same maneuver that the French had already encountered—a well-timed withdrawal that left the Allies to pounce on an empty section of terrain, only to be smashed by an aggressive counter-attack.

Whenever the Germans got wind of a particularly nasty attack, they simply pulled back and let the blow fall harmlessly on the abandoned positions. Then, when the Allied infantry climbed through the broken ter-rain, the defenders emerged from behind the position and methodically eliminated them. Like the French in 1915, the British were amazingly slow to figure out how poor their own security was, and how the defend-ers always knew they were about to attack.[28]

The Messines Ridge offensive, which ultimately cost the BEF perhaps fifty thousand casualties, was an ominous portent. But Haig was opti-mistic, as was the General Staff in London. Plans went ahead for a new battle, Third Ypres, more usually known as Passchendaele, after a small village eight kilometers behind the German lines that was the local objec-tive of the BEF.

By July, the rate of shipping loss had begun to decline, although it was still horrific. But the BEF plans for Third Ypres went on, with all the usual justifications. The aim had been to start in July, but the Germans once again were there first. But this time, instead of attacking with men, they attacked using a new and deadly weapon, and on 17 July 1917, the Germans started heavy shelling of the Ypres positions with dichloroethyl-sulfide gas shells. The Germans called this new and deadly gas, yellow cross, after the emblem on the shells. British troops called it mustard gas, and the French called it Yperite, after where it was first used.

Whatever it was called, its effects at Ypres were "devastating," as General Fries, head of the newly formed American Chemical Warfare

Section, put it.[29] Pershing noted in his diary that the BEF had twenty-six thousand gas casualties in July at Ypres, and on the twenty-sixth, Fifth Army recorded that a single attack had felled one man out of six in an entire division. There was, in other words, a reason why the French tagged the gas Yperite. In July, even though the Messines Ridge fighting was over and Third Ypres hadn't yet begun, the BEF suffered 84,695 casualties (killed, missing, and wounded), which was in point of fact higher than in any of the adjacent months of June, August, or September.

The gas shelling forced the offensive to be delayed (the British attempted to minimize the impact of the gas by blaming the French for the delay), and the actual ground attack didn't begin until 31 July 1917, which meant that most of the fighting would be in August. This was bad news. In northwestern Belgium the water table lies right under the surface. Any time a hole is dug, it begins to fill with water. A massive artillery barrage would therefore create a swamp, even without much rain. August is an unpredictable month for Flanders, and August of 1917 turned out to be unusually wet.

In July the British began their usual multimillion-shell barrage. By 4 August, no serious progress had been made breaking out of the Ypres positions. But casualties had been, by the standards of the BEF, light—less than ten thousand men dead or missing—so Haig was keen to continue on. Ominously, by the fourth, observers who saw the front were using words like "porridge" or "cream cheese" to describe the condition of the ground over which the infantry would have to move.

Clearly there would be no breakthrough, whether the ground was porridge or cement: five days gave the Germans plenty of time to bring up reinforcements. In April and May the French had finally reached the correct decision: when there was no hope of an immediate breakthrough, the offensive had to be aborted. The Chemin des Dames offensive had dragged on for three weeks, but the lesson was clear enough for anyone to see.

Except to the BEF. Haig let Plumer, the only competent senior officer the BEF had, take over from Gough, and Plumer's Second Army managed to force their way through a series of secondary objectives. Plumer was using a crude approximation of von Mudra's slicing tactics, and he was slowly slicing off strips of ground and advancing. But there was nothing surprising in this slow advance: the Germans were simply backing up, and exacting a heavy price for each stage. At this rate it would take years to get through Belgium—assuming that the United Kingdom had the manpower to keep it up.[30]

Lloyd George was dubious, and on 4 September 1917, he held a conference in London whose main objective was to bring a halt to military operations of this sort, and particularly Third Ypres. But the military (navy included) at this point simply presented a united front, even though the submarine threat was subsiding. The civilian argument was that with Russia out of the war and France on the ropes, the British should husband their resources and wait for the Americans. The military simply took the same facts and turned them backward: since everyone else was dropping out, it was imperative that someone show some fight.

The military carried the day and Passchendaele continued on in the mud and rain all through the fall, not winding down until the middle of November. The Imperial General Staff in London claimed that the Germans had lost heavily, and postwar BEF apologists trounced anyone who claimed the contrary. The best estimate is that the BEF lost 399,821 officers and men in casualties of all kinds (killed, wounded, and missing). German losses were heavy as well, but the comparison is revealing. For all of 1917, the BEF had 226,450 officers and men killed. The German figure was 121,622 officers and men killed for the entire front. Whatever was left of the BEF after the Somme and Arras, died in the mud at Passchendaele.[31]

NOTES

1. Lord Hankey, *The Supreme Command* (London: Allen and Unwin, 1961), 680. He's talking about Haig's projects for the summer of 1917.

2. Fayolle, *Carnets secrets de la grande guerre,* ed. Henry Contamine (Paris: Plon, 1964), 190.

3. David Lloyd George, *War Memoirs* (London: Odhams, 1938), 1:538.

4. Most of the grain came from territory (Ukraine) the Germans and Austrians were moving into. The best summary of Russia's prewar production is in Zhores A. Medvedev, *Soviet Agriculture* (New York: Norton, 1987), 237. The idea that Germany and Austria were brought to their knees by the "blockade" is convincingly dealt with in Niall Ferguson, *The Pity of War* (New York: Basic Books, 1999).

5. "We have the formula" is a paraphrase of an actual statement made by Nivelle, and first recorded by Colonel Serrigny on 9 October 1916 at dinner. See [Colonel] Bernard Serrigny, *Trente ans avec Pétain* (Paris: Plon, 1959), 112–13.

6. Data from Eugene Carrias, *L'Armée allemande: Son histoire, son organisation, sa tactique* (Paris: Berger-Levrault, 1938), 206–07.

7. For information on the evolution of German—and also of French—firepower and manpower, see Fernand Gambiez and Martin Suire, *Histoire de la première guerre mondiale* (Paris: Fayard, 1968), 260–1; Pierre Joseph Camena d'Almeida, *L'Armée allemande avant et pendant la guerre de 1914–18* (Paris: Berger-Levrault, 1919), 208–208, 285–86; Service Historiques Armeés, *Inventaire sommaire des archives de la guerre (N 24 and N 25)*. (Troyes: La Renaissance, 1967), 107–24. The figures on BEF versus French weapons strengths are taken from a British government study cited by Denis Winter, *Haig's Command* (New York: Viking, 1991), 148.

8. Both quoted by Gregor Dallas, *At the Heart of a Tiger: Clemenceau and His World, 1841–1929* (New York: Caroll and Graf, 1993), 467. Lyautey's reference was to a comic opera of the same name. See also the slightly different account of Pierre Miquel, Le *Chemin des dames* (Paris: Perrin, 1997), 49.

9. The main reason the Germans pulled back. Nothing suggests that Section IIIb of the German General Staff had gotten any worse at its job, and, so far, as we have seen, the Germans knew the time and place of every Allied offensive.

10. Poincaré, Serrigny, and Ribot all left accounts of what happened, there seems to be little doubt about the sequence of events. The standard French discussion is in Paul Allard, *Les Dessous de la guerre révélés par les comités secrets* (Paris: Les Éditions de France, 1932), 107212. The most elaborate treatment of these meetings and Pétain's speech in English is in Richard Watt, *Dare Call It Treason* (New York: Simon and Schuster, 1963), 165–66. There are brief accounts in John Williams, *Mutiny 1917* (London: Heinemann, 1962), 22–23; Herbert R. Lottman, *Pétain, Hero or Traitor* (New York: Morrow, 1985), 61.

11. A point frequently overlooked; only Pierre Miquel points it out at length in his analysis of what went wrong. See Miquel, 88, 123.

12. Basically, as the war went on, the French used African troops to keep their own losses down. Although recent French analysts have disputed this, see the very thorough analysis in Joe Lunn, *Memoirs of the Maelstrom: A Senegalese Oral History of the First World War* (Portsmouth, N.H.: Heinemann, 1999), which argues that the Senegalese sustained two to three times the losses of the European French infantry (140–47).

13. Speeches in the Chamber make clear that many French deputies were enraged by the slaughter of the African troops. See Allard, 135–40.

14. The most complete and elaborate account is by [Lieutenant-Colonel] Jean Paul Perré, *Battailes et combats des char français: l'année d'apprentissage (1917)* (Paris: Charles-Lavauzelle, 1937), who was there.

15. The most exact accounting is in Miquel, 213–16.

16. See the account in James Cary, *Tanks and Armor in Modern Warfare* (New York: Franklin Watts, 1966), 41–45. As previously noted, the breakdown rate for tanks remained incredibly high. In August 1918 four out of five tanks committed by the BEF were out of action within forty-eight hours. See Peter Beale, *Death by Design: The Fate of British Tank Crews in the Second World War* (Gloucestershire: Sutton, 1998), 19.

17. See the brilliant account by Alexander McKee, *Vimy Ridge* (New York: Stein and Day,

1967), the first writer formally to make the comparison between BEF tactics in World War I and Japanese tactics in World War II (167).

18. According to Lieutenant E.J. Rule of the 14th Battalion, as quoted by Laffin, *British Butchers and Bunglers of World War One,* 106.

19. The figure refers to death sentences handed out through courts-martial. Of the 3,080 British soldiers found guilty, only 346 were actually executed. Fewer French soldiers were convicted (about 2,000), but the rate of execution was higher. See the table in David Englander, "Mutinies and Military Morale," *World War I,* ed. Hew Strachan (New York: Oxford University Press, 1998), 192.

20. An enormous mythology sprang up around the "mutiny," the more so since the army refused to let anyone look at the records until the 1960s. Nor is it clear that the records are very helpful. The standard French account is Guy Pedroncini, *Les Mutineries de 1917.* 3rd ed. (Paris: Presses Universitaires de France, 1996). There is an admirably restrained and succinct summation in Englander, 191–203.

21. John J. Pershing, *My Experiences in the World War* (New York: Stokes, 1931), 2:119.

22. Lloyd George, *War Memoirs,* 1:876.

23. These maps are contained in the American Battle Monuments Commission, *American Armies and Battlefields in Europe* (Washington, D.C.: U.S. Government Printing Office, 1938), the most relevant being a large (1 cm=500-meter scale) map entitled "Meuse-Argonne Offensive of the American First Army, September 26th–November 11th, 1918." I have verified the accuracy of the front-line markers by relating it to the terrain using large-scale French surveying maps. The reader who looks closely at the various French maps used will, when comparing the two sets, notice a certain vagueness in the French ones when it comes to landmarks that might identify the course of the lines. In several cases, the French maps show territory as being in French hands when it was actually behind the German lines.

24. Part of the problem is that almost all the maps in use derive from the excellent ones done for Pétain's own account, *La Bataille de Verdun* (Verdun: Fremont, [1931]), and the last map of the RFV in that text is for June 1916 (88–89). To complicate matters further, there are errors in drawing the lines on these maps: e.g., they show Aprémont as being French, when the whole area along the Saint-Mihiel–Aprémont road was still in German hands in 1918. Curiously, the extremely chauvinistic Michelin Guide to the battlefield has this line drawn correctly: *Verdun Argonne 1914–1918* (Clermont-Ferrand: Michelin, 1937), 10.

25. The only thorough account of this offensive is in Louis Gillet, *La Bataille de Verdun* (Paris: G. Van Ouest et Cie., 1921), 253–74. Gillet, like many French writers in the immediate postwar period, had access to much data since destroyed, and his recapitulations are invaluable. The 1937 Michelin Guide, *Verdun Argonne* has invaluable maps of this and the earlier phases of the battle, e.g., 41–44.

26. The crown prince, understandably reticent about the success of this campaign, claims that many of the key trenches were evacuated before the attack because the Germans knew they couldn't hang on to them: *My War Experiences* (New York: McBride, 1923), 286–88; these figures from Gillet (271).

27. See the discussion in Winter 62–64.

28. See the assessment of the documentary evidence that the Germans knew of the attack and had withdrawn in Winter (96, note 13).

29. See the references in Amos A. Fries and Clarence J. West, *Chemical Warfare* (New York: McGraw-Hill, 1921), 22–23, 151, 176.

30. Some recent British historians have argued that the course of the 1917 battles reveals an evolutionary development in British infantry tactics, positing a learning curve, and even going so far as to say that there was "a process of improvement, which, however bloody, ultimately placed it at the technological and tactical cutting edge of the Allied armies on the Western Front by the final months of the war," as Peter Simkins puts it in his foreword to Ian Passingham, *Pillars of Fire: The Battle of Messines Ridge June 1917* (Gloucestershire: Sutton, 1998), i. The fullest expression of this idea is in Paddy Griffith's *Battle Tactics of the Western Front* (London: Saint Edmunsbury, 1994). But this is to demolish straw men—the point is not that the BEF did not improve, the point is that it took too long to learn, started too late, and changed too slowly. Ultimately the point is not sustainable, as it ignores massive evidence to the contrary, and is probably irrelevant, given the German offensive gains of 1918.

31. "On the Somme he [Haig] had sent the flower of British youth to death or mutilation; at Passchendaele he had tipped the survivors into the slough of despond." John Keegan, *The First World War* (New York: Knopf, 1999), 369

15

1917: Caporetto and Cambrai

The truth was, that these strikes, aimed at the morale of the German army, were wearing down the morale of the British.... Crown Prince Rupprecht, who had often been impressed by the staunch bearing of British prisoners, was shocked on 16 August [1917] to hear one of them saying they would gladly have shot the officers who ordered them to attack . . . Whereas the British would formerly hold out though outflanked, now they surrendered easily. The German infantry, on the other hand, was imbued with confidence in its own superiority.
—*C.E.W. Bean, the official Australian historian*[1]

In the German system, the chiefs of staff actually ran the armies. When von Moltke became distressed about the situation in East Prussia in 1914, his first move was to sack the chief of staff and replace him with Ludendorff, his old prewar operations chief, and when the German defenses on the Somme had given way in July 1916, von Falkenhayn removed the Second Army's chief of staff and replaced him with Colonel Lossberg.

As von Hindenburg and Ludendorff had accumulated control of the entire Eastern Front in 1914, Ludendorff had left most of the military planning to Colonel Max Hoffmann and had spent most of his energies (when he wasn't trying to get von Falkenhayn sacked) setting up the civilian administration of the vast territory that had been wrenched away from Imperial Russia. By the end of 1915, this encompassed an area roughly the size of France, and Ludendorff divided it into six administrative regions: Courland, Lithuania, Suwalki, Vilna, Grodno, and Bialystok.

In addition to setting up a police force, he established newspapers, currency, and courts. But the overall thrust of his work was to turn the area into a vast supply depot and machine shop for the armies of *Ober-Ost*. Ludendorff, strangely enough, turned out to be an excellent provincial governor, and by the end of 1915 *Ober-Ost* had evolved into a troika. Von Hindenburg was the figurehead, Ludendorff the actual ruler of the conquered lands, and Hoffmann in charge of the military.

When von Falkenhayn was dismissed in August 1916, Ludendorff left Hoffmann to run the war in the East, von Hindenburg became the titular head of all the armies Germany possessed, and Ludendorff gradually assumed control. "He now attempted to do for all of Germany what he had done in the conquered provinces of the east" is how one biographer puts it.[2]

As the German High Command read the English and American newspapers, it emerged—correctly—that the Allies had no real offensive plans for 1918. There would be no major offensive until the AEF was ready to go into action, because the Allies had run out of men as well as confidence. The British estimated that it took a minimum of fifteen months for a newly raised division to be ready for combat. Simple arithmetic suggested that the earliest point at which the Americans would be ready was sometime in the summer of 1918, and probably not until August of that year. Pétain's oft-expressed goal was a great offensive in 1919, because by then there would be an AEF of two million men in France, and they would have completed their training.

The difference between the two estimates (the summer of 1918 or the spring of 1919) reflected two different military appreciations of the situation. Pershing envisioned an AEF of about a million men that would be able to make a decisive impact on the front. Pétain wanted to wait until the Allies had such overwhelming strength that there would be no possibility of serious German opposition. Militarily, this was sensible enough: an offensive delivered on such a great scale would probably have fewer casualties and would win the war outright.

The diverging Allied points of view were hardly secret. All the Germans had to do was to read the papers to see that an attack delivered in the spring of 1918 would hit the British and the French before the AEF was organized and trained. This led Ludendorff and the German General Staff to a systematic approach to their problems. By January 1917, the application of overwhelming force had destroyed Rumania. Although the abdication of the Tsar and the formation of the Kerensky government in the spring had temporarily led to a renewed optimism about Russia's continued participation in the war, the truth was that there would be no more major offensive operations by the Russian Army, and by the summer of 1917, the Germans and the Austrians so dominated the front that the only question remaining was when Russia would quit the war and under what terms.

As an East Prussian himself, Ludendorff was anxious that the war in the East be wound down to Germany's advantage. Provided the war was concluded by the end of 1917, the OHL would have the entire spring remaining for an offensive in the West, and by the end of the summer, Germany only had one adversary left on the other two fronts: Italy.

THE ITALIAN COLLAPSE

The Italian Front was dangerous for two reasons. During 1917, as Lloyd George became more firmly in control of the government, he was more and more inclined to the idea that a major offensive in Italy might destroy the Habsburg Empire. This was the by now rather hoary dream of forcing the Western Front to implode on the Germans by destroying Austria. In fairness, however, all of the major combatants were edging toward a complete collapse. Russia had simply been the first to go. It was reasonable to assume that someone had to be next in line, and on paper Austria-Hungary was still the weakest of the lot.

The Germans had another worry: the new Habsburg emperor, Charles I (Francis Joseph I having died on 21 November 1916), was more and more inclined to try to opt for a separate peace. Now that Russia had collapsed, and Serbia was no more, why not come to terms with the Italians and let Germany and France and England finish the war alone? But if Italy could be knocked out of the war militarily, the peace move would be a moot point. Germany had plenty of men still left, and hardly needed Habsburg soldiers in France. Heavy weapons were a different matter, but the German High Command could probably force the Austrians to ship their heavy weapons to the West in time to settle accounts there.

At the same time, the Italians, still commanded by Cadorna, continued to mount offensives. In August 1917, Italy was the only one of the four great Allied powers willing or able to attempt yet another break-through offensive, and on 19 August 1917, Cadorna mounted a new offensive aimed at piercing the Austrian positions on the Isonzo. By this time the Italian Army was a sizable force, and Cadorna committed fifty-one divisions to the operation, which went on for a month, finally run-ning down in the latter part of September. Technically, this was the Eleventh Battle of the Isonzo. Here it was the end of the summer of 1917, and in over two years of battles, the Italians had still not broken the Austrian line: at Gorizia (which the Italians had taken in August 1916), the Isonzo is roughly twelve kilometers from the 1914 Austro-Italian bor-der, and that would pretty much mark the limit of the Italian advance.

While the Italians regrouped for another big push, Austria and Germany decided to solve the Italian problem once and for all. The Germans had learned quickly on the Western Front, and particularly after the Somme, that it was infinitely preferable to go over to the attack and get in the first blow than it was to stand on the defense and try to with-stand it. What was needed was a cadre of new troops to make the blow possible.

So the German General Staff contributed seven divisions and their alpine expert, Krafft von Dellmensingen. This new army, the Fourteenth, acting in conjunction with the Austrian Tenth Army, would attack out of the upper Isonzo valley on a thirty-odd kilometer section of the front located between Flitsch (Plezo) and Tolmin (Tolmino). The aim was to force the Italians back to the Tagliamento River. Given that in its most northerly loop the Tagliamento was about thirty kilometers from the start line, this was an ambitious plan.

But the Austrian High Command, which had committed twenty-six divisions to the operation, was eager for an even more decisive solution. When the Fourteenth and Tenth Armies attacked out of the northeast, the First and Second Armies, which had been holding the lower Isonzo valley, would attack from the east, and the Eleventh Army would attack out of the Trentino in the same direction as in May 1916.

In terms of sheer numbers, the Italians had the advantage, as they had at least forty-one divisions in the region to thirty-three for the attack-ers. But the Germans had new tactics to deploy. As we have seen, early on in 1915, German gunners had realized that the best way to begin an offense was with a short heavy bombardment, which stunned the enemy and obliterated his entire position (hopefully) in one huge massive blow. Instead of the week-long bombardments of the Allies, the Germans had gone for opening barrages of a few hours: the initial barrage at Verdun had basically only been eight hours. Then, as the infantry probed, the barrage lifted and moved on.

The French had mastered part of this—the creeping barrage that went ahead of the infantry—but not the short heavy smashing part. The shorter the bombardment, the less time the defenders had to organize themselves, or, for that matter, to satisfy themselves that this was the preface to the attack. At Verdun, for example, the French General Staff had initially been convinced that the offensive was a feint, primarily because the barrage was so short.

Hitherto, the problem gunners had faced was that they had to register their guns on the targets, that is, they had to fire a round and then judge where it had hit. Establishing where the round had landed in relation to the target area took time. So the simple fact of registration made the guns vulnerable. In positional warfare, there were only so many places a shell could come from. The receivers could locate the guns and begin counter battery work. And the mere fact of registration—or of a series of registrations—could be telling. By late 1916 the French (although not the British) had become expert in this sort of game, and German gunners had been forced to adapt.

So during 1917, German gunners had been experimenting with a radically new idea—firing without prior registration. With an accurate aerial map, in theory one could hit the target on the first shot, using nothing more complicated than spherical trigonometry, provided one was careful and accurate. On the other hand, some of the most significant targets behind the enemy lines didn't demand precision aiming to begin with: a high-explosive shell that landed in a fuel depot or an ammunition dump didn't have to land squarely in the center of it to start a conflagration, and the heavier the shells (and hence the greater their explosive payload) the less accuracy required, because the blast radius was a function of the explosive payload.

When, in the summer of 1917, Hoffmann had persuaded Ludendorff that Riga was a viable target (and that its capture would bring the Russian negotiators to their senses), Ludendorff had released half a dozen divisions to him, and the Germans had used this tactic in their Riga offensive for the first time on a large scale. But this attack went in at the start of October, and the Austro-German offensive began a few weeks later; clearly this was another instance of the spontaneous innovation and rapid diffusion of tactical ideas that characterized the German army.[3]

To complicate matters still further, German gunners would fire gas shells as well as high explosive. So on 24 October 1917, the gunners suddenly opened up, with little warning. The Italian positions on the Isonzo simply dissolved. On 2 November 1917 desperate attempts to form a defensive line on the Tagliamento River failed, and by the seventh, what was left of the Italian Army was on the south bank of the Piave River, a formidable obstacle to any further advance.

Basically the Piave, in the course of the first seventy-odd kilometers from its mouth in the Adriatic north to Feltre, divides the region of Friuli–Venezia Giulia from Veneto. In their offensive, the Austrian and German armies simply seized all of Friuli–Venezia Giulia. Lloyd George estimated it at ten thousand square miles. Habsburg troops were fifty kilometers from Padua, less than thirty kilometers from Venice itself. It was Saint-Mihiel all over again, except on a much larger scale.

Hastily, the Allies put together a total of eight British and French divisions and shipped them to Italy, where, as the Tenth Army, they stiffened the middle of the new defensive line, enabling them to claim that the outcome of the Battle of Caporetto (as the disaster was misleadingly called) had been salvaged. But that was to lose sight of the whole reason for the Italian enterprise, which was to break Austria-Hungary and Germany by stretching them to the breaking point. Shifting an entire army out of the Western Front and putting them in action in Italy was certainly a strange way of accomplishing that aim.

The defensive line held, but why would the Austrians and the Germans have wanted to continue their offensive? There was no point in going any farther to the south or west: the breakthrough pushed the front so far back that for all practical purposes the war in Italy was over. And the Italian Army was devastated, no longer capable of offensive action, as some simple calculations make clear. Cadorna, the Italian commander, had started off in August 1917 with fifty-one divisions in Friulia–Venezia Giulia. Losses in Eleventh Isonzo aren't clear, but by the end of October, the Italian *Commando Supremo* supposedly only had forty-one divisions there, which, if true, would indicate casualties on the order of one hundred thousand men.[4]

Lloyd George promptly went to Italy to make sure the government didn't quit the war on the spot. As a result he was able to do what no political figure had been able to do until now, which was to see for himself how bad the situation actually was. His conclusions were depressing. There were "600,000 in dead, wounded and prisoners and missing (including those who threw their arms away in the debacle and were scattered over the face of Northern Italy)."[5] Interestingly enough, the usual casualty figure is thought to be under 350,000, with about 265,000 soldiers prisoners of war. The difference between the two totals (600,000 as opposed to 350,000) suggests that finally someone was beginning to grasp the Allied achievements with numbers. Soldiers who had thrown their arms away and run could be rounded up and gotten to fight—eventually. But for the time being, the Italians had no army to speak of.[6]

Like their adversaries the Austrians, the Italians had earned themselves a poor reputation among French and British officers. In both cases it was totally undeserved. The French Army had been in combat only eight months longer than the Italian Army, and both the French and British Armies would concede large tracts of French territory in the face of the coming German offensives. By November 1918 Italian losses officially came to 460,000 men killed and 570,000 taken prisoner. By November 1917, Italy basically had no army in the field.

CAMBRAI

In the face of this disaster, Pétain, like Pershing, stuck to his original objectives. But Haig and the Imperial General Staff in London felt that now was the time for the BEF to show that it had not been beaten down at Third Ypres. Fuller, who ran the staff of the BEF Tank Corps, had proposed a great tank attack, a "theatrical blow . . . to restore British prestige" before the winter set in.[7] He proposed an attack against Saint-Quentin, a perfect area for armored operations, and which additionally had the virtue of possibly collapsing a portion of the center of the German line.

As a spoiling attack of the sort the Germans themselves had been practicing for years, this was an excellent move. But Haig was opposed to Saint-Quentin. It was too far away from Flanders (he was still fixated on the idea of a breakthrough out of Ypres), and, worse still, it would mean cooperation with the French. Since part of the Imperial General Staff misrepresentations to the War Cabinet involved suppressing the actual status of the French, who under Pétain had by now (November 1917) completed three successful offensive operations on the Western Front, it was hardly possible to mount a large joint operation without embarrassing questions being asked—or embarrassing comparisons being made, as had been done after the Somme.

The BEF now had a sizable tank force, and the ground around Cambrai was, even in the view of armored advocates like Fuller, eminently suitable terrain as well. The Germans had withdrawn to a line about twelve kilometers to the southwest of the town during February and March 1917, and so the ground behind the German positions was rolling pasture, not some moonscape full of refuse and water-filled craters. The ground over which the tanks would advance—provided the gunners were prevented from their usual orgy of crater building—was in good shape as well.

The problem with Cambrai was that the front was too narrow, and it was too constricted. There were canals on both sides of the front, so the attack, if successful, would be hemmed in. Even Foch realized that mounting an offensive with both sides hemmed in by canals was a bad idea, and said so (the British Cabinet only learned this alarming bit of news well after the fact). Moreover, for the attack to be successful in breaking through to Cambrai, a good twelve kilometers behind the lines, there had to be a massive follow-up, what Fayolle, with justification, had termed the task of moving an army through an army.[8]

Fayolle had also observed that this business of moving one army through another was far from simple, and this was the reason behind Fuller's choice of Saint-Quentin. If the attack was successful, there was room to maneuver through and spread out. At Cambrai, the BEF was in the position of having to move everything through a bottleneck created by the canals. Not only was there not enough room to do this, but Haig lacked the troops. The War Cabinet had pulled out four divisions from the BEF and sent them to Italy, and Haig was unwilling to move other troops out of the Ypres positions, where apparently he still had vague plans of some future offensive taking place.

So the advocates of armor were successful in only one area: the offensive opened without the usual weeklong barrage, which gave it a terrific advantage akin to the one that had prevailed earlier on the Isonzo. On 20 November 1917, the BEF attacked with nineteen divisions, spearheaded by 378 tanks. Compared to the Somme and Third Ypres, where there had been no meaningful advance at all, Cambrai at first looked like a serious breakthrough. The offensive rolled right through the German lines and got to within a few kilometers of Cambrai.

From that point on (about 23 November) Cambrai developed into two entirely different battles. Given the disasters of the past, a quick advance of ten kilometers on a front of any size was an immense victory. Church bells were rung. The Hindenburg line had been broken at its strongest point (why any competent officer would have preferred to attack his adversary at the point where he was strongest is an interesting question). The Germans had at last been defeated. All of the British Imperial Staff's prognostications about the Germans being on the ropes were really true. All Haig needed was more men and he would win the war.

Reality was rather more distressing. The French had learned at the Chemin des Dames that in the intervening months since the Somme, German troops in defensive positions had developed a series of nasty ways in which to disable tanks. The new light mortar, in widespread use by the infantry since the end of 1915, could disable one of the slow-moving behemoths, while the 12.98-millimeter rifle the Germans had already been using in small quantities to shoot through armored loopholes fired an extremely potent armor-piercing bullet. Since the Germans had already integrated their field artillery and their infantry into joint operations, gunners could also be relied on to destroy tanks: the ordinary 77-millimeter field gun had enough punch to blow a hole through the thinly armored vehicles. But when it came down to it, the infantry were managing well enough on their own: Fully half of all French tank personnel casualties came from small arms fire.[9]

Nor had the mechanical reliability, cross-country capabilities, and speed of the British tanks been much improved since the Somme. The British Tanks Corps now learned exactly the same lesson as the French had six months earlier. Half of the underpowered and unwieldy monsters were destroyed or abandoned on the battlefield, with about sixty being picked off by German gunners.[10] Tanks, like heavy guns, wear out with use, and the first tanks wore out quickly and needed refitting. An attack with nearly four hundred vehicles was initially impressive, but when, after forty-eight hours, there were only sixty or seventy still operating, armored operations in the modern sense of the word had obviously ceased. On the twenty-sixth the survivors were withdrawn for repairs, but by then the attack had bogged down completely. The British fought their way most of the distance to Cambrai, but they lacked both the leadership and the manpower to secure what they had taken. But Haig, who had taken personal direction of the attack, persisted in letting the infantry try to continue on its own.

When Lloyd George spoke of the false and misleading reports made to the War Cabinet by his officers, in one sense he was being unfair: the British High Command apparently believed that their boundless optimism represented the true state of affairs with respect to the Germans.[11] The whole idea of Cambrai was based on the assumption that the Germans had been beaten so badly, were so weakened, that they could do little more than hold on by their fingernails. Then, too, the British were aware that the Germans had heavy responsibilities elsewhere: while the planning was going on for Cambrai, they probably knew that the OHL had mounted an offensive at Riga in early October, and had shifted troops to Italy as well. Even if they weren't completely whipped psychologically, the British General Staff believed the Germans should have been out of men—a perennial pipe dream that never went away.

Instead, four days after the attack stalled, the Germans launched a major counterattack. In addition to the six or seven divisions holding the line, they brought in fourteen more from other parts of the front, and completely smashed the shattered infantry divisions, one of which, the Twelfth, simply broke and ran, while two others were wiped out. By 7 December 1917, the Germans had not only ejected the British from the forward positions gained in the initial fighting, but had thrown them out of a whole section of their start line. This was a tactic, it will be remembered, that had first been observed in the spring of 1915 during one phase of the Battle of the Woëvre at the Tranchée de Calonne: the initial French attack had been quite successful, but the defenders had promptly countered and thrown the surprised French out of the initial positions in their own line.

Cambrai was a disaster in other ways as well. The Germans had been working on tank development for over a year. There were two reasons for their slow progress. One was that the Germans realized the power-to-weight ratio problem and were trying to get around it by coupling two engines together (the first working German vehicle was in service by February 1918). The other reason was that after each engagement the battlefield was littered with abandoned Allied tanks. When the Germans moved back across the BEF start line at the southern edge, and established themselves in part of the British lines (which now became the

German forward positions), they cleared the way for their own people to start retrieving abandoned vehicles. When the Germans next went into action, they had as many or more repossessed British tanks as they had tanks of their own design.

The army's handling of the news about Cambrai—continuing to claim it was a great victory even while the Germans were smashing their way back to the start line—fatally weakened Haig's position with the government. It also encouraged the War Cabinet to consider a revolutionary step—a serious alliance with the French and the Americans—something the British General Staff, and particularly Haig and Robertson, had blocked at every turn.

Inside the military, Cambrai was seen as a near miss, not a defeat, and the army consoled itself yet again with its two-part fallback position. Subjectively, it was claimed the Germans were running out of fight. Objectively, they were losing the war of attrition. The argument was also made that Great Britain had no real choice, since, after the April and May 1917 collapse of the French Army, the French had simply stopped fighting.

None of this was true. The aggressive German counterattack at Cambrai strongly suggests the German Army was far from losing its will to continue the fight. And anecdotally, the evidence was to the contrary. One British officer saw the essential tragedy of his soldiers, and put it in his report. If his men advanced standing up, "they were an easy target." But if they advanced by crawling, they "were exhausted in a few minutes." As the authors of one recent study of Third Ypres put it, "Even today the vision of Haig's army crawling into battle in an attempt to stay alive induces a sense of inexpressible melancholy."[12]

Postwar, the War Office listed BEF deaths at Cambrai as 10,042; in November and December 1917, the German Army reported 13,047 fatalities for the entire Western Front. In 1917, the French Army had 136,200 men killed, and the BEF 190,015 killed. Counting the Belgian war dead for the year, the Allied total came to almost 350,000 men. During the same period, 121,622 German soldiers were killed on the Western Front.[13] "How the devil can we finish this war?" General Fayolle confided to his diary (256).

NOTES

1. As quoted by Philip Warner, *Passchendaele, The Tragic Victory of 1917* (New York: Atheneum, 1988), 182–83.

2. D.J. Goodspeed, *Ludendorff: Soldier, Dictator, Revolutionary* (London: Rupert Hart-Davis, 1966), 157.

3. Subsequently the British would claim the new tactics had been developed by an Eastern commander, von Hutier, who had first tried them out at Riga. The effect was to try to make it seem they were caught off-guard by "new" tactics used for the first time in the March 1918 offensive. This has been thoroughly debunked by Bruce I. Gudmundsson in *Stormtroop Tactics: Innovation in the German Army, 1914–1918* (New York: Praeger, 1989); my own claim is that the tactics were developed even earlier. See his prefatory remarks for the discussion of von Hutier and appendix C for the discussion of Laffargue, a French officer whom British propagandists tried to claim had developed the new infantry tactics.

4. The only reliable source on this campaign is Gunther E. Rothenberg, *The Army of Francis-Joseph* (West Lafayette, Ind.: Purdue University Press, 1976), 206–8. The Italian Official History stops at the end of 1916. Rommel's account of the fighting is his most memorable tale. See Erwin Rommel, *Infantry Attacks* (*Greift an: Erlebnisse und Erfahrungen*), (Mechanicsburg, Pa.: Stackpole Books, 1990), (first published as *Infanterie*), 230 ff.

5. The quote is from David Lloyd George, War Memoirs (London: Odhams, 1938), 2:1390. The implication is that more soldiers ran away, or temporarily went missing, than were taken prisoner or killed, which is probably true, and certainly squares with Rommel's account (see note 4).

6. Total strength was supposed to be 1.5 million. Given the losses in Eleventh Isonzo, Italy had lost a staggering 50 percent of its army (700,000 men) in a couple of months. But since Cadorna had only a maximum of sixty-one divisions, it would seem that most of the Italian Army at this point had either gone AWOL or was a casualty of war, since sixty-one divisions is well under 700,000 men.

7. Lloyd George emphasized those same words (2:1334); they are an exceedingly curious choice to use in speaking of an offensive, but revealing as to the mind-set of the BEF's staff. Cambrai is one of the most misrepresented battles of the war. For the traditional view of it as a smashing British victory, see Bryan Cooper, *The Battle of Cambrai* (New York: Stein and Day, 1967). In *The First World War* (New York: Knopf, 1999), John Keegan is considerably more circumspect (370–71).

8. Fayolle, *Carnets secrets de la grande guerre*, ed. Henry Contamine (Paris: Plon, 1964), 109. Fayolle had written this all down in June 1915.

9. Fritz Heigl, *Taschenbuch der Tanks* (Munich: J.F. Lehmanns, 1926), 353. See his discussion on the weaknesses of tanks (322–33).

10. Of the tanks, 71 were abandoned for mechanical reasons, 43 bogged down, and 65 were hit and destroyed. The pattern continued: on 12 August 1918, 480 of the 688 tanks the BEF had sent into action in August were fit only for scrap—an admission that comes from British armored enthusiast Ivor Halstead in his propaganda tract written for World War II, *The Truth About Our Tanks* (London: Lindsay Drummond, 1942), 58. See the sympathetic dis-

cussions in Crow, 130, as well as James Cary, *Tanks and Armor in Modern Warfare* (New York: Franklin Watts, 1966), 50.

11. This scathing blast, in 2:1313, appears at the start of the introduction to this book. Lloyd George sometimes gives the impression that he was unaware of BEF casualties. But, as Robin Prior and Trevor Wilson have demonstrated, this was not the case. See *Passchendaele, The Untold Story* (New Haven: Yale University Press, 1996), 187. On the other hand, since the government was being told that German losses were, by comparison, so large as to be fatally crippling, his claims are not disingenuous.

12. The example quoted, from a report made by an officer of the 58th Division, is found in Prior and Wilson, 176, and their memorable summary directly follows. As they point out, this officer's observations were left out of the report prepared by his superior, a practical example of how the bad news was progressively eliminated as reports made their way up the chain of command.

13. Postwar, various attempts were made to adjust the figures for Cambrai so that the losses were more or less equal, or even slightly to the British advantage. For the actual losses, see War Office [United Kingdom], *Statistics of the Military Effort of the British Empire During the Great War, 1914–1920* (London: His Majesty's Stationery Office, 1922), 327. British figures for 1917 taken from *Australian Medical History*, 2:261, as this corrects errors and omissions in the official British reports: initial reports for the BEF dead in 1917 were slightly over a quarter of a million men. German data taken from Heeressanitatsinspektion des Reichsministeriums, *Sanitätsbericht über das deutsche Heer im Weltkrieg 1914/18* (Berlin: Reichsministerium, 1935), 3: Tables 149–50. French figures taken from Service Historiques des Armeés, *Inventaire sommaire des Archives de la Guerre (N 24 and N 25)* (Troyes: La Renaissance, 1967), annexe 7, corrected for live prisoners using Louis Marin's Report to the Chamber of Deputies (633: 1920, 88, as summarized by Michel Huber in *La Population de la France pendant la guerre* (New Haven: Yale University Press, 1931), 135. The number of German soldiers who died in 1917 on all fronts from all causes is less than the Allied dead on the Western Front alone.

16

1917–1918: The Great Race

*General, these are American regulars. In a hundred and fifty years
they have never been beaten.*
　　　　　　　　—*Preston Brown to General Degoutte, 1 June 1918.*[1]

Unlike Italy and Rumania, persuaded to enter the war so they would
get a piece of Austria, America believed itself to have declared war on
Germany in April 1917 for nobler reasons. To make the world safe for
democracy, as the slogan went. At bottom, however, the Allies had
manipulated the American government with the same expertise they had
shown from the start of the war. President Wilson, a Germanophobe long
before 1914, was already predisposed to aid Great Britain. Although
scrupulously neutral in public (Irish Americans being an important part
of any Democratic politician's constituency), in private he was
unabashedly partisan. His administration did nothing to stop the Allies
from borrowing large sums to finance their war efforts.

During the course of the war, the Allies were able to borrow $10.5
billion from sources in the United States, and $3.5 billion of that sum was
raised before the United States actually entered the war.[2] Such enormous
figures are meaningless without a context, of course, but in 1914, France
and Great Britain combined appropriated only 671 million dollars for
defense.[3] In other words, the Allies borrowed enough money to enable
them to maintain their 1914 defense budgets (which in both cases represented a vast increase over the prewar years) for the entire course of the
war. In 1919, Great Britain's national debt was £7.5 billion, of which

£1.2 billion was an obligation to pay back the American loans.[4]

Loans were only one part of the complex pattern of aid extended by the United States before 1917. American manufacturers made war materials to Allied specifications and shipped them to the Allies. To name two obvious examples: British infantry used rifles produced by Winchester and Remington, and those rifles fired ammunition produced in the United States. British gunners manned eight-inch howitzers built by the Midvale Steel and Ordnance Company in Nicetown, Pennsylvania. Given that in the first two years of the war, Great Britain was able to produce only 700,000 rifles, and was desperate for heavy weapons, the American production was significant.[5]

More important still was the American supply of explosives. The actual explosive ingredient in artillery shells was a mixture of trinitrotoluol, popularly known as TNT. Amatol, the British high explosive, was a mixture of trinitrotoluol and ammonium nitrate. Trinitrotoluol is derived from toluol, a substance somewhat difficult to obtain. In 1914 it came primarily as a by product of coke ovens, and most of the French ovens had been lost to the Germans in August and September of 1914. The production of toluol was thus a bottleneck in the development of artillery shells. In 1914, American toluol capacity was about 700,000 pounds a month. At the start of 1917, it was six million pounds a month. Given that as late as 1916 Great Britain was only able to produce 76,000 tons of high explosives, the American supply of toluol was highly significant.[6] In this and in many other ways, the Allied armies of 1915 and 1916 were as heavily dependent on American industrial products as the Allied governments were on American cash.

The extent of the aid given before America's formal declaration of war has traditionally been passed over in silence. Neither Allied apologists nor American defenders of President Wilson have been anxious to draw attention to the massive level of American support, since it is invariably claimed that the United States was provoked into going to war by German actions against American citizens. Wilson testified before Congress that their country would have gotten into the war anyway. He was careful not to add that one reason was his sympathy for the English, which he went to great lengths to conceal.[7]

Bryan, Wilson's first secretary of state, genuinely wanted America to remain neutral, but he was undercut at every turn, and resigned in protest over the handling of the *Lusitania* sinking. Already, even at that point,

British propagandists at Wellington House had been so successful at selling the British version of the war that when a senator pointed out—correctly—that the *Lusitania* was carrying armaments to Great Britain, he was saved from impeachment only by the testimony of the Harbor Master of the Port of New York. The United States was a cobelligerent long before it declared war.

The hows and whys of Wilson's secret tilt to the British, together with the mechanics of the Anglo-French propaganda effort in the United States, are a fascinating subject, but one outside our purview. But enough has been said to establish that the Germans were quite aware of the American tilt toward the Allies. From their point of view, the issue was not if America would join with Great Britain, but when this would happen, and what effect it would have on the war.

Some Germans professed to sneer at the idea of an American Army having any impact on the field of battle. After all, in 1917, the entire army hardly came to 150,000 men, less even than Belgium's. But to a generation of young German officers who had grown up reading tales of the Wild West, and who had studied the Civil War (which German staff officers all had done), the idea of having to fight a country where the average farmhouse probably had as many guns as the average German infantry platoon was far from reassuring.

The crux of the matter, quite simply, was this. Could America get an army into the field before the Germans could win the war in the West outright? It had taken Great Britain, which in its own estimation had the most professional army in the world in 1914, nearly two years before it was able to deploy a force big enough to mount a sustained offensive effort. British officers, who by their own reckoning were second to none in the raising of large armies from scratch, estimated it took fifteen months to form an infantry division and get it ready for the battlefield. Given what the results to date had been of the British effort, the German General Staff reasonably assumed that an American army wouldn't be able to take the field until August 1918 at the earliest, and that probably there wouldn't be an American offensive until the following year.

So while Pétain patiently rebuilt the demoralized French armies and Haig and Robertson completed their destruction of the BEF, Germany and the United States embarked on what can only be described as a great race to determine the war's outcome. If, as Pétain and the civilians of the Painlevé government believed, it was necessary to wait for American troops to arrive in France and win the war, the obvious question was how long would it take for the United States to create a great army and get it into action. In April 1917, the Germans thus had a window of opportunity to win outright. But it was a window of indeterminate length, and clearly, much depended on how efficiently and rapidly the Americans proceeded.

PERSHING AND THE AMERICAN EXPEDITIONARY FORCE

The man selected to command the AEF brought a new, and for the British, a deeply disturbing personality into the dynamics of Allied command. Like Joffre, von Falkenhayn, and Haig, John J. Pershing was a thoroughly political soldier. In 1906, he had been catapulted from captain to brigadier general, passing over past eight hundred–odd officers who had seniority. Clearly, being the son-in-law of a senior Republican senator (Warren of Wyoming) had its advantages.

There were significant differences between Pershing on the one hand and his Allied colleagues (and German adversaries) on the other. In addition to his West Point education, Pershing—surprisingly—had a degree in law and had spent four years teaching military science at a major American university. In fact, he had started out as a teacher, and had gone to West Point to get a free education.

He thus had an intellectual side that his opposite numbers lacked, as well as a unique understanding of the complex relationship between the army, the government, and the population at large. There was a breadth of military experience as well: he had served as a military attaché and been an observer during the Russo-Japanese War. Like Haig, Pershing had been in combat, and like Joffre, he had been held responsible command positions, both in the Philippines and in Mexico, so he understood the basic problems of reconciling the military with the political, of balancing the need to conform to the government's policy while still making decisions on his own. He had the background for the task, which made him unique among the senior commanders of the war, none of whom had experience doing what they were now called on to do. Armies being inherently hierarchical, Pershing had another advantage as well. Although he was only fifty-seven, he was the senior officer: he had made general when Pétain and Foch and Haig—and Ludendorff—were all still colonels.[8]

Moreover, as the British and French shortly found to their consternation, Pershing had a level of authority that no one else had. Haig, as we have seen, hardly had the confidence of the prime minister and the Cabinet, who controlled him through the Chief of the Imperial General Staff (the CIGS). In January 1918, the government was able to force Robertson, the CIGS, to quit, and his successor, Wilson, was no supporter of Haig. Neither was the man Haig had replaced, French, who was now giving the British Cabinet unofficial advice. London was right across the Channel; Haig had an unhappy group of politicians sitting on his doorstep.

The French picture was bizarre. Pétain, the actual army commander, had control over the troops, but not over the direction of the war effort. By contrast, Foch, who had been named the overall Allied commander in successive stages, had no real authority over any body of troops. On paper he was the supreme commander of all the Allied forces, but none of the actual army commanders (Haig, Pershing, Pétain) had much inclination to obey his orders, and Pershing, who by July 1918 had most of the Allied fighting strength, would simply ignore him.

Moreover, Clemenceau, who had become premier, was a virulent anti-Catholic, deeply distrustful both of Foch's clerical ties and Pétain's growing popularity with the rank and file. For that matter, neither the British nor the French governments were on solid ground politically. Not only was Pershing the only one of the top commanders who enjoyed the "entire confidence" of his country's leader, to quote from a French report on the subject, but his real boss, Wilson, as American president, had "powers more extensive than those of any other ruler," to continue the wording of the report.[9]

Given the problems Pershing faced, this was no bad thing. When he arrived in France at the end of June 1917, he had three major tasks. The first was to create an American Army in France and lead it into action. Given that the United States had never planned for an army of over half a million men, and had never given any thought to their deployment in Europe, this task alone was a difficult one. Not only did the men have to be trained and equipped, they had to be transported to France, and an infrastructure had to be created to maintain them. Virtually all of this had to be created from the ground up, as the French simply did not have the facilities to maintain and supply an entirely new army. As the mutiny in 1917 had made clear, the country hardly had the infrastructure to support its own troops.

Pershing also had to deal with a restive and highly opinionated War Department, which was jealous of its prerogatives and determined to manage the war from the other side of the Atlantic, while at the same time there were other, more senior officers who were deeply jealous of Pershing's authority and thought that all or part of it should have been given to them. Pershing probably got along with Pétain as well as he did because they both had similar problems.

But Pershing had something his French colleague lacked, the support of Wilson, and, perhaps even better, the appearance of that support. This became vitally important, because the British and the French, albeit in different ways, were basically opposed to the creation of an independent American force in France. Over the course of the next sixteen months after June 1917, the British and the French continuously tried to scuttle the concept of the AEF.

Part of the reason for their failure was that Pershing would prove himself to be stubborn. He was willing to stand up to Foch, Haig, Lloyd George, and Clemenceau, either together or separately. He also proved himself remarkably adept politically: time and time again, either the War Department or the Allies thought they had reduced his authority and power, only to find that they hadn't.

But the main reason for Pershing's success with the AEF was that he moved faster than the Allies did. Less than two weeks after his arrival in France, Pershing had established the assembly and training area for the AEF and cabled the manpower requirements back to Washington. He—and the Allies—needed a million men in France by May 1918, and he aimed to assemble the AEF behind Verdun and the Saint-Mihiel salient, thus ensuring that in the projected Allied offensive that would (hopefully once and for all) win the war, the AEF would be at the most important point in the line, the center. Shortly, the one million men in June became two million men by the end of the year.

This was the key decision. The Americans would have to go into action from wherever they had been trained and assembled. So putting them in Lorraine ensured that the AEF would be the major player in the great offensive to come. Pétain saw clearly that the best way to end the war was to carry it through onto German soil. The fastest route into

Germany was through Lorraine—one of the main reasons Bismarck had annexed a portion of it in 1871. Offensives in Champagne-Artois, regardless of their initial success, would mean the Allies would have to fight their way across Belgium before they could strike into Germany. And the German shortening of their line in early 1917 had set an ominous precedent. A.J.P. Taylor would later sum up the problem concisely, in speaking of Messines Ridge: "Two years of preparation and a million pounds of explosive had advanced the British front two miles. How long would it take at this rate to get to Berlin?"[10] But a successful breakthrough in Lorraine would quickly take the Allies into Germany itself.[11] With two million Americans, Pétain was convinced there would be a breakthrough. Immediately on arriving in France, Pershing's staff began planning for an offensive through Lorraine, the operation that would, fourteen months later, be known as the Saint-Mihiel offensive.

Pétain then went one step further. Trying to make sure that the AEF would have the best possible French instructors, he turned the job over to the surviving French alpine troops.[12] While the British exhorted new recruits to use the bayonet, the French, having learned the hard way that the bayonet and the rifle were of little use, taught the Americans the usefulness of grenades. This disparity in training methods started in the United States. Over a third of the British officers sent there to assist in the training of the Americans were specialists in bayonets and riflery, while three fifths of the French instructors were specialists in artillery, hand grenades, and small-unit tactics.[13]

So the AEF was basically (five divisions excepted) trained to use French weapons by French instructors. Not unnaturally, this meant the tactics employed would be those the French had gradually learned under Pétain, which were, as we have seen, adaptations of those developed earlier in the war by the Germans themselves, notably by von Mudra in the Argonne. Although Pershing himself deplored the lack of emphasis on marksmanship in this training, his recorded protests are excellent signs that the French instruction was having an effect.

Leadership on the battlefield (or behind it) cannot be trained. It is sometimes the case that fledgling officers who do well in training fail miserably on the battlefield, while the reverse is true as well: Ulysses S. Grant did badly at West Point, and Max Hoffman, often considered the great strategic genius of the German Army, spent most of his early days in what could charitably be described as a drunken stupor. Regardless of

Pershing's deficiencies as army commander, the AEF had some outstanding junior officers, Patton, Marshall, and MacArthur being the three most well known. Although deeply troubled by growing pains, the AEF had a surprisingly talented leadership, and Pershing's condescension toward the Allies, although impolitic, was quite correct. As we shall see below, the AEF's intelligence operation was vastly better than France's when it came to the essentials.

The newly constituted staff of the AEF made one other decision of great significance. They decided to establish the basic infantry division at about twenty-eight thousand men, the size of the typical Allied Army Corps. Each division would have four regiments, each with three battalions of four infantry companies and a machine gun company. At a point when the French infantry divisions were stabilizing downward to about nine thousand men, the AEF planned to have nearly eighteen thousand combat infantry in each division. If the French were willing to bulk out these units with their own tanks and heavy weapons (which they were), one American division would be the equivalent of three of the under-strength French units and probably four of the under-gunned British ones, since each American division would have its own heavy weapons.[14]

Artillery was of crucial importance. The United States had planned for a war in which it would need an army of half a million men. It had more than enough rifles for this army, but only nine hundred guns, almost all of them three-inch (75 millimeter) field guns, which was barely sufficient even by prewar standards: the Americans needed over three thousand field guns almost immediately. Fortunately, by the middle of 1917, France was producing modern heavy weapons like the Schneider 155 millimeter howitzer and the Filloux 155 millimeter gun, as well as the Renault light tank. French industry could now produce such weapons in quantity, provided it could import the necessary raw materials, since it had lost most of its steel-making capacity in the first two months of the war.

It therefore made sense to equip American units with French-built weapons, trading them for American raw materials, while the United States developed its own manufacturing system.[15] The Allies were already dependent on the United States for basic materials: In 1917, half of the United Kingdom's smokeless powder was supplied by the United States, and American shells and explosives, manufactured in enormous quantities, enabled the Allies to supply the AEF without fear of exhausting their own stocks. As a result, the AEF was almost totally equipped with French guns and tanks, and dependent on the French for technical support, which meant that the French continued a close involvement with the AEF.

At the level of grand strategy the system worked well, but it gave rise to the notion that the AEF was only capable of functioning as an independent army because it was using weapons loaned to it by France and Great Britain. In reality the United States equipped its army with weapons it had purchased abroad through barter, just as the Allied war effort itself was being subsidized by American loans.

This perception was exacerbated by the difficulties caused by the War Department. Instead of a million men, the War Department was prepared to send over only 650,000 at most, even though it quickly became clear that a million-man army was too small—what was needed in France was an army of two million men. This was a battle the War Department lost. On the technical side, however, the War Department's technical experts, like their counterparts in France and Great Britain, generally prevailed. The AEF could have been equipped with its own field guns and its own machine guns—the American three-inch (75 millimeter) field gun was a perfectly satisfactory weapon—but instead of concentrating on mass production of existing designs, the War Department's experts squandered their energies on fruitless attempts to copy the French 75 millimeter weapon. [16]

The supply of weaponry for the American divisions being formed and trained in France was also impeded by a fundamental disagreement about the status of these units and how they would be used—the first of the many attempts to abort the AEF before it was ever born. The French wanted the men to be put into action immediately, without any prior training in France. So did the British, but with a crucial difference. The French wanted them to be slotted in at the regimental level to bulk out their under-strength divisions. But the British wanted them amalgamated into British units under British command—so long as the troops were white. [17]

Pershing saw that this was militarily unwise, politically foolish, and constitutionally out of the question. But initially the Allies had a lever: the Americans would travel to Europe in Allied ships, which meant that they were competing with supplies the Allies needed to maintain themselves in the war. At the war's end, American vessels had transported about 45 percent of the troops sent to France; but this statistic is misleading, as the

American effort became significant only after July 1918.[18] Up until that point, the main source of naval transport was the United Kingdom, which gave the British a valuable lever to use in their attempts to amalgamate the Americans into the BEF.

To the British, the logical solution was not to ship entire divisions over, but to ship riflemen and machine gunners. This would give them manpower to replace their losses. Coincidentally, it would mean the American troops would lack the support necessary for their divisions to function, and so they would have to be incorporated into Allied units and serve under Allied officers.

By contrast, Pershing wanted entire divisions which would train together and then go into action as a separate force under American command. By January 1918, the Allies were extremely annoyed. The AEF had a quarter of a million soldiers in France, and the only ones in line were still basically in training. Pershing kept claiming the Americans would only go into action as an army. The British and the French both knew what this meant: an intact army of two million men—or even a million and a half—would constitute a decisive force on the battlefield. If the AEF went into action on its own, the Americans would claim they had won the war. So the Allies, and particularly the British, wanted control of the troops.[19]

This was hardly a concession to Pershing's vanity. One key reason why the BEF had been so ineffective in 1915 and 1916 was that its leaders, in their eagerness to get into the fighting and make a difference, had basically wiped out the original cadre in the first four months of the war. So the BEF, which had then come perilously close to destroying itself in 1916 all over again, was constantly having to start over again from scratch, minus the all-important cadre of experienced veterans (to train the newcomers) and experienced officers (to control the battlefield). Whether he understood the BEF predicament or was simply obstinate on general principles, Pershing was determined that the AEF would enter combat only in autonomous tactical units, and that its main contribution to the war would be as an expeditionary force operating as army groups.[20]

During 1917, Haig and Robertson had operated as though the BEF could win the war on its own, with or without the French, and certainly without the Americans. The French Army is a broken reed, Haig smugly informed Pershing during their first meeting. But after the slaughter of Passchendaele, Pétain might well have retorted that it was the BEF that was the broken reed. As we have seen, from September 1917 on, the Lloyd George administration in London was beginning to have serious doubts as to the outcome of the war. What after April 1917 had looked like a race between the Germans and the Americans as to who would be ready first had now become a more ominous race: would Haig and Robertson destroy the BEF before the AEF was ready to fight?

The simplest solution was to treat the newly arriving American soldiers as replacement soldiers. The rationale was twofold. First, there was the British claim that the Americans didn't have the staff or the officers to run a million-man army properly. At bottom the French felt the same way, the chief difference being that Pétain was trying to control the snobbishness of his officers, and Haig wasn't.

And once the great German offensive of March 1918 started, the Allies, who had become totally hysterical, resorted to a "Pershing's stubbornness will lose the war" mode. Only the prompt infusion of large numbers of American soldiers into the Allied armies could save the day. It is interesting to speculate how long America would have remained in the war had this scheme been put into effect, particularly given the British casualty rate.

Neither of the Anglo-French claims has much merit. As we shall see, once the fighting started in 1918, it was immediately clear that, Pétain and a few commanders excepted, the fabled Allied superiority in leadership and organization was entirely mythical. And while it is true that both countries were running dangerously short of men, this was because they had consciously diverted manpower to peripheral theaters. They could easily have made up their shortfall by withdrawing their quarter-of-a-million-man army from the Balkans and the Tenth Army from Italy, not to mention the sizable British forces in the Near East.

The argument against this, at the level of grand strategy, was that these forces were necessary to keep large numbers of Central Powers soldiers tied down who would otherwise have been shipped to France. This is to turn the problem inside out. Now that Russia was out of the war, the only reason Austria was still in it was Italy. If the Allies had abandoned Italy and left it to sue for peace (the worst possible case), only seven German divisions would have been shifted to France—while the Allies had shipped ten divisions there and hundreds of their scarce heavy guns simply to stabilize the front.

It is difficult to imagine Austria making more than a token contribution to the Western Front under such circumstances. Consequently, Pershing refused to budge. When American units entered the lines, they did so at the divisional level and above. Their major effort would be as an independent army fighting their own war.

By March 1918, when the Germans began their final offensive, there were nearly half a million Americans in France. Based on the British example, one could expect that there would be at least a million of them there by midsummer, and twice that many by the end of the year. A prudent expectation would be for a faster rate, but if the Germans were going to win the war they needed to win it before the end of July, as after that, they would be faced with a brand-new army as large or larger than any in the West.

Although there was internal wrangling over where to strike first, the German approach was sensible enough. The basic problem of offensives in the West was that a drive on Paris would expose the German flanks, while a drive to the West above Paris would leave France largely intact. The problem was solved sequentially. First, the Germans would defeat the BEF so badly that there would be no possibility of a flank attack. Then they would smash through the French and take Paris. By now von Falkenhayn's logic was implicitly accepted by everyone: armies of a million men were not destroyed. But they could certainly be hit so badly the fight would be taken out of them, and this is exactly what the first German offensive did.

The BEF staff was expecting an attack, but right up to the highest levels they were confident it could be stopped. They believed they had beaten the Germans so badly in 1917 that there was hardly any fight left in them. Moreover, after the debacle of Cambrai, the British had worked on defensive organization. A group of generals had studied captured German documents (written by a major and a colonel), had suitably modified them to fit in with the superior British understanding of such matters, and a much changed and revised version of the German defensive tactics had been put into effect.[21]

The problem was twofold. On the one hand, the British failed to grasp the key basis of German defensive success, the holding back of most of the infantry so that the attackers would be sucked into a trap, blasted by artillery, exhausted by their trek, and then wiped out by the developing counterattack. In actual practice, most British infantry were too far forward. On the other hand, British practice was such that there was no possibility of giving low-level unit commanders the authority they needed to determine when and where to fight. German tactics worked because the Germans decentralized decision making downward. Simply copying their troop dispositions hardly solved the problem.

Over and above this was the complete lack of comprehension as to the tactics that the Germans had steadily been developing over the years. Since the Allies refused to admit there was another way to fight the war, they simply denied that the Germans had developed an alternative. As we have seen, when Pétain brought this up to Joffre in May 1916, it was used as yet another sign of his defeatism. Sarrail, the first Allied general to experience an early version of these tactics in the Argonne, was sacked for incompetence and then sent to Salonika: whether he was incompetent or not, the army was thus denied whatever insights he had into the German offensive tactics von Mudra and the crown prince's Fifth Army had employed against him. Since the Allies always claimed to be beating the Germans decisively, no one bothered to look closely at what their opponents were actually doing.

THE THREE GREAT GERMAN OFFENSIVES

The first of the last great German offensives in the West began on 21 March 1918, and was directed at the British Third and Fifth Armies, who, with French aid were occupying the section of the front between Arras and Laon. The Allies had assumed the Germans would probably attack there. What they had failed to reckon with was the speed of the offensive. After the usual short bombardment, which saturated the whole position with gas and high-explosive shells, and was, as was by now the German practice, initiated without any prior registration shots, the Germans jumped off against the entire line from just northwest of Laon to Arras.

In forty-eight hours the attack had simply destroyed the British Third and Fifth Armies, and the Germans were past Peronne, an advance of roughly twenty-five kilometers along a wide front. The reason for the breakthrough was, quite simply, that the British commanders had practically all their troops in the forward positions. When those were immediately smashed by the barrage and then rolled over by the infantry, there

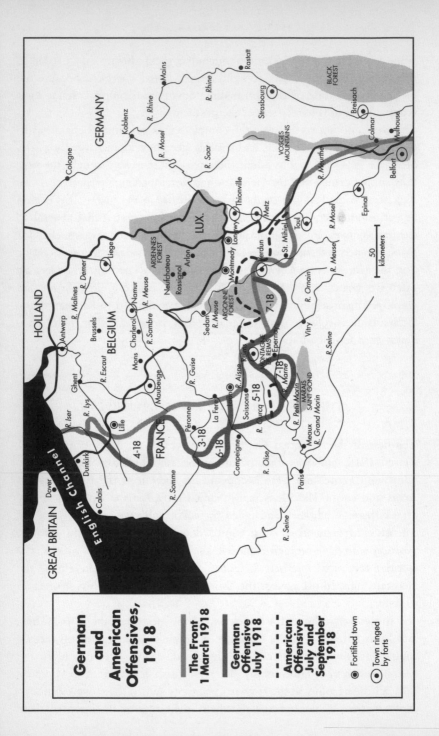

German and American Offensives, 1918

The Front 1 March 1918

German Offensive July 1918

American Offensive July and September 1918

Fortified town

Town ringed by forts

GREAT BRITAIN

English Channel

Dover
Calais
Dunkirk

HOLLAND

R. Iser
R. Lys
R. Escaut
R. Demer
R. Malines

Antwerp
Ghent
Brussels
BELGIUM
Mons
Lille
4-18

Liege
Namur
Charleroi
R. Sambre
R. Meuse
Maubeuge
Péronne
3-18
La Fère
6-18
Compiegne
R. Guise

FRANCE

R. Somme
R. Oise
R. Ourcq 5-18
Soissons
Meaux
R. Petit Morin
R. Grand Morin
MARAIS SAINT-GOND
R. Grand Morin
Paris
R. Seine

R. Aisne
Reims
MONTAGNE DE REIMS
Epernay
R. Marne 7-18
Vitry
R. Ornain
R. Seine

Sedan
R. Meuse
ARGONNE FOREST
Montmedy
Rossignol
Arlon
Neufchâteau
ARDENNES FOREST
LUX.
7-18
Verdun
St. Mihiel
Toul
R. Mosel
R. Meuse
Epinal
R. Meurthe

Longwy
Longuyon
Thionville
Metz

Koblenz
Cologne
GERMANY
R. Mosel
R. Saar
R. Rhine
Mains
Rastatt

Strasbourg
BLACK FOREST
Breisach
Colmar
Mulhouse
Belfort
VOSGES MOUNTAINS
R. Rhine

50 kilometers

were no troops behind them to plug the gap. So much for studying German methods.

As usual, Haig, who was still fixated on Flanders, had most of his troops north of the battle zone, so it was left to Pétain to move his own reserves into the rear and seal off the rupture. Unlike Haig, Pétain had a large reserve, and he had earmarked four divisions to rescue the BEF (Haig had made a similar undertaking, although where these troops were to be found is another matter).

For all practical purposes, the Germans had now cut the front in two. The main lateral rail lines, which could be used to move men and matériel behind the front lines all converged on Amiens. Of the three practicable lines, the Germans had severed the one that ran through Chaulnes and the one running through Montdidier, leaving only the one that ran up from Paris. When Haig tried to move men south, or Pétain north, they would have to go west, thus drawing them away from the lines. Given the speed of the German offensives, this meant that reinforcements would be too far away from the battlefield to have any impact on it.

In terms of morale, the effect was catastrophic. Although officially, the British were fighting hard and desperately, in actuality the troops, once overrun and surrounded, simply quit. Whole battalions surrendered their positions intact as the offensive flowed around them: the BEF lost 165,000 men in the first ten days of fighting, a high proportion of them prisoners.[22] The survivors, once regrouped, now faced a heartbreaking prospect: having to fight the Somme and Cambrai once again. For the German advance had rolled over the old Somme battlefield, and pushed a large section of the Western Front farther west.

The panic at the BEF was August 1914 all over again. Haig, like French, saw only one option, to pull out to the Channel and hang on there, thus leaving everyone else to finish the war as best they could. This was hardly a better solution in 1918 than in 1914, as the government realized. The Allied governments called a meeting. On 26 March, at Doullens, they announced a solution. Foch, who was on paper already the supreme commander, would now be the only person allowed to say who moved where, thus cutting off Haig's intention of pulling out entirely.[23] A few days later, on 3 April, at another meeting, the details of Foch's position were ironed out.

While the Allies rewrote Foch's job description, the German General Staff unrolled a new operation, an offensive that would deploy out of

Lille and move north, threatening the whole Ypres salient. On 9 April, they attacked and took another piece of Flanders. If the Germans broke through to the Channel, the troops in the salient would be cut off. So the BEF had no choice but to defend the newly exposed flank. But since they were already desperately short of men, this meant there was no real possibility of breaking the huge westward bulge the Germans had won in March.

The Germans had neatly turned the tables on the Allies. The territory won was a huge buffer zone that would shield their armies during their next offensive, should the British attack, and by the middle of April there was no real possibility of the BEF doing that. In a roughly five-week period in March and April 1918, the BEF had almost 150,000 dead and missing, or about the level of Third Ypres—which lasted five months. The French had dead and missing of nearly 60,000. German losses had been heavy as well: about 105,000 killed and missing. The problem for the Allies was simply this: not only had the Germans suffered far fewer losses but their army was now larger than it had been when the offensive started, with a ration strength of just over four million men.[24] When coupled with the massive casualties sustained during Third Ypres, the BEF was virtually finished as an offensive force.

When Clemenceau and Poincaré had asked Pétain to explain what the Germans were doing, he had replied, briefly, that their aim was first to beat the English and then to beat the French. Typically, Clemenceau, who probably disliked Pétain even more than Poincaré did, saw this as evidence of his defeatism. There was no room at the top for a realistic assessment of the war—something that Foch, whose vocabulary apparently consisted of only one word ("attack"), grasped intuitively.

But Pétain had gotten the German plan right. Nor was there much that could be done about it. The Germans now had an enormous stretch of the front from Laon to Reims and over to Verdun, where they could mount an attack. The French didn't have the men to defend the whole line adequately. The best Pétain could do was to hope that when the attack came the AEF would be able to seal it off.

Actually, there was no certainty that the Germans would even attack there. They had done so well to the north that it was easy to argue they would simply push on through to the Channel and run the BEF back to England. Foch, ever keen to mount an attack, was now trying to put together a projected offensive that would throw the Germans back to their start line, which meant he was demanding troops be sent west and north.

The French General Staff obliged him by projecting that the next attack would come there, mainly because they had still not grasped the speed with which the Germans could switch the directions of their attacks, a failing that is probably attributable to their delusionary thinking earlier in the war. Having convinced themselves they were winning—and that the Germans were always on the defensive—they hadn't bothered to notice the speed with which the Germans could throw together counterattacks as well as offensives. Now, belatedly, they were learning.

But not fast enough: the French intelligence bureau confidently predicted there would be another German attack, which would enlarge the existing salient and try to rupture the front. Four years into the war, and they were still getting it incredibly wrong.

Over at Pershing's headquarters, a young ex-cotton dealer turned intelligence officer, Samuel Hubbard, looked at all the available information and concluded that the Germans were going to turn south, and would launch an offensive across the Chemin des Dames at the end of May.[25] Despite the fact that the Allied intelligence estimates had been continuously wrong for the last forty-five months of the war, Hubbard's analysis was disregarded. How could the Americans, who had just arrived on the scene, be better at this than the French and the British, who had been doing it for years? Besides, everyone knew that the AEF's staff was a shambles, its commanders completely incompetent, their ineptitude exceeded only by their pride and their touchiness about taking the advice of professional soldiers who knew better.

General Duchêne, commander of the French Sixth Army, which was holding the front along the ridge, was, like the British Fifth Army's Gough, one of those who knew better. Like Gough, he rejected the concept of defense in depth, and had almost all of his ten divisions (six French and four British) in the main line.

On 27 May 1918, the Germans, to the consternation and surprise of everyone except Captain Hubbard, smashed across the ridge. Like Verdun and Saint-Mihiel, it was another in a long series of surprise offensives that caught everyone completely unawares. By the twenty-ninth, the Germans had taken Soissons, and the French were simply melting away. The Germans were making for the Marne, and got there by 5 June, driving about fifty kilometers straight toward Paris. As gloomy French officers told their American counterparts, it was now August 1914, and with the same sort of astronomical casualties: since the start of the March offensive, the French had lost 167,000 men killed and missing—more than their losses at Verdun over many months of fighting.

The rapidity of the German advance was as astonishing to the French as earlier it had been to the British. In a few days the Germans were at the Marne, and gearing up for another big push. The logic of the sequence of offensives now became clear. The Germans had drawn the Allies north, and had then attacked south. What was more, the success of their northern attacks precluded any possibility of relieving the pressure on the Marne by an offensive to the north.

Thus far, Pétain's prediction to Clemenceau had been quite accurate: first they'll beat the British, and then they'll beat us, he had said. Clemenceau saw this as defeatism, and Haig, ever the opportunist when it came to his reputation, quickly built on French gossip and portrayed Pétain as a broken wreck, while he became the architect of victory. But Pétain was simply telling the truth; he had more confidence in the Americans than Clemenceau did.

A REAL MIRACLE OF THE MARNE

As the French government prepared to abandon the capital, and as French staff officers gloomily told their American counterparts that if the Germans took Paris the war would be over, troops from the American Second and Third Divisions moved past the debris of the French Sixth Army, and up into the southwestern corner of the German salient, to the west of Château-Thierry.[26] Although in negotiations Pershing appeared cheerfully willing to let the Allies wipe themselves out rather than subordinate American units to them, in actual practice he was quite willing to contribute to the common defense if he saw any sense in the plan—and if his troops were operating as autonomous units. By 3 June, the Americans were in action.

In fact, the Second Division promptly found itself in one of the bloodiest battles in the history of the United States Army. The German commanders opposite saw immediately that the American intervention was decisive. General Böhm sent a message to the men of his Twenty-eighth Division that the stakes in the fighting had nothing to do with insignificant pieces of ground; it was, he said, the simple question of whether the Americans were better than the Germans.[27] He had no need to remind his men that they had already proven themselves better than the British or the French. They already knew that.

The Second Division the Germans were worried about was unique: one of its two infantry brigades was composed of Marines. When war had been declared, they had lobbied for a place at the head of the line, and, Marines being Marines, a detachment was added to the Second Division, where it replaced one of the two infantry brigades. By a quirk of censorship, the actions of the Marines were passed through the censors while the actions of the army troops were not. So in the ensuing battle, the Marine brigade got all the publicity, even though the army brigade did just as much fighting.

The first American effort took place on 6 June 1918, at the Bois de Belleau, an insignificant forest to the northwest of Château-Thierry. The German position consisted of three small hills (142, 169, and 192). Although the elevation was slight, the hills—and particularly the main one (the American cemetery is at its base)—rise sharply out of the rolling landscape. Like the Vauquois, Belleau Wood was an ideal defensive position.

The course of the battle was simple: the Germans, realizing the American advance, installed themselves on the crests. The Americans, who initially didn't realize the Germans were there in force, mounted an infantry attack, unsupported by artillery, just as the French had done at the Vauquois. Somewhat to the amazement of the Germans defending, the Americans proceeded to push them off the hills and take possession of the territory.

Tactically, the engagement was a minor one, but when the French government renamed Belleau Wood, where the Marines went into action, the Bois de la Brigade de Marine, they had a point. It was the American Second and Third Divisions, collectively, that stopped the German advance to the south, and thus saved France. It was the Marines who forced the Germans to consider the possibility they might lose the war outright. The cost was terrible. The Marines suffered over five thousand casualties, the bloodiest engagement in the history of the corps until Tarawa. Over the course of the June fighting, the Second Division lost nearly ten thousand men, about the same as the losses of the entire Anglo-

American invasion force at Normandy in 1944. Belleau Wood has some claim to be the bloodiest battle the United States has ever fought.[28]

As might be expected from units that had only recently been assembled, the whole operation was a mess of misdirection, error, and failure from beginning to end. And the American muddle was hardly helped by the French. At the divisional and corps level, the French commands simply collapsed in the face of the German attack, just as the British had done earlier. They had no clear idea what was going on and were of only marginal competence even in the best of circumstances. Like Foch, they confused attitude with action, and were cheerfully willing to sacrifice the infantry to prove that they had the proper sort of dash.

Nor was there much of any real importance about Belleau Wood. It was simply one of the thousands of small forests that the war turned into an abbatoir. That being said, Belleau Wood was a crucial engagement. Böhm was right. For years, the Allies had thrown their elite troops into action against the Germans: the cream of the prewar BEF at Mons and le Cateau, the colonial infantry at Rossignol, the French alpine troops at le Linge and Hartmannswillerkopf, the finest of the Russian Guards divisions at Tannenberg—to name a few of the more notorious. And in every instance, these elite troops had been massacred without any real gains other than what was fabricated by propagandists. No elite infantry, operating as infantry, had ever beaten the Germans out of a defensive position they had determined to hold. The Australians and Canadians had come close in 1917, but they had been reinforced by millions of pounds of high explosives, and assaulted positions that had already—in theory anyway—been blown sky high. The Second Division was going to have to fight its way in on its own.

The Germans knew this, and they also knew that it was important to hit the Americans hard and show them—and the world—who was master of the battlefield. In his orders, von Conta, the German corps commander, had specifically spoken of the need to inflict heavy casualties on the American troops. Afterward, his staff grimly recorded their appreciation: "The personnel must be called excellent.... a very good division, if not [in the sense of "possibly even"] an assault division.... attacks of the marines carried out smartly and ruthlessly. The moral effect of our fire did not materially check the advance of the infantry. The nerves of the Americans are still unshaken."[29]

In other words, the Germans lost more than a few hectares of forest.

For the first time, they lost territory they had been fighting desperately to hold, and lost it so decisively they were unable to regain it. In the Argonne, France's more perceptive officers had noted that although the gains were insignificant, they gave the Germans moral ascendancy over the battlefield. Haig could claim that the slaughter of his infantry at Third Ypres was taking the fight out of his opponents, but as the participants themselves realized, it was the other way around.

For four years, the Germans had dominated the battlefield. The spring of 1918, when Allied troops simply surrendered by the battalion, marked the logical result of that ascendancy. Belleau Wood was an insignificant engagement, but it marked the turning point of the war. The Germans had beaten the British and the French. Now they found themselves up against a troubling new adversary.

And it was an adversary whose numbers were growing by leaps and bounds. When the Germans struck again, for the last time, in July, there were nine hundred thousand American troops in France, nearly half a million of them combat troops. The July offensives stalled, and by the eighteenth, a combined Franco-American offensive operation had attacked into the salient bulging below the Soissons-Reims line. On the twentieth, the German General Staff planners, deeply upset by what had happened, staged their own version of a mutiny, suggesting that the army withdraw to its 1917 positions and start negotiating an armistice.

Ludendorff, shaken, went into a denial reminiscent of the world the Allied generals lived in.[30] Since the Allies had failed to break through, they probably couldn't break through, the Germans could sit on their gains and plan for another round. While Ludendorff recuperated, the Americans kept on attacking, slowly moving up past Fère-en-Tardenois. This was an ominous turn of events. The Germans could afford to lose territory—and they were inflicting casualties. But the one thing they certainly did not want to do was to give the AEF units the experience of offensive success.

The offensive begun there was not by any means an exclusively American affair. In fact, quantitatively, most of the ground regained was taken by the French. But it was the American drive to Fismes, and the developing side offensive from the west, also American, that forced the withdrawals. The AEF would attack through the center and the French would take the flanks.

NOTES

1. As quoted by Robert Asprey, *At Belleau Wood* (New York: Putnam, 1965), 100.

2. Figures taken from the *Times* (London), 23 January 1925: 12. The $3.5 billion figure includes moneys loaned after November 1918.

3. Data taken from Quincy Wright, *A Study of War* University of Chicago Press, 1942), Table 58 (1:670–71).

4. Figures in Martin Middlebrook, *The First Day on the Somme* (New York: Norton, 1972), 257. Niall Ferguson, as I understand his rather complex argument in *The Pity of War* (New York: Basic Books, 1999), makes the contrary case: "It is often assumed that foreign lending made a decisive difference to the outcome of the First World War" (326). Given the ratio of the American loans to the amount of funds expended (the entire French national budget in 1914 was only $1.002 billion) this argument simply doesn't hold up. Great Britain might have been able to continue the war without foreign loans, but France could not have, and without France, there was no possibility that Great Britain could beat Germany.

5. For rifle production, see Ferguson, 260. Given that the United States was neutral, a certain coyness surrounds the American data. But see the surprisingly candid revelations in Benedict Crowell and Robert Wilson, *The Arms of Industry* (New Haven, Conn.: Yale University Press, 1921). The discussion of rifles is in 1:228–233, of the howitzer, 1:94–95. Crowell was the assistant secretary of war and director of munitions from 1917 on.

6. Information on high explosives from Crowell and Wilson, 1:158–59; British data from Ferguson, 260.

7. The relevant congressional testimony is reprinted in H. C. Peterson, *Propaganda for War: The Campaign Against American Neutrality, 1914–1917* (Norman: University of Oklahoma Press, 1939), 271. Wilson was hardly the only figure to be conned by Allied propaganda. See the extensive discussion in Stewart Halsey Ross, *Propaganda for War: How the United States Was Conditioned to Fight the Great War of 1914–1918* (Jefferson, N.C.: McFarland, 1996), 145–214.

8. Although many of these details are to be found in Donald Smythe's excellent *Pershing: General of the Armies* (Bloomington: Indiana University Press, 1986), no one has yet commented on the importance of Pershing's seniority—or his legal background—in dealing with the Allies.

9. As quoted in John J. Pershing, *My Experiences in the World War* (New York: Stokes, 1931), 2:67.

10. A. J. P. Taylor, *Illustrated History of the First World War* (New York: Putnam, 1964), 145.

11. To military historians of World War II, this is a commonplace. See John Nelson Ricard's remarks in *Patton at Bay: The Lorraine Campaign* (Westport, Conn.: Praeger, 1999), 60–62.

12. Although often tagged simply as a "division," by American historians, as we saw in the chapter on the Vosges fighting, these Alpine divisions were simply the grouping of the traditionally independent alpine battalions, whose organization and history are recorded in Jean Mabire, *Chasseurs alpins: des Vosqes aux Djebels, 1914–1964* (Paris: Presses de la Cité, 1984), esp. 432–44.

13. See the discussion in Colonel Leonard Ayres in *The War with Germany, A Statistical Summary* (Washington, D.C.: Government Printing Office, 1919), 31.

14. The BEF was woefully under-gunned when it came to such mainstays as automatic weapons (French troops typically deployed three to four times as many automatic weapons as the British), and when American troops encountered British training methods they were surprised to find the emphasis was totally on the bayonet—only their French instructors bothered about such trivia as grenades.

15. The only extensive discussion is in Ayres (73–100), who has all the figures.

16. For the American problems with the 75 millimeter gun, see Bruce I. Gudmundsson, *On Artillery* (New York: Praeger, 1993) 29–36. Such problems had nothing to do with Pershing, and in fact continued up until the end of the next war, the most notorious example being the unwillingness to equip American tanks with a high velocity gun comparable to German and Russian designs. Both the French and the British armies had similar problems: French soldiers entered the war without a modern howitzer as a result. See the discussions in Joffre, *Mémoires du maréchal Joffre* (Paris: Plon, 1932), 4–5, 66–69. The British situation was even worse, since the various experts refused to use anything created abroad. See the pungent comments in Edward Louis Spears, *Liaison 1914: A Narrative of the Great Retreat.* 1st ed. (London: Heinemann, 1930), 109–110.

17. When the War Department proposed to send a division of black troops to England for training, the British military attaché in Washington protested and Milner, the minister of war, wrote to Pershing observing that there "would be a good deal of administrative trouble" if "the British Army had to undertake the training of a colored division" (Pershing, 2:45–46).

18. See the tables in Ayres, who is surprisingly reticent about specifying the extent to which the AEF was initially transported by the British (37–46).

19. "Let the Americans send men by divisions, or nominally so, without any equipment or transport. . . . When you have got them here and concentrated them in lumps, you can use them when and where you like." Report by a British liaison officer, as recorded by James H. Hallas, *Squandered Victory: The American First Army at St. Mihiel* (London: Praeger, 1995), esp. 261–65.

20. See the extensive discussions in Smythe, esp. 113–19. American historians writing about the AEF have been strangely receptive to taking British (and to a lesser extent, French) claims about Pershing and the competency of the Americans at face value, often seeming to assume that the BEF possessed a level of skill it clearly never did. See, for example, David F. Trask, *The AEF and Coalition Warmaking, 1917–1918* (Lawrence, Kansas: University of Kansas Press, 1993), who attributes to Foch and Haig a level of military competency totally at odds with their command record—and with which few analysts of their performance would agree.

21. See the account in Martin Samuels, *Doctrine and Dogma: German and British Infantry Tactics in the First World War* (New York: Greenwood, 1992), 17–19.

22. Figures from Martin Middlebrook, *The First Day on the Somme* (New York: Norton, 1972), 246.

23. Postwar, Haig successfully rewrote all this to show that everything was his doing and that it was Pétain who was in a funk and had to be superseded by Foch. Winter, in *Haig's Command* (New York: Viking, 1991), effectively demolishes this myth (183–188).

24. Official British calculations of losses are found in War Office [United King-dom], *Statistics of the Military Effort of the British Empire During the Great War, 1914–1920* (London: His Majesty's Stationery Office, 1922), 241. French data from Service *historiques des armeés, Inventaire sommaire des archives de la guerre* (N 24 and N 25) (Troyes: La Renaissance, 1967), annexe 6. German figures in Heeres-sani-täts-inspektion des Reichs-ministeriums, *Sanitätsbericht über das deutsche Heer in Weltkrieg 1914/18,* (Berlin: Reichsministerium, 1935), 3: Tables 158.

25. See the account in Asprey, 63–64. Asprey's account is echoed by Byron Farwell in *Over There* (New York: Norton, 1999), 164–165.

26. As reported to Pershing by Major Paul Clark; see Asprey, 90.

27. "An American success along our front, even if only temporary, may have the most unfavorable influence on the attitude of the Entente and the duration of the war. In the coming battles, therefore, it is not a question of the possession of this or that village or woods. . . . it is a question of whether the claim that the American Army is the equal or even superior of the German Army is to be made good." As quoted by Asprey, 285.

28. The American cemetery at Belleau Wood has 2,289 single graves and com-memorates 1,060 missing—the highest number of missing for any American military cemetery of this war.

29. American Battle Monuments Commission, *American Armies and Battlefields in Europe: A History, Guide, and Reference Book* (Washington, D.C.: U.S. Government Printing Office, 1938), 31.

30. His behavior during the July fighting was bizarre. In addition to long periods of speechlessness and incoherence, he had taken to reading long passages from the *Prayer Book of the Moravian Brethren*—not for spiritual guidance, apparently, but for military advice. See the account in D. J. Goodspeed, *Ludendorff: Soldier, Dictator, Revolutionary* (London: Rupert Hart-Davis, 1966), 197–205.

17

1918: The AEF and the End of the War

*The old Boche is learning the art and science of retiring, and with
practice he will become perfect. I wish to goodness we had four or
five thousand more tanks.*

—The Chief of the Imperial General Staff,
to Sir Douglas Haig, 21 August 1918.[1]

Pershing was now planning a major offensive effort. So was Foch.
Having spent months browbeating everyone about the necessity of
attacking, he was now finally able to mount an attack back into the territory the Germans had gotten in March and April. Sensibly, the Germans
began to retreat, letting the Allies attack against abandoned positions.
The right wing of the German front consisted of hundreds of kilometers
of buffer zone. They could withdraw their troops step by step, simply
wearing the Allies down. And in fact, the Germans were able to retreat
faster than the Allies could advance.

Foch had already pressured Haig into participating in an offensive
that was aimed at rolling back the German gains around Amiens, and this
had gone in on 8 August. It was successful because the Germans had
already begun to withdraw. Once their offensives had stalled, the salient
they had taken was largely indefensible. But it gave them a marvelous
buffer zone through which to retreat. When Bean, who would become the
official Australian historian, surveyed the projected battleground on the
morning of the eighth, he saw nothing but abandoned territory ahead of
him. The Germans had already withdrawn, taking their heavy guns with

them, retreating in such good order that the Allies, lacking these four or five thousand tanks, were hard-pressed to follow.

The Allied problem was that the Germans had broken through the lines so decisively that they could withdraw at their leisure, then turn and fight whenever they chose. And turn and fight they did: Although British apologists have traditionally represented the BEF offensives of the last three months of the war as a victorious advance which decisively broke their enemy, British casualty returns suggest the contrary. In the last five months of the war (July through November) the BEF had three times as many men killed as on the Somme, or over one hundred thousand men killed, while French figures came to 161,000, and American to about sixty thousand.[2]

Although British losses were almost twice the American losses, the amount of the front being held by the two armies was almost the same. In early July, the BEF occupied 148 kilometers of the front, and the AEF occupied 100 kilometers; but by September the ratio had become 150:126, and by September, the AEF was holding a greater section of the front (157 kilometers) than was the BEF (140 kilometers).[3]

While statistical data such as these can be misleading, they suggest the magnitude of the American achievement, the more so considering that in September of 1918 the AEF was involved in intensive combat. The reason for this lay in the nature of the front, which had always been shaped roughly like an S, with the top and bottom curves pulled back toward the vertical. In their spring and summer offensives, the Germans had simply bent the upper curve through ninety degrees or so. When they began to withdraw, their forces had the option of a slow retreat through hundreds of kilometers of French and Belgian territory, and this is precisely what happened.

But at the pivot point of the S, the German lines were still fairly close to the lateral rail lines that allowed them to shuttle men and equipment behind their front. A breakthrough there would segment the German armies, deprive them of their great advantage of being able to shuttle troops and guns from one area to the next so as to beat off Allied advances. Pershing and Pétain, who wanted to win the war outright in the same way Grant had beaten the Confederacy, saw punching up through this hinge as the first step. Once the line was pierced, a great Franco-American offensive into Lorraine and Alsace would bring with it the opportunity to win the war on their terms.

The question was whether the Germans could outlast the Allies, wear them down so they would be willing to end the war. As long as Foch kept trying to chase them through Artois and Flanders, the Germans would win. At some point they could turn and destroy their opponents, since as the line shortened their superiority would grow. So the sensible strategy was Pétain's—attack hard against the center of the line and break the front in two.

This was what Pershing, who now had the only capable army, proposed to do. The first step was to retake the Saint-Mihiel salient and the Woëvre plain. Although for various reasons the offensive is simply known as Saint-Mihiel, the area of operations extended from Haudimont south to below the town, and then over to the Moselle at Pont-à-Mousson. So this was the scene of three of the worst French disasters of the war, and, as a result, an area where repeated French efforts had gotten them nowhere. Psychologically, the offensive was important. it would show the Americans they could operate successfully where the French had failed, erase the black mark on the French record, and shake the defending Germans.

It also had a more serious military purpose. In the panic of Verdun, the French had evacuated the whole part of the front known as the Woëvre (which was distinct from the plain itself). As noted earlier, that evacuation more or less destroyed any major offensive efforts at Verdun: as long as the Germans held the heights of the Meuse below the city, no serious attack could be mounted to the north and east, which was, unfortunately, the best place for an attack. Although officially the French had gotten back all the ground lost during the 1916 German offensive during Nivelle's attacks at the end of the year, the truth was that as late as September of 1918, the Germans still had possession of a solid half of what they had gained in the February–June 1916 offensive at Verdun, and all of the ground gained during their September 1914 offensive, which took Saint-Mihiel.

The center of the line, then, was like a sequential puzzle. To break through and sever the rail connections, it was necessary to roll northward up the Meuse valley. That could be done only with control of the heights of the Meuse and the buttes of the Argonne to the west. That in turn could be taken only if the Woëvre plain adjacent to the Verdun sector of the front was taken, and that in turn demanded the conquest of Saint-Mihiel. So the first step was Saint-Mihiel.

The Aisne-Marne offensive and the events of July had at last awak-
ened the French General Staff to a truly horrifying possibility: the AEF
might be able to win the war on its own, and Pershing's Saint-Mihiel
offensive would certainly start the ball rolling. All the more so as the projected Anglo-French operations in September were in areas of no great
importance.

This was worrisome in the extreme: Saint-Mihiel had been one long
French disaster; Foch had no interest in letting the Americans take it
back. So the supreme commander strolled into Pershing's headquarters
and proposed the AEF do something quite different. Instead of attacking
as a major force at Saint-Mihiel, the AEF would be split up and dispersed
among French units, who would engage in what sounds suspiciously like
a rehash of First Artois.[4]

Pershing's response revealed pretty clearly the extent to which Foch
actually had any real authority over anyone. He simply said no. The
German successes since March had made it obvious to Pershing that the
French had no idea of how to beat the Germans. Nor did they have any
claim to their fabled superiority in staffing. The only thing the AEF had
seen in the spring of 1918 was mass panic and constant ineptitude.

The Americans would be deployed as a whole, and they would be
deployed at Saint-Mihiel, or, basically, nowhere. The fact that Foch gave
in makes clear just how important the AEF had become on the Western
Front. Having given in, however, Foch then insisted that the AEF mount
another offensive that would fit in with his real strategic goals, and that
this offensive would have to take place almost immediately after the start
of Saint-Mihiel. Charitably, Foch may have felt he was simply testing the
AEF to rise to the occasion. But what he was proposing was, by Allied
standards, impossible. Only the German Army so far had demonstrated
the ability to mount a series of attacks in different directions using the
same resources.

Moreover, the Argonne was the worst place on the Western Front for
offensive operations, and Foch's plan would basically require the AEF to
mount a repeat of Sarrail's 1915 Argonne offensive and Pétain's 1917
Verdun operation, both at the same time, against an enemy primed and
waiting for them. The behavior of the senior Allied generals at this time
suggests men more afraid the Americans would beat the Germans than
that the Germans would win the war.

Wilson, in London, sent messages demanding that the operation be stopped because the AEF lacked the competency to mount a major offensive on its own. Foch's proposal was aimed at dismantling the AEF; Wilson's message at keeping it out of action. This was preposterous since the only Allied general to mount an offensive operation against the Germans that had met basic parameters for success was Pétain.

Unfortunately for their collective efforts, when the Saint-Mihiel offensive was launched, on 12 September, it was a major success. Part of this was attributable to the fact that the Germans had always planned to evacuate the bottom part of the theater when attacked. And, of course, it was promptly claimed that this and this alone enabled the Americans to do so well. The reality was more complex. The AEF was using Pétain's tactics (which were von Mudra's), but with the manpower that Pétain had lacked. A short, massive bombardment that covered the entire wedge of the salient was followed by a massive assault along both sides.

The weakness of the position had always been that a broadly based assault could break through the ends of the salient, pinching off the defenders from the rest of the front. Only an assault of overwhelming strength would suffice, because otherwise the German defenders would shuttle reinforcements along behind their lines and quickly pinch off any threatened breakthrough. Foch's proposal for a reduced attack along the south face of the position was a recipe for a costly failure.

The other reason for the success of the American offensive was its speed. As the Germans had demonstrated, for a breakthrough to succeed the advancing infantry not only had to be well through the initial defensive lines in a short time, but the infantry had to be in a condition to mount an aggressive defense of the territory they had taken. That in turn meant that the artillery supporting the advancing infantry had to suppress the enemy artillery to keep it from destroying the positions the infantry was occupying. At the same time, the advancing infantry, properly reinforced, had to be able to move on past the next lines of defenses. Only then could a breakthrough take place.

With the exception of Pétain's two offensives in 1917, the French and the British had never been able to do this on any scale in sustained fashion. In 1915, as we have seen, the French attempt to reduce the Saint-Mihiel salient (the Battle of the Woëvre) had ended in a failure that was costly in terms of manpower and morale. The American success, therefore, was equally decisive. The Germans had already begun to concede that American soldiers were determined adversaries on the battlefield, but the general assumption was that they would be less capable of serious offensive operations than the British. Saint-Mihiel proved the contrary. Von Hindenburg, who could read maps as well as anyone, termed Saint-Mihiel a major defeat, and Ludendorff demonstrated symptoms of a nervous breakdown.[5]

In getting Pershing to agree to a second major offensive to be mounted within ten days of Saint-Mihiel, Foch had ensured that if there was an American breakthrough at Saint-Mihiel, there would be no chance to exploit it. Strategically speaking, this was a serious mistake, although Foch probably supposed that the AEF would at most enjoy a modest success and never thought of a serious exploitation of a breakthrough.

Postwar, von Gallwitz, who had commanded the German defenders at Saint-Mihiel, observed that an attack there would have been "much more important than the successes gained along the Meuse and in the Argonne."[6] Some of America's more able junior officers, men like Douglas MacArthur, George S. Patton, and George Marshall, felt strongly that the AEF could have broken out of the salient and, properly reinforced, brought the war to a speedy end.[7] Surprisingly little attention has been devoted to this possibility, but on the balance, it is probably correct.

Although some American commanders, notably Liggett, argued that the AEF would have been unable to reduce the German fortifications at Metz, this claim is a red herring: the Metz fortifications did not cover the northernmost part of the Woëvre plain, which gradually rises to become the Heights of the Meuse to the east of Verdun. The Americans would have been able to advance straight north to the west of Metz, and to the northeast on the other side of the city. Given the troops and guns assembled for Saint-Mihiel, Pershing had the resources to pursue this strategy, which would have been less costly of American lives than the Meuse-Argonne offensive Foch had insisted on. Moreover, by July 1918 the French had a sizable group of super-heavy guns, including two monster 520-millimeter Schneider weapons that had been specifically developed to destroy the Metz forts.[8]

It was also claimed that the Woëvre was unsuitable for such an offensive. But, as we have already seen, in September of 1914 the Germans had been able to move their heavy motorized artillery all the way across the plain to Saint-Mihiel, so it is difficult to argue that the same feat, at the same time of the year, was impossible. Moreover, the heavy railroad guns the French would have used in this offensive were all rail guns that would have relied on the existing rail lines running up the Meuse and the Mosel Rivers.

Moreover, the exploitation MacArthur and Patton wanted would have given the Allies an advantage that they in fact did not possess in October and November 1918. To the Germans, northern Lorraine was Lothringen, historically and culturally Germanic. A success around Metz would have put Allied armies on territory the Germans regarded as German, a goal which Joffre had pursued in August 1914.

In terms of strategy, this approach had much to recommend it, not least its endorsement by some of the AEF's most able officers. By contrast, Meuse-Argonne (the front from Sainte-Menehould to the Meuse) was the quintessential Allied objective. Of all the places on the line, the Argonne was the most difficult one to attack. There was the terrain itself. Then there was the fact that the Germans over the last four years had dug themselves in.[9] In theory, if the AEF broke through, they could punch a hole all the way past the main lateral rail line the German Army needed to keep the front supplied. They could then keep on going, roll right back up the Meuse, as Joffre had tried to do in August 1914. A major breakthrough here could be catastrophic for Germany—although hardly on the same scale as a deployment around Metz.

The American speed at switching from one offense to the other had stunned the Allies and heartened the French. But once the offensive began, and the AEF had tough going, a host of military experts declared them completely inept. The slow progress through the Argonne, as the Germans gave way elsewhere, allowed the British in particular to suggest that they won the war and the Americans were merely helpful.[10]

All through October the Americans slowly fought their way through the Argonne, systematically reversing the gains von Mudra had made in 1914 and 1915. If Belleau Wood was one of the bloodier engagements in the history of the American Army, then Meuse-Argonne was certainly one of the bloodiest campaigns. In September, the AEF had about five thousand soldiers killed outright, and in October the number climbed to twenty-two thousand. The American cemetery at Romagnes-sous-Montfaucon has 14,240 graves; it is bigger than the cemetery at Normandy.

But these casualties have to be put in perspective. The BEF, which was essentially just chasing the German withdrawal, had twenty-nine thousand men killed and missing in September and forty-four thousand in October; the French had twenty-three thousand men killed and missing in

September and nearly forty thousand in October—and it should be realized that at this point the nominal combat strengths of the three Allied armies were nearly equal.[11]

But the AEF was slowly forcing the Germans back. As our account of the fighting there in chapters six, seven, and eight, has made clear, the fact that in a month of hard fighting the Americans were able to move on through the area and break through is astonishing, a major tribute to the AEF and to the French officers and alpine troops who mostly trained it.

Meanwhile, a few kilometers to the west, American infantry divisions serving with the French attacked straight up from Souain and broke through German lines, which had held since 1915. It is no coincidence that the French military cemetery at Souain is one of the largest French military cemeteries in the world, with the remains of 30,743 French soldiers, while the ossuary of the Navarin, right up the road, holds the remains of another ten thousand.

Champagne-Ardennes, far more than Verdun or Artois, was the graveyard of the French army: 111,659 soldiers are buried there, and another 35,902 are buried in the cemeteries in the Argonne. Over 10 percent of all known French war dead are here, all of them killed in the catastrophic failed offensives of 1915.[12] If the Argonne was the graveyard of France's military hopes and abilities, Champagne was literally the graveyard of its troops. In both, American arms had proven decisive, and it is no coincidence that it was after the American intervention began that, for the first time, the German prisoner count began to climb.

WILSON ENDS THE WAR

The AEF's Argonne offensive precipitated a complete collapse at the German General Staff. On 26 September, when the Americans broke through and advanced, Ludendorff became so distraught there is suspicion he suffered a stroke, and the staff's liaison with the government urged that Germany end the war. On 5 October, the new chancellor, Prince Maximilian of Baden, told the Reichstag that an immediate armistice was necessary.

In their final days, the men governing Wilhelmine Germany finally managed to put together a coherent and successful foreign policy. They simply ignored France and Great Britain, and sent President Wilson a message indicating they would accept his Fourteen Points. This was logical: the United States had the army that was defeating them. But it was also a shrewd assessment of the former Princeton history professor. Wilson was more than willing to accede, provided his political goals were met. So Ludendorff was forced to resign, Wilhelm abdicated, and Germany, once the details started to leak, simply unraveled over the course of a few days in late October.

Germany was slowly collapsing, as was Austria, but the Max initiative (nicknamed after the new and short-lived chancellor, Prince Max of Baden) had driven a stake into the heart of the alliance. The collective leadership of France and Great Britain was furious that the Germans were negotiating independently with Wilson on the basis of a document (the Fourteen Points) for which they had nothing but contempt, and no interest at all in accepting as the basis for anything.

Taken literally, Wilson's ideas would mean that everyone from the Irish to the Tyroleans would have a say in determining how they were governed, which was hardly what the Allies intended. The French had no more interest in letting the Alsatians decide on their own government than the Italians did the inhabitants of the South Tyrol, or the Serbs the Slovenes and the Croats—and that was simply the start of a long list that would ultimately have included most of Europe.

From a purely military point of view, Pétain realized—as did Pershing—that Germany was nowhere near beaten, nor would it be until the German Army had been. Their idea was to stick to the original plan and mount a massive invasion of Germany, using Lorraine as the base. In other words, the success of the Saint-Mihiel offensive would be the basis for the operations MacArthur and Patton had so desired. Consequently, for reasons both good and bad, the Allies wanted to continue the war. The Germans, who wanted to preserve their army and their military cadre intact, saw an opportunity for doing that by dealing with Wilson. And Wilson, who was determined to end it, had all the cards. Or, more accurately, the Allies had lost most of theirs.

So on 29 October 1918, Wilson's trusted adviser, Colonel House, put it to the Allied leadership directly: if Germany accepted the Fourteen Points, and the Allies did not, then the United States might well have to negotiate a peace directly with the Central Powers. House was more than Wilson's closest adviser. In modern parlance, he might be called the president's

National Security Adviser. Everyone knew he spoke for Wilson. And even though Wilson was in the process of losing control over the Senate (in the fall 1918 elections the Republicans obtained a one-seat majority), to European politicians Wilson appeared to be emperor of America.

Clemenceau was nothing if not a realist, and he cared little for diplomatic niceties.[13] He knew blackmail when he saw it as well as any French politician of the Third Republic, and promptly asked House point blank if that meant a separate peace between the United States and Germany. That is to say, will the United States dump Great Britain and France? When House, who was an ardent Anglophile, replied that it might well mean that, the Allies caved in.

It was true that the armies of the two German Empires were melting away. But their armies were still entirely on enemy territory, and they were still surprisingly intact. Too intact for their broken opponents to contemplate fighting them further on their own. With 345,000 men killed or missing, the BEF that had survived Third Ypres had perished during the spring and summer of 1918. The same could be said of the French, who had 340,000 men either dead or missing in this same period, or about twice the comparable German losses.[14] Without Pershing's two million Americans, there was no army capable of beating Germany. Wilson's terms became the Allied terms.

Suddenly, the Great War was over. Peace had broken out.

NOTES

1. As quoted by Peter Beale in *Death by Design: The Fate of British Tank Crews in the Second World War* (Phoenix Mill, England: Sutton, 1998) 20.

2. See the tables in War Office [United Kingdom], *Statistics of the Military Effort of the British Empire During the Great War, 1914–1920* (London: His Majesty's Stationery Office, 1922), 325–27. The same tables give the Somme casualties for the period 1 July–30 November 1916 as 498,054. On a daily basis, BEF losses for the 1918 period were about 14 percent higher than in 1916. By contrast, French losses during February–June of 1916 were 442,000. Losses for the first three reporting periods of the war (1914, and the two six-month periods of 1915) were substantially higher, being 982,000, 815,000, and 649,000 respectively. See the redaction in Michel Huber, *La population de la France pendant la guerre* (New Haven, Conn.: Yale University Press, 1931), 412–19.

3. These figures computed by Colonel Leonard Ayres, The War with Germany, *A Statistical Summary* (Washington, D.C.: U.S. Government Printing Office, 1919), 103.

4. Smythe attempts a sympathetic account of what Foch was proposing; unfortunately, his key assumption (the Saint-Mihiel salient led to nowhere), is untenable. See the extensive analysis in Hallas, *Squandered Victory,* esp. 261–65.

5. See the entertaining summary in Smythe 187, who quotes the impression of a German officer, who said that Ludendorff was "so overcome by the events of the day as to be unable to carry on a clear and comprehensive discussion."

6. Gallwitz quote is reprinted in Hallas 261.

7. See the brief excerpts from each officer reprinted in Hallas, 261–264. Pershing was also convinced that the attack should have been pushed farther.

8. See the summary in Guy le Hallé, *Verdun, les forts de la victoire* (Paris: Citedis, 1998), 16–17.

9. Subsequent historians have made a fetish out of the "fortifications" of the "Siegfried Line," characterizing places like Montfaucon as though they were fortresses. On-site inspection of the ruins reveals a contrary impression: the stone buildings of French farms and towns would do well enough on their own. As one contemporary officer put it: "particularly after they collapse the upper part so that the basement has about ten feet of rubble over it."

10. Having failed to prevent the formation of the AEF, British officers engaged in serious attempts to destroy it: General Wilson tried to get Pershing's Saint-Mihiel offensive canceled, charging that the AEF lacked the staff and the offensive would be stopped with "cruel losses" (see the discussion in Smythe, 180). In late September, Clemenceau began a ferocious barrage of criticisms, demanding that Pershing be removed from command and that President Wilson be told the "truth." (Smythe 201–2). By 12 October representations had been made to Lloyd George as well. It is difficult to give much credence to these charges, given the French and British collapse in the spring of 1918.

11. American data, from Ayres (120) is confusingly displayed and probably low. The Germans never completed the monthly returns for August through November of 1918, but the evidence available suggests that most of the "losses" claimed were actually prisoners who had decided—like their superiors on the staff—that the war was over now that the Americans had arrived in force.

12. Numbers taken from information posted at the cemeteries. As many men died in military hospitals in the interior, and since obviously the number of graves in an area is not the same as the number of soldiers who fell there, the percent-age is simply intended to be a grisly illustration of how awful this section of the front was.

13. In 1919, during the Versailles negotiations, when Hyams, the Belgian secretary for foreign affairs, asked him if there was anything Clemenceau wanted him to do, the old reprobate brusquely suggested he go drown himself. So much for Allied outrage over the rape of Belgium. See Charles L. Mee, *The End of Order, Versailles 1919* (New York: Dutton, 1980), 197–99. The interchange between House and the Allies actually took place. See the account in Stephen Bonsal, *Unfinished Business* (New York: Doubleday, 1944), 2–3.

14. The American and Italian Expeditionary Forces, and the Belgian Army, had well over 100,000, for a total of about 750,000 men killed and missing. As noted above, the most complete German accounting of 1918 losses came to 230,243 dead and missing, but stopped at 31 July. The imbalance is too great to be affected seriously by the incomplete nature of the

German report: for example, only about one fifth of French losses for 1918 were in the final three months of the war, so it is highly unlikely that German losses on the battlefield exceeded 300,000 men. British data from the Official History, corrected for certain omissions and displayed in more elaborate form in Arthur Grahame Butler et al., The Australian Medical Services in the War of 1914–18 (Melbourne: Australian War Memorial, 1930-43) 2:261. French data from Inventaire sommaire des archives de la guerre (N 24 and N 25), (Troyes: La Renaissance, 1967) annexe 6. German figures are found in Sanitatsbericht uber das deutsche Heer im Weltkrie 1914/18, 3: Table 158. Italian figures of 9,000 taken from information posted at the Italian Expeditionary Force cemetery at Bligny. American losses of 85,252 are taken from information posted at the Meuse-Argonne cemetery, and are somewhat different from those given by Colonel Ayres, 123–124.

Epilogue

Pseudoreality Prevails

World history undoubtedly comes into being like all the other stories. Authors can never really think of anything new, and they all copy from each other. That is why all politicians study history instead of biology or whatever. So much for authors.

—*Robert Musil*[1]

The Americans buried their dead, erecting some of the most impressive cemeteries and monuments of the war, clear signs of their awareness of the dimensions of their victory. The victory columns at Montfaucon and Montsec can be seen for kilometers. At Varennes-en-Argonne, the state of Pennsylvania built a monument approximately the size of an aircraft carrier. From the slight ridge in the ground of Champagne on which the French Navarin monument sits, with its ossuary of ten thousand remains, it is possible to see the slight rise in the ground which is Blanc Mont, a low smudge on the horizon with an American column rising out of the trees, celebrating a victory the French failed to achieve in four years of slaughter.

The Americans buried their dead, built their monuments, and went home (not in quite that order). They then forgot entirely about the war. The War Department spent the next seven years doing a disappearing act on the casualties, and did so with such success that few Americans realized the magnitude of either the losses or the victories. But then the Americans had other problems. As one returning veteran remarked rather ruefully, "We went to war to save democracy and got back home only to find we couldn't get anything to drink."

One of the eagles in the American cemetery at Thiaucourt, where the remains of 4,437 soldiers killed in the September 1918 Saint-Mihiel offensive are interred. In sharp contrast to the French and British cemeteries, the American ones are celebrations of power and victory.

For the Europeans, the problem was more serious than Prohibition. In December 1918, General Fayolle, in Germany, summed up the problem precisely.

> The country does not project an image of a vanished people. Everything breathes order, prosperity, richness. Germany is not at all exhausted. If left alone, they will start the war all over again, in ten years, if not before.[2]

Like von Falkenhayn, who had believed France would crack in six months, Fayolle's estimate of the time lapse was way off. But also like von Falkenhayn, he was basically right: the French Army cracked and broke in April 1917, and in September 1939, Germany started a new war.

So while Haig created a legend of how he—or anyway the British Army—had won the war by knocking the fight out of the Germans, the actual events passed rapidly into myth and folklore. As usual, Jean Dutourd puts it best: "While our soil was being littered with statues of dying soldiers in cheap stone, Gallic cocks in brass, and weeping angels cast in concrete, the war veterans were reducing their epic to the level of street-corner gossip."[3]

For France the epic had a horrifying ending. Louis Marin's report to the Chamber of Deputies confirmed what André Maginot had suspected and Abel Ferry had deduced. France had almost exactly 1.4 million war dead. The United Kingdom had slightly over 900,000 war dead (and admitted officially that about 750,000 of them died on the Western Front), including nearly 57,000 Canadians and just over 59,000 Australians. Colonel Ayres, the War Department's chief statistician, revealed that there were roughly 122,500 American military personnel deaths. Eighty-five thousand American soldiers and Marines died on the Western Front.[4]

Ayres believed that 102,000 Belgian soldiers had been killed. His counterparts in the British War Office believed the figure to be closer to 46,000, and a more authoritative postwar Belgian figure is 40,367. By actual count, there are 22,953 Belgian military graves from the war.[5] Nearly 10,000 Italian and 2,000 Portuguese soldiers died on the Western Front. The Allies had almost exactly 2.4 million dead, the overwhelming majority of them killed on the Western Front.

Postwar, the German Medical Services established the following: 590,902 soldiers had been killed on the Western Front up to 31 July 1918, and for all fronts, 1,202,042 soldiers had either been killed outright, or had subsequently died, while an examination of the army's own figures gave a total of 1,621,034 dead through 31 December 1918; there are 768,000 German soldiers interred in France.[6] There is a striking imbalance between the number of German and Allied soldiers killed, and this would be so even with substantially higher German losses. Germany lost fewer soldiers fighting on all fronts than the Allies did fighting on the Western Front. On the Western Front, the ratio was at least two to one, and probably higher.

The French and Belgian governments tried to make plans for the next war. In January 1920 Foch was eased out and replaced by Pétain. Over the next three years the army and the government hammered out a coherent plan for national defense. General Guillaumat, a veteran of the Salonika standoff with the Bulgarians, carried the torch for Foch and Joffre, arguing that the best policy was an army with strong offensive powers, which would carry the battle to the enemy.

But the plan finally adopted bore a curious resemblance to the one from the 1870s: given France's losses, and the loss of confidence in the army, the best way to defend France was through building more fortifications. Although generally seen as a sign of France's defeatism and despair, this was a logical response which—unlike the criticisms of its opponents—actually took into acount what had happened during the war itself. The French General Staff had gutted the defense system Séré de Rivières had constructed, partly on the basis of false information about what had happened to the forts themselves. But by 1923 enough studies had been done to establish that, other than a few basic problems in design, the reason the system had failed was because it had not actually been used.

True, the Belgian forts, and the older French ones, had succumbed to heavy artillery, but even there an analysis of the actual damage done suggested that this could have been prevented easily enough. The French sandwich technique had proven largely impervious to the heaviest and most powerful shells, and the main deficiencies of the existing system could easily be remedied. Positive flow ventilation could ensure that the defenders weren't asphyxiated by dust and fumes. A more effective use of subsidiary fortlets and underground extensions would prevent infantry attacks from developing with much greater sucess than the moat-and-wall technique of Vauban that had been used in the earlier forts, and better positioning and protection would make them even more invulnerable.

The biggest problem had been not with the hardware in 1914, but with the men inside (when there garrisons inside at all). But this could be remedied as well, by garrisoning the forts in the same way that submarines or major warships were staffed, and through proper training. On 31 December 1925, Painlevé established a commission thereafter known by the acronym CORF, which basically laid down the blueprints for the new system of fortifications. General Guillaumat presided over CORF, Pétain approved much of the actual details, and André Maginot, who had succeeded Painlevé, rustled up the funds from the Chamber. France being France, the CORF fortifications became known as the Maginot Line, giving rise to a folkloric tradition in which the wounded veteran of Verdun had built the whole thing virtually on his own. Despite the folklore, France finally had a rational defense policy that took into account the realities of modern warfare.

As France, so Belgium: the Liège fortifications were expanded by the addition of a great new fort, which commanded the Meuse crossing just three kilometers to the north of where the Germans had crossed in 1914. Eben Emael, completed in 1935, was the most modern fortification in the world. The Belgians had corrected their mistakes as thoroughly as had the French. Belgian officers who went through the newly completed fort were convinced it was invulnerable.

At dawn on 11 May 1940, seventy-eight *Pioniere* from the German Seventh Airborne Division landed on the fort by glider. They were armed with a fearsome new weapon, shaped charge explosives in fifty-kilogram bundles, and promptly blew enormous holes in the turrets. The fort was out of commission in twenty-eight hours. When the commandant tried to organize a defense, the garrison bolted.

Eleven years later, in 1951, France inaugurated the formal opening of the Marne Monument. Designed by Marshal Foch himself, it is a thirty-three-meter red sandstone column designed to resemble a menhir of the ancient Gauls, with an art deco ensemble of harps, trumpets, thunderbolts, and the angel of victory growing out of the top. Quotations from Marshal Joffre chiseled in faux-runic lettering are scattered over the column, and at its base is an impressive greater than life-sized bas-relief that shows the men responsible for the victory of the Marne.

The bas-relief violates perspective: Joffre, who stands in the center, clasping the arm of a French soldier, is twice the size of the real man. The soldier is markedly smaller, the seven generals responsible for the triumph smaller still (although still life-sized). Foch is at Joffre's right hand, while Gallieni, the general most responsible for seizing the moment, is off at far left. The spurious historicity and lack of perspective combine to suggest something empty and lifeless, a forced celebration of an event long forgotten. And indeed the history of the monument is not without its own symbolism. Work wasn't begun until 1931, well after Foch's death, the monument wasn't completed until 1939, and not dedicated until 1951.

The Marne Monument is about thirty kilometers south of Épernay, France, about eight kilometers north of Sezannes. Three thousand five hundred meters to the northwest of it is the French military cemetery of Soizy-aux-Bois, where 1,692 French soldiers—the poilus the monument supposedly celebrates—were hastily thrown into two communal graves and then forgotten. The two graves are not identified as such—they appear to be simply two raised embankments of hard earth with masonry around them. Whatever plaque was once erected has largely been obliterated by time, and the small cross in the center is in even worse shape. The cemetery at Soizy, barren, exposed at the side of the road, reeks of neglect and abandonment, even by the relaxed standards of French cemeteries.

Seventy-eight hundred meters to the southeast is another cemetery. It is named after the village of Connantre, but it stands distant from the hamlet, out in the middle of one of those enormous fields that characterize the flat landscape of Haut Marne. It is a consolidated cemetery in which the remains of 8,896 German soldiers are buried. Like all German cemeteries of this war, it is beautifully landscaped and meticulously maintained. The cemetery is surrounded on all sides by a thick row of trees, making it a place of obvious repose and meditation. The names of the men who died in 1914 in this area, and who were collected from various points and placed in a common grave here, are engraved on massive brass tablets facing the entrance. Behind the tablets is a more intimate monument, an austere and surprisingly minimalist Pietà in a soft rose stone. Behind the monument are crosses marking where 1,298 German soldiers who died in the Second Battle of the Marne lie buried. There are always flowers on at least one grave, or a wreath beneath the sculpture. Like the perfectly manicured lawns, the massive plaques and markers, the flowers signify that these men are remembered.

No greater contrast could be imagined: between the meticulous German commemoration of its sons who rest in foreign soil, and France's neglect of its own children who fought to save it; between the funereal pomposity of Foch's monument and the melancholy intimacy of these cemeteries.

If an anthropologist from Mars were to visit here and study these cemeteries carefully, he would conclude that a great war had been fought here, and that clearly one side had been victorious. He would be right.

NOTES

1. Robert Musil, *The Man Without Qualities,* trans. Sophie Wilkins and Burton Pike (New York: Knopf, 1995), 1:390. The title of the epilogue, "Pseudoreality Prevails" is taken from their translation of one of Musil's chapters (83). Literally the title is *"Seinesgleichen Geschieht."* but "Pseudoreality Prevails" is a wondrously funny tag in its own right, and certainly reflects the philosophical and historical sense of what Musil was about.

2. Fayolle, *Carnets secrets de la grande guerre,* ed Henry Contamine (Paris: Plon, 1964), 322. Fayolle's comments were paralleled by those of Americans who were in Germany at the same time.

3. Jean Dutourd, *The Taxis of the Marne,* trans. Harold King (New York: Simon and Schuster, 1957), 195.

4. British data taken from War Office [United Kingdom], *Statistics of the Military Effort of the British Empire During the Great War, 1914–1920* (London: His Majesty's Stationery Office, 1922), 237. This data was corrected for certain omissions and displayed in more elaborate form in Arthur Grahame Butler et al., *The Australian Medical Services in the War of 1914–18* (Melbourne: Australian War Memorial, 1930–43), 2:261. It is sometimes claimed that there were no official French figures for losses in the war. Not so. See the French data derived from extensive government reports made to the French Chamber, as redacted and analyzed in Michel Huber, *La Population de la France pendant la guerre* (New Haven: Yale University Press, 1931), 412–19; also summarized in Service Historiques des Armeés, *Inventaire sommaire des archives de la guerre* (N 24 and N 25) (Troyes: La Renaissance, 1967), annexe 6. Although the majority of the American remains were sent back to the United States, according to current information from the Battlefield Monuments Commission, initially approximately 81,000 Americans were buried (mostly in France) and another 4,500 were never found or identified.

5. Information obtained from M. Patrick de Wolf, who is compiling a master list of Belgian war graves.

6. German data taken from Heeressanitatsinspektion des Reichsministeriums, *Sanitätsbericht über das deutsche Heer im Weltkrieg 1914/18,* 3 vols. (Berlin: Reichsministerium, 1935), 3:13 and Tables 155–58. There are higher figures given on pages 12–13, but these figures include live prisoners of war whom the statisticians continued to list as "missing" since they had no way of knowing how many there were. I have excluded them for the simple reason that (1) there were well over seven hundred thousand German prisoners of war in France alone by November 1918, a figure so high that it strongly suggests that the vast majority of the German missing were actually alive; and (2) we have fairly accurate figures for the Allied war dead with the missing separated out. In other words, the figures for the missing could be put back in and added to the totals of the known dead, producing much larger numbers, but the ratio of loss between the two sides would stay pretty much the same. According to the *Volksbund Deutsche Kriegsgräberfürsorge,* which maintains the German military cemeteries, there are 768,000 German graves from the 1914–1918 war on the Western Front—a number obviously consistent with these other German figures (the figure quoted is taken from their publications titled *Mittelfrankreich,* published in October 1989, and available at the military cemetery of Noyers-Pont-Maugis [France]). Although a book could be written about the numbers and the reporting, the conclusion remains the same, which is why in May 1940 the German Army was so much larger than the Allied armies. Many British analysts have refused to accept the German data as being reliable, arguing that the wounded were undercounted. Not so, and since these figures are for the dead, the issue is irrelevant. *The Australian Medical Services* (note 45) demonstrates the intrinsic consistency of the German data, which both the War Office researchers and Churchill regarded as being highly reliable.

An Essay on Sources

And so, here's the way that history will be written in fifty years, when, the witnesses having died, conscientious historians, anxious to take advantage of good sources, will read the archives of the GQG. Let's shout at them all at once: "A risky business." Let's put them all on guard against this vast enterprise which, day by day, as I watched, destroyed the truth, and right before my eyes. And if those historians don't take that into account, they will make us completely doubt history.

—*Jean de Pierrefeu*[1]

INTRODUCTION

This essay, which students of the war wishing to expand their knowledge of the subject may find useful, may be thought of as informally divided into four parts. The first enumerates the key sources that define my assumptions: casualties, weapons, doctrines and plans, eyewitness accounts. The second section lists the important sources for key events during the war in chronological order from 1914 to 1918. The third section lists general works of value: postwar works on tactics, biographies, general histories, and the like. The fourth part discusses, briefly, such things as maps, archives, and on-site work. There is no attempt to be exhaustive; rather the essay directs the reader to points of interest: a complete listing of the many works dealing with the war would be a separate volume in itself.[2]

CASUALTIES

I have used both the official casualty reports of the combatants, and the reports of the military medical services, which often provide a more accurate and complete accounting. The medical reports are the most useful and conclusive, as well as the most ignored. The most comprehensive of these is Heeressanitätsinspektion des Reichsministeriums, *Sanitätsbericht über das deutsche Heer im Weltkrieg 1914/18,* 3 vols. (Berlin: Reichsministerium, 1935).[3] French casualty figures were first compiled during the war for the Secret Committee by Abel Ferry, and reprinted in Abel Ferry, *La Guerre vue d'en bas et d'en haut* (Paris: Grasset, 1920). The final official figures were contained in Senate Report in 1919, and are also summarized in the French Army Historical Service Archives (see below). In the 1930s the French statistician Michel Huber compiled a massive analysis of all aspects of the war, and this work, based on the official data, should be the standard source for any serious study of the war: Michel Huber, *La Population de la France pendant la guerre* (New Haven: Yale University Press, 1931). Contrary to what is often said, the official French history is very good at presenting data on French losses for key offensives. The data recorded by the French Medical Services is basically unavailable, but Huber, who had access to it, reproduces the important parts, along with virtually every other statistic of any importance.

Basic data for the BEF is found in War Office [United Kingdom], *Statistics of the Military Effort of the British Empire During the Great War, 1914–1920* (London: His Majesty's Stationery Office, 1922). Subsequent generations of British historians have completely ignored the data supplied by their own government's statisticians regarding comparative losses. The British Official History goes to great lengths to contradict the data, and the British Medical History is completely subordinated to the propagandistic ends of Edmonds, the official historian. However, the official Australian medical historian corrected this record (see below), as well as providing much other comparative data of great importance, and the official accounts of the other Commonwealth forces are excellent: Battlefields Memorial Commission, *Canadian Battlefield Memorials* (Ottawa: Acland, 1929); Arthur Grahame Butler et al., *The Australian Medical Services in the War of 1914–18,* 3 vols. (Melbourne: Australian War Memorial, 1930–43). (Vol. 1: Gallipoli, Siani, Palestine, New Guinea; vol. 2: Western Front); A. Fortescue Duguid, *Official History of Canadian Forces in the Great War* (Ottawa: Patenaude, 1938); William Richard Feasby, *Official History of the Canadian Medical Services, 1939–45* (Ottawa: Cloutier, 1953); Andrew

Macphail, *Official History of the Canadian Forces in the Great War: The Medical Services* (Ottawa: Acland, 1925).

A book could be written on how the War Department bungled casualty reporting for the AEF, finally, in 1926, making the United States the only country to misrepresent its losses officially and systematically. Fortunately, the earlier and more accurate reports are still extant, particularly those of the Surgeon General for 1919 and 1920. Colonel Ayres, the War Department head statistician, produced the only other useful report: Leonard P. Ayres, *The War with Germany: A Statistical Summary* (Washington, D.C.: U.S. Government Printing Office, 1919).[4]

The information on Italian and Austro-Hungarian casualties on the Western Front comes from the burial records of the cemeteries on the front where those soldiers are buried. Italian records are from the cemetery at Bligny, south of Reims, where 3,453 of the estimated 9,000 Italian war dead are interred. Austro-Hungarian dead, almost exclusively consisting of soldiers from Erdély/Siebenbürgen, are scattered among the German military cemeteries in the Meuse-Argonne region. Information on Belgian casualties may be found in Henri Bernard, *L'an 14 et la campagne des illusions* (Brussels: La Renaissance du Livre, 1983); my analysis is supplemented by the researches of M. Patrick DeWolf, who is currently preparing an exhaustive compilation of all Belgian war dead and has thus far found information on over twenty thousand of them.

WEAPONS

The indispensable volume here is Général [Firmin Émile] Gascouin, *L'Évolution de l'artillerie pendant la guerre* (Paris: Flammarion, 1920), supplemented by Général [Alexandre] Percin, *L'Artillerie aux manoeuvres de Picardie en 1910* (Paris: Berger-Levrault, 1911). There is invaluable photographic and documentary material located in the Fort de la Pompelle, outside Reims, particularly on mortars, whose history is described in great detail by Général Jean-Joseph Roquerol in *Histoire des crapouillots* (Paris: Payot, 1935). From the German side, the best view is Theodor Spiess, *Minenwerfer im Grosskampf* (Munich: J.F. Lehmann, 1933). The photographs of German and Allied equipment are extremely revealing, and make clear the extent to which the Allies lagged behind throughout the entire war. Information on explosive power and range of shells is taken from French Army intelligence data: 2eme Bureau, GQG, *Artillerie allemande: Les Projectiles* (Paris: Inprimerie National, 1917).

See also John S. Hammond and Dawson Olmstead, *Gunner's Handbook for Field Artillery* (New York: Dutton, 1917); Jules Paloque, *Artillerie de campagne* (Paris: O. Doin et Fils, 1909); Major James E. Hicks, *French Military Weapons 1717 to 1938* (New Milford, Conn.: N. Flayderman, 1964); David Nash, *German Artillery 1914–1918* (London: Altmark, 1970); Lieutenant-Colonel Émile Rimailho, *Artillerie de campagne* (Paris: Gauthier-Villars, 1924); Paul Gaston Dubois, *L'Artillerie de campagne dans la guerre actuel* (Paris: Fournier, 1916); and Ludwig Jedlicka, *Unser Heer: 300 Jahre österreichisch Soldatentum in Krieg und Frieden* (Vienna: Fürlinger, 1963). A useful debunking of the BEF's weapons is in Leslie W. C. S. Barnes, *Canada's Guns* (Ottawa: Canadian War Museum, 1979).

The key source for mechanization and armor is [Lieutenant-Colonel] Jean Paul Perré, *Battailes et combats des chars français: L'Année d'apprentissage (1917)* (Paris: Charles-Lavauzelle, 1937). There are numerous popular works in English, the most useful of which is Duncan Crow, ed., *AFV's of World War One* (Windsor, Canada: Profile, 1970). Of the very few systematic studies of chemical warfare, the most useful and comprehensive is Rudolph Hanslian and Franz Bergendorff, *Der Chemische Krieg* (Berlin: E.S. Mittlerer & Son, 1925), which should be supplemented by Amos A. Fries and Clarence J. West, *Chemical Warfare* (New York: McGraw-Hill, 1921) as well as Julius Meyer, *Der Gaskampf und die Chemische Kampfstoffe* (Leipzig: Hirzel, 1926).

The role of airpower in the war is misunderstood. The general impression is that when the war began, no power had an air force, nor any idea how to use one. Not so. See Alex Imrie's misleadingly titled *Pictorial History of the German Army Air Service* (London: Ian Allen, 1971). The strategic side of German airpower is discussed with surprising thoroughness in Jules Poirier, *Les Bombardements de Paris (1914–1918)* (Paris: Payot, 1930) and Maurice Thiéry, *Paris bombardé par zeppelins, gothas, et berthas* (Paris: Éditions de Boccard, 1921). Subject to the limitations described in the first sentence of this paragraph, the analysis in R.D.S. Higham's *Air Power: A Concise History* (New York: St. Martin's, 1972) is revelatory.

DOCTRINES AND PLANS

The war plans of France and Germany (and Austria and Russia) are deeply misunderstood. The basic material on France is archival.[5] Fatally for most historians, von Schlieffen's plan was not published until Gerard Ritter, *Der Schlieffenplan: Kritik eines Mythos* (Munich: Oldenbourg, 1956). When the work was translated into English, there were major errors: *The Schlieffen Plan: Critique of a Myth,* trans. Andrew and Eva Wilson (New York: Praeger, 1958).

The subject of infantry doctrine is equally confused. Fortunately there are two studies that illuminate the problems perfectly: Douglas Porch, *The March to the Marne: The French Army 1871–1914* (New York: Cambridge University Press, 1981) and Martin Samuels, *Doctrine and Dogma: German and British Infantry Tactics in the First World War* (New York: Greenwood, 1992). Joffre's comments (contained only in the French text of his memoirs) are also significant, and any discussion of how the combatants fought in theory should be viewed in the light of some of the numerous accounts of eyewitnesses (discussed below).

ORGANIZATION AND STRUCTURE OF THE ARMIES

The basic information on the structure and organization of the French Army and presently contained in their archives, is summarized at great length and invaluable detail in *Inventaire sommaire des archives de la guerre.*[6] See also the indispensable compilation of German troops movements by Général Edmond Buat, *L'Armée allemande pendant la guerre de 1914–18* (Paris: Chapelot, 1920).

Most of the best information about the German Army was compiled by their French adversaries. The most useful studies: Pierre Joseph Camena d'Almeida, *L'Armée allemande avant et pendant la guerre de 1914–18* (Paris: Berger-Levrault, 1919); Eugene Carrias, *L'Armée allemande: Son histoire, son organisation, sa tactique* (Paris: Berger-Levrault, 1938): Didier Lainé, *L'Armée allemande en 1914* (Paris: Chromos, 1984); Felix Martin and F. Pont, *L'Armée allemande: Étude d'organisation* (Paris: Chapelot, 1903); [Sidney Rau], *L'État militaire des principales puissances étrangères en 1900* (Nancy: Berger-Levrault, 1900). The official Bavarian account of the first part of the war is invaluable: Karl Dueringer (Bayerischen Kriegsarchiv), *Die Schlacht in Lothringen und in den Vogesen 1914,* 2 vols. (Munich: Max Schick, 1929).

The role and composition of the elite or special units played an important part in the war is unexplored. Two key works are: Jean Mabire, *Chasseurs alpins: Des Vosges aux Djebels, 1914–1964* (Paris: Presses de la Cité, 1984); Paul Heinrici, *Das Ehrenbuch der Deutschen Pioniere* (Berlin: Wilhelm Rolf, [1931]).

MEMOIRS AND EYEWITNESSES

The indispensable book for any serious study of any level of personal experience narrative in this war is Jean-Norton Cru's *Témoins* (Paris: Les Étincelles, 1928), recently reissued as a paperback by the University of Nancy. In addition to his comprehensive evaluation of combat accounts, Norton Cru, a Franco-American combat veteran with a doctorate in history, provides invaluable data about the service records of the writers, establishing whether or not the writer actually witnessed the events he wrote about. Although the emphasis is on French witnesses, Norton Cru provides valuable insights into German, British, and American observers, as well as discussions of the works of some senior commanders.

The most important accounts were those journals and documents that the writer kept secretly; in the first three cases, the writer died before his thoughts could be corrected or changed: Fayolle, *Carnets secrets de la grande guerre,* ed. Henry Contamine (Paris: Plon, 1964); Abel Jules Ferry, *Les Carnets secrets d'Abel Ferry 1914–1918* (Paris: Grasset, 1957); [Général] Joseph-Simon Gallieni, *Les Carnets de Gallieni,* publiés par son fils Gaëtan Gallieni, notes de P.B. Gheusi (Paris: Albin Michel, 1932). All three men were privileged witnesses who had access to information the ordinary officer or journalist did not: Gallieni, as the ranking officer in the French Army (his recommendation elevated Joffre); Ferry, as an undersecretary to the Viviani Cabinet, who was also a serving officer and a member of the Chamber; and Fayolle, one of the few successful generals of the war, saw and recorded the thoughts of Pétain and Foch with unparalleled candor.

I disagree strongly with the notion that the published memoirs that appeared after the war are next to useless since they are so patently self-serving. On the contrary, the most damning evidence demonstrating conclusively how poorly the Allied leadership grasped the war is to be found in the memoirs of Joffre and Lloyd George. In its French edition (the English translation pulled out the first half of his account and reprinted it as appendix at the back, thus destroying much of the book's impact) Joffre's account is the most valuable; Herbillon's is telling in key places, and Serrigny gives a valuable indication as to what Pétain thought and said. Poincaré's gives unintentionally telling illustrations: Colonel Herbillon, *Souvenirs d'un officier de liaison pendant le guerre mondial,* 2 vols. (Paris: Tallandier, 1930); Maréchal [Joseph-Jacques-Césaire] Joffre, *Mémoires du maréchal Joffre* (Paris: Plon, 1932); [Colonel] Bernard Serrigny, *Trente ans avec Pétain* (Paris: Plon, 1959); Raymond Poincaré, *Au service de la France,* 6 vols. (Paris: Plon, 1931).

On the British side, in addition to Lloyd George's memoirs, there are useful things to be found in Lord Hankey and in Allardice Riddell, but the real mother lode of how the British totally failed to grasp the war is the private diaries of Colonel Repington, the military affairs correspondent for *The Times*, who knew everyone and recorded what they said and what he thought: Lord Hankey, *The Supreme Command* (London: Allen and Unwin, 1961); David Lloyd George, *War Memoirs*, 2 vols. (London: Odhams, 1938); George Allardice Riddell, *Lord Riddell's War Diary, 1914–1918* (London: Nicholson and Watson, 1933); [Colonel] Charles à Court Repington, *The First World War 1914–1918, Personal Experiences of Colonel Repington*, 2 vol. (London: Constable, 1920).

Of the senior German commanders, the only accounts of substance I found were Erich von Falkenhayn, *Die Oberste Heeresleitung 1914–1916* (Berlin: E. S. Mittlerer, 1920), and Kronprinz Wilhelm, *Meine Erinnerungen aus Deutschlands Heldenkampf* (Berlin: E. S. Mittlerer & Son, 1923). The standard English translations of both are seriously flawed in key places. Although the recollections of Ludendorff and Max Hoffmann are frequently cited, Ludendorff's account, which was written at a point when his mental stability should really be questioned, is more a fiction than a memoir. Despite the fact that it is a consciously toned down and carefully contrived work, Pershing's account of his experiences is surprisingly useful: John J. Pershing, *My Experiences in the World War*, 2 vols. (New York: Stokes, 1931).

EYEWITNESSES TO COMBAT

Norton-Cru found more than four hundred accounts, and ranked them according to their value as testimony. I found little to quarrel with in his assessments. Of the many important accounts, I cite only a few: Jean Bernier's autobiographical novel, *La Percée* (Paris: Albin Michel, 1920); Georges Boucheron, *L'Assaut: l'Argonne et Vauquois avec le 10e division* (Paris: Perrin, 1917); Paul Cazin, *L'Humaniste à la guerre* (Paris: Plon, 1920); André Pézard, *Nous autres à Vauquois* [1915–1916] (Paris: Renaissance du Livre, 1917; reissued 1974); Maurice Genevoix, *Ceux de 14* [contains Sous Verdun, Nuits de Guerre, La Boue, and Les Éparges in an "édition définitive"] (Paris: Flammarion, 1974); Paul Lintier, Ma pièce (Paris: Plon, 1916); Jean Galtier-Boissière, *En rase campagne* (Paris: Berger-Levrault, 1917); Henry Morel-Journel, *Journal d'un officier de la 74e division* (Montbrison: Brassert, 1922).

Norton-Cru excluded the accounts of field grade officers in his work, although some of his better witnesses were promoted during the war. Some of what was written is of considerable value, notably the letters of Colonel Emil Driant (see below under biographies), and the rather prickly account of his defense of Fort de Vaux by Commandant Raynal: *Le drame du Fort de Vaux, journal du Commandant Raynal* (Verdun: Éditions Lorraines, no date).

An enormous body of work has been done compiling the accounts of English and American combat eyewitnesses, most of it lacking any critical framework and of dubious value. The French equivalent, very well done, is Gérard Canini, *Combattre à Verdun et souffrance quotidien* (Nancy: Presses Universitaires, 1988).

I found three English accounts and one German account of great use, however. Rommel and Montgomery became two of the outstanding generals of the Second World War. Consequently, what they said about the first one is intrinsically interesting. Spears, as the BEF liaison with the French, was a privileged witness, and made all the more so by his record of distinguished service in the next war. Bernard Law Montgomery, *The Memoirs of Field-Marshal the Viscount Montgomery of Alamein, K. G.* (New York: World Publishing, 1958); Edward Louis Spears, *Liaison 1914: A Narrative of the Great Retreat.* 1st ed. (London: Heinemann, 1930). Like everyone else interested in this subject, I grew up reading Robert Graves's *Good-bye to All That* (New York: Blue Ribbon Books, 1930), which remains the definitive English personal experience narrative. So, too, for Erwin Rommel, *Infantry Attacks* (Mechanicsburg, Pa.: Stackpole Books, 1990), 230 [first published as *Infanterie Greift an: Erlebniesse und Erfahrungen* (Potsdam: Voggenreiter, 1937)].

Like Rommel, whose account of his experiences is cast as a manual for infantry tactics, the best German witnesses tended to write monographs on arms and equipment, or accounts of campaigns. An excellent example of the first tendency would be Oberleutnant D. R. Schindler, who compiled an authoritative work on German heavy weapons: *Eine 42cm Mörser-Batterie im Weltkrieg* (Breslau: Hofmann, 1934). Bernhard Kellermann's *Der Krieg im Argonnerwald* (Berlin: Julius Bard, 1921), is a good instance of the latter. One of the most comprehensive compilations of eyewitness accounts—valuable in its own right as the basic source book on the *Pioniere* (Germany's combat engineers)—is Heinrici, *Das Ehrenbuch der Deutschen Pioniere*.

Two completely forgotten but incredibly vivid works by Americans, which colored my view of the initial fighting considerably, are W. Hervey Allen, *Towards the Flame* (New York: Doran, 1925), and John W. Thomason, Jr., *Fix Bayonets* (New York: Scribner's, 1926).

CONTEMPORARY ACCOUNTS

By far the most useful source is the magazine published by the *New York Times* during this period (*New York Times Current History: The European War*), which gives an excellent idea of what both the Allies and independent observers believed was happening. In the initial weeks of the war, before French censorship took hold, it was possible to file objective reports from the front, particularly in Belgium. The best of these: Irvin S. Cobb, *Paths of Glory: Impressions of the War Written at the Front* (New York: George Doran, 1915); Henry Hamilton Fyfe, *My Seven Selves* (London: Allen and Unwin, 1935); Granville Roland Fortescue, *At the Front with Three Armies: My Adventures in the Great War* (London: A. Melrose, 1915); Geoffrey Winthrop Young, *From the Trenches: Louvain to the Aisne, First Record of an Eyewitness* (New York: Stokes, 1914); Harold Ashton, *First from the Front* (London: A. C. Pearson, 1914). There is a comprehensive account of the work of these correspondents in Emmet Crozier, *American Reporters on the Western Front, 1914–1918* (New York: Oxford University Press, 1959). The only interesting account of the German side is by the famous Swedish explorer Sven Anders Hedin, *With the German Armies in the West,* translated by H. G. de Walterstorff (London: J. Lane, 1915), intended by Lane as a wake-up call to a complacent British public.

Despite the censored passages, Jules Poirier's *Reims* (Paris: Payot, 1917) is an invaluable source for day-by-day news about the war in August 1914—unlike many of the wartime writers, Poirier was a good analyst as well.

FORTIFICATIONS AND THE WAR IN BELGIUM

The two authoritative accounts of the fighting for the Belgian forts are curiously neglected, even though between them they contain all the primary materials: Colonel A. de Schrÿver [Chef d'État-Major de la 3 me Division d'Armée], *La Bataille de Liège (août 1914)* (Liège: Vaillant-Carmanne, 1922), and Colonel Robert Normand, *Défense de Liège, Namur, Anvers en 1914* (Paris: L. Fournier, 1923). Also of great importance is rather misleadingly titled Henri Bernard's, *L'An 14 et la campagne des illusions* (Brussels: La Renaissance du Livre, 1983)— the book is actually the notes made by his father, who was a battalion commander in the Belgian Army in 1914, but with useful notes by his son, who taught at the École Royale Militaire.

See also Commandement de l'Armée, *Operations de l'armée belge pendant la campagne 1914–1918* (English) (Brussels: ICM, 1930); Commandement de l'Armée, *La guerre de 1914: L'Action de l'armée Belge pour la défense du pays et le respect de sa neutralité: Rapport du commandement de l'armée (periode du 31 juillet au 31 décembre 1914)* (Paris: Libraire Chapelot, 1915); Major Tasnier and Major R. van Overstraeten, *L'Armée Beige dans la guerre mondiale* (Brussels: Henri Bertelles, 1923).

The most comprehensive discussions of fortifications: Guy Le Hallé, *Verdun, les forts de la victoire* (Paris: CITÉDIS, 1998); Colonel Robert Normand, *Défense de Liège, Namur, Anvers en 1914* (Paris: Fournier, 1923); Stéphane Gaber, *La Lorraine fortifilée* (Metz: Éditions Serpenoise, 1997). Some of the most informative work on the fortifications of 1914 is to be found in the French monographs on the postwar CORF fortifications, particularly Étienne Anthérieu, *Grandeur et sacrifice de la ligne Maginot* (Paris: G. Durassié, 1962); Louis Claudel, *La Ligne Maginot: Conception—réalisation* (Saint-Maurice: Association Saint-Maurice, 1974); Jean-Yves Mary, *La Ligne Maginot: Ce qu'elle était, ce qu'il en reste* (Paris: SERCAP, 1980).

THE INITIAL FIGHTING

Almost every French text on the war touches on the opening fighting. The seminal work is Henry Contamine, *La Revanche, 1871–1914* (Paris: Berger-Levrault, 1957). Additionally, I found the following works to be of great help in detailing the actual combat: Joseph Bedier, *L'Effort française* (Paris: Renaissance du Livre, 1919), Erhard von Mutius, *Die Schlacht bei Longwy* (Berlin: Stalling, 1919), Reichsarchiv, *Von Nancy bis zum Camp des Romains 1914* (Berlin: Stalling, 1925) (band 6 of *Schlachten des Weltkrieges*), Hermann Gackenholz, *Entscheidung in Lothringen, 1914* (Berlin: Junker and Dunnhaupt, 1933). The Bavarian archival account is indispensable: Dueringer, *Die Schlacht in Lothringen*.

FIGHTING IN 1915

The indispensable French account is by Général Daille: *Histoire de la guerre mondiale: Joffre et la guerre d'usure, 1915–1916,* vol. 2. (Paris: Payot, 1936). See also

Charles Aimond, *La guerre de 1914–1918 dans la Meuse* (Verdun: Martin-Colaardelle, 1922); Ernest Beauguitte, *Vauquois* (Paris: Berger-Levrault, 1921); Yves Buffetaut in *La Bataille de Verdun, de l'Argonne à la Woëvre* (Tours: Éditions Heimdale, 1990); Armand Durlewanger, *Sites militaires en Alsace* (Strasbourg: La Nuée Bleue, 1991); and Le Linge 1915 (Colmar: S. A. E. P. Ingersheim, 1980); [Captain] René Ernest Louis Feriet, *La Butte de Vauquois, 1914–1918* (Paris:Payot, 1937); Louis Gurial, *"Je les grignote ..." Champagne 1914–1915* (Paris: Hachette, 1965); Henry Jacques Hardouin, *L'Épopée garibaldienne* (Paris: Debresse, 1939); Général J[ean-Joseph] Rouquerol, *La Guerre en Argonne and Les hauts de Meuse et Saint-Mihiel* (Paris: Payot, 1939).

1916: VERDUN

The indispensable source book for Verdun is (still) Jacques-Henri Lefebvre, *Verdun, Le Plus Grande Bataille de l'Histoire.* 10th ed. (Verdun: Éditions du Mémorial, 1993). Of the numerous French works on this battle, I list only a few of the most significant and useful: Henry Corda, *La Bataille de Verdun, 1916: Ses enseignements et ses consequences: conferences faites en 1921 aux sociéte d'officiers suisses* (Paris: Gauthier-Villars, 1921); Alain Denizot, *Verdun, 1914–1916* (Paris: Éditiones Latines, 1996); Louis Gillet, *La Bataille de Verdun* (Paris: G. Van Ouest et cie., 1921); Paul Heuzé, *La Voie Sacreé* (Paris: Renaissance du Livre, 1919); Lieutenant-Colonel Marchal, *La Bataille de Verdun expliquée sur le terrain* (Verdun: Fremont et Fils, 1920); Charles Paquet, *Dans l'attendé de la ruée: Verdun* (janvier–février 1916) (Paris: Berger-Levrault, 1928); Jules Poirier, *La Bataille de Verdun, 21 février—18 décembre 1916* (Paris: Chiron, 1922); Colonel [Paul] Rocolle, *"Preliminaires de la Bataille de Verdun,"* Revue historique des armées, 1975 2(4), 29–58 and *"Douaumont 1916–un sujet de réflexion,"* Revue historique des armées, 1977 3(3), 55–82; Général J[ean-Joseph] Rouquerol, *Le Drame de Douaumont, 21 février–24 octobre 1916* (Paris: Payot, 1931); Jacques Becker, *Verdun: Le Premier choc de l'attaque allemande* (Paris: Berger-Levrault, 1920).

I cannot say I found much of value in German. Werth, *Verdun: Die Schlacht und der Mythos* (Bergische Gladbach: Gustav Lübbe Verlag, 1979), an impressionistic and even journalistic work; but there is much that is invaluable in Wilhelm Ziegler, *Verdun* (Hamburg: Hanseatische Verlagsanstalt, 1936); Werner Beumelburg, *Schlachten des Weltkriegs: Douaumont* (Oldenburg: Stalling, 1925);

Paul C. Ettighoffer, *Verdun, das grosse Gericht* (Bayreuth: Hestia Verlag, 1964).

It is an axiom that the best study in English is Alistair Horne's *The Price of Glory: Verdun, 1916*. (New York: St. Martin's 1963). Unfortunately, there is hardly anything in it that stands up to investigation. Although brilliantly written, the factually and conceptually flawed narrative is also disfigured by characterizations such as "an excitable, impressionable race like the French" (31). A much better general account is Georges Blond, *Verdun*, translated by Francis Frenaye (New York: Macmillan, 1964). Pétain's own account must be read carefully—like Pershing, Pétain was not about to incite controversy: *La Bataille de Verdun* (Verdun: Fremont, 1931). The maps, widely reprinted, have serious errors.

1916: THE SOMME AND ELSEWHERE

In addition to the Austrian and Italian Official Histories, the work of Gunther E. Rothenberg, *The Army of Francis Joseph* (West Lafayette, Ind.: Purdue University Press, 1976) is indispensable, as is Norman Stone's *The Eastern Front, 1914–1917* (London: Hodder and Stoughton, 1975). The case study on Rumania prepared for use at West Point contains much valuable data (reprinted by Relevance 1.2 [Fall 1996]), as does Henri Berthelot, *Mémoirs et Correspondence, 1916–1919,* ed. Glen E. Torrey (New York: Columbia University Press, 1987).

I found the following a useful corrective to the standard English accounts of the Somme: Marcel Carnoy, *Les Batailles de la Somme* (Paris: Tallandier, 1988). Lynn Macdonald, *The Somme* (London: Michael Joseph, 1983), is an excellent work, and Malcolm Brown, *The Imperial War Museum Book of the Somme* (London: Sidgwick and Jackson, 1996), has much of interest, but the best discussion of the battle is in John Keegan, *The Face of Battle* (New York: Viking, 1976).

1917 AND AFTER

The basic guide to the Nivelle offensive is René Courtois, *Le Chemin des dames* (Paris: Tallandier, 1992), while Pierre Miquel, *Le Chemin des dames* (Paris: Perrin, 1997), provides an excellent overview of the politics as well as an analysis of the fighting. Although little more than a propagandistic picture book (the text is almost entirely captions), Yves Buffetaut's *The 1917 Spring Offensives* (Paris: Histoire et Collections, 1997) has invaluable photographic evidence. The only account of Pétain's offensives in 1917 are to be found in Gillet and Poirier (above). The literature on the BEF during this period is enormous, repetitive, and mostly without merit. The exceptions: Keegan's treatment in *The First World War* (New York: Knopf, 1999); John Laffin, *British Butchers and Bunglers of World War One* (Phoenix Mill: Sutton, 1989)—a work whose reception has unfortunately been colored by the sensationalist title; Robin Prior and Trevor Wilson, *Passchendaele, The Untold Story* (New Haven: Yale University Press, 1996); and Alexander McKee's astonishingly good *Vimy Ridge* (New York: Stein and Day, 1967).

There are numerous valuable accounts of the AEF's struggles, the most recent being the best: Byron Farwell's *Over There* (New York: Norton, 1999). Robert Asprey, *At Belleau Wood* (New York: G.P. Putnam's Sons, 1965), is a stimulating account of the battle. The works of American historians have been marred by a surprising naiveté with respect to the claims of British apologists as to the success and competence of the AEF. James H. Hallas, in his study of the Saint-Mihiel offensive, is the exception: *Squandered Victory* (London: Praeger, 1995). My own perceptions of the AEF and the Allies have been heavily influenced by the mentor of my early years, David Amacker (formerly, Lieutenant, U.S.A.), a member of the Wilson delegation at Versailles and one of the interpreters there. See the discussion in Stephen Bonsal, *Unfinished Business* (Garden City, N.Y.: Doubleday, 1944), 22–23.

PUBLIC OPINION AND POLICY

Although this is a military history, political issues and popular perceptions often shaped the battlefield (as they usually do). Public opinion in France was manipulated to an extent never before seen. See, in particular, Paul Allard, *Les Dessous de la guerre, révélés par les comités secrets* (Paris: Éditions de France, 1932); Marcel Berger and Paul Allard, *Les Secrets de la censure pendant la guerre* (Paris: Éditions des Portiques, 1932). English and Americans were bombarded with supposedly objective works, often written by well-known scholars, which presented the official view of the war. See, among many such works, Charles Sarolea, *How Belgium Saved Europe* (London: Heinemann, 1915). The correlation of these "histories" with the historical record is a fascinating topic.

Although no British study details how the government controlled the war, there are several reasonable studies of British propaganda efforts, of which the best is arguably M. L. Sanders and Philip M. Taylor, *British Propaganda During the First World War, 1914–18* (London: Macmillan, 1982). A surprising number of works detail American policies during the war, including H. C. Peterson, *Propaganda for War: The Campaign Against American Neutrality, 1914–1917* (Norman, Okla.: University of Oklahoma Press, 1939), Stewart Halsey Ross, *Propaganda for War: How the United States Was Conditioned to Fight the Great War of 1914–1918* (Jefferson, N. C.: McFarland, 1996). George T. Blakey's *Historians on the Homefront* (Lexington, Ky.: University of Kentucky Press, 1970) should be the required first text for any study of what has been written about the war.

DEDUCTIONS AND INSIGHTS

Analysis of the war is dominated in English by the recollections of the major figures, e.g., Ludendorff, and the writings of a few Englishmen, e.g., Liddell-Hart. After Rommel's own account, a better starting point is Hugo Freytag-Loringhoven, *Deductions from the World War* (New York: G. P. Putnam's Sons, 1918); Pascal Marie Lucas, *Evolution of Tactical Ideas* (Paris: Berger-Levrault, 1923); Paul Henri Maisonneuve, *L'Infanterie sous le feu: Étude critique sur le combat* (Paris: Berger-Levrault, 1925).

Works dealing with World War II are generally overlooked by historians of World War I. Ironically, one of the most insightful works on German infantry doctrine is the United States Army's official discussion of German Army doctrine (*Training Manual 30–450*), published in 1941, which clearly links the aggressive and casualty-conscious Wehrmacht of 1939–1940 with the army of 1914: War Department [United States], *Handbook on German Military Forces* (Washington, D.C.: War Department, 1941). A close second would be Samuel Lyman Atwood Marshall, *Men Against Fire: The Problem of Battle Command in Future Wars* (New York: William Morrow, 1964 [1947]), which by inference explains a great deal.

As mentioned earlier, accounts of the so-called Maginot Line are highly instructive in understanding the achievements and failures of the pre-1914 fortifications. So too with accounts of tank development between the wars. See, in particular: André Duvignac, *Histoire de l'armée motorisée* (Paris: Imprimerie Nationale,

1947); Fritz Heigl, *Taschenbuch der Tanks* (Munich: J. F. Lehmanns, 1926). Peter Beale's sensationalist-titled *Death by Design: The Fate of British Tank Crews in the Second World War* (Phoenix Mill: Sutton, 1998) is an invaluable account of British armored design with much illuminating detail about the Great War.

In the 1990s a growing body of English analysts have attempted, in the face of all evidence to the contrary, to argue that Haig and the BEF did reasonably well, the key texts being Paddy Griffiths, *Battle Tactics of the Western Front* (London: St. Edmunsbury, 1994); Ian Passingham, *Pillars of Fire: The Battle of Messines Ridge June 1917* (Phoenix Mill: Sutton, 1998). But such essays demolish straw men—the point is not that the BEF did not improve, the point is that it took too long to learn, started too late, and changed too slowly. The point is not sustainable, and probably irrelevant, given the German offensive gains of 1918.

GENERAL HISTORIES

In French, I found the following of great interest, in addition to the works of Contamine and Daille (cited above): Jean Galtier-Boissière, *Histoire de la grande guerre* (Paris: Le Crapouillot, 1932–33); Fernand Gambiez and Martin Suire, *Histoire de la première guerre mondiale* (Paris: Fayard, 1968); Louis Koeltz, *La Guerre de 1914–1918* (Paris: Sirey, 1966). Although the point of view is far too politically charged, as well as ideologically unbalanced, there is much of great value in Holger Herwig's *The First World War* (London: Arnold, 1997).

In English, hardly anyone departs from the framework laid down by the chief British propagandist, John Buchan, who was the second director of his country's official propaganda service. His eminently readable four-volume *A History of the Great War* (Boston: Houghton Mifflin, 1922) in turn follows the leads established by one of the Allies' most determined supporters, Frank H. Simonds, *History of the World War* (New York: Doubleday, 1917). The most entertaining and insightful general history to come after that is A. J. P. Taylor's witty Illustrated *History of the First World War* (New York: G. P. Putnam's Sons, 1964).

Like Taylor, Winston Churchill often draws the wrong conclusions, but until recently he was the only historian to question the propagandistic accounts of historians. *The World Crisis, 1916–1918* (New York: Charles Scribner's Sons, 1927) is a major work, undeserving of the vicious attacks directed at it. See the defense by Robin Prior, *Churchill's World Crisis as History* (London: Croom Helm, 1983).

Although it is not really a history of the war, Niall Ferguson's *The Pity of*

War (New York: Basic Books, 1999) is the first work of any intellectual substance on the general issues of the war to appear since Churchill. The reader will notice that Ferguson's arguments and mine frequently converge on the same conclusion, although using drastically different methods to arrive there.

BIOGRAPHY

At one point in *The Dogma of the Battle of Annihilation* (Westport, Conn.: Greenwood, 1986) the Israeli officer Jehuda Wallach remarks that the biographies of the men of the Great War are mostly gossip, to which I would add a hearty amen. In English, two notable exceptions are: Denis Winter, *Haig's Command* (New York: Viking, 1991) and Donald Smythe, *Pershing: General of the Armies* (Bloomington, Ind.: Indiana University Press, 1986). Although it frequently does not pass Wallach's test, Lamar Cecil's biography of Wilhelm II (Chapel Hill: University of North Carolina Press, 1996) is a useful corrective to the simplistic and propagandistic views of Germany and the higher levels of the German command.

In French, I found the following to be surprisingly insightful: Arthur Conte, *Joffre* (Paris: Oliver Orban, 1991); Pierre Varillon, *Joffre* (Paris: Libraire Arthème Fayard, 1956). Gaston Jolivet, *Le Colonel Driant* (Paris: Delagrave, 1919) (the only source for Colonel Driant's wartime letters) (see above); Captaine P[aul] Lyet, *Joffre et Galliéni à la Marne* (Paris: Berger-Levrault, 1938); Raymond Recouly, *Joffre* (New York: Appleton, 1931).

Some of the best work on the French has been done outside of France. I found Gregor Dallas, *At the Heart of a Tiger: Clemenceau and His World, 1841–1929* (New York: Caroll and Graf, 1993) to have valuable insights into the internal politics of the government, while Stephan Ryan's *Pétain the Soldier* (Cranbury, N.J.: Barnes, 1969) is a first-rate work. D. J. Goodspeed's *Ludendorff: Soldier, Dictator, Revolutionary* (London: Rupert Hart-Davis, 1966) is a valuable corrective to the usual treatment, although in many respects it hardly goes far enough.

MAPS AND GUIDES

The best situation maps are to be found in the German Official History (above) and in the maps contained in the misnamed American Battle Monuments

Commission, *American Armies and Battlefields in Europe* (Washington, D.C.: U.S. Government Printing Office, 1938). I matched these on site using very-large-scale (1 cm:250 m) maps obtained from the French National Institute of Geography.

In general, in this war one simply ignores the claims made by the combatants and goes straight to the maps. After the war, the Michelin Tire Company published a series of guides to the various battlefields in French and in English, and I found these invaluable accounts of how the French wished the war had gone. All were published directly by Michelin in Clermont-Ferrand: *L'Alsace et les combats des Vosges* (1914–1918) (1920); *Argonne 1914–1918* (1919); *La Bataille de la Somme 1916–1917* (1920); *La Bataille de Verdun 1914–1918* (1921), *The Battle of Verdun 1914–1918* (1919), *Les Batailles de la Somme (1916–1917)* (1920), *Metz et la bataille de Morhange* (1919).

ON-SITE WORK AND ARCHIVES

The most valuable information, which provided me with the basis for this study, was what I saw on the ground, not what I extracted from libraries and archives. Printed and archival materials generally provided confirmation rather than insight, if that. Much that is weak in military history is weak owing to an ignorance of the conditions on the ground, together with a rather touching naïveté about the importance of documents and unpublished materials buried in archives. "I had to chuckle when I saw the location of the regiment on one of the maps [of the Corps Combat Study]," Colonel James Stacy wrote. "Its true location was about twenty miles to the rear."[7] That Colonel Stacy was talking about an American report written in 1951, not a British or French one written in 1915, pretty much says it all when it comes to the subject of documentary evidence.

A familiarity with the ground also establishes how deeply connected certain areas are: an observer on the top of the Vauquois can see the ossuary at Verdun and also the American monument at Monfaucon, which seems a perfect instance of how interrelated the seemingly separate theaters actually were.

In many parts of the French section of the line the trench systems are still intact, as are most of the forts and the German defensive complexes. Additionally, in the various monuments, marks, and military cemeteries, I found a great deal of valuable evidence as to how the war was actually fought and by whom, including such curiosities as information about the Italian detachment of 1918.

In understanding weapons, words are a poor substitute for seeing. I found the artillery collections at the Fort de la Pompelle, at the Verdun Memorial, the city of Verdun, the town of Vauquois, the Austrian Army Museum (Vienna), the Bavarian Army Museum (at Ingolstadt), and the Foreign Legion Museum (Aubagne), extremely helpful. So, too, with the half a dozen French officers I encountered, who provided me with rather graphic demonstrations of certain basic principles of gunnery and locomotion, and who, for obvious reasons, must remain anonymous.

Historians operate under the conviction that archival research is the be all and end all of their profession. Indeed the author of one of the many pedestrian studies of the war dismisses one of the few actually good ones with the remark that it is based only on printed sources. But in France, where no one trusted either the archives or the records (or the archivists), the tradition was to publish what you found so it couldn't disappear, and I doubt there is anything of any substance not in print. On the basis of his researches into Haig, Denis Winter claims that the American archives, like the British, were rifled, and I'm inclined to believe him. Most historians seem rather naïve about the behavior of bureaucracies—and armies are definitely bureaucracies: reports are written to advance careers, to cover up for mistakes, to shift the blame elsewhere, and to advance a certain point of view.

Photographic archival evidence, on the contrary, is invaluable. The National Archives, strangely enough, has an enormous collection of German photographs, and, even more peculiarly, a collection of German wartime picture postcards, and I found these to be extremely valuable evidence. So, too, with exhibits at Pompelle (excellent material on mortars), Le Linge, and the Verdun Battlefield Museum.

The official publications of the various combatants before and during the war, frequently overlooked, are extremely useful as indicators of what it was thought was actually going on. English historians routinely cite a French intelligence document on the German Army that was translated into English by both the American and British Army as U.S. Army General Staff, Military Intelligence Division, *Histories of the 251 Divisions of the German Army which Participated in the War (1914–1918)* (Washington, D.C.: U.S. Government Printing Office, 1920). This document is comically unreliable and conceptually defective. German regiments are in the wrong divisions, the dates of major offensive operations are sometimes wrong (135), and the assessments of battle worthiness fly in the face of their known campaign record (143); and see also, Hallas (listed above, 119), for a practical example. Perhaps more seriously, the reports consistently omit references to the most potent German units, such as the *Pioniere* and the *Jäger*. At bottom what they reveal is an obsession with rifles and horses rather than firepower, while the whole idea of subdividing divisions into categories such as first rate and mediocre is to mistake the nature of modern warfare.

On the contrary, official United States Army publications postwar (noted above) often are quite useful. So, too, the somewhat misleadingly titled *American Armies and Battlefields in Europe: A History, Guide, and Reference Book* (Washington, D.C.: U.S. Government Printing Office, 1938), as well as Colonel Ayres's invaluable statistical abstract (mentioned above). The British Army published its own guide to the French Army, and the July 1914 edition is extremely revealing: War Office, *Handbook of the French Army, 1914* (London: War Office, 1914). To read it is to comprehend why the war went so badly for the Allies.

NOTES

1. As quoted by Jean Galtier-Boissière in *Histoire de la grande guerre* (Paris: Crapouillot, [1932?], 295. Presumably the quote is taken from Jean de Pierrefeu's, *G.Q.G. Secteur.* 1st ed. (Paris: Les Éditions G. Crés et cie., 1922), but I have yet to find it in the editions I've been able to locate.

2. I have made no attempt, either in the notes in the text, or in this essay, to provide an intensive critical appreciation of all the research on the war. This is particularly the case for a number of recent works, mostly by German scholars, which in my view add little to the enormous body of French writing. In any event, a number of exhaustive compilations of such studies already exists, for example, Dennis E. Showalter, *German Military History, 1648–1982: A Critical Bibliography* (New York: Garland, 1984).

3. The monthly casualties for the Western Front are found in vol. 3, pt. 1. As noted in the text, this is the data Churchill used for his calculations in *The World Crisis 1916–1918* (New York: Charles Scribner's Sons, 1927).

4. See also the report of the Adjutant General, American Expeditionary Forces: Summary of Casualties Among Members of the American Expeditionary Forces During the World War (W 3.2: Am3/2), as well as U.S. Army, *United States Army in the World War, 1917–1919*, 15: Reports of Commander in Chief (Washington, D.C.: Department of the Army, 1948). Correspondence in the Congressional Archives makes clear both the dissatisfaction of key officers with the official report and the War Department insistence on manipulating the figures.

5. See the summary in Service Historiques des Armeés, *Inventaire sommaire des archives de la guerre (N 24 and N 25)* (Troyes: La Renaissance, 1967).

6. The summaries are confusingly titled. See in particular, *N 24 et N 25* (Troyes: La Renaissance, 1967); [Jean Nicot] Service Historique, *Inventaire sommaire des archives de la guerre 1914–1918, Groupes de division: 21N corps d'armeé: 22N; Places et regions forti-fieés: 23N; Divisions et brigades: 24N; Regiments: 25N* (Troyes: La Renaissance, 1969).

7. Taken from a handwritten memorandum prepared by Colonel Stacy for his son, John Stacy, and now in his possession. Colonel Stacy (then a major) was the executive officer of the 23rd Infantry Regiment in Korea, where he received the DSC and the Croix de Guerre.

INDEX

Page numbers in *italics* refer to maps and illustrations.

Hoffmann, Max, 74, 97, 289–90, 293, 309
Holland, 15, 32, 118–19, 121
horses, 45, 55
House, Edward M., 335–36
howitzers, 5, 24, 39–46, *39*, 48, 77, 130, 146, 149, 273
75 millimeter, 24, 39–46, *39*, 48, 55, 72, 75, 116, 129–30, 134, 145, 149, 185, 207, 234, 274, 311
105 millimeter, 24, *42*, 43–44, 46, 48, 58, 149, 159
120 millimeter, 24, *40, 42, 57*, 94, 116, 134
150 millimeter, *43*, 44, 46, 48, 57, 61–62, 116, 116, 159, 207, 269
155 millimeter, *39–40*, 44–45, 134, 273, 310
210 millimeter, 44–46, 57–61, 94, 113, 116, 157, 159, 207
305 millimeter, 48–49, 61, 83, 95, 109, 116–17, 151
420 millimeter, 48–49, 58–61, 83, 94, 111, 117, 219
Hubbard, Samuel, 319
Hungary, 254–55

indirect fire, 41, 155–56
infantry, 19–20, 38, 38, 41, 46, 90–91, 99, 111, 133, 149, 157–60, 221, 274, 293, 297, 331–32
combat described by, xi, 62, 119, 147, 169, 235–36, 299
in combined-arms operations, 38, 45–46, 48–49, 145, 173–77, 209, 269, 297–98
ethnic composition of, 151, 156, 258–59, 273–74, 311
morale of, 5–6, 26, 95, 102, 119, 151–53, 158, 172, 222–25, 273–74
in siege warfare, 61, 95, 116–19, 128–29, 173–74
training of, 24, 26, 88, 234, 309, 314–15

intelligence, 34–35, 146, 153, 158, 173, 182–84, 191, 198, 201–2, 241, 254, 270, 282, 290, 298, 310, 314–15, 319
Isonzo valley, 150–51, 153, 197–98, 247–48, 255, 292, 294–96
Italian Expeditionary Force, 177, 254
Italian Front, 5, 8, 148–53, 193, 197–98, 246, 247–48, 251, 291–96, 298
Italian General Staff, 150–51, 247, 294
Italy, 18, 148–50, 182, 201, 217, 242, 245–46, 254, 291–92, 294–95, 313, 341

Jäger, 32, 58, 154, 174–75
Jaurès, Jean Léon, 200
Joffre, Joseph Jacques, 5–6, 20–24, 51, 62, 70, 77–78, 85, 87, 97–99, 102, 109, 113, 115, 129, 156, 166–69, 182, 188–92, 200, 203, 207, 257, 270, 306, 342
in leadership crises, 73, 75, 84, 158–59, 259, 262–64
offensive doctrine of, 21–22, 125, 190, 262, 269, 269, 315, 341
strategic goals of, 185–87, 194, 196–98, 229, 231, 233, 256, 281, 333
journalists, 63, 77, 181–82, 188
justice, military, 97–98, 111, 224, 277

Kagohls, 208
Kastas, 208–9
Keegan, John, 1
Kerensky, Alexander, 291
Khrushchev, Nikita, 8
Kitchener, Horatio, Lord, 117, 181–82
Kluck, Alexander von, 83, 85, 87–89, 97, 103
Knobelsdorf, Konstantin von, 75, 216
Kolomea, 250–51
Krafft von Dellmensingen, Konrad, 292
Krupp armament works, 175